COMPILATION OF SELECTED AEROSPACE LAWS

VOLUME 2: TITLE 51 UNITED STATES CODE
OTHER LEGISLATION

Updated through the 118th Congress

Includes provisions of:

Provisions of Title 51, U.S.C. –National and Commercial Space Programs • Internal Revenue Code of 1986 • Acts Relating to Washington Area Airports • Counter UAS Authorities • Atomic Energy Defense Act • Homeland Security Act of 2002 • American Security Drone Act of 2023 • Title VII of the Trade Act • International Security and Development Cooperation Act of 1985 • Railway Labor Act • FAA Reauthorization Act of 2018 • FAA Extension, Safety, and Security Act of 2016 • FAA Modernization and Reform Act of 2012 • European Union Emissions Trading Scheme Prohibition Act of 2011 • Airline Safety and Federal Aviation Administration Extension Act of 2010 • Intelligence Reform and Terrorism Prevention Act of 2004 • Vision 100—Century of Aviation Reauthorization Act • Aviation and Transportation Security Act • Air Transportation Safety and System Stabilization Act • Wendell H. Ford Aviation Investment and Reform Act for the 21st Century • Federal Aviation Reauthorization Act of 1996 • NOTAM Improvement Act of 2023 • Consolidated Appropriations Resolution, 2003 •

Prepared By M. TWINCHEK
2025

Forward

T his Compilation of Selected Laws is a resource for those interested in laws governing civil aerospace. This compilation includes laws governing civil aviation, aviation safety, airport improvement, the Federal Aviation Administration(FAA), the National Transportation Safety Board, aviation security, essential air service, commercial airlines, general aviation, unmanned aircraft systems, aviation labor, international aviation, commercial space transportation, air traffic management, and general FAA operations.

The materials included comes from publicly available, open source information, prepared for the public by the Office of the Legislative Counsel of the U.S. House of Representatives and the Office of the Law Revision Counsel.

Items listed as a Statute Compilation do not appear in the U.S. Code or that have been classified to a title of the U.S. Code that has not been enacted into positive law. Each Statute Compilation incorporates the amendments made to the underlying statute since it was originally enacted and are current as of the date noted.

This compilation is not an official document and should not be cited as evidence of any law. The official version of Federal law is found in the United States Statutes at Large and in the U.S. Code, the legal effect of which is established in sections 112 and 204, respectively, of title 1, United States Code.

A special thanks is extended to the Office of Law Revision Counsel and the House Office of the Legislative Counsel for providing the U.S. Code and statute compilations; and to the Government Publications Office for hosting and making these available for use to the public. An additional thank you is offered to the staff of the House and Senate Committees who were gracious in responding to inquiries and providing background information to the legislation included.

Questions and comments may be directed to:
M. Twinchek
Email: mtwinchek@outlook.com

Contents

Selected Provisions of the Internal Revenue Code of 1986

Current through Public Law 118-78

TITLE 51—NATIONAL AND COMMERCIAL SPACE PROGRAMS

This title was enacted by Pub. L. 111–314, §3, Dec. 18, 2010, 124 Stat. 3328

* * * * * * *

Subtitle V—Programs Targeting Commercial Opportunities

Subtitle V—Programs Targeting Commercial Opportunities

CHAPTER 501—SPACE COMMERCE

SUBCHAPTER I—GENERAL

* * * * * * *

SUBCHAPTER I—GENERAL

§50101. DEFINITIONS

In this chapter:

(1) COMMERCIAL PROVIDER.—The term "commercial provider" means any person providing space transportation services or other space-related activities, primary control of which is held by persons other than Federal, State, local, and foreign governments.

(2) PAYLOAD.—The term "payload" means anything that a person undertakes to transport to, from, or within outer space, or in suborbital trajectory, by means of a space transportation vehicle, but does not include the space transportation vehicle itself except for its components which are specifically designed or adapted for that payload.

(3) SPACE-RELATED ACTIVITIES.—The term "space-related activities" includes research and development, manufacturing, processing, service, and other associated and support activities.

(4) SPACE TRANSPORTATION SERVICES.—The term "space transportation services" means the preparation of a space transportation vehicle and its payloads for transportation to, from, or within outer space, or in suborbital trajectory, and the conduct of transporting a payload to, from, or within outer space, or in suborbital trajectory.

(5) SPACE TRANSPORTATION VEHICLE.—The term "space transportation vehicle" means any vehicle constructed for the purpose of operating in, or transporting a payload to, from, or within, outer space, or in suborbital trajectory, and includes any component of such vehicle not specifically designed or adapted for a payload.

(6) STATE.—The term "State" means each of the several States of the Union, the District of Columbia, the Commonwealth of Puerto Rico, the Virgin Islands, Guam, American Samoa, the Commonwealth of the Northern Mariana Islands, and any other commonwealth, territory, or possession of the United States.

(7) UNITED STATES COMMERCIAL PROVIDER.—The term "United States commercial provider" means a commercial provider, organized under the laws of the United States or of a State, that is—

(A) more than 50 percent owned by United States nationals; or

(B) a subsidiary of a foreign company and the Secretary of Transportation finds that—

(i) such subsidiary has in the past evidenced a substantial commitment to the United States market through—

(I) investments in the United States in long-term research, development, and manufacturing (including the manufacture of major components and subassemblies); and

(II) significant contributions to employment in the United States; and

(ii) the country or countries in which such foreign company is incorporated or organized, and, if appropriate, in which it principally conducts its business, affords reciprocal treatment to companies described in subparagraph (A) comparable to that afforded to such foreign company's subsidiary in the United States, as evidenced by—

(I) providing comparable opportunities for companies described in subparagraph (A) to participate in Government-sponsored research and development similar to that authorized under this chapter;

(II) providing no barriers, to companies described in subparagraph (A) with respect to local investment opportunities, that are not provided to foreign companies in the United States; and

(III) providing adequate and effective protection for the intellectual property rights of companies described in subparagraph (A).

(Pub. L. 111–314, §3, Dec. 18, 2010, 124 Stat. 3394.)

* * * * * * *

CHAPTER 509—COMMERCIAL SPACE LAUNCH ACTIVITIES

§50901. FINDINGS AND PURPOSES

(a) FINDINGS.—Congress finds that—

(1) the peaceful uses of outer space continue to be of great value and to offer benefits to all mankind;

(2) private applications of space technology have achieved a significant level of commercial and economic activity and offer the potential for growth in the future, particularly in the United States;

(3) new and innovative equipment and services are being sought, produced, and offered by entrepreneurs in telecommunications, information services, microgravity research, human space flight, and remote sensing technologies;

(4) the private sector in the United States has the capability of developing and providing private launching, reentry, and associated services that would complement the launching, reentry, and associated capabilities of the United States Government;

(5) the development of commercial launch vehicles, reentry vehicles, and associated

services would enable the United States to retain its competitive position internationally, contributing to the national interest and economic well-being of the United States;

(6) providing launch services and reentry services by the private sector is consistent with the national security and foreign policy interests of the United States and would be facilitated by stable, minimal, and appropriate regulatory guidelines that are fairly and expeditiously applied;

(7) the United States should encourage private sector launches, reentries, and associated services and, only to the extent necessary, regulate those launches, reentries, and services to ensure compliance with international obligations of the United States and to protect the public health and safety, safety of property, and national security and foreign policy interests of the United States;

(8) space transportation, including the establishment and operation of launch sites, reentry sites, and complementary facilities, the providing of launch services and reentry services, the establishment of support facilities, and the providing of support services, is an important element of the transportation system of the United States, and in connection with the commerce of the United States there is a need to develop a strong space transportation infrastructure with significant private sector involvement;

(9) the participation of State governments in encouraging and facilitating private sector involvement in space-related activity, particularly through the establishment of a space transportation-related infrastructure, including launch sites, reentry sites, complementary facilities, and launch site and reentry site support facilities, is in the national interest and is of significant public benefit;

(10) the goal of safely opening space to the American people and their private commercial, scientific, and cultural enterprises should guide Federal space investments, policies, and regulations;

(11) private industry has begun to develop commercial launch vehicles capable of carrying human beings into space and greater private investment in these efforts will stimulate the Nation's commercial space transportation industry as a whole;

(12) space transportation is inherently risky, and the future of the commercial human space flight industry will depend on its ability to continually improve its safety performance;

(13) a critical area of responsibility for the Department of Transportation is to regulate the operations and safety of the emerging commercial human space flight industry;

(14) the public interest is served by creating a clear legal, regulatory, and safety regime for commercial human space flight; and

(15) the regulatory standards governing human space flight must evolve as the industry matures so that regulations neither stifle technology development nor expose crew, government astronauts, or space flight participants to avoidable risks as the public comes to expect greater safety for crew, government astronauts, and space flight participants from the industry.

(b) PURPOSES.—The purposes of this chapter are—

(1) to promote economic growth and entrepreneurial activity through use of the space environment for peaceful purposes;

(2) to encourage the United States private sector to provide launch vehicles, reentry vehicles, and associated services by—

(A) simplifying and expediting the issuance and transfer of commercial licenses;

(B) facilitating and encouraging the use of Government-developed space technology; and

(C) promoting the continuous improvement of the safety of launch vehicles designed to carry humans, including through the issuance of regulations, to the extent permitted by this chapter;

(3) to provide that the Secretary of Transportation is to oversee and coordinate the conduct of commercial launch and reentry operations, issue permits and commercial licenses and transfer commercial licenses authorizing those operations, and protect the public health and safety, safety of property, and national security and foreign policy interests of the United States; and

(4) to facilitate the strengthening and expansion of the United States space transportation infrastructure, including the enhancement of United States launch sites and launch-site support facilities, and development of reentry sites, with Government, State, and private sector involvement, to support the full range of United States space-related activities.

(Pub. L. 103–272, §1(e), July 5, 1994, 108 Stat. 1330, §70101 of title 49; Pub. L. 105–303, title I, §102(a)(2), Oct. 28, 1998, 112 Stat. 2846; Pub. L. 108–492, §2(a), Dec. 23, 2004, 118 Stat. 3974; renumbered §70101 then §50901 of title 51, Pub. L. 111–314, §4(d)(2), (3)(A), Dec. 18, 2010, 124 Stat. 3440; Pub. L. 114–90, title I, §112(a), Nov. 25, 2015, 129 Stat. 711.)

§50902. DEFINITIONS

In this chapter—

(1) "citizen of the United States" means—

(A) an individual who is a citizen of the United States;

(B) an entity organized or existing under the laws of the United States or a State; or

(C) an entity organized or existing under the laws of a foreign country if the controlling interest (as defined by the Secretary of Transportation) is held by an individual or entity described in subclause (A) or (B) of this clause.

(2) "crew" means any employee of a licensee or transferee, or of a contractor or subcontractor of a licensee or transferee, who performs activities in the course of that employment directly relating to the launch, reentry, or other operation of or in a launch vehicle or reentry vehicle that carries human beings.

(3) "executive agency" has the same meaning given that term in section 105 of title 5.

(4) "government astronaut" means an individual who—

(A) is designated by the National Aeronautics and Space Administration under section 20113(n);

(B) is carried within a launch vehicle or reentry vehicle in the course of his or her employment, which may include performance of activities directly relating to the launch, reentry, or other operation of the launch vehicle or reentry vehicle; and

(C) is either—

(i) an employee of the United States Government, including the uniformed services, engaged in the performance of a Federal function under authority of law or an Executive act; or

(ii) an international partner astronaut.

(5) "international partner astronaut" means an individual designated under Article 11 of the International Space Station Intergovernmental Agreement, by a partner to that agreement other than the United States, as qualified to serve as an International Space Station crew member.

(6) "International Space Station Intergovernmental Agreement" means the Agreement Concerning Cooperation on the International Space Station, signed at Washington January 29, 1998 (TIAS 12927).

(7) "launch" means to place or try to place a launch vehicle or reentry vehicle and any payload or human being from Earth—

(A) in a suborbital trajectory;

(B) in Earth orbit in outer space; or

(C) otherwise in outer space,

including activities involved in the preparation of a launch vehicle or payload for launch, when those activities take place at a launch site in the United States.

(8) "launch property" means an item built for, or used in, the launch preparation or launch of a launch vehicle.

(9) "launch services" means—

(A) activities involved in the preparation of a launch vehicle, payload, crew (including crew training), government astronaut, or space flight participant for launch; and

(B) the conduct of a launch.

(10) "launch site" means the location on Earth from which a launch takes place (as defined in a license the Secretary issues or transfers under this chapter) and necessary facilities at that location.

(11) "launch vehicle" means—

(A) a vehicle built to operate in, or place a payload or human beings in, outer space; and

(B) a suborbital rocket.

(12) "obtrusive space advertising" means advertising in outer space that is capable of being recognized by a human being on the surface of the Earth without the aid of a telescope or other technological device.

(13) "payload" means an object that a person undertakes to place in outer space by means of a launch vehicle or reentry vehicle, including components of the vehicle specifically designed or adapted for that object.

(14) except in section 50904(c), "permit" means an experimental permit issued under section 50906.

(15) "person" means an individual and an entity organized or existing under the laws of a State or country.

(16) "reenter" and "reentry" mean to return or attempt to return, purposefully, a reentry vehicle and its payload or human beings, if any, from Earth orbit or from outer space to Earth.

(17) "reentry services" means—

(A) activities involved in the preparation of a reentry vehicle and payload, crew (including crew training), government astronaut, or space flight participant, if any, for reentry; and

(B) the conduct of a reentry.

(18) "reentry site" means the location on Earth to which a reentry vehicle is intended to return (as defined in a license the Secretary issues or transfers under this chapter).

(19) "reentry vehicle" means a vehicle designed to return from Earth orbit or outer space to Earth, or a reusable launch vehicle designed to return from Earth orbit or outer space to Earth, substantially intact.

(20) "space flight participant" means an individual, who is not crew or a government astronaut, carried within a launch vehicle or reentry vehicle.

(21) "space support vehicle flight" means a flight in the air that—

(A) is not a launch or reentry; but

(B) is conducted by a space support vehicle.

(22) "space support vehicle" means a vehicle that is—

(A) a launch vehicle;

(B) a reentry vehicle; or

(C) a component of a launch or reentry vehicle.

(23) "State" means a State of the United States, the District of Columbia, and a territory or possession of the United States.

(24) unless and until regulations take effect under section 50922(c)(2), "suborbital rocket" means a vehicle, rocket-propelled in whole or in part, intended for flight on a suborbital trajectory, and the thrust of which is greater than its lift for the majority of the rocket-powered portion of its ascent.

(25) "suborbital trajectory" means the intentional flight path of a launch vehicle, reentry vehicle, or any portion thereof, whose vacuum instantaneous impact point does not leave the surface of the Earth.

(26) "third party" means a person except—

(A) the United States Government or the Government's contractors or subcontractors involved in launch services or reentry services;

(B) a licensee or transferee under this chapter;

(C) a licensee's or transferee's contractors, subcontractors, or customers involved in launch services or reentry services;

(D) the customer's contractors or subcontractors involved in launch services or reentry services; or

(E) crew, government astronauts, or space flight participants.

(27) "United States" means the States of the United States, the District of Columbia, and the territories and possessions of the United States.

(Pub. L. 103–272, §1(e), July 5, 1994, 108 Stat. 1331, §70102 of title 49; Pub. L. 104–287, §5(92), Oct. 11, 1996, 110 Stat. 3398; Pub. L. 105–303, title I, §102(a)(3), Oct. 28, 1998, 112 Stat. 2846; Pub. L. 106–391, title III, §322(a), Oct. 30, 2000, 114 Stat. 1598; Pub. L. 108–492, §2(b), Dec. 23, 2004, 118 Stat. 3975; renumbered §70102 then §50902 of title 51 and amended Pub. L. 111–314, §4(d)(2), (3)(B), (5)(A), (B), Dec. 18, 2010, 124 Stat. 3440, 3441; Pub. L. 114–90, title I, §112(c), (e)–(j), Nov. 25, 2015, 129 Stat. 712, 713; Pub. L. 115–254, div. B, title V, §581(a), Oct. 5, 2018, 132 Stat. 3397.)

§50903. GENERAL AUTHORITY

(a) GENERAL.—The Secretary of Transportation shall carry out this chapter.

(b) FACILITATING COMMERCIAL LAUNCHES AND REENTRIES.—In carrying out this chapter, the Secretary shall—

(1) encourage, facilitate, and promote commercial space launches and reentries by the private sector, including those involving space flight participants; and

(2) take actions to facilitate private sector involvement in commercial space transportation activity, and to promote public-private partnerships involving the United States Government, State governments, and the private sector to build, expand, modernize, or operate a space launch and reentry infrastructure.

(c) SAFETY.—In carrying out the responsibilities under subsection (b), the Secretary shall encourage, facilitate, and promote the continuous improvement of the safety of launch vehicles designed to carry humans, and the Secretary may, consistent with this chapter, promulgate regulations to carry out this subsection.

(d) EXECUTIVE AGENCY ASSISTANCE.—When necessary, the head of an executive agency shall assist the Secretary in carrying out this chapter.

(Pub. L. 103–272, §1(e), July 5, 1994, 108 Stat. 1332, §70103 of title 49; Pub. L. 105–303, title I, §102(a)(4), Oct. 28, 1998, 112 Stat. 2847; Pub. L. 108–492, §2(c)(1), (2), Dec. 23, 2004, 118 Stat. 3976; renumbered §70103 then §50903 of title 51, Pub. L. 111–314, §4(d)(2), (3)(C), Dec. 18, 2010, 124 Stat. 3440.)

§50904. RESTRICTIONS ON LAUNCHES, OPERATIONS, AND REENTRIES

(a) REQUIREMENT.—A license issued or transferred under this chapter, or a permit, is required for the following:

(1) for a person to launch a launch vehicle or to operate a launch site or reentry site, or to reenter a reentry vehicle, in the United States.

(2) for a citizen of the United States (as defined in section 50902(1)(A) or (B) of this title) to launch a launch vehicle or to operate a launch site or reentry site, or to reenter a reentry vehicle, outside the United States.

(3) for a citizen of the United States (as defined in section 50902(1)(C) of this title) to launch a launch vehicle or to operate a launch site or reentry site, or to reenter a reentry vehicle, outside the United States and outside the territory of a foreign country unless there is an agreement between the United States Government and the government of the foreign country providing that the government of the foreign country has jurisdiction over the launch or operation or reentry.

(4) for a citizen of the United States (as defined in section 50902(1)(C) of this title) to launch a launch vehicle or to operate a launch site or reentry site, or to reenter a reentry vehicle, in the territory of a foreign country if there is an agreement between the United States Government and the government of the foreign country providing that the United States Government has jurisdiction over the launch or operation or reentry.

Notwithstanding this subsection, a permit shall not authorize a person to operate a launch site or reentry site.

(b) COMPLIANCE WITH PAYLOAD REQUIREMENTS.—The holder of a license or permit under this chapter may launch or reenter a payload only if the payload complies with all requirements of the laws of the United States related to launching or reentering a payload.

(c) PREVENTING LAUNCHES AND REENTRIES.—The Secretary of Transportation shall establish whether all required licenses, authorizations, and permits required for a payload have been obtained. If no license, authorization, or permit is required, the Secretary may prevent the launch or reentry if the Secretary decides the launch or reentry would jeopardize the public health and safety, safety of property, or national security or foreign policy interest of the United States.

(d) SINGLE LICENSE OR PERMIT.—The Secretary of Transportation shall ensure that only 1 license or permit is required from the Department of Transportation to conduct activities involving crew, government astronauts, or space flight participants, including launch and reentry, for which a license or permit is required under this chapter. The Secretary shall ensure that all Department of Transportation regulations relevant to the licensed or permitted activity are satisfied.

(Pub. L. 103–272, §1(e), July 5, 1994, 108 Stat. 1332, §70104 of title 49; Pub. L. 105–303, title I, §102(a)(5), Oct. 28, 1998, 112 Stat. 2847; Pub. L. 108–492, §2(c)(3)–(5), Dec. 23, 2004, 118 Stat. 3976; renumbered §70104 then §50904 of title 51 and amended Pub. L. 111–314, §4(d)(2), (3)(D), (5)(C)–(E), Dec. 18, 2010, 124 Stat. 3440, 3441; Pub. L. 114–90, title I, §112(k), Nov. 25, 2015, 129 Stat. 713.)

§50905. LICENSE APPLICATIONS AND REQUIREMENTS

(a) APPLICATIONS.—(1) A person may apply to the Secretary of Transportation for a license or transfer of a license under this chapter in the form and way the Secretary prescribes. Consistent with the public health and safety, safety of property, and national security and foreign policy interests of the United States, the Secretary, not later than 180 days after accepting an application in accordance with criteria established pursuant to subsection (b)(2)(D),[1] shall issue or transfer a license if the Secretary decides in writing that the applicant complies, and will continue to comply, with this chapter and regulations prescribed under this chapter. The Secretary shall inform the applicant of any pending issue and action required to resolve the issue if the Secretary has not made a decision not later than 120 days after accepting an application in accordance with criteria established pursuant to subsection (b)(2)(D). The Secretary shall transmit to the Committee on Science of the House of Representatives and the Committee on Commerce, Science, and Transportation of the Senate a written notice not later than 30 days after any occurrence when the Secretary has not taken action on a license application within the deadline established by this subsection.

(2) In carrying out paragraph (1), the Secretary may establish procedures for safety approvals of launch vehicles, reentry vehicles, safety systems, processes, services, or personnel (including approval procedures for the purpose of protecting the health and safety of crew, government astronauts, and space flight participants, to the extent permitted by subsections (b) and (c)) that may be used in conducting licensed commercial space launch or reentry activities.

(b) REQUIREMENTS.—(1) Except as provided in this subsection, all requirements of the laws of the United States applicable to the launch of a launch vehicle or the operation of a launch site or a reentry site, or the reentry of a reentry vehicle, are requirements for a license or permit under this chapter.

(2) The Secretary may prescribe—

(A) any term necessary to ensure compliance with this chapter, including on-site verification that a launch, operation, or reentry complies with representations stated in the application;

(B) any additional requirement necessary to protect the public health and safety, safety of property, national security interests, and foreign policy interests of the United States;

(C) by regulation that a requirement of a law of the United States not be a requirement

13

for a license or permit if the Secretary, after consulting with the head of the appropriate executive agency, decides that the requirement is not necessary to protect the public health and safety, safety of property, and national security and foreign policy interests of the United States;

(D) additional license requirements, for a launch vehicle carrying a human being for compensation or hire, necessary to protect the health and safety of crew, government astronauts, or space flight participants, only if such requirements are imposed pursuant to final regulations issued in accordance with subsection (c); and

(E) regulations establishing criteria for accepting or rejecting an application for a license or permit under this chapter within 60 days after receipt of such application.

(3) The Secretary may waive a requirement, including the requirement to obtain a license, for an individual applicant if the Secretary decides that the waiver is in the public interest and will not jeopardize the public health and safety, safety of property, and national security and foreign policy interests of the United States. The Secretary may not grant a waiver under this paragraph that would permit the launch or reentry of a launch vehicle or a reentry vehicle without a license or permit if a human being will be on board.

(4) The holder of a license or a permit under this chapter may launch or reenter crew only if—

(A) the crew has received training and has satisfied medical or other standards specified in the license or permit in accordance with regulations promulgated by the Secretary;

(B) the holder of the license or permit has informed any individual serving as crew in writing, prior to executing any contract or other arrangement to employ that individual (or, in the case of an individual already employed as of the date of enactment of the Commercial Space Launch Amendments Act of 2004, as early as possible, but in any event prior to any launch in which the individual will participate as crew), that the United States Government has not certified the launch vehicle as safe for carrying crew or space flight participants; and

(C) the holder of the license or permit and crew have complied with all requirements of the laws of the United States that apply to crew.

(5) The holder of a license or a permit under this chapter may launch or reenter a space flight participant only if—

(A) in accordance with regulations promulgated by the Secretary, the holder of the license or permit has informed the space flight participant in writing about the risks of the launch and reentry, including the safety record of the launch or reentry vehicle type, and the Secretary has informed the space flight participant in writing of any relevant information related to risk or probable loss during each phase of flight gathered by the Secretary in making the determination required by section 50914(a)(2) and (c);

(B) the holder of the license or permit has informed any space flight participant in writing, prior to receiving any compensation from that space flight participant or (in the case of a space flight participant not providing compensation) otherwise concluding any agreement to fly that space flight participant, that the United States Government has not certified the launch vehicle as safe for carrying crew or space flight participants;

(C) in accordance with regulations promulgated by the Secretary, the space flight participant has provided written informed consent to participate in the launch and reentry

14

and written certification of compliance with any regulations promulgated under paragraph (6)(A); and

(D) the holder of the license or permit has complied with any regulations promulgated by the Secretary pursuant to paragraph (6).

(6)(A) The Secretary may issue regulations requiring space flight participants to undergo an appropriate physical examination prior to a launch or reentry under this chapter. This subparagraph shall cease to be in effect three years after the date of enactment of the Commercial Space Launch Amendments Act of 2004.

(B) The Secretary may issue additional regulations setting reasonable requirements for space flight participants, including medical and training requirements. Such regulations shall not be effective before the expiration of 3 years after the date of enactment of the Commercial Space Launch Amendments Act of 2004.

(c) SAFETY REGULATIONS.—

(1) IN GENERAL.—The Secretary may issue regulations governing the design or operation of a launch vehicle to protect the health and safety of crew, government astronauts, and space flight participants.

(2) REGULATIONS.—Regulations issued under this subsection shall—

(A) describe how such regulations would be applied when the Secretary is determining whether to issue a license under this chapter;

(B) apply only to launches in which a vehicle will be carrying a human being for compensation or hire;

(C) be limited to restricting or prohibiting design features or operating practices that—

(i) have resulted in a serious or fatal injury (as defined in 49 CFR 830, as in effect on November 10, 2004) to crew, government astronauts, or space flight participants during a licensed or permitted commercial human space flight; or

(ii) contributed to an unplanned event or series of events during a licensed or permitted commercial human space flight that posed a high risk of causing a serious or fatal injury (as defined in 49 CFR 830, as in effect on November 10, 2004) to crew, government astronauts, or space flight participants; and

(D) be issued with a description of the instance or instances when the design feature or operating practice being restricted or prohibited contributed to a result or event described in subparagraph (C).

(3) FACILITATION OF STANDARDS.—The Secretary shall continue to work with the commercial space sector, including the Commercial Space Transportation Advisory Committee, or its successor organization, to facilitate the development of voluntary industry consensus standards based on recommended best practices to improve the safety of crew, government astronauts, and space flight participants as the commercial space sector continues to mature.

(4) COMMUNICATION AND TRANSPARENCY.—Nothing in this subsection shall be construed to limit the authority of the Secretary to discuss potential regulatory approaches, potential performance standards, or any other topic related to this subsection with the commercial space industry, including observations, findings, and recommendations from the Commercial Space Transportation Advisory Committee, or its successor organization, prior to the issuance of a notice of proposed rulemaking.

Such discussions shall not be construed to permit the Secretary to promulgate industry regulations except as otherwise provided in this section.

(5) INTERIM VOLUNTARY INDUSTRY CONSENSUS STANDARDS REPORTS.—

(A) IN GENERAL.—Not later than December 31, 2016, and every 30 months thereafter until December 31, 2021, the Secretary, in consultation and coordination with the commercial space sector, including the Commercial Space Transportation Advisory Committee, or its successor organization, shall submit to the Committee on Commerce, Science, and Transportation of the Senate and the Committee on Science, Space, and Technology of the House of Representatives a report on the progress of the commercial space transportation industry in developing voluntary industry consensus standards that promote best practices to improve industry safety.

(B) CONTENTS.—The report shall include, at a minimum—

(i) any voluntary industry consensus standards that have been accepted by the industry at large;

(ii) the identification of areas that have the potential to become voluntary industry consensus standards that are currently under consideration by the industry at large;

(iii) an assessment from the Secretary on the general progress of the industry in adopting voluntary industry consensus standards;

(iv) any lessons learned about voluntary industry consensus standards, best practices, and commercial space launch operations;

(v) any lessons learned associated with the development, potential application, and acceptance of voluntary industry consensus standards, best practices, and commercial space launch operations; and

(vi) recommendations, findings, or observations from the Commercial Space Transportation Advisory Committee, or its successor organization, on the progress of the industry in developing voluntary industry consensus standards that promote best practices to improve industry safety.

(6) REPORT.—Not later than 270 days after the date of enactment of the SPACE Act of 2015, the Secretary, in consultation and coordination with the commercial space sector, including the Commercial Space Transportation Advisory Committee, or its successor organization, shall submit to the Committee on Commerce, Science, and Transportation of the Senate and the Committee on Science, Space, and Technology of the House of Representatives a report specifying key industry metrics that might indicate readiness of the commercial space sector and the Department of Transportation to transition to a safety framework that may include regulations under paragraph (9) that considers space flight participant, government astronaut, and crew safety.

(7) REPORTS.—Not later than March 31 of each of 2018 and 2022, the Secretary, in consultation and coordination with the commercial space sector, including the Commercial Space Transportation Advisory Committee, or its successor organization, shall submit to the Committee on Commerce, Science, and Transportation of the Senate and the Committee on Science, Space, and Technology of the House of Representatives a report that identifies the activities, described in this subsection and subsection (d) most appropriate for a new safety framework that may include regulatory action, if any, and a proposed transition plan for such safety framework.

(8) INDEPENDENT REVIEW.—Not later than December 31, 2022, an independent

systems engineering and technical assistance organization or standards development organization contracted by the Secretary shall submit to the Committee on Commerce, Science, and Transportation of the Senate and the Committee on Science, Space, and Technology of the House of Representatives an assessment of the readiness of the commercial space industry and the Federal Government to transition to a safety framework that may include regulations. As part of the review, the contracted organization shall evaluate—

(A) the progress of the commercial space industry in adopting voluntary industry consensus standards as reported by the Secretary in the interim assessments included in the reports under paragraph (5);

(B) the progress of the commercial space industry toward meeting the key industry metrics identified by the report under paragraph (6), including the knowledge and operational experience obtained by the commercial space industry while providing services for compensation or hire; and

(C) whether the areas identified in the reports under paragraph (5) are appropriate for regulatory action, or further development of voluntary industry consensus standards, considering the progress evaluated in subparagraphs (A) and (B) of this paragraph.

(9) LEARNING PERIOD.—Beginning on January 1, 2025, the Secretary may propose regulations under this subsection without regard to subparagraphs (C) and (D) of paragraph (2). The development of any such regulations shall take into consideration the evolving standards of the commercial space flight industry as identified in the reports published under paragraphs (5), (6), and (7).

(10) RULE OF CONSTRUCTION.—Nothing in this subsection shall be construed to limit the authority of the Secretary to issue requirements or regulations to protect the public health and safety, safety of property, national security interests, and foreign policy interests of the United States.

(d) PROCEDURES AND TIMETABLES.—The Secretary shall establish procedures and timetables that expedite review of a license or permit application and reduce the regulatory burden for an applicant.

(Pub. L. 103–272, §1(e), July 5, 1994, 108 Stat. 1333, §70105 of title 49; Pub. L. 105–303, title I, §102(a)(6), Oct. 28, 1998, 112 Stat. 2848; Pub. L. 108–492, §2(c)(6)–(15), Dec. 23, 2004, 118 Stat. 3976–3979; renumbered §70105 then §50905 of title 51 and amended Pub. L. 111–314, §4(d)(2), (3)(E), (5)(F), Dec. 18, 2010, 124 Stat. 3440, 3441; Pub. L. 112–95, title VIII, §827, Feb. 14, 2012, 126 Stat. 133; Pub. L. 114–55, title I, §102(e), Sept. 30, 2015, 129 Stat. 523; Pub. L. 114–90, title I, §§111, 112(l), Nov. 25, 2015, 129 Stat. 709, 713; Pub. L. 118–15, div. B, title II, §2202(k), Sept. 30, 2023, 137 Stat. 83; Pub. L. 118–34, title I, §102(k), Dec. 26, 2023, 137 Stat. 1114; Pub. L. 118–41, title I, §102(k), Mar. 8, 2024, 138 Stat. 22; Pub. L. 118–63, title XI, §1111, May 16, 2024, 138 Stat. 1419.)

§50906. EXPERIMENTAL PERMITS

(a) A person may apply to the Secretary of Transportation for an experimental permit under this section in the form and manner the Secretary prescribes. Consistent with the protection of the public health and safety, safety of property, and national security and foreign policy interests of the United States, the Secretary, not later than 120 days after receiving an application pursuant to this section, shall issue a permit if the Secretary decides in writing that the applicant complies, and will continue to comply, with this chapter and regulations prescribed under this chapter. The Secretary shall inform the applicant of any pending issue and action required to resolve the issue if the Secretary has not made a decision not later than 90 days after receiving an application. The Secretary shall transmit to the Committee on Science of the House of Representatives and Committee on Commerce, Science, and Transportation of the Senate a written notice not later than 15 days after any occurrence when the Secretary has failed to act on a permit within the deadline established by this section.

(b) In carrying out subsection (a), the Secretary may establish procedures for safety approvals of launch vehicles, reentry vehicles, safety systems, processes, services, or personnel that may be used in conducting commercial space launch or reentry activities pursuant to a permit.

(c) In order to encourage the development of a commercial space flight industry, the Secretary may when issuing permits use the authority granted under section 50905(b)(2)(C).

(d) The Secretary may issue a permit only for reusable suborbital rockets or reusable launch vehicles that will be launched into a suborbital trajectory or reentered under that permit solely for—

(1) research and development to test design concepts, equipment, or operating techniques;

(2) showing compliance with requirements as part of the process for obtaining a license under this chapter; or

(3) crew training for a launch or reentry using the design of the rocket or vehicle for which the permit would be issued.

(e) Permits issued under this section shall—

(1) authorize an unlimited number of launches and reentries for a particular suborbital rocket or suborbital rocket design, or for a particular reusable launch vehicle or reusable launch vehicle design, for the uses described in subsection (d); and

(2) specify the type of modifications that may be made to the suborbital rocket or launch vehicle without changing the design to an extent that would invalidate the permit.

(f) Permits shall not be transferable.

(g) The Secretary may issue a permit under this section notwithstanding any license issued under this chapter. The issuance of a license under this chapter may not invalidate a permit issued under this section.

(h) No person may operate a reusable suborbital rocket or reusable launch vehicle under a permit for carrying any property or human being for compensation or hire.

(i) For the purposes of sections 50907, 50908, 50909, 50910, 50912, 50914, 50917, 50918, 50919, and 50923 of this chapter—

(1) a permit shall be considered a license;

(2) the holder of a permit shall be considered a licensee;

(3) a vehicle operating under a permit shall be considered to be licensed; and

(4) the issuance of a permit shall be considered licensing.

This subsection shall not be construed to allow the transfer of a permit.

(Added Pub. L. 108–492, §2(c)(16), Dec. 23, 2004, 118 Stat. 3979, §70105a of title 49; renumbered §70105a then §50906 of title 51 and amended Pub. L. 111–314, §4(d)(2), (3)(F), (5)(G), (H), Dec. 18, 2010, 124 Stat. 3440–3442; Pub. L. 114–90, title I, §104, Nov. 25, 2015, 129 Stat. 706.)

§50907. Monitoring activities

(a) General Requirements.—A licensee under this chapter must allow the Secretary of Transportation to place an officer or employee of the United States Government or another individual as an observer at a launch site or reentry site the licensee uses, at a production facility or assembly site a contractor of the licensee uses to produce or assemble a launch vehicle or reentry vehicle, at a site not owned or operated by the Federal Government or a foreign government used for crew, government astronaut, or space flight participant training, or at a site at which a payload is integrated with a launch vehicle or reentry vehicle. The observer will monitor the activity of the licensee or contractor at the time and to the extent the Secretary considers reasonable to ensure compliance with the license or to carry out the duties of the Secretary under sections 50904(c), 50905, and 50906 of this title. A licensee must cooperate with an observer carrying out this subsection.

(b) Contracts.—To the extent provided in advance in an appropriation law, the Secretary may make a contract with a person to carry out subsection (a) of this section.

(Pub. L. 103–272, §1(e), July 5, 1994, 108 Stat. 1334, §70106 of title 49; Pub. L. 105–303, title I, §102(a)(7), Oct. 28, 1998, 112 Stat. 2848; Pub. L. 108–492, §2(c)(17), Dec. 23, 2004, 118 Stat. 3980; renumbered §70106 then §50907 of title 51 and amended Pub. L. 111–314, §4(d)(2), (3)(G), (5)(I), Dec. 18, 2010, 124 Stat. 3440–3442; Pub. L. 114–90, title I, §112(m), Nov. 25, 2015, 129 Stat. 713.)

§50908. Effective periods, and modifications, suspensions, and revocations, of licenses

(a) Effective Periods of Licenses.—The Secretary of Transportation shall specify the period for which a license issued or transferred under this chapter is in effect.

(b) Modifications.—(1) On the initiative of the Secretary or on application of the licensee, the Secretary may modify a license issued or transferred under this chapter if the Secretary decides the modification will comply with this chapter.

(2) The Secretary shall modify a license issued or transferred under this chapter whenever a modification is needed for the license to be in conformity with a regulation that was issued pursuant to section 50905(c) after the issuance of the license. This paragraph shall not apply to permits.

(c) Suspensions and Revocations.—The Secretary may suspend or revoke a license if the Secretary decides that—

(1) the licensee has not complied substantially with a requirement of this chapter or a regulation prescribed under this chapter; or

(2) the suspension or revocation is necessary to protect the public health and safety, the safety of property, or a national security or foreign policy interest of the United States.

(d) Additional Suspensions.—(1) The Secretary may suspend a license when a previous launch or reentry under the license has resulted in a serious or fatal injury (as defined in 49 CFR 830, as in effect on November 10, 2004) to any human being and the Secretary has determined that continued operations under the license are likely to cause additional serious or fatal injury (as defined in 49 CFR 830, as in effect on November 10, 2004) to any human being.

(2) Any suspension imposed under this subsection shall be for as brief a period as possible and, in any event, shall cease when the Secretary—

(A) has determined that the licensee has taken sufficient steps to reduce the likelihood of a recurrence of the serious or fatal injury; or

(B) has modified the license pursuant to subsection (b) to sufficiently reduce the likelihood of a recurrence of the serious or fatal injury.

(3) This subsection shall not apply to permits.

(e) EFFECTIVE PERIODS OF MODIFICATIONS, SUSPENSIONS, AND REVOCATIONS.—Unless the Secretary specifies otherwise, a modification, suspension, or revocation under this section takes effect immediately and remains in effect during a review under section 50912 of this title.

(f) NOTIFICATION.—The Secretary shall notify the licensee in writing of the decision of the Secretary under this section and any action the Secretary takes or proposes to take based on the decision.

(Pub. L. 103–272, §1(e), July 5, 1994, 108 Stat. 1334, §70107 of title 49; Pub. L. 108–492, §2(c)(18), (19), Dec. 23, 2004, 118 Stat. 3980; renumbered §70107 then §50908 of title 51 and amended Pub. L. 111–314, §4(d)(2), (3)(H), (5)(J), (K), Dec. 18, 2010, 124 Stat. 3440–3442; Pub. L. 114–90, title I, §112(n), Nov. 25, 2015, 129 Stat. 713.)

§50909. PROHIBITION, SUSPENSION, AND END OF LAUNCHES, OPERATION OF LAUNCH SITES AND REENTRY SITES, AND REENTRIES

(a) GENERAL AUTHORITY.—The Secretary of Transportation may prohibit, suspend, or end immediately the launch of a launch vehicle or the operation of a launch site or reentry site, or reentry of a reentry vehicle, licensed under this chapter if the Secretary decides the launch or operation or reentry is detrimental to the public health and safety, the safety of property, or a national security or foreign policy interest of the United States.

(b) EFFECTIVE PERIODS OF ORDERS.—An order under this section takes effect immediately and remains in effect during a review under section 50912 of this title.

(Pub. L. 103–272, §1(e), July 5, 1994, 108 Stat. 1334, §70108 of title 49; Pub. L. 105–303, title I, §102(a)(8), Oct. 28, 1998, 112 Stat. 2848; renumbered §70108 then §50909 of title 51 and amended Pub. L. 111–314, §4(d)(2), (3)(I), (5)(L), Dec. 18, 2010, 124 Stat. 3440–3442.)

§50910. PREEMPTION OF SCHEDULED LAUNCHES OR REENTRIES

(a) GENERAL.—With the cooperation of the Secretary of Defense and the Administrator of the National Aeronautics and Space Administration, the Secretary of Transportation shall act to ensure that a launch or reentry of a payload is not preempted from access to a United States Government launch site, reentry site, or launch property, except for imperative national need, when a launch date commitment or reentry date commitment from the Government has been obtained for a launch or reentry licensed under this chapter. A licensee or transferee preempted from access to a launch site, reentry site, or launch property does not have to pay the Government any amount for launch services, or services related to a reentry, attributable only to the scheduled launch or reentry prevented by the preemption.

(b) IMPERATIVE NATIONAL NEED DECISIONS.—In consultation with the Secretary of Transportation, the Secretary of Defense or the Administrator shall decide when an imperative national need requires preemption under subsection (a) of this section. That decision may not be delegated.

(c) REPORTS.—In cooperation with the Secretary of Transportation, the Secretary of

Defense or the Administrator, as appropriate, shall submit to Congress not later than 7 days after a decision to preempt under subsection (a) of this section, a report that includes an explanation of the circumstances justifying the decision and a schedule for ensuring the prompt launching or reentry of a preempted payload.

(Pub. L. 103–272, §1(e), July 5, 1994, 108 Stat. 1335, §70109 of title 49; Pub. L. 105–303, title I, §102(a)(9), Oct. 28, 1998, 112 Stat. 2849; renumbered §70109 then §50910 of title 51, Pub. L. 111–314, §4(d)(2), (3)(J), Dec. 18, 2010, 124 Stat. 3440, 3441.)

§50911. SPACE ADVERTISING

(a) LICENSING.—Notwithstanding the provisions of this chapter or any other provision of law, the Secretary may not, for the launch of a payload containing any material to be used for the purposes of obtrusive space advertising—

(1) issue or transfer a license under this chapter; or

(2) waive the license requirements of this chapter.

(b) LAUNCHING.—No holder of a license under this chapter may launch a payload containing any material to be used for purposes of obtrusive space advertising.

(c) COMMERCIAL SPACE ADVERTISING.—Nothing in this section shall apply to nonobtrusive commercial space advertising, including advertising on—

(1) commercial space transportation vehicles;

(2) space infrastructure payloads;

(3) space launch facilities; and

(4) launch support facilities.

(Added Pub. L. 106–391, title III, §322(b), Oct. 30, 2000, 114 Stat. 1598, §70109a of title 49; renumbered §70109a then §50911 of title 51, Pub. L. 111–314, §4(d)(2), (3)(K), Dec. 18, 2010, 124 Stat. 3440, 3441.)

§50912. ADMINISTRATIVE HEARINGS AND JUDICIAL REVIEW

(a) ADMINISTRATIVE HEARINGS.—The Secretary of Transportation shall provide an opportunity for a hearing on the record to—

(1) an applicant under this chapter, for a decision of the Secretary under section 50905(a) or 50906 of this title to issue or transfer a license with terms or deny the issuance or transfer of a license;

(2) an owner or operator of a payload under this chapter, for a decision of the Secretary under section 50904(c) of this title to prevent the launch or reentry of the payload; and

(3) a licensee under this chapter, for a decision of the Secretary under—

(A) section 50908(b) or (c) of this title to modify, suspend, or revoke a license; or

(B) section 50909(a) of this title to prohibit, suspend, or end a launch or operation of a launch site or reentry site, or reentry of a reentry vehicle, licensed by the Secretary.

(b) JUDICIAL REVIEW.—A final action of the Secretary under this chapter is subject to judicial review as provided in chapter 7 of title 5.

(Pub. L. 103–272, §1(e), July 5, 1994, 108 Stat. 1335, §70110 of title 49; Pub. L. 105–303, title I, §102(a)(10), Oct. 28, 1998, 112 Stat. 2849; Pub. L. 108–492, §2(c)(20), Dec. 23, 2004, 118 Stat. 3981; renumbered §70110 then §50912 of title 51 and amended Pub. L. 111–314, §4(d)(2), (3)(L), (5)(M)–(P), Dec. 18, 2010, 124 Stat. 3440–3442.)

§50913. ACQUIRING UNITED STATES GOVERNMENT PROPERTY AND SERVICES

(a) GENERAL REQUIREMENTS AND CONSIDERATIONS.—(1) The Secretary of Transportation shall facilitate and encourage the acquisition by the private sector and State governments of—

(A) launch or reentry property of the United States Government that is excess or otherwise is not needed for public use; and

(B) launch services and reentry services, including utilities, of the Government otherwise not needed for public use.

(2) In acting under paragraph (1) of this subsection, the Secretary shall consider the commercial availability on reasonable terms of substantially equivalent launch property or launch services or reentry services from a domestic source, whether such source is located on or off a Federal range.

(b) PRICE.—(1) In this subsection, "direct costs" means the actual costs that—

(A) can be associated unambiguously with a commercial launch or reentry effort; and

(B) the Government would not incur if there were no commercial launch or reentry effort.

(2) In consultation with the Secretary, the head of the executive agency providing the property or service under subsection (a) of this section shall establish the price for the property or service. The price for—

(A) acquiring launch property by sale or transaction instead of sale is the fair market value;

(B) acquiring launch property (except by sale or transaction instead of sale) is an amount equal to the direct costs, including specific wear and tear and property damage, the Government incurred because of acquisition of the property; and

(C) launch services or reentry services is an amount equal to the direct costs, including the basic pay of Government civilian and contractor personnel, the Government incurred because of acquisition of the services.

(3) The Secretary shall ensure the establishment of uniform guidelines for, and consistent implementation of, this section by all Federal agencies.

(c) COLLECTION BY SECRETARY.—The Secretary may collect a payment under this section with the consent of the head of the executive agency establishing the price. Amounts collected under this subsection shall be deposited in the Treasury. Amounts (except for excess launch property) shall be credited to the appropriation from which the cost of providing the property or services was paid.

(d) COLLECTION BY OTHER GOVERNMENTAL HEADS.—The head of a department, agency, or instrumentality of the Government may collect a payment for an activity involved in producing a launch vehicle or reentry vehicle, or the payload of either, for launch or reentry if the activity was agreed to by the owner or manufacturer of the launch vehicle, reentry vehicle, or payload.

(Pub. L. 103–272, §1(e), July 5, 1994, 108 Stat. 1335, §70111 of title 49; Pub. L. 105–303, title I, §102(a)(11), Oct. 28, 1998, 112 Stat. 2849; renumbered §70111 then §50913 of title 51, Pub. L. 111–314, §4(d)(2), (3)(M), Dec. 18, 2010, 124 Stat. 3440, 3441.)

§50914. Liability insurance and financial responsibility requirements

(a) General Requirements.—(1) When a launch or reentry license is issued or transferred under this chapter, the licensee or transferee shall obtain liability insurance or demonstrate financial responsibility in amounts to compensate for the maximum probable loss from claims by—

(A) a third party for death, bodily injury, or property damage or loss resulting from an activity carried out under the license; and

(B) the United States Government against a person for damage or loss to Government property resulting from an activity carried out under the license.

(2) The Secretary of Transportation shall determine the amounts required under paragraph (1)(A) and (B) of this subsection, after consulting with the Administrator of the National Aeronautics and Space Administration, the Secretary of the Air Force, and the heads of other appropriate executive agencies.

(3) For the total claims related to one launch or reentry, a licensee or transferee is not required to obtain insurance or demonstrate financial responsibility of more than—

(A)(i) $500,000,000 under paragraph (1)(A) of this subsection; or

(ii) $100,000,000 under paragraph (1)(B) of this subsection; or

(B) the maximum liability insurance available on the world market at reasonable cost if the amount is less than the applicable amount in clause (A)(i) or (ii) of this paragraph.

(4) An insurance policy or demonstration of financial responsibility under this subsection shall protect the following, to the extent of their potential liability for involvement in launch services or reentry services, at no cost to the Government:

(A) the Government.

(B) executive agencies and personnel, contractors, and subcontractors of the Government.

(C) contractors, subcontractors, and customers of the licensee or transferee.

(D) contractors and subcontractors of the customer.

(E) space flight participants.

(5) Subparagraph (E) of paragraph (4) ceases to be effective September 30, 2025.

(b) Reciprocal Waiver of Claims.—(1)(A) A launch or reentry license issued or transferred under this chapter shall contain a provision requiring the licensee or transferee to make a reciprocal waiver of claims with applicable parties involved in launch services or reentry services under which each party to the waiver agrees to be responsible for personal injury to, death of, or property damage or loss sustained by it or its own employees resulting from an activity carried out under the applicable license.

(B) In this paragraph, the term "applicable parties" means—

(i) contractors, subcontractors, and customers of the licensee or transferee;

(ii) contractors and subcontractors of the customers; and

(iii) space flight participants.

(C) Clause (iii) of subparagraph (B) ceases to be effective September 30, 2025.

(2) The Secretary of Transportation shall make, for the Government, executive agencies of the Government involved in launch services or reentry services, and contractors and subcontractors involved in launch services or reentry services, a reciprocal waiver of claims with the licensee or transferee, contractors, subcontractors, crew, space flight participants,

and customers of the licensee or transferee, and contractors and subcontractors of the customers, involved in launch services or reentry services under which each party to the waiver agrees to be responsible for property damage or loss it sustains, or for personal injury to, death of, or property damage or loss sustained by its own employees or by space flight participants, resulting from an activity carried out under the applicable license. The waiver applies only to the extent that claims are more than the amount of insurance or demonstration of financial responsibility required under subsection (a)(1)(B) of this section. After consulting with the Administrator and the Secretary of the Air Force, the Secretary of Transportation may waive, for the Government and a department, agency, and instrumentality of the Government, the right to recover damages for damage or loss to Government property to the extent insurance is not available because of a policy exclusion the Secretary of Transportation decides is usual for the type of insurance involved.

(c) DETERMINATION OF MAXIMUM PROBABLE LOSSES.—The Secretary of Transportation shall determine the maximum probable losses under subsection (a)(1)(A) and (B) of this section associated with an activity under a license not later than 90 days after a licensee or transferee requires a determination and submits all information the Secretary requires. The Secretary shall amend the determination as warranted by new information.

(d) ANNUAL REPORT.—(1) Not later than November 15 of each year, the Secretary of Transportation shall submit to the Committee on Commerce, Science, and Transportation of the Senate and the Committee on Science of the House of Representatives a report on current determinations made under subsection (c) of this section related to all issued licenses and the reasons for the determinations.

(2) Not later than May 15 of each year, the Secretary of Transportation shall review the amounts specified in subsection (a)(3)(A) of this section and submit a report to Congress that contains proposed adjustments in the amounts to conform with changed liability expectations and availability of insurance on the world market. The proposed adjustment takes effect 30 days after a report is submitted.

(e) LAUNCHES OR REENTRIES INVOLVING GOVERNMENT FACILITIES AND PERSONNEL.—The Secretary of Transportation shall establish requirements consistent with this chapter for proof of financial responsibility and other assurances necessary to protect the Government and its executive agencies and personnel from liability, death, bodily injury, or property damage or loss as a result of a launch or operation of a launch site or reentry site or a reentry involving a facility or personnel of the Government. The Secretary may not relieve the Government of liability under this subsection for death, bodily injury, or property damage or loss resulting from the willful misconduct of the Government or its agents.

(f) COLLECTION AND CREDITING PAYMENTS.—The head of a department, agency, or instrumentality of the Government shall collect a payment owed for damage or loss to Government property under its jurisdiction or control resulting from an activity carried out under a launch or reentry license issued or transferred under this chapter. The payment shall be credited to the current applicable appropriation, fund, or account of the department, agency, or instrumentality.

(g) FEDERAL JURISDICTION.—Any claim by a third party or space flight participant for death, bodily injury, or property damage or loss resulting from an activity carried out under the license shall be the exclusive jurisdiction of the Federal courts.

(Pub. L. 103–272, §1(e), July 5, 1994, 108 Stat. 1336, §70112 of title 49; Pub. L. 104–287, §5(74), (93), Oct.

11, 1996, 110 Stat. 3396, 3398; Pub. L. 105–303, title I, §102(a)(12), Oct. 28, 1998, 112 Stat. 2850; Pub. L. 108–492, §2(c)(21), Dec. 23, 2004, 118 Stat. 3981; renumbered §70112 then §50914 of title 51, Pub. L. 111–314, §4(d)(2), (3)(N), Dec. 18, 2010, 124 Stat. 3440, 3441; Pub. L. 114–90, title I, §§103(a)(1), 106, 107, Nov. 25, 2015, 129 Stat. 706, 707.)

§50915. PAYING CLAIMS EXCEEDING LIABILITY INSURANCE AND FINANCIAL RESPONSIBILITY REQUIREMENTS

(a) GENERAL REQUIREMENTS.—(1) To the extent provided in advance in an appropriation law or to the extent additional legislative authority is enacted providing for paying claims in a compensation plan submitted under subsection (d) of this section, the Secretary of Transportation shall provide for the payment by the United States Government of a successful claim (including reasonable litigation or settlement expenses) of a third party against a person described in paragraph (3)(A) resulting from an activity carried out under the license issued or transferred under this chapter for death, bodily injury, or property damage or loss resulting from an activity carried out under the license. However, claims may be paid under this section only to the extent the total amount of successful claims related to one launch or reentry—

(A) is more than the amount of insurance or demonstration of financial responsibility required under section 50914(a)(1)(A) of this title; and

(B) is not more than $1,500,000,000 (plus additional amounts necessary to reflect inflation occurring after January 1, 1989) above that insurance or financial responsibility amount.

(2) The Secretary may not provide for paying a part of a claim for which death, bodily injury, or property damage or loss results from willful misconduct by the licensee or transferee. To the extent insurance required under section 50914(a)(1)(A) of this title is not available to cover a successful third party liability claim because of an insurance policy exclusion the Secretary decides is usual for the type of insurance involved, the Secretary may provide for paying the excluded claims without regard to the limitation contained in section 50914(a)(1).

(3)(A) A person described in this subparagraph is—

(i) a licensee or transferee under this chapter;

(ii) a contractor, subcontractor, or customer of the licensee or transferee;

(iii) a contractor or subcontractor of a customer; or

(iv) a space flight participant.

(B) Clause (iv) of subparagraph (A) ceases to be effective September 30, 2025.

(b) NOTICE, PARTICIPATION, AND APPROVAL.—Before a payment under subsection (a) of this section is made—

(1) notice must be given to the Government of a claim, or a civil action related to the claim, against a party described in subsection (a)(1) of this section for death, bodily injury, or property damage or loss;

(2) the Government must be given an opportunity to participate or assist in the defense of the claim or action; and

(3) the Secretary must approve any part of a settlement to be paid out of appropriations of the Government.

(c) WITHHOLDING PAYMENTS.—The Secretary may withhold a payment under subsection

25

(a) of this section if the Secretary certifies that the amount is not reasonable. However, the Secretary shall deem to be reasonable the amount of a claim finally decided by a court of competent jurisdiction.

(d) SURVEYS, REPORTS, AND COMPENSATION PLANS.—(1) If as a result of an activity carried out under a license issued or transferred under this chapter the total of claims related to one launch or reentry is likely to be more than the amount of required insurance or demonstration of financial responsibility, the Secretary shall—

(A) survey the causes and extent of damage; and

(B) submit expeditiously to Congress a report on the results of the survey.

(2) Not later than 90 days after a court determination indicates that the liability for the total of claims related to one launch or reentry may be more than the required amount of insurance or demonstration of financial responsibility, the President, on the recommendation of the Secretary, shall submit to Congress a compensation plan that—

(A) outlines the total dollar value of the claims;

(B) recommends sources of amounts to pay for the claims;

(C) includes legislative language required to carry out the plan if additional legislative authority is required; and

(D) for a single event or incident, may not be for more than $1,500,000,000.

(3) A compensation plan submitted to Congress under paragraph (2) of this subsection shall—

(A) have an identification number; and

(B) be submitted to the Senate and the House of Representatives on the same day and when the Senate and House are in session.

(e) CONGRESSIONAL RESOLUTIONS.—(1) In this subsection, "resolution"—

(A) means a joint resolution of Congress the matter after the resolving clause of which is as follows: "That the Congress approves the compensation plan numbered _____ submitted to the Congress on _____ XX, 20____.", with the blank spaces being filled appropriately; but

(B) does not include a resolution that includes more than one compensation plan.

(2) The Senate shall consider under this subsection a compensation plan requiring additional appropriations or legislative authority not later than 60 calendar days of continuous session of Congress after the date on which the plan is submitted to Congress.

(3) A resolution introduced in the Senate shall be referred immediately to a committee by the President of the Senate. All resolutions related to the same plan shall be referred to the same committee.

(4)(A) If the committee of the Senate to which a resolution has been referred does not report the resolution within 20 calendar days after it is referred, a motion is in order to discharge the committee from further consideration of the resolution or to discharge the committee from further consideration of the plan.

(B) A motion to discharge may be made only by an individual favoring the resolution and is highly privileged (except that the motion may not be made after the committee has reported a resolution on the plan). Debate on the motion is limited to one hour, to be divided equally between those favoring and those opposing the resolution. An amendment to the motion is not in order. A motion to reconsider the vote by which the motion is agreed to or disagreed to is not in order.

(C) If the motion to discharge is agreed to or disagreed to, the motion may not be renewed and another motion to discharge the committee from another resolution on the same plan may not be made.

(5)(A) After a committee of the Senate reports, or is discharged from further consideration of, a resolution, a motion to proceed to the consideration of the resolution is in order at any time, even though a similar previous motion has been disagreed to. The motion is highly privileged and is not debatable. An amendment to the motion is not in order. A motion to reconsider the vote by which the motion is agreed to or disagreed to is not in order.

(B) Debate on the resolution referred to in subparagraph (A) of this paragraph is limited to not more than 10 hours, to be divided equally between those favoring and those opposing the resolution. A motion further to limit debate is not debatable. An amendment to, or motion to recommit, the resolution is not in order. A motion to reconsider the vote by which the resolution is agreed to or disagreed to is not in order.

(6) The following shall be decided in the Senate without debate:

(A) a motion to postpone related to the discharge from committee.

(B) a motion to postpone consideration of a resolution.

(C) a motion to proceed to the consideration of other business.

(D) an appeal from a decision of the chair related to the application of the rules of the Senate to the procedures related to a resolution.

(f) APPLICATION.—This section applies to a license issued or transferred under this chapter for which the Secretary receives a complete and valid application not later than September 30, 2025. This section does not apply to permits.

(Pub. L. 103–272, §1(e), July 5, 1994, 108 Stat. 1338, §70113 of title 49; Pub. L. 104–287, §5(94), Oct. 11, 1996, 110 Stat. 3398; Pub. L. 105–303, title I, §102(a)(13), Oct. 28, 1998, 112 Stat. 2850; Pub. L. 106–74, title IV, §433, Oct. 20, 1999, 113 Stat. 1097; Pub. L. 106–377, §1(a)(1) [title IV, §429], Oct. 27, 2000, 114 Stat. 1441, 1441A–56; Pub. L. 106–405, §§5(b), 6(a), Nov. 1, 2000, 114 Stat. 1752; Pub. L. 108–428, §1, Nov. 30, 2004, 118 Stat. 2432; Pub. L. 108–492, §2(c)(22), (23), Dec. 23, 2004, 118 Stat. 3981; Pub. L. 111–125, §1, Dec. 28, 2009, 123 Stat. 3486; renumbered §70113 then §50915 of title 51 and amended Pub. L. 111–314, §4(d)(2), (3)(O), (5)(Q), (R), Dec. 18, 2010, 124 Stat. 3440–3442; Pub. L. 112–273, §3, Jan. 14, 2013, 126 Stat. 2454; Pub. L. 113–76, §8, Jan. 17, 2014, 128 Stat. 7; Pub. L. 114–90, title I, §§102(d), 103(a)(2), Nov. 25, 2015, 129 Stat. 706.)

§50916. DISCLOSING INFORMATION

The Secretary of Transportation, an officer or employee of the United States Government, or a person making a contract with the Secretary under section 50907(b) of this title may disclose information under this chapter that qualifies for an exemption under section 552(b)(4) of title 5 or is designated as confidential by the person or head of the executive agency providing the information only if the Secretary decides withholding the information is contrary to the public or national interest.

(Pub. L. 103–272, §1(e), July 5, 1994, 108 Stat. 1340, §70114 of title 49; renumbered §70114 then §50916 of title 51 and amended Pub. L. 111–314, §4(d)(2), (3)(P), (5)(S), Dec. 18, 2010, 124 Stat. 3440–3442.)

§50917. ENFORCEMENT AND PENALTY

(a) PROHIBITIONS.—A person may not violate this chapter, a regulation prescribed under this chapter, or any term of a license issued or transferred under this chapter.

(b) GENERAL AUTHORITY.—(1) In carrying out this chapter, the Secretary of Transportation may—

(A) conduct investigations and inquiries;

(B) administer oaths;

(C) take affidavits; and

(D) under lawful process—

(i) enter at a reasonable time a launch site, reentry site, production facility, assembly site of a launch vehicle or reentry vehicle, crew or space flight participant training site, or site at which a payload is integrated with a launch vehicle or reentry vehicle to inspect an object to which this chapter applies or a record or report the Secretary requires be made or kept under this chapter; and

(ii) seize the object, record, or report when there is probable cause to believe the object, record, or report was used, is being used, or likely will be used in violation of this chapter.

(2) The Secretary may delegate a duty or power under this chapter related to enforcement to an officer or employee of another executive agency with the consent of the head of the agency.

(c) CIVIL PENALTY.—(1) After notice and an opportunity for a hearing on the record, a person the Secretary finds to have violated subsection (a) of this section is liable to the United States Government for a civil penalty of not more than $100,000. A separate violation occurs for each day the violation continues.

(2) In conducting a hearing under paragraph (1) of this subsection, the Secretary may—

(A) subpena witnesses and records; and

(B) enforce a subpena in an appropriate district court of the United States.

(3) The Secretary shall impose the civil penalty by written notice. The Secretary may compromise or remit a penalty imposed, or that may be imposed, under this section.

(4) The Secretary shall recover a civil penalty not paid after the penalty is final or after a court enters a final judgment for the Secretary.

(Pub. L. 103–272, §1(e), July 5, 1994, 108 Stat. 1341, §70115 of title 49; Pub. L. 105–303, title I, §102(a)(14), Oct. 28, 1998, 112 Stat. 2850; Pub. L. 108–492, §2(c)(24), Dec. 23, 2004, 118 Stat. 3981; renumbered §70115 then §50917 of title 51, Pub. L. 111–314, §4(d)(2), (3)(Q), Dec. 18, 2010, 124 Stat. 3440, 3441.)

§50918. CONSULTATION

(a) MATTERS AFFECTING NATIONAL SECURITY.—The Secretary of Transportation shall consult with the Secretary of Defense on a matter under this chapter affecting national security. The Secretary of Defense shall identify and notify the Secretary of Transportation of a national security interest relevant to an activity under this chapter.

(b) MATTERS AFFECTING FOREIGN POLICY.—The Secretary of Transportation shall consult with the Secretary of State on a matter under this chapter affecting foreign policy. The Secretary of State shall identify and notify the Secretary of Transportation of a foreign policy interest or obligation relevant to an activity under this chapter.

(c) OTHER MATTERS.—In carrying out this chapter, the Secretary of Transportation shall consult with the head of another executive agency—

(1) to provide consistent application of licensing requirements under this chapter;

(2) to ensure fair treatment for all license applicants; and

(3) when appropriate.

(Pub. L. 103–272, §1(e), July 5, 1994, 108 Stat. 1341, §70116 of title 49; renumbered §70116 then §50918 of title 51, Pub. L. 111–314, §4(d)(2), (3)(R), Dec. 18, 2010, 124 Stat. 3440, 3441.)

§50919. RELATIONSHIP TO OTHER EXECUTIVE AGENCIES, LAWS, AND INTERNATIONAL OBLIGATIONS

(a) EXECUTIVE AGENCIES.—Except as provided in this chapter, a person is not required to obtain from an executive agency a license, approval, waiver, or exemption to launch a launch vehicle or operate a launch site or reentry site, or to reenter a reentry vehicle.

(b) FEDERAL COMMUNICATIONS COMMISSION AND SECRETARY OF COMMERCE.—This chapter does not affect the authority of—

(1) the Federal Communications Commission under the Communications Act of 1934 (47 U.S.C. 151 et seq.); or

(2) the Secretary of Commerce under chapter 601 of this title.

(c) STATES AND POLITICAL SUBDIVISIONS.—A State or political subdivision of a State—

(1) may not adopt or have in effect a law, regulation, standard, or order inconsistent with this chapter; but

(2) may adopt or have in effect a law, regulation, standard, or order consistent with this chapter that is in addition to or more stringent than a requirement of, or regulation prescribed under, this chapter.

(d) CONSULTATION.—The Secretary of Transportation is encouraged to consult with a State to simplify and expedite the approval of a space launch or reentry activity.

(e) FOREIGN COUNTRIES.—The Secretary of Transportation shall—

(1) carry out this chapter consistent with an obligation the United States Government assumes in a treaty, convention, or agreement in force between the Government and the government of a foreign country; and

(2) consider applicable laws and requirements of a foreign country when carrying out this chapter.

(f) LAUNCH NOT AN EXPORT; REENTRY NOT AN IMPORT.—A launch vehicle, reentry vehicle, or payload that is launched or reentered is not, because of the launch or reentry, an export or import, respectively, for purposes of a law controlling exports or imports, except that payloads launched pursuant to foreign trade zone procedures as provided for under the Foreign Trade Zones Act (19 U.S.C. 81a–81u) shall be considered exports with regard to customs entry.

(g) NONAPPLICATION.—

(1) IN GENERAL.—This chapter does not apply to—

(A) a launch, reentry, operation of a launch vehicle or reentry vehicle, operation of a launch site or reentry site, or other space activity the Government carries out for the Government; or

(B) planning or policies related to the launch, reentry, operation, or activity under subparagraph (A).

(2) RULE OF CONSTRUCTION.—The following activities are not space activities the Government carries out for the Government under paragraph (1):

(A) A government astronaut being carried within a launch vehicle or reentry vehicle under this chapter.

(B) A government astronaut performing activities directly relating to the launch, reentry, or other operation of the launch vehicle or reentry vehicle under this chapter.

(Pub. L. 103–272, §1(e), July 5, 1994, 108 Stat. 1342, §70117 of title 49; Pub. L. 104–287, §5(95), Oct. 11, 1996, 110 Stat. 3398; Pub. L. 105–303, title I, §102(a)(15), Oct. 28, 1998, 112 Stat. 2850; renumbered §70117 then §50919 of title 51 and amended Pub. L. 111–314, §4(d)(2), (3)(S), (5)(T), Dec. 18, 2010, 124 Stat. 3440–3442; Pub. L. 114–90, title I, §112(o), Nov. 25, 2015, 129 Stat. 713.)

§50920. User fees

The Secretary of Transportation may collect a user fee for a regulatory or other service conducted under this chapter only if specifically authorized by this chapter.

(Pub. L. 103–272, §1(e), July 5, 1994, 108 Stat. 1342, §70118 of title 49; renumbered §70118 then §50920 of title 51, Pub. L. 111–314, §4(d)(2), (3)(T), Dec. 18, 2010, 124 Stat. 3440, 3441.)

§50921. Office of Commercial Space Transportation

There are authorized to be appropriated to the Secretary of Transportation for the activities of the Office of the Associate Administrator for Commercial Space Transportation—

(1) $11,941,000 for fiscal year 2005;
(2) $12,299,000 for fiscal year 2006;
(3) $12,668,000 for fiscal year 2007;
(4) $13,048,000 for fiscal year 2008; and
(5) $13,440,000 for fiscal year 2009.

(Pub. L. 103–272, §1(e), July 5, 1994, 108 Stat. 1343, §70119 of title 49, Pub. L. 105–303, title I, §102(b), Oct. 28, 1998, 112 Stat. 2851; Pub. L. 106–405, §3(a), Nov. 1, 2000, 114 Stat. 1752; Pub. L. 108–360, title III, §301, Oct. 25, 2004, 118 Stat. 1680; renumbered §70119 then §50921 of title 51, Pub. L. 111–314, §4(d)(2), (3)(U), Dec. 18, 2010, 124 Stat. 3440, 3441.)

§50922. Regulations

(a) In General.—The Secretary of Transportation, within 9 months after the date of the enactment of this section, shall issue regulations to carry out this chapter that include—

(1) guidelines for industry and State governments to obtain sufficient insurance coverage for potential damages to third parties;

(2) procedures for requesting and obtaining licenses to launch a commercial launch vehicle;

(3) procedures for requesting and obtaining operator licenses for launch;

(4) procedures for requesting and obtaining launch site operator licenses; and

(5) procedures for the application of government indemnification.

(b) Reentry.—The Secretary of Transportation, within 6 months after the date of the enactment of this section, shall issue a notice of proposed rulemaking to carry out this chapter that includes—

(1) procedures for requesting and obtaining licenses to reenter a reentry vehicle;

(2) procedures for requesting and obtaining operator licenses for reentry; and

(3) procedures for requesting and obtaining reentry site operator licenses.

(c) Amendments.—(1) Not later than 12 months after the date of enactment of the

Commercial Space Launch Amendments Act of 2004, the Secretary shall publish proposed regulations to carry out that Act, including regulations relating to crew, space flight participants, and permits for launch or reentry of reusable suborbital rockets. Not later than 18 months after such date of enactment, the Secretary shall issue final regulations.

(2)(A) Starting 3 years after the date of enactment of the Commercial Space Launch Amendments Act of 2004, the Secretary may issue final regulations changing the definition of suborbital rocket under this chapter. No such regulation may take effect until 180 days after the Secretary has submitted the regulation to the Congress.

(B) The Secretary may issue regulations under this paragraph only if the Secretary has determined that the definition in section 50902 does not describe, or will not continue to describe, all appropriate vehicles and only those vehicles. In making that determination, the Secretary shall take into account the evolving nature of the commercial space launch industry.

(d) EFFECTIVE DATE.—(1) Licenses for the launch or reentry of launch vehicles or reentry vehicles with human beings on board and permits may be issued by the Secretary prior to the issuance of the regulations described in subsection (c).

(2) As soon as practicable after the date of enactment of the Commercial Space Launch Amendments Act of 2004, the Secretary shall issue guidelines or advisory circulars to guide the implementation of that Act until regulations are issued.

(3) Notwithstanding paragraphs (1) and (2), no licenses for the launch or reentry of launch vehicles or reentry vehicles with human beings on board or permits may be issued starting three years after the date of enactment of the Commercial Space Launch Amendments Act of 2004 unless the final regulations described in subsection (c) have been issued.

(Added Pub. L. 105–303, title I, §102(a)(16), Oct. 28, 1998, 112 Stat. 2850, §70120 of title 49; amended Pub. L. 108–492, §2(c)(25), Dec. 23, 2004, 118 Stat. 3981; renumbered §70120 then §50922 of title 51 and amended Pub. L. 111–314, §4(d)(2), (3)(V), (5)(U), Dec. 18, 2010, 124 Stat. 3440–3442.)

§50923. REPORT TO CONGRESS

The Secretary of Transportation shall submit to Congress an annual report to accompany the President's budget request that—

(1) describes all activities undertaken under this chapter, including a description of the process for the application for and approval of licenses under this chapter and recommendations for legislation that may further commercial launches and reentries; and

(2) reviews the performance of the regulatory activities and the effectiveness of the Office of Commercial Space Transportation.

(Added Pub. L. 105–303, title I, §102(a)(16), Oct. 28, 1998, 112 Stat. 2851, §70121 of title 49; renumbered §70121 then §50923 of title 51, Pub. L. 111–314, §4(d)(2), (3)(W), Dec. 18, 2010, 124 Stat. 3440, 3441.)

CHAPTER 511—SPACE TRANSPORTATION INFRASTRUCTURE MATCHING GRANTS

§51101. Definitions

In this chapter—

(1) the definitions in section 50501 of this title apply.

(2) "commercial space transportation infrastructure development" includes—

(A) construction, improvement, design, and engineering of space transportation infrastructure in the United States; and

(B) technical studies to define how new or enhanced space transportation infrastructure can best meet the needs of the United States commercial space transportation industry.

(3) "project" means a project (or separate projects submitted together) to carry out commercial space transportation infrastructure development, including the combined submission of all projects to be undertaken at a particular site in a fiscal year.

(4) "project grant" means a grant of an amount by the Secretary of Transportation to a sponsor for one or more projects.

(5) "public agency" means a State or an agency of a State, a political subdivision of a State, or a tax-supported organization.

(6) "sponsor" means a public agency that, individually or jointly with one or more other public agencies, submits to the Secretary under this chapter an application for a project grant.

(Pub. L. 103–272, §1(e), July 5, 1994, 108 Stat. 1343, §70301 of title 49; renumbered §70301 then §51101 of title 51 and amended Pub. L. 111–314, §4(d)(2), (4)(A), (6)(A), Dec. 18, 2010, 124 Stat. 3440–3442.)

§51102. Grant authority

(a) General Authority.—To ensure the resiliency of the space transportation infrastructure of the United States, the Secretary of Transportation may make project grants to sponsors as provided in this chapter.

(b) Limitations.—The Secretary may make a project grant under this chapter only if—

(1) at least 10 percent of the total cost of the project will be paid by the private sector; and

(2) the grant will not be for more than 50 percent of the total cost of the project.

(Pub. L. 103–272, §1(e), July 5, 1994, 108 Stat. 1343, §70302 of title 49; renumbered §70302 then §51102 of title 51, Pub. L. 111–314, §4(d)(2), (4)(B), Dec. 18, 2010, 124 Stat. 3440, 3441.)

§51103. GRANT APPLICATIONS

(a) GENERAL.—A sponsor may submit to the Secretary of Transportation an application for a project grant. The application must state the project to be undertaken and be in the form and contain the information the Secretary requires.

(b) CONSIDERATIONS AND CONSULTATION.—(1) In selecting proposed projects for grants under this section, the Secretary of Transportation shall consider—

(A) the contribution of the project to industry capabilities that serve the United States Government's space transportation needs;

(B) the extent of industry's financial contribution to the project;

(C) the extent of industry's participation in the project;

(D) the positive impact of the project on the international competitiveness of the United States space transportation industry;

(E) the extent of State contributions to the project; and

(F) the impact of the project on launch operations and other activities at Government launch ranges.

(2) The Secretary of Transportation shall consult with the Secretary of Defense, the Administrator of the National Space and Aeronautics Administration, and the heads of other appropriate agencies of the Government about paragraph (1)(A) and (F) of this subsection.

(c) REQUIREMENTS.—The Secretary of Transportation may approve an application only if the Secretary is satisfied that—

(1) the project will contribute to the purposes of this chapter;

(2) the project is reasonably consistent with plans (existing at the time of approval of the project) of public agencies that are—

(A) authorized by the State in which the project is located; and

(B) responsible for the development of the area surrounding the project site;

(3) if the application proposes to use Government property, the specific consent of the head of the appropriate agency has been obtained;

(4) the project will be completed without unreasonable delay;

(5) the sponsor submitting the application has the legal authority to engage in the project; and

(6) any additional requirements prescribed by the Secretary have been met.

(d) PREFERENCE FOR INDUSTRY CONTRIBUTIONS.—The Secretary of Transportation shall give preference to applications for projects for which there will be greater industry financial contributions, all other factors being equal.

(Pub. L. 103–272, §1(e), July 5, 1994, 108 Stat. 1344, §70303 of title 49; renumbered §70303 then §51103 of title 51, Pub. L. 111–314, §4(d)(2), (4)(C), Dec. 18, 2010, 124 Stat. 3440, 3441.)

§51104. ENVIRONMENTAL REQUIREMENTS

(a) POLICY.—It is the policy of the United States that projects selected under this chapter shall provide for the protection and enhancement of the natural resources and the quality of the environment of the United States. In carrying out this policy, the Secretary of Transportation shall consult with the Secretary of the Interior and the Administrator of the Environmental Protection Agency about a project that may have a significant effect on natural resources, including fish and wildlife, natural, scenic, and recreational assets, water and air quality, and other factors affecting the environment. If the Secretary of Transportation finds that a project will have a significant adverse effect, the Secretary may approve the application for the project only if, after a complete review that is a matter of public record, the Secretary makes a written finding that no feasible and prudent alternative to the project exists and that all reasonable steps have been taken to minimize the adverse effect.

(b) PUBLIC HEARING REQUIREMENT.—The Secretary of Transportation may approve an application only if the sponsor of the project certifies to the Secretary that an opportunity for a public hearing has been provided to consider the economic, social, and environmental effects of the project and its consistency with the goals of any planning carried out by the community. When a hearing is held under this paragraph, the sponsor shall submit a copy of the transcript of the hearing to the Secretary.

(c) COMPLIANCE WITH AIR AND WATER QUALITY STANDARDS.—(1) The Secretary of Transportation may approve an application only if the chief executive officer of the State in which the project is located certifies in writing to the Secretary that there is reasonable assurance that the project will be located, designed, constructed, and operated to comply with applicable air and water quality standards. If the Administrator has not prescribed those standards, certification shall be obtained from the Administrator. Notice of certification or refusal to certify shall be provided not later than 60 days after the Secretary receives the application.

(2) The Secretary of Transportation shall condition the approval of an application on compliance with applicable air and water quality standards during construction and operation.

(d) COMPLIANCE WITH LAWS AND REGULATIONS.—The Secretary of Transportation may require a certification from a sponsor that the sponsor will comply with all applicable laws and regulations. The Secretary may rescind at any time acceptance of a certification from a sponsor under this subsection. This subsection does not affect any responsibility of the Secretary under another law, including—

(1) section 303 of title 49;

(2) title VI of the Civil Rights Act of 1964 (42 U.S.C. 2000d et seq.);

(3) title VIII of the Act of April 11, 1968 (42 U.S.C. 3601 et seq.);

(4) the National Environmental Policy Act of 1969 (42 U.S.C. 4321 et seq.); and

(5) the Uniform Relocation Assistance and Real Property Acquisition Policies Act of 1970 (42 U.S.C. 4601 et seq.).

(Pub. L. 103–272, §1(e), July 5, 1994, 108 Stat. 1344, §70304 of title 49; renumbered §70304 then §51104 of title 51 and amended Pub. L. 111–314, §4(d)(2), (4)(D), (6)(B), Dec. 18, 2010, 124 Stat. 3440, 3441, 3443.)

§51105. AUTHORIZATION OF APPROPRIATIONS

Not more than $10,000,000 may be appropriated to the Secretary of Transportation to make grants under this chapter. Amounts appropriated under this section remain available until expended.

(Pub. L. 103–272, §1(e), July 5, 1994, 108 Stat. 1345, §70305 of title 49; renumbered §70305 then §51105 of title 51, Pub. L. 111–314, §4(d)(2), (4)(E), Dec. 18, 2010, 124 Stat. 3440, 3441.)

* * * * * * *

CHAPTER 515—OFFICE OF SPACEPORTS

Sec.[1]

51501.[1]   Establishment of Office of Spaceports.[1]

[1] *Editorially supplied. Section added by Pub. L. 115–254 without corresponding amendment of chapter analysis.*

§51501. ESTABLISHMENT OF OFFICE OF SPACEPORTS

(a) ESTABLISHMENT OF OFFICE.—Not later than 90 days after the date of enactment of this section, the Secretary of Transportation shall identify, within the Office of Commercial Space Transportation, a centralized policy office to be known as the Office of Spaceports.

(b) FUNCTIONS.—The Office of Spaceports shall—

(1) support licensing activities for operation of launch and reentry sites;

(2) develop policies that promote infrastructure improvements at spaceports;

(3) provide technical assistance and guidance to spaceports;

(4) promote United States spaceports within the Department; and

(5) strengthen the Nation's competitiveness in commercial space transportation infrastructure and increase resilience for the Federal Government and commercial customers.

(c) RECOGNITION.—In carrying out the functions assigned in subsection (b), the Secretary shall recognize the unique needs and distinctions of spaceports that host— [1]

(1) launches to or reentries from orbit; and

(2) are involved in suborbital launch activities.

(d) DIRECTOR.—The head of the Office of the Associate Administrator for Commercial Space Transportation shall designate a Director of the Office of Spaceports.

(e) DEFINITION.—In this section the term "spaceport" means a launch or reentry site that is operated by an entity licensed by the Secretary of Transportation.

(Added Pub. L. 115–254, div. B, title V, §580(b)(1), Oct. 5, 2018, 132 Stat. 3395.)

[1] *So in original. The dash probably should follow "that" and the word "host" probably should appear at the beginning of par. (1).*

* * * * * * *

SELECTED PROVISIONS OF THE INTERNAL REVENUE CODE OF 1986

CURRENT THROUGH PUBLIC LAW 118-78

TITLE 26—INTERNAL REVENUE CODE

* * * * * * *

Subtitle D—Miscellaneous Excise Taxes

* * * * * * *

CHAPTER 31—RETAIL EXCISE TAXES

* * * * * * *

Subchapter B—Special Fuels

Sec.

* * * * * * *

4042.   Tax on fuel used in commercial transportation on inland waterways.

* * * * * * *

§4041. IMPOSITION OF TAX

(a) * * *

* * * * * * *

(c) CERTAIN LIQUIDS USED AS A FUEL IN AVIATION.—

(1) IN GENERAL.—

There is hereby imposed a tax upon any liquid for use as a fuel other than aviation gasoline—

(A) sold by any person to an owner, lessee, or other operator of an aircraft for use in such aircraft, or

(B) used by any person in an aircraft unless there was a taxable sale of such fuel under subparagraph (A).

(2) EXEMPTION FOR PREVIOUSLY TAXED FUEL.—

No tax shall be imposed by this subsection on the sale or use of any liquid for use as a fuel other than aviation gasoline if tax was imposed on such liquid under section 4081 (other than such tax at the Leaking Underground Storage Tank Trust Fund financing rate) and the tax thereon was not credited or refunded.

(3) RATE OF TAX.—

The rate of tax imposed by this subsection shall be 21.8 cents per gallon (4.3 cents per gallon with respect to any sale or use for commercial aviation).

(d) ADDITIONAL TAXES TO FUND LEAKING UNDERGROUND STORAGE TANK TRUST FUND.—

(1) TAX ON SALES AND USES SUBJECT TO TAX UNDER SUBSECTION (A).—

In addition to the taxes imposed by subsection (a), there is hereby imposed a tax of 0.1 cent a gallon on the sale or use of any liquid (other than liquefied petroleum gas and other than liquefied natural gas) if tax is imposed by subsection (a)(1) or (2) on such sale or use. No tax shall be imposed under the preceding sentence on the sale or use of any liquid if tax was imposed with respect to such liquid under section 4081 at the Leaking Underground Storage Tank Trust Fund financing rate.

(2) LIQUIDS USED IN AVIATION.—

In addition to the taxes imposed by subsection (c), there is hereby imposed a tax of 0.1 cent a gallon on any liquid (other than gasoline (as defined in section 4083))—

(A) sold by any person to an owner, lessee, or other operator of an aircraft for use as a fuel in such aircraft, or

(B) used by any person as a fuel in an aircraft unless there was a taxable sale of such liquid under subparagraph (A).

No tax shall be imposed by this paragraph on the sale or use of any liquid if there was a taxable sale of such liquid under section 4081.

(3) DIESEL FUEL USED IN TRAINS.—

In the case of any sale for use or use after December 31, 2006, there is hereby imposed a tax of 0.1 cent per gallon on any liquid other than gasoline (as defined in section 4083)—

(A) sold by any person to an owner, lessee, or other operator of a diesel-powered train for use as a fuel in such train, or

(B) used by any person as a fuel in a diesel-powered train unless there was a taxable sale of such fuel under subparagraph (A).

No tax shall be imposed by this paragraph on the sale or use of any liquid if tax was imposed on such liquid under section 4081.

(4) TERMINATION.—

The taxes imposed by this subsection shall not apply during any period during which the Leaking Underground Storage Tank Trust Fund financing rate under section 4081 does not apply.

(5) NONAPPLICATION OF EXEMPTIONS OTHER THAN FOR EXPORTS.—

For purposes of this section, the tax imposed under this subsection shall be determined without regard to subsections (b)(1)(A), (f), (g), (h), and (l). The preceding sentence shall not apply with respect to subsection (g)(3) and so much of subsection (g)(1) as relates to vessels (within the meaning of section 4221(d)(3)) employed in foreign trade or trade between the United States and any of its possessions.

[(e) Repealed.]

(f) EXEMPTION FOR FARM USE.—

(1) EXEMPTION.—

Under regulations prescribed by the Secretary, no tax shall be imposed under this section on any liquid sold for use or used on a farm for farming purposes.

(2) USE ON A FARM FOR FARMING PURPOSES.—

For purposes of paragraph (1) of this subsection, use on a farm for farming purposes shall be determined in accordance with paragraphs (1), (2), and (3) of section 6420(c).

(g) OTHER EXEMPTIONS.—

Under regulations prescribed by the Secretary, no tax shall be imposed under this section—

(1) on any liquid sold for use or used as supplies for vessels or aircraft (within the meaning of section 4221(d)(3));

(2) with respect to the sale of any liquid for the exclusive use of any State, any political subdivision of a State, or the District of Columbia, or with respect to the use by any of the foregoing of any liquid as a fuel;

(3) upon the sale of any liquid for export, or for shipment to a possession of the United States, and in due course so exported or shipped;

(4) with respect to the sale of any liquid to a nonprofit educational organization for its exclusive use, or with respect to the use by a nonprofit educational organization of any liquid as a fuel; and

(5) with respect to the sale of any liquid to a qualified blood collector organization (as defined in section 7701(a)(49)) for such organization's exclusive use in the collection, storage, or transportation of blood.

For purposes of paragraph (4), the term "nonprofit educational organization" means an educational organization described in section 170(b)(1)(A)(ii) which is exempt from income tax under section 501(a). The term also includes a school operated as an activity of an organization described in section 501(c)(3) which is exempt from income tax under section 501(a), if such school normally maintains a regular faculty and curriculum and normally has a regularly enrolled body of pupils or students in attendance at the place where its educational activities are regularly carried on.

(h) EXEMPTION FOR USE BY CERTAIN AIRCRAFT MUSEUMS.—

(1) EXEMPTION.—

Under regulations prescribed by the Secretary, no tax shall be imposed under this section on any liquid sold for use or used by an aircraft museum in an aircraft or vehicle owned by such museum and used exclusively for purposes set forth in paragraph (2)(C).

(2) DEFINITION OF AIRCRAFT MUSEUM.—

For purposes of this subsection, the term "aircraft museum" means an organization—
(A) described in section 501(c)(3) which is exempt from income tax under section 501(a),
(B) operated as a museum under charter by a State or the District of Columbia, and
(C) operated exclusively for the procurement, care, and exhibition of aircraft of the type used for combat or transport in World War II.

[(i) Repealed.]

(j) SALES BY UNITED STATES, ETC..—

The taxes imposed by this section shall apply with respect to liquids sold at retail by the United States, or by any agency or instrumentality of the United States, unless sales by such agency or instrumentality are by statute specifically exempted from such taxes.

[(k) Repealed.]

(l) EXEMPTION FOR CERTAIN USES.—

No tax shall be imposed under this section on any liquid sold for use in, or used in, a helicopter or a fixed-wing aircraft for purposes of providing transportation with respect to which the requirements of subsection (f) or (g) of section 4261 are met.

(m) CERTAIN ALCOHOL FUELS.—

(1) IN GENERAL.—

In the case of the sale or use of any partially exempt methanol or ethanol fuel the rate of the tax imposed by subsection (a)(2) shall be—
(A) after September 30, 1997, and before October 1, 2028—
(i) in the case of fuel none of the alcohol in which consists of ethanol, 9.15 cents per gallon, and
(ii) in any other case, 11.3 cents per gallon, and
(B) after September 30, 2028—
(i) in the case of fuel none of the alcohol in which consists of ethanol, 2.15 cents per gallon, and
(ii) in any other case, 4.3 cents per gallon.

(2) PARTIALLY EXEMPT METHANOL OR ETHANOL FUEL.—

The term "partially exempt methanol or ethanol fuel" means any liquid at least 85 percent of which consists of methanol, ethanol, or other alcohol produced from natural gas.

* * * * * * *

CHAPTER 32—MANUFACTURERS EXCISE TAXES

* * * * * * *

Subchapter A—Automotive and Related Items

* * * * * * *

PART III—PETROLEUM PRODUCTS

* * * * * * *

SUBPART A—MOTOR AND AVIATION FUELS

Sec.

4081.	Imposition of tax.
4082.	Exemptions for diesel fuel and kerosene.
4083.	Definitions; special rule; administrative authority.

* * * * * * *

§4081. IMPOSITION OF TAX

(a) TAX IMPOSED.—

(1) Tax on removal, entry, or sale

(A) In general

There is hereby imposed a tax at the rate specified in paragraph (2) on—

(i) the removal of a taxable fuel from any refinery,

(ii) the removal of a taxable fuel from any terminal,

(iii) the entry into the United States of any taxable fuel for consumption, use, or warehousing, and

(iv) the sale of a taxable fuel to any person who is not registered under section 4101 unless there was a prior taxable removal or entry of such fuel under clause (i), (ii), or (iii).

(B) Exemption for bulk transfers to registered terminals or refineries

(I) IN GENERAL

The tax imposed by this paragraph shall not apply to any removal or entry of a taxable fuel transferred in bulk by pipeline or vessel to a terminal or refinery if the person removing or entering the taxable fuel, the operator of such pipeline or vessel (except as provided in clause (ii)), and the operator of such terminal or refinery are registered under section 4101.

(II) Nonapplication of registration to vessel operators entering by deep-draft vessel

For purposes of clause (i), a vessel operator is not required to be registered with respect to the entry of a taxable fuel transferred in bulk by a vessel described in section 4042(c)(1).

(2) Rates of tax

(A) In general

The rate of the tax imposed by this section is—

(i) in the case of gasoline other than aviation gasoline, 18.3 cents per gallon,

(ii) in the case of aviation gasoline, 19.3 cents per gallon, and

(iii) in the case of diesel fuel or kerosene, 24.3 cents per gallon.

(B) Leaking Underground Storage Tank Trust Fund tax

The rates of tax specified in subparagraph (A) shall each be increased by 0.1 cent per gallon. The increase in tax under this subparagraph shall in this title be referred to as the Leaking Underground Storage Tank Trust Fund financing rate.

(C) Taxes imposed on fuel used in aviation.—

In the case of kerosene which is removed from any refinery or terminal directly into the fuel tank of an aircraft for use in aviation, the rate of tax under subparagraph (A)(iii) shall be—

(i) in the case of use for commercial aviation by a person registered for such use under section 4101, 4.3 cents per gallon, and

(ii) in the case of use for aviation not described in clause (i), 21.8 cents per gallon.

(D) Diesel-water fuel emulsion.—

In the case of diesel-water fuel emulsion at least 14 percent of which is water and with respect to which the emulsion additive is registered by a United States manufacturer with the Environmental Protection Agency pursuant to section 211 of the Clean Air Act (as in effect on March 31, 2003), subparagraph (A)(iii) shall be applied by substituting "19.7 cents" for "24.3 cents". The preceding sentence shall not apply to the removal, sale, or use of diesel-water fuel emulsion unless the person so removing, selling, or using such fuel is registered under section 4101.

(3) Certain refueler trucks, tankers, and tank wagons treated as terminal.—

(A) In general.—

For purposes of paragraph (2)(C), a refueler truck, tanker, or tank wagon shall be treated as part of a terminal if—

(i) such terminal is located within an airport,

(ii) any kerosene which is loaded in such truck, tanker, or wagon at such terminal is for delivery only into aircraft at the airport in which such terminal is located,

(iii) such truck, tanker, or wagon meets the requirements of subparagraph (B) with respect to such terminal, and

(iv) except in the case of exigent circumstances identified by the Secretary in regulations, no vehicle registered for highway use is loaded with kerosene at such terminal.

(B) REQUIREMENTS.—

A refueler truck, tanker, or tank wagon meets the requirements of this subparagraph with respect to a terminal if such truck, tanker, or wagon—

(i) has storage tanks, hose, and coupling equipment designed and used for the purposes of fueling aircraft,

(ii) is not registered for highway use, and

(iii) is operated by—

(I) the terminal operator of such terminal, or

(II) a person that makes a daily accounting to such terminal operator of each delivery of fuel from such truck, tanker, or wagon.

(C) REPORTING.—

The Secretary shall require under section 4101(d) reporting by such terminal operator of—

(i) any information obtained under subparagraph (B)(iii)(II), and

(ii) any similar information maintained by such terminal operator with respect to deliveries of fuel made by trucks, tankers, or wagons operated by such terminal operator.

(D) APPLICABLE RATE.—

For purposes of paragraph (2)(C), in the case of any kerosene treated as removed from a terminal by reason of this paragraph—

(i) the rate of tax specified in paragraph (2)(C)(i) in the case of use described in such paragraph shall apply if such terminal is located within a secured area of an airport, and

(ii) the rate of tax specified in paragraph (2)(C)(ii) shall apply in all other cases.

(4) LIABILITY FOR TAX ON KEROSENE USED IN COMMERCIAL AVIATION.—

For purposes of paragraph (2)(C)(i), the person who uses the fuel for commercial aviation shall pay the tax imposed under such paragraph. For purposes of the preceding sentence, fuel shall be treated as used when such fuel is removed into the fuel tank.

(b) Treatment of removal or subsequent sale by blender.—

(1) In general.—

There is hereby imposed a tax at the rate determined under subsection (a) on taxable fuel removed or sold by the blender thereof.

(2) Credit for tax previously paid.—

If—

(A) tax is imposed on the removal or sale of a taxable fuel by reason of paragraph (1), and

(B) the blender establishes the amount of the tax paid with respect to such fuel by reason of subsection (a),

the amount of the tax so paid shall be allowed as a credit against the tax imposed by reason of paragraph (1).

(c) Later separation of fuel from diesel-water fuel emulsion.—

If any person separates the taxable fuel from a diesel-water fuel emulsion on which tax was imposed under subsection (a) at a rate determined under subsection (a)(2)(D) (or with respect to which a credit or payment was allowed or made by reason of section 6427), such person shall be treated as the refiner of such taxable fuel. The amount of tax imposed on any removal of such fuel by such person shall be reduced by the amount of tax imposed (and not credited or refunded) on any prior removal or entry of such fuel.

(d) Termination.—

(1) In general

The rates of tax specified in clauses (i) and (iii) of subsection (a)(2)(A) shall be 4.3 cents per gallon after September 30, 2028.

(2) Aviation fuels.—

The rates of tax specified in subsection (a)(2)(A)(ii) and (a)(2)(C)(ii) shall be 4.3 cents per gallon—

(A) after December 31, 1996, and before the date which is 7 days after the date of the enactment of the Airport and Airway Trust Fund Tax Reinstatement Act of 1997, and

(B) after September 30, 2028.

(3) Leaking Underground Storage Tank Trust Fund financing rate.—

The Leaking Underground Storage Tank Trust Fund financing rate under subsection (a)(2) shall apply after September 30, 1997, and before October 1, 2028.

(e) Refunds in certain cases.—

Under regulations prescribed by the Secretary, if any person who paid the tax imposed by this section with respect to any taxable fuel establishes to the satisfaction of the Secretary that a prior tax was paid (and not credited or refunded) with respect to such taxable fuel, then an amount equal to the tax paid by such person shall be allowed as a refund (without interest) to such person in the same manner as if it were an overpayment of tax imposed by this section.

§4082. EXEMPTIONS FOR DIESEL FUEL AND KEROSENE

(a) IN GENERAL.—

The tax imposed by section 4081 shall not apply to diesel fuel and kerosene—
(1) which the Secretary determines is destined for a nontaxable use,
(2) which is indelibly dyed by mechanical injection in accordance with regulations which the Secretary shall prescribe, and
(3) which meets such marking requirements (if any) as may be prescribed by the Secretary in regulations.
Such regulations shall allow an individual choice of dye color approved by the Secretary or chosen from any list of approved dye colors that the Secretary may publish.

(b) NONTAXABLE USE.—

For purposes of this section, the term "nontaxable use" means—
(1) any use which is exempt from the tax imposed by section 4041(a)(1) other than by reason of a prior imposition of tax,
(2) any use in a train, and
(3) any use described in section 4041(a)(1)(C)(iii)(II).
The term "nontaxable use" does not include the use of kerosene in an aircraft and such term shall not include any use described in section 6421(e)(2)(C).

(c) EXCEPTION TO DYEING REQUIREMENTS.—

Paragraph (2) of subsection (a) shall not apply with respect to any diesel fuel and kerosene—
(1) removed, entered, or sold in a State for ultimate sale or use in an area of such State during the period such area is exempted from the fuel dyeing requirements under subsection (i) of section 211 of the Clean Air Act (as in effect on the date of the enactment of this subsection) by the Administrator of the Environmental Protection Agency under paragraph (4) of such subsection (i) (as so in effect), and
(2) the use of which is certified pursuant to regulations issued by the Secretary.

(d) ADDITIONAL EXCEPTIONS TO DYEING REQUIREMENTS FOR KEROSENE.—

(1) USE FOR NON-FUEL FEEDSTOCK PURPOSES.—

Subsection (a)(2) shall not apply to kerosene—
(A) received by pipeline or vessel for use by the person receiving the kerosene in the manufacture or production of any substance (other than gasoline, diesel fuel, or special fuels referred to in section 4041), or

    (B) to the extent provided in regulations, removed or entered—

        (i) for such a use by the person removing or entering the kerosene, or

        (ii) for resale by such person for such a use by the purchaser,

but only if the person receiving, removing, or entering the kerosene and such purchaser (if any) are registered under section 4101 with respect to the tax imposed by section 4081.

(2) WHOLESALE DISTRIBUTORS.—

    To the extent provided in regulations, subsection (a)(2) shall not apply to kerosene received by a wholesale distributor of kerosene if such distributor—

    (A) is registered under section 4101 with respect to the tax imposed by section 4081 on kerosene, and

    (B) sells kerosene exclusively to ultimate vendors described in section 6427(l)(5)(B) with respect to kerosene.

(e) KEROSENE REMOVED INTO AN AIRCRAFT.—

    In the case of kerosene (other than kerosene with respect to which tax is imposed under section 4043) which is exempt from the tax imposed by section 4041(c) (other than by reason of a prior imposition of tax) and which is removed from any refinery or terminal directly into the fuel tank of an aircraft—

    (1) the rate of tax under section 4081(a)(2)(A)(iii) shall be zero, and

    (2) if such aircraft is employed in foreign trade or trade between the United States and any of its possessions, the increase in such rate under section 4081(a)(2)(B) shall be zero.

    For purposes of this subsection, any removal described in section 4081(a)(3)(A) shall be treated as a removal from a terminal but only if such terminal is located within a secure area of an airport.

(f) EXCEPTION FOR LEAKING UNDERGROUND STORAGE TANK TRUST FUND FINANCING RATE.—

(1) IN GENERAL.—

    Subsection (a) shall not apply to the tax imposed under section 4081 at the Leaking Underground Storage Tank Trust Fund financing rate.

(2) EXCEPTION FOR EXPORT, ETC..—

    Paragraph (1) shall not apply with respect to any fuel if the Secretary determines that such fuel is destined for export or for use by the purchaser as supplies for vessels (within the meaning of section 4221(d)(3)) employed in foreign trade or trade between the United States and any of its possessions.

(g) REGULATIONS.—

    The Secretary shall prescribe such regulations as may be necessary to carry out this section, including regulations requiring the conspicuous labeling of retail diesel fuel and kerosene pumps and other delivery facilities to assure that persons are aware of which fuel is available only for nontaxable uses.

(h) CROSS REFERENCE.—

For tax on train and certain bus uses of fuel purchased tax-free, see subsections (a)(1) and (d)(3) of section 4041.

§4083. DEFINITIONS; SPECIAL RULE; ADMINISTRATIVE AUTHORITY

* * * * * * *

(b) COMMERCIAL AVIATION.—

For purposes of this subpart, the term "commercial aviation" means any use of an aircraft in a business of transporting persons or property for compensation or hire by air, unless properly allocable to any transportation exempt from the taxes imposed by sections 4261 and 4271 by reason of section 4281 or 4282 or by reason of subsection (h) or (i) of section 4261. Such term shall not include the use of any aircraft before October 1, 2028, if tax is imposed under section 4043 with respect to the fuel consumed in such use or if no tax is imposed on such use under section 4043 by reason of subsection (c)(5) thereof.

* * * * * * *

CHAPTER 33—FACILITIES AND SERVICES

* * * * * * *

Subchapter C—Transportation by Air

* * * * * * *

PART I—PERSONS

* * * * * * *

§4261. IMPOSITION OF TAX

(a) IN GENERAL.—

There is hereby imposed on the amount paid for taxable transportation of any person a tax equal to 7.5 percent of the amount so paid.

(b) DOMESTIC SEGMENTS OF TAXABLE TRANSPORTATION.—

(1) IN GENERAL.—

There is hereby imposed on the amount paid for each domestic segment of taxable transportation by air a tax in the amount of $3.00.

(2) DOMESTIC SEGMENT.—

For purposes of this section, the term "domestic segment" means any segment consisting of 1 takeoff and 1 landing and which is taxable transportation described in section 4262(a)(1).

(3) CHANGES IN SEGMENTS BY REASON OF REROUTING.—

If—

(A) transportation is purchased between 2 locations on specified flights, and

(B) there is a change in the route taken between such 2 locations which changes the number of domestic segments, but there is no change in the amount charged for such transportation,

the tax imposed by paragraph (1) shall be determined without regard to such change in route.

(c) USE OF INTERNATIONAL TRAVEL FACILITIES.—

(1) IN GENERAL.—

There is hereby imposed a tax of $12.00 on any amount paid (whether within or without the United States) for any transportation of any person by air, if such transportation begins or ends in the United States.

(2) EXCEPTION FOR TRANSPORTATION ENTIRELY TAXABLE UNDER SUBSECTION (A).—

This subsection shall not apply to any transportation all of which is taxable under subsection (a) (determined without regard to sections 4281 and 4282).

(3) SPECIAL RULE FOR ALASKA AND HAWAII.—

In any case in which the tax imposed by paragraph (1) applies to a domestic segment beginning or ending in Alaska or Hawaii, such tax shall apply only to departures and shall be at the rate of $6.

(d) BY WHOM PAID.—

Except as provided in section 4263(a), the taxes imposed by this section shall be paid by the person making the payment subject to the tax.

(e) SPECIAL RULES.—

(1) Segments to and from rural airports

(A) EXCEPTION FROM SEGMENT TAX.—

The tax imposed by subsection (b)(1) shall not apply to any domestic segment beginning or ending at an airport which is a rural airport for the calendar year in which such segment begins or ends (as the case may be).

(B) RURAL AIRPORT.—

For purposes of this paragraph, the term "rural airport" means, with respect to any calendar year, any airport if—

(i) there were fewer than 100,000 commercial passengers departing by air (in the case of any airport described in clause (ii)(III), on flight segments of at least 100 miles) during the second preceding calendar year from such airport, and

    (ii) such airport—

        (I) is not located within 75 miles of another airport which is not described in clause (i),

        (II) is receiving essential air service subsidies as of the date of the enactment of this paragraph, or

        (III) is not connected by paved roads to another airport.

(2) Amounts paid outside the United States

In the case of amounts paid outside the United States for taxable transportation, the taxes imposed by subsections (a) and (b) shall apply only if such transportation begins and ends in the United States.

(3) Amounts paid for right to award free or reduced rate air transportation.—

(A) In general.—

Any amount paid (and the value of any other benefit provided) to an air carrier (or any related person) for the right to provide mileage awards for (or other reductions in the cost of) any transportation of persons by air shall be treated for purposes of subsection (a) as an amount paid for taxable transportation, and such amount shall be taxable under subsection (a) without regard to any other provision of this subchapter.

(B) Controlled group.—

For purposes of subparagraph (A), a corporation and all wholly owned subsidiaries of such corporation shall be treated as 1 corporation.

(C) Regulations.—

The Secretary shall prescribe rules which reallocate items of income, deduction, credit, exclusion, or other allowance to the extent necessary to prevent the avoidance of tax imposed by reason of this paragraph. The Secretary may prescribe rules which exclude from the tax imposed by subsection (a) amounts attributable to mileage awards which are used other than for transportation of persons by air.

(4) Inflation adjustment of dollar rates of tax.—

(A) In general.—

In the case of taxable events in a calendar year after the last nonindexed year, the $3.00 amount contained in subsection (b) and each dollar amount contained in subsection (c) shall be increased by an amount equal to—

    (i) such dollar amount, multiplied by

    (ii) the cost-of-living adjustment determined under section 1(f)(3) for such calendar year by substituting the year before the last nonindexed year for "calendar year 2016" in subparagraph (A)(ii) thereof.

If any increase determined under the preceding sentence is not a multiple of 10 cents, such increase shall be rounded to the nearest multiple of 10 cents.

(B) Last nonindexed year.—

For purposes of subparagraph (A), the last nonindexed year is—

(i) 2002 in the case of the $3.00 amount contained in subsection (b), and

(ii) 1998 in the case of the dollar amounts contained in subsection (c).

(C) Taxable event.—

For purposes of subparagraph (A), in the case of the tax imposed by subsection (b), the beginning of the domestic segment shall be treated as the taxable event.

(D) Special rule for amounts paid for domestic segments beginning after 2002.—

If an amount is paid during a calendar year for a domestic segment beginning in a later calendar year, then the rate of tax under subsection (b) on such amount shall be the rate in effect for the calendar year in which such amount is paid.

(5) Amounts paid for aircraft management services.—

(A) In general.—

No tax shall be imposed by this section or section 4271 on any amounts paid by an aircraft owner for aircraft management services related to—

(i) maintenance and support of the aircraft owner's aircraft, or

(ii) flights on the aircraft owner's aircraft.

(B) Aircraft management services.—

For purposes of subparagraph (A), the term "aircraft management services" includes—

(i) assisting an aircraft owner with administrative and support services, such as scheduling, flight planning, and weather forecasting,

(ii) obtaining insurance,

(iii) maintenance, storage and fueling of aircraft,

(iv) hiring, training, and provision of pilots and crew,

(v) establishing and complying with safety standards, and

(vi) such other services as are necessary to support flights operated by an aircraft owner.

(C) Lessee treated as aircraft owner.—

(i) In general.—

For purposes of this paragraph, the term "aircraft owner" includes a person who leases the aircraft other than under a disqualified lease.

(ii) Disqualified lease.—

For purposes of clause (i), the term "disqualified lease" means a lease from a person providing aircraft management services with respect to such aircraft (or a related person (within the meaning of section 465(b)(3)(C)) to the person providing such services), if such lease is for a term of 31 days or less.

(D) Pro rata allocation.—

In the case of amounts paid to any person which (but for this subsection) are subject to the tax imposed by subsection (a), a portion of which consists of amounts described in subparagraph (A), this paragraph shall apply on a pro rata basis only to the portion which consists of amounts described in such subparagraph.

(f) Exemption for certain uses.—

No tax shall be imposed under subsection (a) or (b) on air transportation—

(1) by helicopter for the purpose of transporting individuals, equipment, or supplies in the exploration for, or the development or removal of, hard minerals, oil, or gas, or

(2) by helicopter or by fixed-wing aircraft for the purpose of the planting, cultivation, cutting, or transportation of, or caring for, trees (including logging operations),

but only if the helicopter or fixed-wing aircraft does not take off from, or land at, a facility eligible for assistance under the Airport and Airway Development Act of 1970, or otherwise use services provided pursuant to section 44509 or 44913(b) or subchapter I of chapter 471 of title 49, United States Code, during such use. In the case of helicopter transportation described in paragraph (1), this subsection shall be applied by treating each flight segment as a distinct flight.

(g) Exemption for air ambulances providing certain emergency medical transportation.—

No tax shall be imposed under this section or section 4271 on any air transportation for the purpose of providing emergency medical services—

(1) by helicopter, or

(2) by a fixed-wing aircraft equipped for and exclusively dedicated on that flight to acute care emergency medical services.

(h) Exemption for skydiving uses.—

No tax shall be imposed by this section or section 4271 on any air transportation exclusively for the purpose of skydiving.

(i) Exemption for seaplanes.—

No tax shall be imposed by this section or section 4271 on any air transportation by a seaplane with respect to any segment consisting of a takeoff from, and a landing on, water, but only if the places at which such takeoff and landing occur have not received and are not receiving financial assistance from the Airport and Airways Trust Fund.

(j) Exemption for aircraft in fractional ownership aircraft programs.—

No tax shall be imposed by this section or section 4271 on any air transportation if tax is imposed under section 4043 with respect to the fuel used in such transportation. This subsection shall not apply after September 30, 2028.

(k) Application of Taxes.—

(1) In general.—

The taxes imposed by this section shall apply to—

(A) transportation beginning during the period—

(i) beginning on the 7th day after the date of the enactment of the Airport and Airway Trust Fund Tax Reinstatement Act of 1997, and

(ii) ending on September 30, 2028, and

(B) amounts paid during such period for transportation beginning after such period.

(2) Refunds.—

If, as of the date any transportation begins, the taxes imposed by this section would not have applied to such transportation if paid for on such date, any tax paid under paragraph (1)(B) with respect to such transportation shall be treated as an overpayment.

§4262. Definition of taxable transportation

(a) Taxable transportation; in general.—

For purposes of this part, except as provided in subsection (b), the term "taxable transportation" means—

(1) transportation by air which begins in the United States or in the 225–mile zone and ends in the United States or in the 225–mile zone; and

(2) in the case of transportation by air other than transportation described in paragraph (1), that portion of such transportation which is directly or indirectly from one port or station in the United States to another port or station in the United States, but only if such portion is not a part of uninterrupted international air transportation (within the meaning of subsection (c)(3)).

(b) Exclusion of certain travel.—

For purposes of this part, the term "taxable transportation" does not include that portion of any transportation by air which meets all 4 of the following requirements:

(1) such portion is outside the United States;

(2) neither such portion nor any segment thereof is directly or indirectly—

(A) between (i) a point where the route of the transportation leaves or enters the continental United States, or (ii) a port or station in the 225-mile zone, and

(B) a port or station in the 225-mile zone;

(3) such portion—

(A) begins at either (i) the point where the route of the transportation leaves the United States, or (ii) a port or station in the 225-mile zone, and

(B) ends at either (i) the point where the route of the transportation enters the United States, or (ii) a port or station in the 225-mile zone; and

(4) a direct line from the point (or the port or station) specified in paragraph (3)(A), to the point (or the port or station) specified in paragraph (3)(B), passes through or over a point which is not within 225 miles of the United States.

(c) DEFINITIONS.—

For purposes of this section—

(1) CONTINENTAL UNITED STATES.—

The term "continental United States" means the District of Columbia and the States other than Alaska and Hawaii.

(2) 225-MILE ZONE.—

The term "225-mile zone" means that portion of Canada and Mexico which is not more than 225 miles from the nearest point in the continental United States.

(3) UNINTERRUPTED INTERNATIONAL AIR TRANSPORTATION.—

The term "uninterrupted international air transportation" means any transportation by air which is not transportation described in subsection (a)(1) and in which—

(A) the scheduled interval between (i) the beginning or end of the portion of such transportation which is directly or indirectly from one port or station in the United States to another port or station in the United States and (ii) the end or beginning of the other portion of such transportation is not more than 12 hours, and

(B) the scheduled interval between the beginning or end and the end or beginning of any two segments of the portion of such transportation referred to in subparagraph (A)(i) is not more than 12 hours.

For purposes of this paragraph, in the case of personnel of the United States Army, Air Force, Navy, Marine Corps, and Coast Guard traveling in uniform at their own expense when on official leave, furlough, or pass, the scheduled interval described in subparagraph (A) shall be deemed to be not more than 12 hours if a ticket for the subsequent portion of such transportation is purchased within 12 hours after the end of the earlier portion of such transportation and the purchaser accepts and utilizes the first accommodations actually available to him for such subsequent portion.

(d) TRANSPORTATION.—

For purposes of this part, the term "transportation" includes layover or waiting time and movement of the aircraft in deadhead service.

(e) AUTHORITY TO WAIVE 225-MILE ZONE PROVISIONS.—

(1) IN GENERAL.—

If the Secretary of the Treasury determines that Canada or Mexico has entered into a qualified agreement—

(A) the Secretary shall publish a notice of such determination in the Federal Register, and

(B) effective with respect to transportation beginning after the date specified in such notice, to the extent provided in the agreement, the term "225-mile zone" shall not include part or all of the country with respect to which such determination is made.

(2) Termination of Waiver.—

If a determination was made under paragraph (1) with respect to any country and the Secretary of the Treasury subsequently determines that the agreement is no longer in effect or that the agreement is no longer a qualified agreement—

(A) the Secretary shall publish a notice of such determination in the Federal Register, and

(B) subparagraph (B) of paragraph (1) shall cease to apply with respect to transportation beginning after the date specified in such notice.

(3) Qualified Agreement.—

For purposes of this subsection, the term "qualified agreement" means an agreement between the United States and Canada or Mexico (as the case may be)—

(A) setting forth that portion of such country which is not to be treated as within the 225-mile zone, and

(B) providing that the tax imposed by such country on transportation described in subparagraph (A) will be at a level which the Secretary of the Treasury determines to be appropriate.

(4) Requirement that Agreement be Submitted to Congress.—

No notice may be published under paragraph (1)(A) with respect to any qualified agreement before the date 90 days after the date on which a copy of such agreement was furnished to the Committee on Ways and Means of the House of Representatives and the Committee on Finance of the Senate.

§4263. Special Rules

(a) Payments Made Outside the United States for Prepaid Orders.—

If the payment upon which tax is imposed by section 4261 is made outside the United States for a prepaid order, exchange order, or similar order, the person furnishing the initial transportation pursuant to such order shall collect the amount of the tax.

(b) Tax Deducted Upon Refunds.—

Every person who refunds any amount with respect to a ticket or order which was purchased without payment of the tax imposed by section 4261 shall deduct from the amount refundable, to the extent available, any tax due under such section as a result of the use of a portion of the transportation purchased in connection with such ticket or order, and shall report to the Secretary the amount of any such tax remaining uncollected.

(c) Payment of Tax.—

Where any tax imposed by section 4261 is not paid at the time payment for transportation is made, then, under regulations prescribed by the Secretary, to the extent that such tax is not collected under any other provision of this subchapter, such tax shall be paid by the carrier providing the initial segment of such transportation which begins or ends in the United States.

(d) APPLICATION OF TAX.—

The tax imposed by section 4261 shall apply to any amount paid within the United States for transportation of any person by air unless the taxpayer establishes, pursuant to regulations prescribed by the Secretary, at the time of payment for the transportation, that the transportation is not transportation in respect of which tax is imposed by section 4261.

(e) ROUND TRIPS.—

In applying this subchapter to a round trip, such round trip shall be considered to consist of transportation from the point of departure to the destination, and of separate transportation thereafter.

(f) TRANSPORTATION OUTSIDE THE NORTHERN PORTION OF THE WESTERN HEMISPHERE.—

In applying this subchapter to transportation any part of which is outside the northern portion of the Western Hemisphere, if the route of such transportation leaves and reenters the northern portion of the Western Hemisphere, such transportation shall be considered to consist of transportation to a point outside such northern portion, and of separate transportation thereafter. For purposes of this subsection, the term "northern portion of the Western Hemisphere" means the area lying west of the 30th meridian west of Greenwich, east of the international dateline, and north of the Equator, but not including any country of South America.

PART II—PROPERTY

§4271. IMPOSITION OF TAX

(a) IN GENERAL.—

There is hereby imposed upon the amount paid within or without the United States for the taxable transportation (as defined in section 4272) of property a tax equal to 6.25 percent of the amount so paid for such transportation. The tax imposed by this subsection shall apply only to amounts paid to a person engaged in the business of transporting property by air for hire.

(b) By whom paid

(1) IN GENERAL.—

Except as provided by paragraph (2), the tax imposed by subsection (a) shall be paid by the person making the payment subject to tax.

(2) Payments made outside the United States

If a payment subject to tax under subsection (a) is made outside the United States and the person making such payment does not pay such tax, such tax—

(A) shall be paid by the person to whom the property is delivered in the United States by the person furnishing the last segment of the taxable transportation in respect of which such tax is imposed, and

(B) shall be collected by the person furnishing the last segment of such taxable transportation.

(c) Determination of amounts paid in certain cases.—

For purposes of this section, in any case in which a person engaged in the business of transporting property by air for hire and one or more other persons not so engaged jointly provide services which include taxable transportation of property, and the person so engaged receives, for the furnishing of such taxable transportation, a portion of the receipts from the joint providing of such services, the amount paid for the taxable transportation shall be treated as being the sum of (1) the portion of the receipts so received, and (2) any expenses incurred by any of the persons not so engaged which are properly attributable to such taxable transportation and which are taken into account in determining the portion of the receipts so received.

(d) Application of tax.—

(1) In general.—

The tax imposed by subsection (a) shall apply to—

(A) transportation beginning during the period—

(i) beginning on the 7th day after the date of the enactment of the Airport and Airway Trust Fund Tax Reinstatement Act of 1997, and

(ii) ending on September 30, 2028, and

(B) amounts paid during such period for transportation beginning after such period.

(2) Refunds.—

If, as of the date any transportation begins, the taxes imposed by this section would not have applied to such transportation if paid for on such date, any tax paid under paragraph (1)(B) with respect to such transportation shall be treated as an overpayment.

§4272. Definition of taxable transportation, etc.

(a) In general.—

For purposes of this part, except as provided in subsection (b), the term "taxable transportation" means transportation by air which begins and ends in the United States.

(b) Exceptions.—

For purposes of this part, the term "taxable transportation" does not include—

(1) that portion of any transportation which meets the requirements of paragraphs (1), (2), (3), and (4) of section 4262(b), or

(2) under regulations prescribed by the Secretary, transportation of property in the course of exportation (including shipment to a possession of the United States) by continuous movement, and in due course so exported.

(c) EXCESS BAGGAGE OF PASSENGERS.—

For purposes of this part, the term "property" does not include excess baggage accompanying a passenger traveling on an aircraft operated on an established line.

(d) TRANSPORTATION.—

For purposes of this part, the term "transportation" includes layover or waiting time and movement of the aircraft in deadhead service.

PART III—SPECIAL PROVISIONS APPLICABLE TO TAXES ON TRANSPORTATION BY AIR

§4281. SMALL AIRCRAFT ON NONESTABLISHED LINES

(a) IN GENERAL.—

The taxes imposed by sections 4261 and 4271 shall not apply to transportation by an aircraft having a maximum certificated takeoff weight of 6,000 pounds or less, except when such aircraft is operated on an established line or when such aircraft is a jet aircraft.

(b) MAXIMUM CERTIFICATED TAKEOFF WEIGHT.—

For purposes of this section, the term "maximum certificated takeoff weight" means the maximum such weight contained in the type certificate or airworthiness certificate.

(c) SIGHTSEEING.—

For purposes of this section, an aircraft shall not be considered as operated on an established line at any time during which such aircraft is being operated on a flight the sole purpose of which is sightseeing.

(d) JET AIRCRAFT.—

For purposes of this section, the term "jet aircraft" shall not include any aircraft which is a rotorcraft or propeller aircraft.

§4282. TRANSPORTATION BY AIR FOR OTHER MEMBERS OF AFFILIATED GROUP

(a) GENERAL RULE.—

Under regulations prescribed by the Secretary, if—
 (1) one member of an affiliated group is the owner or lessee of an aircraft, and
 (2) such aircraft is not available for hire by persons who are not members of such group,
no tax shall be imposed under section 4261 or 4271 upon any payment received by one member of the affiliated group from another member of such group for services furnished to such other member in connection with the use of such aircraft.

(b) AVAILABILITY FOR HIRE.—

For purposes of subsection (a), the determination of whether an aircraft is available for hire by persons who are not members of an affiliated group shall be made on a flight-by-flight basis.

(c) AFFILIATED GROUP.—

For purposes of subsection (a), the term "affiliated group" has the meaning assigned to such term by section 1504(a), except that all corporations shall be treated as includible corporations (without any exclusion under section 1504(b)).

* * * * * * *

Subchapter E—Special Provisions Applicable to Services and Facilities Taxes

Sec.

§4291. CASES WHERE PERSONS RECEIVING PAYMENT MUST COLLECT TAX

Except as otherwise provided in section 4263(a), every person receiving any payment for facilities or services on which a tax is imposed upon the payor thereof under this chapter shall collect the amount of the tax from the person making such payment.

[§4292. REPEALED.]

§4293. EXEMPTION FOR UNITED STATES AND POSSESSIONS

The Secretary of the Treasury may authorize exemption from the taxes imposed by section 4041, section 4051, chapter 32 (other than the taxes imposed by sections 4064 and 4121) and subchapter B of chapter 33, as to any particular article, or service or class of articles or services, to be purchased for the exclusive use of the United States, if he determines that the imposition of such taxes with respect to such articles or services, or class of articles or services will cause substantial burden or expense which can be avoided by granting tax exemption and that full benefit of such exemption, if granted, will accrue to the United States.

* * * * * * *

CHAPTER 65—ABATEMENTS, CREDITS, AND REFUNDS

* * * * * * *

Subchapter B—Rules of Special Application

§6427. FUELS NOT USED FOR TAXABLE PURPOSES

* * * * * * *

(d) Use by certain aircraft museums or in certain other aircraft uses.—

Except as provided in subsection (k), if—

(1) any gasoline on which tax was imposed by section 4081, or

(2) any fuel on the sale of which tax was imposed under section 4041,

is used by an aircraft museum (as defined in section 4041(h)(2)) in an aircraft or vehicle owned by such museum and used exclusively for purposes set forth in section 4041(h)(2)(C), or is used in a helicopter or a fixed-wing aircraft for a purpose described in section 4041(l), the Secretary shall pay (without interest) to the ultimate purchaser of such gasoline or fuel an amount equal to the aggregate amount of the tax imposed on such gasoline or fuel.

* * * * * * *

(l) Nontaxable uses of diesel fuel and kerosene.—

(1) In general.—

Except as otherwise provided in this subsection and in subsection (k), if any diesel fuel or kerosene on which tax has been imposed by section 4041 or 4081 is used by any person in a nontaxable use, the Secretary shall pay (without interest) to the ultimate purchaser of such fuel an amount equal to the aggregate amount of tax imposed on such fuel under section 4041 or 4081, as the case may be, reduced by any payment made to the ultimate vendor under paragraph (4)(C)(i).

(2) Nontaxable use.—

For purposes of this subsection, the term "nontaxable use" means any use which is exempt from the tax imposed by section 4041(a)(1) other than by reason of a prior imposition of tax.

(3) Refund of certain taxes on fuel used in diesel-powered trains.—

For purposes of this subsection, the term "nontaxable use" includes fuel used in a diesel-powered train. The preceding sentence shall not apply with respect to—

(A) the Leaking Underground Storage Tank Trust Fund financing rate under sections 4041 and 4081, and

(B) so much of the rate specified in section 4081(a)(2)(A) as does not exceed the rate applicable under section 4041(a)(1)(C)(ii).

The preceding sentence shall not apply in the case of fuel sold for exclusive use by a State or any political subdivision thereof.

(4) Refunds for kerosene used in aviation.—

(A) Kerosene used in commercial aviation.—

In the case of kerosene used in commercial aviation (as defined in section 4083(b)) (other than supplies for vessels or aircraft within the meaning of section 4221(d)(3)), paragraph (1) shall not apply to so much of the tax imposed by section 4041 or 4081, as the case may be, as is attributable to—

(i) the Leaking Underground Storage Tank Trust Fund financing rate imposed by such section, and

(ii) so much of the rate of tax specified in section 4041(c) or 4081(a)(2)(A)(iii), as the case may be, as does not exceed 4.3 cents per gallon.

(B) KEROSENE USED IN NONCOMMERCIAL AVIATION.—

In the case of kerosene used in aviation that is not commercial aviation (as so defined) (other than any use which is exempt from the tax imposed by section 4041(c) other than by reason of a prior imposition of tax), paragraph (1) shall not apply to—

(i) any tax imposed by subsection (c) or (d)(2) of section 4041, and

(ii) so much of the tax imposed by section 4081 as is attributable to—

(I) the Leaking Underground Storage Tank Trust Fund financing rate imposed by such section, and

(II) so much of the rate of tax specified in section 4081(a)(2)(A)(iii) as does not exceed the rate specified in section 4081(a)(2)(C)(ii).

(C) Payments to ultimate, registered vendor

(I) IN GENERAL.—

With respect to any kerosene used in aviation (other than kerosene described in clause (ii) or kerosene to which paragraph (5) applies), if the ultimate purchaser of such kerosene waives (at such time and in such form and manner as the Secretary shall prescribe) the right to payment under paragraph (1) and assigns such right to the ultimate vendor, then the Secretary shall pay the amount which would be paid under paragraph (1) to such ultimate vendor, but only if such ultimate vendor—

(I) is registered under section 4101, and

(II) meets the requirements of subparagraph (A), (B), or (D) of section 6416(a)(1).

(II) PAYMENTS FOR KEROSENE USED IN NONCOMMERCIAL AVIATION.—

The amount which would be paid under paragraph (1) with respect to any kerosene to which subparagraph (B) applies shall be paid only to the ultimate vendor of such kerosene. A payment shall be made to such vendor if such vendor—

(I) is registered under section 4101, and

(II) meets the requirements of subparagraph (A), (B), or (D) of section 6416(a)(1).

(5) Registered vendors to administer claims for refund of diesel fuel or kerosene sold to State and local governments

(A) IN GENERAL.—

Paragraph (1) shall not apply to diesel fuel or kerosene used by a State or local government.

(B) Sales of kerosene not for use in motor fuel.—

Paragraph (1) shall not apply to kerosene (other than kerosene used in aviation) sold by a vendor—

(i) for any use if such sale is from a pump which (as determined under regulations prescribed by the Secretary) is not suitable for use in fueling any diesel-powered highway vehicle or train, or

(ii) to the extent provided by the Secretary, for blending with heating oil to be used during periods of extreme or unseasonable cold.

(C) Payment to ultimate, registered vendor.—

Except as provided in subparagraph (D), the amount which would (but for subparagraph (A) or (B)) have been paid under paragraph (1) with respect to any fuel shall be paid to the ultimate vendor of such fuel, if such vendor—

(i) is registered under section 4101, and

(ii) meets the requirements of subparagraph (A), (B), or (D) of section 6416(a)(1).

(D) Credit card issuer.—

For purposes of this paragraph, if the purchase of any fuel described in subparagraph (A) (determined without regard to the registration status of the ultimate vendor) is made by means of a credit card issued to the ultimate purchaser, the Secretary shall pay to the person extending the credit to the ultimate purchaser the amount which would have been paid under paragraph (1) (but for subparagraph (A)), but only if such person meets the requirements of clauses (i), (ii), and (iii) of section 6416(a)(4)(B). If such clause (i), (ii), or (iii) is not met by such person extending the credit to the ultimate purchaser, then such person shall collect an amount equal to the tax from the ultimate purchaser and only such ultimate purchaser may claim such amount.

* * * * * * *

CHAPTER 75—CRIMES, OTHER OFFENSES, AND FORFEITURES

* * * * * * *

§7275. Penalty for offenses relating to certain airline tickets and advertising

(a) Tickets.—

In the case of transportation by air all of which is taxable transportation (as defined in section 4262), the ticket for such transportation shall show the total of—

(1) the amount paid for such transportation, and

(2) the taxes imposed by subsections (a) and (b) of section 4261.

(b) ADVERTISING.—

In the case of transportation by air all of which is taxable transportation (as defined in section 4262) or would be taxable transportation if section 4262 did not include subsection (b) thereof, any advertising made by or on behalf of any person furnishing such transportation (or offering to arrange such transportation) which states the cost of such transportation shall—

(1) state such cost as the total of (A) the amount to be paid for such transportation, and (B) the taxes imposed by sections 4261(a), (b), and (c), and

(2) if any such advertising states separately the amount to be paid for such transportation or the amount of such taxes, state such total at least as prominently as the more prominently stated of the amount to be paid for such transportation or the amount of such taxes and shall describe such taxes substantially as: "user taxes to pay for airport construction and airway safety and operations".

(c) Non-tax charges

(1) IN GENERAL.—

In the case of transportation by air for which disclosure on the ticket or advertising for such transportation of the amounts paid for passenger taxes is required by subsection (a)(2) or (b)(1)(B), if such amounts are separately disclosed, it shall be unlawful for the disclosure of such amounts to include any amounts not attributable to such taxes.

(2) Inclusion in transportation cost

Nothing in this subsection shall prohibit the inclusion of amounts not attributable to the taxes imposed by subsection (a), (b), or (c) of section 4261 in the disclosure of the amount paid for transportation as required by subsection (a)(1) or (b)(1)(A), or in a separate disclosure of amounts not attributable to such taxes.

(d) PENALTY.—

Any person who violates any provision of subsection (a), (b), or (c) is, for each violation, guilty of a misdemeanor, and upon conviction thereof shall be fined not more than $100.

* * * * * * *

Subtitle I—Trust Fund Code

§9500. SHORT TITLE

This subtitle may be cited as the "Trust Fund Code of 1981".

CHAPTER 98—TRUST FUND CODE

* * * * * * *

Subchapter A—Establishment of Trust Funds

Sec.

* * * * * * *

9502.   Airport and Airway Trust Fund.

9503.   Highway Trust Fund.

* * * * * * *

§9502. Airport and Airway Trust Fund

(a) Creation of Trust Fund.—

There is established in the Treasury of the United States a trust fund to be known as the "Airport and Airway Trust Fund", consisting of such amounts as may be appropriated, credited, or paid into the Airport and Airway Trust Fund as provided in this section, section 9503(c)(5), or section 9602(b).

(b) Transfers to Airport and Airway Trust Fund.—

There are hereby appropriated to the Airport and Airway Trust Fund amounts equivalent to—

(1) the taxes received in the Treasury under—

(A) section 4041(c) (relating to aviation fuels),

(B) section 4043 (relating to surtax on fuel used in aircraft part of a fractional ownership program),

(C) sections 4261 and 4271 (relating to transportation by air), and

(D) section 4081 with respect to aviation gasoline and kerosene to the extent attributable to the rate specified in section 4081(a)(2)(C), and

(2) the amounts determined by the Secretary of the Treasury to be equivalent to the amounts of civil penalties collected under section 47107(m) of title 49, United States Code.

There shall not be taken into account under paragraph (1) so much of the taxes imposed by section 4081 as are determined at the rate specified in section 4081(a)(2)(B).

(c) Appropriation of additional sums

There are hereby authorized to be appropriated to the Airport and Airway Trust Fund such additional sums as may be required to make the expenditures referred to in subsection (d) of this section.

(d) Expenditures from Airport and Airway Trust Fund.—

(1) Airport and airway program.—

Amounts in the Airport and Airway Trust Fund shall be available, as provided by appropriation Acts, for making expenditures before October 1, 2028, to meet those obligations of the United States—

(A) incurred under title I of the Airport and Airway Development Act of 1970 or of the Airport and Airway Development Act Amendments of 1976 or of the Aviation Safety and Noise Abatement Act of 1979 or under the Fiscal Year 1981 Airport Development Authorization Act or the provisions of the Airport and Airway

Improvement Act of 1982 or the Airport and Airway Safety and Capacity Expansion Act of 1987 or the Federal Aviation Administration Research, Engineering, and Development Authorization Act of 1990 or the Aviation Safety and Capacity Expansion Act of 1990 or the Airport and Airway Safety, Capacity, Noise Improvement, and Intermodal Transportation Act of 1992 or the Airport Improvement Program Temporary Extension Act of 1994 or the Federal Aviation Administration Authorization Act of 1994 or the Federal Aviation Reauthorization Act of 1996 or the provisions of the Omnibus Consolidated and Emergency Supplemental Appropriations Act, 1999 providing for payments from the Airport and Airway Trust Fund or the Interim Federal Aviation Administration Authorization Act or section 6002 of the 1999 Emergency Supplemental Appropriations Act, Public Law 106–59, or the Wendell H. Ford Aviation Investment and Reform Act for the 21st Century or the Aviation and Transportation Security Act or the Vision 100—Century of Aviation Reauthorization Act or any joint resolution making continuing appropriations for the fiscal year 2008 or the Department of Transportation Appropriations Act, 2008 or the Airport and Airway Extension Act of 2008 or the Federal Aviation Administration Extension Act of 2008 or the Federal Aviation Administration Extension Act of 2008, Part II or the Federal Aviation Administration Extension Act of 2009 or any joint resolution making continuing appropriations for the fiscal year 2010 or the Fiscal Year 2010 Federal Aviation Administration Extension Act or the Fiscal Year 2010 Federal Aviation Administration Extension Act, Part II or the Federal Aviation Administration Extension Act of 2010 or the Airport and Airway Extension Act of 2010 or the Airport and Airway Extension Act of 2010, Part II or the Airline Safety and Federal Aviation Administration Extension Act of 2010 or the Airport and Airway Extension Act of 2010, Part III or the Airport and Airway Extension Act of 2010, Part IV or the Airport and Airway Extension Act of 2011 or the Airport and Airway Extension Act of 2011, Part II or the Airport and Airway Extension Act of 2011, Part III or the Airport and Airway Extension Act of 2011, Part IV or the Airport and Airway Extension Act of 2011, Part V or the Airport and Airway Extension Act of 2012 or the FAA Modernization and Reform Act of 2012 or the Airport and Airway Extension Act of 2015 or the Airport and Airway Extension Act of 2016 or the FAA Extension, Safety, and Security Act of 2016 or the Disaster Tax Relief and Airport and Airway Extension Act of 2017 or the Airport and Airway Extension Act of 2018 or the Airport and Airway Extension Act of 2018, Part II or the FAA Reauthorization Act of 2018 or title II of division B of the Continuing Appropriations Act, 2024 and Other Extensions Act or the Airport and Airway Extension Act of 2023, Part II or the Airport and Airway Extension Act of 2024 or the Airport and Airway Extension Act of 2024, Part II or the FAA Reauthorization Act of 2024;

(B) heretofore or hereafter incurred under part A of subtitle VII of title 49, United States Code, which are attributable to planning, research and development, construction, or operation and maintenance of—

(i) air traffic control,

(ii) air navigation,

(iii) communications, or

(iv) supporting services,

for the airway system; or

    (C) for those portions of the administrative expenses of the Department of Transportation which are attributable to activities described in subparagraph (A) or (B).

Any reference in subparagraph (A) to an Act shall be treated as a reference to such Act and the corresponding provisions (if any) of title 49, United States Code, as such Act and provisions were in effect on the date of the enactment of the last Act referred to in subparagraph (A).

(2) Transfers from Airport and Airway Trust Fund on Account of Certain Refunds.——

The Secretary of the Treasury shall pay from time to time from the Airport and Airway Trust Fund into the general fund of the Treasury amounts equivalent to the amounts paid after August 31, 1982, in respect of fuel used in aircraft, under section 6420 (relating to amounts paid in respect of gasoline used on farms), 6421 (relating to amounts paid in respect of gasoline used for certain nonhighway purposes), or 6427 (relating to fuels not used for taxable purposes) (other than subsection (l)(4) thereof).

(3) Transfers from the Airport and Airway Trust Fund on Account of Certain Section 34 Credits.——

The Secretary of the Treasury shall pay from time to time from the Airport and Airway Trust Fund into the general fund of the Treasury amounts equivalent to the credits allowed under section 34 (other than payments made by reason of paragraph (4) of section 6427(l)) with respect to fuel used after August 31, 1982. Such amounts shall be transferred on the basis of estimates by the Secretary of the Treasury, and proper adjustments shall be made in amounts subsequently transferred to the extent prior estimates were in excess of or less than the credits allowed.

(4) Transfers for Refunds and Credits not to exceed Trust Fund Revenues attributable to Fuel Used.——

The amounts payable from the Airport and Airway Trust Fund under paragraph (2) or (3) shall not exceed the amounts required to be appropriated to such Trust Fund with respect to fuel so used.

(5) Transfers from Airport and Airway Trust Fund on Account of Refunds of Taxes on Transportation by Air.——

The Secretary of the Treasury shall pay from time to time from the Airport and Airway Trust Fund into the general fund of the Treasury amounts equivalent to the amounts paid after December 31, 1995, under section 6402 (relating to authority to make credits or refunds) or section 6415 (relating to credits or refunds to persons who collected certain taxes) in respect of taxes under sections 4261 and 4271.

(6) Transfers from the Airport and Airway Trust Fund on

ACCOUNT OF CERTAIN AIRPORTS.—

The Secretary of the Treasury may transfer from the Airport and Airway Trust Fund to the Secretary of Transportation or the Administrator of the Federal Aviation Administration an amount to make a payment to an airport affected by a diversion that is the subject of an administrative action under paragraph (3) or a civil action under paragraph (4) of section 47107(m) of title 49, United States Code.

(e) LIMITATION ON TRANSFERS TO TRUST FUND.—

(1) IN GENERAL.—

Except as provided in paragraph (2), no amount may be appropriated or credited to the Airport and Airway Trust Fund on and after the date of any expenditure from the Airport and Airway Trust Fund which is not permitted by this section. The determination of whether an expenditure is so permitted shall be made without regard to—

(A) any provision of law which is not contained or referenced in this title or in a revenue Act; and

(B) whether such provision of law is a subsequently enacted provision or directly or indirectly seeks to waive the application of this subsection.

(2) EXCEPTION FOR PRIOR OBLIGATIONS.—

Paragraph (1) shall not apply to any expenditure to liquidate any contract entered into (or for any amount otherwise obligated) before October 1, 2028, in accordance with the provisions of this section.

(f) ADDITIONAL TRANSFER TO TRUST FUND.—

Out of money in the Treasury not otherwise appropriated, there is hereby appropriated $14,000,000,000 to the Airport and Airway Trust Fund.

§9503. HIGHWAY TRUST FUND

(a) CREATION OF TRUST FUND.—

There is established in the Treasury of the United States a trust fund to be known as the "Highway Trust Fund", consisting of such amounts as may be appropriated or credited to the Highway Trust Fund as provided in this section or section 9602(b).

(b) TRANSFER TO HIGHWAY TRUST FUND OF AMOUNTS EQUIVALENT TO CERTAIN TAXES AND PENALTIES.—

(1) CERTAIN TAXES.—

There are hereby appropriated to the Highway Trust Fund amounts equivalent to the taxes received in the Treasury before October 1, 2028, under the following provisions—

(A) section 4041 (relating to taxes on diesel fuels and special motor fuels),

(B) section 4051 (relating to retail tax on heavy trucks and trailers),

(C) section 4071 (relating to tax on tires),

(D) section 4081 (relating to tax on gasoline, diesel fuel, and kerosene), and

(E) section 4481 (relating to tax on use of certain vehicles).

For purposes of this paragraph, taxes received under sections 4041 and 4081 shall be determined without reduction for credits under section 6426 and taxes received under section 4081 shall be determined without regard to tax receipts attributable to the rate specified in section 4081(a)(2)(C).

(2) LIABILITIES INCURRED BEFORE OCTOBER 1, 2028.—

There are hereby appropriated to the Highway Trust Fund amounts equivalent to the taxes which are received in the Treasury after September 30, 2028, and before July 1, 2029, and which are attributable to liability for tax incurred before October 1, 2028, under the provisions described in paragraph (1).

[(3) Repealed.]

(4) CERTAIN TAXES NOT TRANSFERRED TO HIGHWAY TRUST FUND.—

For purposes of paragraphs (1) and (2), there shall not be taken into account the taxes imposed by—

(A) section 4041(d),

(B) section 4081 to the extent attributable to the rate specified in section 4081(a)(2)(B),

(C) section 4041 or 4081 to the extent attributable to fuel used in a train, or

(D) in the case of gasoline and special motor fuels used as described in paragraph (3)(D) or (4)(B) of subsection (c), section 4041 or 4081 with respect to so much of the rate of tax as exceeds—

(i) 11.5 cents per gallon with respect to taxes imposed before October 1, 2001,

(ii) 13 cents per gallon with respect to taxes imposed after September 30, 2001, and before October 1, 2003, and

(iii) 13.5 cents per gallon with respect to taxes imposed after September 30, 2003, and before October 1, 2005.

(5) CERTAIN PENALTIES.—

(A) IN GENERAL.—

There are hereby appropriated to the Highway Trust Fund amounts equivalent to the penalties paid under sections 6715, 6715A, 6717, 6718, 6719, 6720A, 6725, 7232, and 7272 (but only with regard to penalties under such section related to failure to register under section 4101).

(B) PENALTIES RELATED TO MOTOR VEHICLE SAFETY.—

(I) IN GENERAL.—

There are hereby appropriated to the Highway Trust Fund amounts equivalent to covered motor vehicle safety penalty collections.

(II) COVERED MOTOR VEHICLE SAFETY PENALTY COLLECTIONS

For purposes of this subparagraph, the term "covered motor vehicle safety penalty collections" means any amount collected in connection with a civil penalty under section 30165 of title 49, United States Code, reduced by any award authorized by the Secretary of Transportation to be paid to any person in connection with information provided by such person related to a violation of chapter 301 of such title which is a predicate to such civil penalty.

(6) LIMITATION ON TRANSFERS TO HIGHWAY TRUST FUND.—

(A) IN GENERAL.—

Except as provided in subparagraph (B), no amount may be appropriated to the Highway Trust Fund on and after the date of any expenditure from the Highway Trust Fund which is not permitted by this section. The determination of whether an expenditure is so permitted shall be made without regard to—

(i) any provision of law which is not contained or referenced in this title or in a revenue Act, and

(ii) whether such provision of law is a subsequently enacted provision or directly or indirectly seeks to waive the application of this paragraph.

(B) EXCEPTION FOR PRIOR OBLIGATIONS.—

Subparagraph (A) shall not apply to any expenditure to liquidate any contract entered into (or for any amount otherwise obligated) before October 1, 2026, in accordance with the provisions of this section.

(c) EXPENDITURES FROM HIGHWAY TRUST FUND.—

(1) FEDERAL-AID HIGHWAY PROGRAM.—

Except as provided in subsection (e), amounts in the Highway Trust Fund shall be available, as provided by appropriation Acts, for making expenditures before October 1, 2026, to meet those obligations of the United States heretofore or hereafter incurred which are authorized to be paid out of the Highway Trust Fund under the Infrastructure Investment and Jobs Act or any other provision of law which was referred to in this paragraph before the date of the enactment of such Act (as such Act and provisions of law are in effect on the date of the enactment of such Act).

(2) FLOOR STOCKS REFUNDS.—

The Secretary shall pay from time to time from the Highway Trust Fund into the general fund of the Treasury amounts equivalent to the floor stocks refunds made before July 1, 2029, under section 6412(a). The amounts payable from the Highway Trust Fund under the preceding sentence shall be determined by taking into account only the portion of the taxes which are deposited into the Highway Trust Fund.

(3) Transfers from the Trust Fund for motorboat fuel taxes.—

(A) Transfer to Land and Water Conservation Fund.—

(i) In general.—

The Secretary shall pay from time to time from the Highway Trust Fund into the land and water conservation fund provided for in chapter 2003 of title 54 amounts (as determined by the Secretary) equivalent to the motorboat fuel taxes received on or after October 1, 2005, and before October 1, 2028.

(ii) Limitation.—

The aggregate amount transferred under this subparagraph during any fiscal year shall not exceed $1,000,000.

(B) Excess funds transferred to Sport Fish Restoration and Boating Trust Fund.—

Any amounts in the Highway Trust Fund—
(i) which are attributable to motorboat fuel taxes, and
(ii) which are not transferred from the Highway Trust Fund under subparagraph (A),

shall be transferred by the Secretary from the Highway Trust Fund into the Sport Fish Restoration and Boating Trust Fund.

(C) Motorboat fuel taxes.—

For purposes of this paragraph, the term "motorboat fuel taxes" means the taxes under section 4041(a)(2) with respect to special motor fuels used as fuel in motorboats and under section 4081 with respect to gasoline used as fuel in motorboats, but only to the extent such taxes are deposited into the Highway Trust Fund.

(D) Determination.—

The amount of payments made under this paragraph after October 1, 1986 shall be determined by the Secretary in accordance with the methodology described in the Treasury Department's Report to Congress of June 1986 entitled "Gasoline Excise Tax Revenues Attributable to Fuel Used in Recreational Motorboats."

(4) Transfers from the Trust Fund for small-engine fuel taxes.—

(A) In general.—

The Secretary shall pay from time to time from the Highway Trust Fund into the Sport Fish Restoration and Boating Trust Fund amounts (as determined by him) equivalent to the small-engine fuel taxes received on or after December 1, 1990, and before October 1, 2028.

(B) Small-engine fuel taxes

For purposes of this paragraph, the term "small-engine fuel taxes" means the taxes under section 4081 with respect to gasoline used as a fuel in the nonbusiness use of small-engine outdoor power equipment, but only to the extent such taxes are deposited into the Highway Trust Fund.

(5) TRANSFERS FROM THE TRUST FUND FOR CERTAIN AVIATION FUEL TAXES.—

The Secretary shall pay at least monthly from the Highway Trust Fund into the Airport and Airway Trust Fund amounts (as determined by the Secretary) equivalent to the taxes received on or after October 1, 2005, under section 4081 with respect to so much of the rate of tax as does not exceed—

(A) 4.3 cents per gallon of kerosene subject to section 6427(l)(4)(A) with respect to which a payment has been made by the Secretary under section 6427(l), and

(B) 21.8 cents per gallon of kerosene subject to section 6427(l)(4)(B) with respect to which a payment has been made by the Secretary under section 6427(l).

Transfers under the preceding sentence shall be made on the basis of estimates by the Secretary, and proper adjustments shall be made in the amounts subsequently transferred to the extent prior estimates were in excess of or less than the amounts required to be transferred. Any amount allowed as a credit under section 34 by reason of paragraph (4) of section 6427(l) shall be treated for purposes of subparagraphs (A) and (B) as a payment made by the Secretary under such paragraph.

(d) ADJUSTMENTS OF APPORTIONMENTS.—

(1) ESTIMATES OF UNFUNDED HIGHWAY AUTHORIZATIONS AND NET HIGHWAY RECEIPTS.—

The Secretary of the Treasury, not less frequently than once in each calendar quarter, after consultation with the Secretary of Transportation, shall estimate—

(A) the amount which would (but for this subsection) be the unfunded highway authorizations at the close of the next fiscal year, and

(B) the net highway receipts for the 48-month period beginning at the close of such fiscal year.

(2) PROCEDURE WHERE THERE IS EXCESS UNFUNDED HIGHWAY AUTHORIZATIONS.—

If the Secretary of the Treasury determines for any fiscal year that the amount described in paragraph (1)(A) exceeds the amount described in paragraph (1)(B)—

(A) he shall so advise the Secretary of Transportation, and

(B) he shall further advise the Secretary of Transportation as to the amount of such excess.

(3) ADJUSTMENT OF APPORTIONMENTS WHERE UNFUNDED AUTHORIZATIONS EXCEED 4 YEARS' RECEIPTS.—

(A) DETERMINATION OF PERCENTAGE.—

If, before any apportionment to the States is made, in the most recent estimate made by the Secretary of the Treasury there is an excess referred to in paragraph (2)(B), the Secretary of Transportation shall determine the percentage which—

(i) the excess referred to in paragraph (2)(B), is of

(ii) the amount authorized to be appropriated from the Trust Fund for the fiscal year for apportionment to the States.

If, but for this sentence, the most recent estimate would be one which was made on a date which will be more than 3 months before the date of the apportionment, the Secretary of the Treasury shall make a new estimate under paragraph (1) for the appropriate fiscal year.

(B) ADJUSTMENT OF APPORTIONMENTS.—

If the Secretary of Transportation determines a percentage under subparagraph (A) for purposes of any apportionment, notwithstanding any other provision of law, the Secretary of Transportation shall apportion to the States (in lieu of the amount which, but for the provisions of this subsection, would be so apportioned) the amount obtained by reducing the amount authorized to be so apportioned by such percentage.

(4) APPORTIONMENT OF AMOUNTS PREVIOUSLY WITHHELD FROM APPORTIONMENT.—

If, after funds have been withheld from apportionment under paragraph (3)(B), the Secretary of the Treasury determines that the amount described in paragraph (1)(A) does not exceed the amount described in paragraph (1)(B) or that the excess described in paragraph (1)(B) is less than the amount previously determined, he shall so advise the Secretary of Transportation. The Secretary of Transportation shall apportion to the States such portion of the funds so withheld from apportionment as the Secretary of the Treasury has advised him may be so apportioned without causing the amount described in paragraph (1)(A) to exceed the amount described in paragraph (1)(B). Any funds apportioned pursuant to the preceding sentence shall remain available for the period for which they would be available if such apportionment took effect with the fiscal year in which they are apportioned pursuant to the preceding sentence.

(5) DEFINITIONS.—

For purposes of this subsection—

(A) Unfunded highway authorizations

The term "unfunded highway authorizations" means, at any time, the excess (if any) of—

(i) the total potential unpaid commitments at such time as a result of the apportionment to the States of the amounts authorized to be appropriated from the Highway Trust Fund, over

(ii) the amount available in the Highway Trust Fund at such time to defray such commitments (after all other unpaid commitments at such time which are payable from the Highway Trust Fund have been defrayed).

(B) NET HIGHWAY RECEIPTS.—

The term "net highway receipts" means, with respect to any period, the excess of—
    (i) the receipts (including interest) of the Highway Trust Fund during such period, over
    (ii) the amounts to be transferred during such period from such Fund under subsection (c) (other than paragraph (1) thereof).

(6) MEASUREMENT OF NET HIGHWAY RECEIPTS.—

For purposes of making any estimate under paragraph (1) of net highway receipts for periods ending after the date specified in subsection (b)(1), the Secretary shall treat—
    (A) each expiring provision of subsection (b) which is related to appropriations or transfers to the Highway Trust Fund to have been extended through the end of the 48-month period referred to in paragraph (1)(B), and
    (B) with respect to each tax imposed under the sections referred to in subsection (b)(1), the rate of such tax during the 48-month period referred to in paragraph (1)(B) to be the same as the rate of such tax as in effect on the date of such estimate.

(7) REPORTS.—

Any estimate under paragraph (1) and any determination under paragraph (2) shall be reported by the Secretary of the Treasury to the Committee on Ways and Means of the House of Representatives, the Committee on Finance of the Senate, the Committees on the Budget of both Houses, the Committee on Public Works and Transportation of the House of Representatives, and the Committee on Environment and Public Works of the Senate.

(e) ESTABLISHMENT OF MASS TRANSIT ACCOUNT.—

(1) CREATION OF ACCOUNT.—

There is established in the Highway Trust Fund a separate account to be known as the "Mass Transit Account" consisting of such amounts as may be transferred or credited to the Mass Transit Account as provided in this section or section 9602(b).

(2) TRANSFERS TO MASS TRANSIT ACCOUNT.—

The Secretary of the Treasury shall transfer to the Mass Transit Account the mass transit portion of the amounts appropriated to the Highway Trust Fund under subsection (b) which are attributable to taxes under sections 4041 and 4081 imposed after March 31, 1983. For purposes of the preceding sentence, the term "mass transit portion" means, for any fuel with respect to which tax was imposed under section 4041 or 4081 and otherwise deposited into the Highway Trust Fund, the amount determined at the rate of—
    (A) except as otherwise provided in this sentence, 2.86 cents per gallon,
    (B) 1.43 cents per gallon in the case of any partially exempt methanol or ethanol fuel (as defined in section 4041(m)) none of the alcohol in which consists of ethanol,
    (C) 1.86 cents per energy equivalent of a gallon of diesel (as defined in section

4041(a)(2)(D)) in the case of liquefied natural gas,

(D) 2.13 cents per energy equivalent of a gallon of gasoline (as defined in section 4041(a)(2)(C)) in the case of liquefied petroleum gas, and

(E) 9.71 cents per MCF (determined at standard temperature and pressure) in the case of compressed natural gas.

(3) EXPENDITURES FROM ACCOUNT.—

Amounts in the Mass Transit Account shall be available, as provided by appropriation Acts, for making capital or capital related expenditures (including capital expenditures for new projects) before October 1, 2026, in accordance with the Infrastructure Investment and Jobs Act or any other provision of law which was referred to in this paragraph before the date of the enactment of such Act (as such Act and provisions of law are in effect on the date of the enactment of such Act).

(4) LIMITATION.—

Rules similar to the rules of subsection (d) shall apply to the Mass Transit Account.

(5) Portion of certain transfers to be made from account

(A) IN GENERAL.—

Transfers under paragraphs (2) and (3) of subsection (c) shall be borne by the Highway Account and the Mass Transit Account in proportion to the respective revenues transferred under this section to the Highway Account (after the application of paragraph (2)) and the Mass Transit Account.

(B) HIGHWAY ACCOUNT.—

For purposes of subparagraph (A), the term "Highway Account" means the portion of the Highway Trust Fund which is not the Mass Transit Account.

(f) Determination of Trust Fund balances after September 30, 1998

(1) IN GENERAL.—

For purposes of determining the balances of the Highway Trust Fund and the Mass Transit Account after September 30, 1998, the opening balance of the Highway Trust Fund (other than the Mass Transit Account) on October 1, 1998, shall be $8,000,000,000. The Secretary shall cancel obligations held by the Highway Trust Fund to reflect the reduction in the balance under this paragraph.

(2) RESTORATION OF FOREGONE INTEREST.—

Out of money in the Treasury not otherwise appropriated, there is hereby appropriated—

(A) $14,700,000,000 to the Highway Account (as defined in subsection (e)(5)(B)) in the Highway Trust Fund; and

(B) $4,800,000,000 to the Mass Transit Account in the Highway Trust Fund.

(3) INCREASE IN FUND BALANCE.—

There is hereby transferred to the Highway Account (as defined in subsection (e)(5)(B)) in the Highway Trust Fund amounts appropriated from the Leaking Underground Storage Tank Trust Fund under section 9508(c)(2).

(4) ADDITIONAL APPROPRIATIONS TO TRUST FUND.—

Out of money in the Treasury not otherwise appropriated, there is hereby appropriated to—

(A) the Highway Account (as defined in subsection (e)(5)(B)) in the Highway Trust Fund—

(i) for fiscal year 2013, $6,200,000,000, and

(ii) for fiscal year 2014, $10,400,000,000, and

(B) the Mass Transit Account in the Highway Trust Fund, for fiscal year 2014, $2,200,000,000.

(5) ADDITIONAL SUMS.—

Out of money in the Treasury not otherwise appropriated, there is hereby appropriated—

(A) $7,765,000,000 to the Highway Account (as defined in subsection (e)(5)(B)) in the Highway Trust Fund; and

(B) $2,000,000,000 to the Mass Transit Account in the Highway Trust Fund.

(6) ADDITIONAL INCREASE IN FUND BALANCE.—

There is hereby transferred to the Highway Account (as defined in subsection (e)(5)(B)) in the Highway Trust Fund amounts appropriated from the Leaking Underground Storage Tank Trust Fund under section 9508(c)(3).

.—(7) Additional sums.—

Out of money in the Treasury not otherwise appropriated, there is hereby appropriated—

(A) $6,068,000,000 to the Highway Account (as defined in subsection (e)(5)(B)) in the Highway Trust Fund; and

(B) $2,000,000,000 to the Mass Transit Account in the Highway Trust Fund.

(8) FURTHER TRANSFERS TO TRUST FUND<.—/h4>

Out of money in the Treasury not otherwise appropriated, there is hereby appropriated—

(A) $51,900,000,000 to the Highway Account (as defined in subsection (e)(5)(B)) in the Highway Trust Fund; and

(B) $18,100,000,000 to the Mass Transit Account in the Highway Trust Fund.

(9) ADDITIONAL INCREASE IN FUND BALANCE.—

There is hereby transferred to the Highway Account (as defined in subsection (e)(5)(B)) in the Highway Trust Fund amounts appropriated from the Leaking

Underground Storage Tank Trust Fund under section 9508(c)(4).

(10) FURTHER TRANSFERS TO TRUST FUND.—

Out of money in the Treasury not otherwise appropriated, there is hereby appropriated—

(A) $10,400,000,000 to the Highway Account (as defined in subsection (e)(5)(B)) in the Highway Trust Fund; and

(B) $3,200,000,000 to the Mass Transit Account in the Highway Trust Fund.

(11) FURTHER TRANSFERS TO TRUST FUND.—

Out of money in the Treasury not otherwise appropriated, there is hereby appropriated—

(A) $90,000,000,000 to the Highway Account (as defined in subsection (e)(5)(B)) in the Highway Trust Fund; and

(B) $28,000,000,000 to the Mass Transit Account in the Highway Trust Fund.

(12) TREATMENT OF AMOUNTS.—

Any amount appropriated or transferred under this subsection to the Highway Trust Fund shall remain available without fiscal year limitation.

* * * * * * *

Subchapter B—General Provisions

Sec.
9601.   Transfer of amounts.
9602.   Management of Trust Funds.

§9601. TRANSFER OF AMOUNTS.—

The amounts appropriated by any section of subchapter A to any Trust Fund established by such subchapter shall be transferred at least monthly from the general fund of the Treasury to such Trust Fund on the basis of estimates made by the Secretary of the Treasury of the amounts referred to in such section. Proper adjustments shall be made in the amounts subsequently transferred to the extent prior estimates were in excess of or less than the amounts required to be transferred.

§9602. MANAGEMENT OF TRUST FUNDS.—

(a) REPORT.—

It shall be the duty of the Secretary of the Treasury to hold each Trust Fund established by subchapter A, and (after consultation with any other trustees of the Trust Fund) to report to the Congress each year on the financial condition and the results of the operations of each such Trust Fund during the preceding fiscal year and on its expected condition and operations during the next 5 fiscal years. Such report shall be printed as a House document of the session of the Congress to which the report is made.

(b) INVESTMENT.—

(1) IN GENERAL.—

It shall be the duty of the Secretary of the Treasury to invest such portion of any Trust Fund established by subchapter A as is not, in his judgment, required to meet current withdrawals. Such investments may be made only in interest-bearing obligations of the United States. For such purpose, such obligations may be acquired—

(A) on original issue at the issue price, or

(B) by purchase of outstanding obligations at the market price.

(2) SALE OF OBLIGATIONS.—

Any obligation acquired by a Trust Fund established by subchapter A may be sold by the Secretary of the Treasury at the market price.

(3) INTEREST ON CERTAIN PROCEEDS.—

The interest on, and the proceeds from the sale or redemption of, any obligations held in a Trust Fund established by subchapter A shall be credited to and form a part of the Trust Fund.

* * * * * * *

ACTS RELATING TO WASHINGTON AREA AIRPORTS

ACT OF JUNE 29, 1940

ACT OF JUNE 29, 1940-(Washington Airports)

[54 Stat. 686]

[This Act has not been amended]

AN ACT To provide for the administration of the Washington National Airport, and for other purposes.

Be it enacted by the Senate and House of Representatives of the United States of America in Congress assembled,

That for the purposes of this Act—

SEC. 1. (a) "Secretary" means the Secretary of Transportation.

(b) "Airport" means the Ronald Reagan Washington National Airport, which shall consist of, and include, the tract of land, together with all structures, improvements, and other facilities located thereon, lying partly in the District of Columbia and partly in the State of Virginia, particularly described as follows:

Commencing at a point of beginning, said point being the intersection of the property line of property owned by the Richmond, Fredericksburg and Potomac Railroad Company, and dredging base line at station 0+18.99 referenced south 6,808.21, west 9,078.02, running in a southeasterly direction on a bearing of south 22°51'18" east a distance of 6,270.91 feet, more or less, to station 62+89.90 of said dredging base line. Thence 13°30' right on a bearing of south 9°21'18" east a distance of 1,332.29 feet, more or less, to station 76+22.19 of said base line. Thence 11°04'19" right on a bearing of south 1°43'01" west a distance of 1,231.20 feet, more or less, to station 88+53.39 of said base line. Thence 12°40'41" right on a bearing of south 14°23'42" west a distance of 2,409.32 feet, more or less, to station 112+62.71 on said base line. Thence 1°15'44.3" right on a bearing of south 15°39'26.3" west a distance of 4,938.38

feet, more or less, to United States Coast and Geodetic Survey Station WATER, referenced south 22,220.86, west 8,395.54. Thence 17°09'25.6" left on a bearing of south 1°29'59.3" east a distance of 85.58 feet, more or less, to a corner of the property line between the United States of America and Smoot Sand and Gravel Corporation. Thence 85°59'59.3" right on a bearing of south 84°30'00" west a distance of 1,516.41 feet, more or less, to a monument located at a corner on the property line of the Richmond, Fredericksburg and Potomac Railroad Company, said monument being referenced south 22,451.75, west 9,902.73. Thence 85°50'06.7" right on a bearing of north 8°09'54" west a distance of 442.68 feet, more or less. Thence 5°00'12" left on a bearing of north 13°10'06" west a distance of 578.64 feet, more or less. Thence 4°57'25" left on a bearing of north 18°07'31" west a distance of 462.94 feet, more or less. Thence 1°34'50" left on a bearing of north 19°42'21" west a distance of 943.56 feet, more or less, to the point of a curve having an angle of 27°52'45" right radius 1,241.15 feet, long chord 597.98 feet, on a bearing of north 5°45'58" west. Thence along the arc of said curve a distance of 603.92 feet, more or less, to the point of tangency of said curve. Thence along a tangent to said curve on a bearing of north 8°10'24" east a distance of 232.33 feet, more or less, to the point of a curve having an angle of 36°59'09" left, radius 1,046 feet, long chord 663.56 feet on a bearing of north 10°19'10.5" west. Thence along the arc of said curve a distance of 675.22 feet, more or less, to the point of tangency of said curve. Thence along a tangent to said curve on a bearing of north 28°48'45" west a distance of 256.75 feet, more or less. Thence 30°33'10" left on a bearing of north 59°21'55" west a distance of 287.84 feet, more or less. Thence 40°45'20" right on a bearing of north 18°36'35" west a distance of 1,142.08 feet, more or less. Thence 5°43'29" right on a bearing of north 12°53'06" west a distance of 118.02 feet, more or less, to the point of a curve having an angle of 26°20'50" right, radius 3,665.71 feet, long chord 1,670.85 feet on a bearing of north 0°17'19" east. Thence along the arc of said curve a distance of 1,685.66 feet, more or less, to the point of tangency of said curve. Thence along a tangent to said curve on a bearing of north 13°27'44" east a distance of 2,002.11 feet, more or less, to the point of a curve having an angle of 10°36'25" left, radius 2,864.79 feet, long chord of 529.59 feet

on a bearing of north 8°09'31.5" east. Thence along the arc
of said curve a distance of 530.25 feet, more or less, to the
point of tangency of said curve. Thence along a tangent to said
curve on a bearing of north 2°51'19" east a distance of 124.53
feet, more or less. Thence 6°57'52" left on a bearing of north
4°06'33" west a distance of 571.33 feet, more or less. Thence
7°22'39" left on a bearing of north 11°29'12" west a distance of
811.63 feet, more or less. Thence 8°16'52" right on a bearing
of north 3°12'20" east a distance of 70.41 feet, more or less, to
the point of a curve having an angle of 7°43'12" right, radius
5,479.58 feet, long chord 737.75 feet on a bearing of north
7°03'56" east. Thence along the arc of said curve a distance
of 738.31 feet, more or less, to the point of tangency of said
curve, said point being on the old property line between Mary E.
Cullinane and Milton Hopfenmaier property. Thence along said
property line on a bearing of north 75°11'50" east a distance
of 204.72 feet, more or less, to a monument marked U. S. D.
1–N. P. S., reference south 18,419.16, west 10,829.26. Thence
along the same bearing of north 75°11'50" east a distance of
215 feet, more or less. Thence 34°36'06" left on a bearing of
north 40°35'44" east a distance of 1,509 feet, more or less,
to the point of a curve having an angle of 5°45' left, radius
7,239.41 feet, long chord of 723.20 feet, on a bearing of north
37°53'14" east. Thence along the arc of said curve a distance
of 726.51 feet, more or less, to the point of a compound curve
having an angle of 6°00' left, radius 2,217.01 feet, long chord
of 232.06 feet on a bearing of north 32°10'44" east. Thence
along the arc of said curve a distance of 232.15 feet, more
or less, to the point of a compound curve having an angle
of 57°01'20" left, radius 1,303.74, long chord 1,244.62, on a
bearing of north 0°40'04" east. Thence along the arc of said
curve a distance of 1,297.22 feet, more or less, to the point of
a compound curve having an angle of 7°59'54.3" left, radius
2,217.01 feet, long chord 309.23 feet on a bearing of north
31°49'33" west. Thence along the arc of said curve a distance
of 310 feet, more or less, to the intersection of said curve with
the property line of the Richmond, Fredericksburg and Potomac
Railroad Company and the United States of America. Thence in
a northeasterly direction along a bearing of north 34°30'00" east
a distance of 340 feet, more or less, to the point of beginning;
excepting, however, such portion thereof as the President may,

by Executive order or orders, prescribe, which portion shall be added to, and administered as part of, the Mount Vernon Memorial Highway, authorized by the Act approved May 23, 1928 (45 Stat. 721), as amended.

SEC. 2. The Secretary shall have control over, and responsibility for, the care, operation, maintenance, and protection of the airport, together with the power to make and amend such rules and regulations as he may deem necessary to the proper exercise thereof.

SEC. 3. The Secretary is empowered to lease, upon such terms as he may deem proper, space or property within or upon the airport for purposes essential or appropriate to the operation of the airport.

SEC. 4. (a) The Secretary, and any Department of Transportation employee appointed to protect life and property on the airport, when designated by the Secretary, is hereby authorized and empowered (1) to arrest under a warrant within the limits of the airport any person accused of having committed within the boundaries of the airport any offense against the laws of the United States, or against any rule or regulation prescribed pursuant to this Act; (2) to arrest without warrant any person committing any such offense within the limits of the airport, in his presence; or (3) to arrest without warrant within the limits of the airport any person whom he has reasonable grounds to believe has committed a felony within the limits of the airport.

(b) Any individual having the power of arrest as provided in subsection (a) of this section may carry firearms or other weapons as the Secretary may direct or by regulation may prescribe.

(c) The United States Park Police may, at the request of the Secretary, be assigned by the Director of the National Park Service, in his discretion, subject to the supervision and direction of the Secretary of the Interior, to patrol any area of the airport, and any members of the United States Park Police so assigned are hereby authorized and empowered to make arrests within the limits of the airport for the same offenses, and in the same manner and circumstances, as is provided in this section with respect to employees designated by the Secretary.

SEC. 5. Any person who knowingly and willfully violates any

rule or regulation prescribed under this Act shall be guilty of a misdemeanor, and, upon conviction thereof, shall be fined not more than $500 or imprisoned not more than six months, or both.

SEC. 6. The officer on duty in command of those employees designated by the Secretary as provided in section 4 may accept deposit of collateral from any person charged with the violation of any rule or regulation prescribed under this Act, for appearance in court or before the appropriate United States magistrate judge; and such collateral shall be deposited with the United States magistrate judge at Alexandria, Virginia.

SEC. 7. The Secretary may enter into agreements with the State of Virginia, or with any political subdivision thereof, for such municipal services as the Secretary shall deem necessary to the proper and efficient government of the airport, and he may, from time to time, agree to modifications in any such agreement: *Provided, however,* That where the charge for any such service is established by the laws of the State of Virginia, the Secretary may not pay for such service an amount in excess of the charge so established. There is hereby authorized to be appropriated such sums as may be necessary for the making of payment for services under any such agreement.

ACT OF OCTOBER 31, 1945

CH 443, 59 STAT. 553

ACT OF OCTOBER 31, 1945

[Chapter 443 of 79th Congress; 59 Stat. 553]

[As Amended Through P.L. 105-154, Enacted February 6, 1989]

AN ACT To establish a boundary line between the District of Columbia and the Commonwealth of Virginia, and for other purposes.

Be it enacted by the Senate and House of Representatives of the United States of America in Congress assembled,

TITLE I–BOUNDARY LINE BETWEEN THE DISTRICT OF COLUMBIA AND THE COMMONWEALTH OF VIRGINIA

* * * * * * *

SEC. 11. Unless the context otherwise requires, the definitions of the words and phrases used in this Act shall be the definitions assigned to such words and phrases by the Civil Aeronautics Act of 1938, as amended.

SEC. 106. The provisions of sections 272 to 289, inclusive, of the Criminal Code (U.S.C., title 18, secs. 451-468) shall be applicable to such portions of the George Washington Memorial Parkway and of the Ronald Reagan National Airport as are situated within the Commonwealth of Virginia. Any United States commissioner specially designated for that purpose by the District Court of the United States for the Eastern District of Virginia shall have jurisdiction to try and, if found guilty, to sentence persons charged with petty offenses against the laws of the United States committed on the above-described portions of the said parkway or airport.

The probation laws shall be applicable to persons so tried. For the purposes of this section, the term ``petty offense'' shall be defined as in section 335 of the Criminal Code (U.S.C., title aid shall so elect, however, he shall be tried in the said district court.

SEC. 11. Unless the context otherwise requires, the definitions of the words and phrases used in this Act shall be the definitions assigned to such words and phrases by the Civil Aeronautics Act of 1938, as amended.

SEC. 107. The State of Virginia hereby consents that exclusive jurisdiction in the Ronald Reagan National Airport (as described in sec. 1(b) of the Act of June 29, 1940 (54 Stat. 686)), title to which is now in the United States, shall be in the United States. The conditions upon which this consent is given are the following and none others: (1) There is hereby reserved in the Commonwealth of Virginia the jurisdiction and power to levy a tax on the sale of oil, gasoline, and all other motor fuels and lubricants sold on the Ronald Reagan National Airport for use in over-the-road vehicles such as trucks, busses, and automobiles, except sales to the United States: *Provided,* That the Commonwealth of Virginia shall have no jurisdiction or power to levy a tax on the sale or use of oil, gasoline, or other motor fuels and lubricants for other purposes; (2) there is hereby expressly reserved in the Commonwealth of Virginia the jurisdiction and power to serve criminal and civil process on the Ronald Reagan National Airport; and (3) there is hereby reserved in the Commonwealth of Virginia the jurisdiction and power to regulate the manufacture, sale, and use of alcoholic beverages on the Ronald Reagan National Airport (as described in sec. 1(b) of the Act of June 29, 1940 (54 Stat. 686)).

Subject to the limitation on the consent of the State of Virginia as expressed herein exclusive jurisdiction in the Ronald Reagan National Airport shall be in the United States and the same is hereby accepted by the United States.

This Act shall have no retroactive effect except that taxes and contributions in connection with operations, sales and property on and income derived at the Ronald Reagan National Airport heretofore paid either to the Commonwealth of Virginia or the District of Columbia are hereby declared to have been paid to the proper jurisdictions and the Commonwealth of Virginia and the

94

District of Columbia each hereby waives any claim for any such taxes or contributions heretofore assessed or assessable to the extent of any such payment to either jurisdiction.

Any provision of law of the United States or the Commonwealth of Virginia which is to any extent in conflict with this Act is to the extent of such conflict hereby expressly repealed.

ACT OF SEPTEMBER 7, 1950

CH. 905, 64 STAT. 770

ACT OF SEPTEMBER 7, 1950-(Washington Airports)[1]

[Chapter 905 of 81st Congress; 64 Stat. 770]

[As Amended Through P.L. 85–511, Enacted July 11, 1958]

AN ACT To authorize the construction, protection, operation, and maintenance of a public airport in or in the vicinity of the District of Columbia.

Be it enacted by the Senate and House of Representatives of the United States of America in Congress assembled,

That the Secretary of Transportation (hereinafter referred to as the "Secretary") is hereby authorized and directed to construct, protect, operate, improve, and maintain within or in the vicinity of the District of Columbia, a public airport (including all buildings and other structures necessary or desirable therefor).

---

[1] The airport constructed under this Act, known as Dulles International Airport, was renamed Washington Dulles International Airport by Public Law 98–510.

SEC. 2. For the purpose of carrying out this Act, the Secretary is authorized to acquire, by purchase, lease, condemnation, or otherwise (including transfer with or without compensation from Federal agencies or the District of Columbia, or any State or political subdivision thereof), such lands and interests in lands and appurtenances thereto, including avigation easements or air-space rights, as may be necessary or desirable for the construction, maintenance, improvement, operation, and protection of the airport: *Provided further,* That before making commitments for the acquisition of land, or the transfer of any lands, the Secretary shall consult and advise with the National Capital Park and Planning Commission as to the conformity of the proposed location with the Commission's comprehensive plan for the National Capital and its environs, and said Commission shall, upon request, submit a report and recommendations thereon within thirty days: *Provided further,* That the choice of site by the Secretary shall be made only after consultation with the governing body in the county in which the airport is to be located, with respect to the suitability of the site to be selected, and its possible impact on the vicinity.

SEC. 3. For the purposes of this Act, the Secretary is empowered to acquire, by purchase, lease, condemnation, or otherwise (including transfer with or without compensation from Federal agencies or the District of Columbia, or any State or political subdivision thereof), rights-of-way or easements for roads, trails, pipe lines, power lines, railroad spurs, and other similar facilities necessary or desirable for the construction or proper operation of the airport.

The Secretary is authorized to construct any streets, highways, or roadways (including bridges) as may be necessary to provide access to the airport from existing streets, highways, or roadways. Upon completion of construction of any street, highway, or roadway within the District of Columbia, such street, highway, or roadway shall be transferred to the District of Columbia without charge, and thereafter shall be maintained by the District of Columbia. Upon construction of any street, highway, or roadway within a State or political subdivision thereof, such street, highway, or roadway may be transferred to such State or political subdivision thereof, without charge, on the condition that such street, highway, or roadway thereafter be maintained as a public street, highway, or roadway by such State or political subdivision thereof.

SEC. 4. The Secretary shall have control over and responsibility for the care, operation, maintenance, improvement, and protection of the airport, together with the power to make and amend such rules and regulations as he may deem necessary to the proper exercise thereof: *Provided,* That the authority herein contained may be delegated by the Secretary to such official or officials of the Department of Transportation as the Secretary may designate.

SEC. 5. The Secretary is empowered to lease under such conditions as he may deem proper and for such periods as may be desirable space or property within or upon the airport for purposes essential or appropriate to the operation of the airport: *Provided,* That no lease for the use of any hanger or space therein shall extend for a period exceeding three years.

SEC. 6. The Secretary is authorized to contract with any person for the furnishing of supplies or performance of services at or upon the airport necessary or desirable for the proper operation of the airport, including but not limited to, contracts for furnishing food and lodging, sale of aviation fuels, furnishing of aircraft repairs and other aeronautical services, and such other services and supplies as may be necessary or desirable for the traveling public. No such contract, not including contracts involving the construction of permanent buildings or facilities, shall extend for a period of longer than five years, except the restaurant. The provisions of section 3709 of the Revised Statutes shall not apply to contracts authorized under this section, to leases authorized under section 5 hereof, or to contracts for architectural or engineering services necessary for the design and planning of the airport.

SEC. 7. Any executive department, independent establishment, or agency of the Federal Government or the District of Columbia, for the purposes of carrying out this Act, is authorized to transfer to the Secretary, without compensation, upon his request, any lands, interests in lands (including avigation easements or air-space rights), buildings, property, or equipment under its control and in excess of its own requirements, which the Secretary may consider necessary or desirable for the construction, care, operation, maintenance, improvement, or protection of the airport.

SEC. 8. (a) The Secretary, and any Department of Transportation employee appointed to protect life and property on the airport, when designated by the Secretary, is hereby authorized and empowered (1) to arrest under a warrant within the limits of the airport any person accused of having committed within the boundaries of the airport any offense against the laws of the United States, or against any rule or regulation prescribed pursuant to this Act; (2) to arrest without warrant any person committing any such offense within the limits of the airport, in his presence; or (3) to arrest without warrant within the limits of the airport any person whom he has reasonable grounds to believe has committed a felony within the limits of the airport.

(b) Any individual having the power of arrest as provided in subsection (a) of this section may carry firearms or other weapons as the Secretary may direct or by regulation may prescribe.

(c) The United States Park Police may, at the request of the Secretary, be assigned by the Secretary of the Interior, in his discretion, to patrol any area of the airport, and any members of the United States Park Police so assigned are hereby authorized and empowered to make arrests within the limits of the airport for the same offenses and in the same manner and circumstances as are provided in this section with respect to employees designated by the Secretary.

(d) The officer on duty in command of those employees designated by the Secretary as provided in subsection (a) of this section may accept deposit of collateral from any person charged with the violation of any rule or regulation prescribed under this Act, for appearance in court or before the appropriate United States magistrate judge; and such collateral shall be deposited with such United States magistrate judge.

SEC. 9. The Secretary may enter into agreements with the State, or any political subdivision thereof, in which the airport or any portion thereof is situated, for such State or municipal services as the Secretary shall deem necessary to the proper and efficient operation and protection of the airport, and he may, from time to time, agree to modifications in any such agreement: *Provided, however,* That where the charge for any such service is established by the laws of the State, the Secretary may not pay for such service in excess of the charge so established.

SEC. 10. Any person who knowingly and willfully violates any rule, regulation, or order issued by the Secretary under this Act shall be deemed guilty of a misdemeanor and upon conviction thereof shall be subject to a fine of not more than $500 or to imprisonment not exceeding six months, or to both such fine and imprisonment.

SEC. 11. Unless the context otherwise requires, the definitions of the words and phrases used in this Act shall be the definitions assigned to such words and phrases by the Civil Aeronautics Act of 1938, as amended.

SEC. 12. There is hereby authorized to be appropriated such sum as may be necessary for the construction of the airport authorized by this Act, and such sum shall remain available until expended. There are hereby authorized to be appropriated such other sums as may be necessary to carry out the purposes of this Act.

SELECTED PROVISIONS RELATING TO COUNTER-UAS AUTHORITIES

SECTION 130I OF TITLE 10 U.S.C.

PUBLIC LAW 118-78

§130I. PROTECTION OF CERTAIN FACILITIES AND ASSETS FROM UNMANNED AIRCRAFT

(a) AUTHORITY.—Notwithstanding section 46502 of title 49, or any provision of title 18, the Secretary of Defense may take, and may authorize members of the armed forces and officers and civilian employees of the Department of Defense with assigned duties that include safety, security, or protection of personnel, facilities, or assets, to take, such actions described in subsection (b)(1) that are necessary to mitigate the threat (as defined by the Secretary of Defense, in consultation with the Secretary of Transportation) that an unmanned aircraft system or unmanned aircraft poses to the safety or security of a covered facility or asset.

(b) ACTIONS DESCRIBED.—(1) The actions described in this paragraph are the following:

(A) Detect, identify, monitor, and track the unmanned aircraft system or unmanned aircraft, without prior consent, including by means of intercept or other access of a wire communication, an oral communication, or an electronic communication used to control the unmanned aircraft system or unmanned aircraft.

(B) Warn the operator of the unmanned aircraft system or unmanned aircraft, including by passive or active, and direct or indirect physical, electronic, radio, and electromagnetic means.

(C) Disrupt control of the unmanned aircraft system or unmanned aircraft, without prior consent, including by disabling the unmanned aircraft system or unmanned aircraft by intercepting, interfering, or causing interference with wire, oral, electronic, or radio communications used to control the unmanned aircraft system or unmanned aircraft.

(D) Seize or exercise control of the unmanned aircraft system or unmanned aircraft.

(E) Seize or otherwise confiscate the unmanned aircraft system or unmanned aircraft.

(F) Use reasonable force to disable, damage, or destroy the unmanned aircraft system or unmanned aircraft.

(2) The Secretary of Defense shall develop the actions described in paragraph (1) in coordination with the Secretary of Transportation.

(c) FORFEITURE.—Any unmanned aircraft system or unmanned aircraft described in subsection (a) that is seized by the Secretary of Defense is subject to forfeiture to the United States.

(d) REGULATIONS AND GUIDANCE.—(1) The Secretary of Defense and the Secretary of Transportation may prescribe regulations and shall issue guidance in the respective areas of each Secretary to carry out this section.

(2)(A) The Secretary of Defense and the Secretary of Transportation shall coordinate in the development of guidance under paragraph (1).

(B) The Secretary of Defense shall coordinate with the Secretary of Transportation and the Administrator of the Federal Aviation Administration before issuing any guidance or otherwise implementing this section if such guidance or implementation might affect aviation safety, civilian aviation and aerospace operations, aircraft airworthiness, or the use of airspace.

(e) PRIVACY PROTECTION.—The regulations prescribed or guidance issued under subsection (d) shall ensure that—

(1) the interception or acquisition of, or access to, communications to or from an unmanned aircraft system under this section is conducted in a manner consistent with the fourth amendment to the Constitution and applicable provisions of Federal law;

(2) communications to or from an unmanned aircraft system are intercepted, acquired, or accessed only to the extent necessary to support a function of the Department of Defense;

(3) records of such communications are not maintained for more than 180 days unless the Secretary of Defense determines that maintenance of such records—

(A) is necessary to support one or more functions of the Department of Defense; or

(B) is required for a longer period to support a civilian law enforcement agency or by any other applicable law or regulation; and

(4) such communications are not disclosed outside the Department of Defense unless the disclosure—

(A) would fulfill a function of the Department of Defense;

(B) would support a civilian law enforcement agency or the enforcement activities of a regulatory agency of the Federal Government in connection with a criminal or civil investigation of, or any regulatory action with regard to, an action described in subsection (b)(1); or

(C) is otherwise required by law or regulation.

(f) BUDGET.—The Secretary of Defense shall submit to Congress, as a part of the defense budget materials for each fiscal year after fiscal year 2018, a consolidated funding display that identifies the funding source for the actions described in subsection (b)(1) within the Department of Defense. The funding display shall be in unclassified form, but may contain a classified annex.

(g) SEMIANNUAL BRIEFINGS.—(1) On a semiannual basis during the five-year period beginning March 1, 2018, the Secretary of Defense and the Secretary of Transportation, shall jointly provide a briefing to the appropriate congressional committees on the activities carried out pursuant to this section. Such briefings shall include—

(A) policies, programs, and procedures to mitigate or eliminate impacts of such activities to the National Airspace System;

(B) a description of instances where actions described in subsection (b)(1) have been taken;

(C) how the Secretaries have informed the public as to the possible use of authorities under this section; and

(D) how the Secretaries have engaged with Federal, State, and local law enforcement agencies to implement and use such authorities.

(2) Each briefing under paragraph (1) shall be in unclassified form, but may be

accompanied by an additional classified briefing.

(h) RULE OF CONSTRUCTION.—Nothing in this section may be construed to—

(1) vest in the Secretary of Defense any authority of the Secretary of Transportation or the Administrator of the Federal Aviation Administration under title 49; and

(2) vest in the Secretary of Transportation or the Administrator of the Federal Aviation Administration any authority of the Secretary of Defense under this title.

(i) PARTIAL TERMINATION.—(1) Except as provided by paragraph (2), the authority to carry out this section with respect to the covered facilities or assets specified in clauses (iv) through (viii) of subsection (j)(3)(C) shall terminate on December 31, 2023.

(2) The President may extend by 180 days the termination date specified in paragraph (1) if before November 15, 2023, the President certifies to Congress that such extension is in the national security interests of the United States.

(j) DEFINITIONS.—In this section:

(1) The term "appropriate congressional committees" means—

(A) the congressional defense committees;

(B) the Select Committee on Intelligence, the Committee on the Judiciary, and the Committee on Commerce, Science, and Transportation of the Senate; and

(C) the Permanent Select Committee on Intelligence, the Committee on the Judiciary, and the Committee on Transportation and Infrastructure of the House of Representatives.

(2) The term "budget", with respect to a fiscal year, means the budget for that fiscal year that is submitted to Congress by the President under section 1105(a) of title 31.

(3) The term "covered facility or asset" means any facility or asset that—

(A) is identified by the Secretary of Defense, in consultation with the Secretary of Transportation with respect to potentially impacted airspace, through a risk-based assessment for purposes of this section;

(B) is located in the United States (including the territories and possessions of the United States); and

(C) directly relates to the missions of the Department of Defense pertaining to—

(i) nuclear deterrence, including with respect to nuclear command and control, integrated tactical warning and attack assessment, and continuity of government;

(ii) missile defense;

(iii) national security space;

(iv) assistance in protecting the President or the Vice President (or other officer immediately next in order of succession to the office of the President) pursuant to the Presidential Protection Assistance Act of 1976 (18 U.S.C. 3056 note);

(v) air defense of the United States, including air sovereignty, ground-based air defense, and the National Capital Region integrated air defense system;

(vi) combat support agencies (as defined in paragraphs (1) through (4) of section 193(f) of this title);

(vii) special operations activities specified in paragraphs (1) through (9) of section 167(k) of this title;

(viii) production, storage, transportation, or decommissioning of high-yield explosive munitions, by the Department; or

(ix) a Major Range and Test Facility Base (as defined in sections [1] 4173(i) of this title).

(4) The term "defense budget materials", with respect to a fiscal year, means the materials submitted to Congress by the Secretary of Defense in support of the budget for that fiscal year.

(5) The terms "electronic communication", "intercept", "oral communication", and "wire communication" have the meanings given those terms in section 2510 of title 18.

(6) The terms "unmanned aircraft" and "unmanned aircraft system" have the meanings given those terms in section 44801 of title 49.

(Added Pub. L. 114–328, div. A, title XVI, §1697(a), Dec. 23, 2016, 130 Stat. 2639; amended Pub. L. 115–91, div. A, title XVI, §1692, Dec. 12, 2017, 131 Stat. 1788; Pub. L. 116–92, div. A, title XVI, §1694, title XVII, §1731(a)(6), Dec. 20, 2019, 133 Stat. 1791, 1812; Pub. L. 116–283, div. A, title X, §1081(a)(8), title XVIII, §1845(c)(4), Jan. 1, 2021, 134 Stat. 3871, 4247.)

SECTION 528 OF TITLE 14 U.S.C.

PUBLIC LAW 188-78

§528. PROTECTING AGAINST UNMANNED AIRCRAFT

For the purposes of section 210G(k)(3)(C)(iv) of the Homeland Security Act of 2002, the missions authorized to be performed by the United States Coast Guard shall be those related to—

(1) functions of the U.S. Coast Guard relating to security or protection of facilities and assets assessed to be high-risk and a potential target for unlawful unmanned aircraft activity, including the security and protection of—

(A) a facility, including a facility that is under the administrative control of the Commandant; and

(B) a vessel (whether moored or underway) or an aircraft, including a vessel or aircraft—

(i) that is operated by the Coast Guard, or that the Coast Guard is assisting or escorting; and

(ii) that is directly involved in a mission of the Coast Guard pertaining to—

(I) assisting or escorting a vessel of the Department of Defense;

(II) assisting or escorting a vessel of national security significance, a high interest vessel, a high capacity passenger vessel, or a high value unit, as those terms are defined by the Secretary;

(III) section 527(a) of this title;

(IV) assistance in protecting the President or the Vice President (or other officer next in order of succession to the Office of the President) pursuant to the Presidential Protection Assistance Act of 1976 (18 U.S.C. 3056 note);

(V) protection of a National Special Security Event and Special Event Assessment Rating events;

(VI) air defense of the United States, including air sovereignty, ground-based air defense, and the National Capital Region integrated air defense system; or

(VII) a search and rescue operation; and

(2) missions directed by the Secretary pursuant to 210G(k)(3)(C)(iii) [1] of the Homeland Security Act of 2002.

(Added Pub. L. 115–254, div. H, §1603(a), Oct. 5, 2018, 132 Stat. 3529, §104; renumbered §528 and amended Pub. L. 115–282, title I, §§105(b), 123(b)(2), Dec. 4, 2018, 132 Stat. 4200, 4240.)

---

[1] *So in original. Probably should be preceded by "section".*

Section 4510 of the

Atomic Energy Defense Act
50 U.S.C. 2661

Public Law 118-78

* * * * * * *

DIVISION D—ATOMIC ENERGY DEFENSE PROVISIONS

* * * * * * *

TITLE XLV—SAFEGUARDS AND SECURITY MATTERS

Subtitle A—Safeguards and Security

* * * * * * *

SEC. 4510. [50 U.S.C. 2661] PROTECTION OF CERTAIN NUCLEAR FACILITIES AND ASSETS FROM UNMANNED AIRCRAFT.

(a) AUTHORITY.— Notwithstanding any provision of title 18, United States Code, the Secretary of Energy may take such actions described in subsection (b)(1) that are necessary to mitigate the threat (as defined by the Secretary of Energy, in consultation with the Secretary of Transportation) that an unmanned aircraft system or unmanned aircraft poses to the safety or security of a covered facility or asset.

(b) ACTIONS DESCRIBED.— (1) The actions described in this paragraph are the following:

(A) Detect, identify, monitor, and track the unmanned aircraft system or unmanned aircraft, without prior consent, including by means of intercept or other access of a wire, oral, or electronic communication used to control the unmanned aircraft system or unmanned aircraft.

(B) Warn the operator of the unmanned aircraft system or unmanned aircraft, including by passive or active, and direct or indirect physical, electronic, radio, and electromagnetic means.

(C) Disrupt control of the unmanned aircraft system or unmanned aircraft, without prior consent, including by disabling the unmanned aircraft system or unmanned aircraft by intercepting, interfering, or causing interference with wire, oral, electronic, or radio communications used to control the unmanned aircraft system or unmanned aircraft.

(D) Seize or exercise control of the unmanned aircraft system or unmanned aircraft.

(E) Seize or otherwise confiscate the unmanned aircraft system or unmanned aircraft.

(F) Use reasonable force to disable, damage, or destroy the unmanned aircraft system or unmanned aircraft.

(2) The Secretary of Energy shall develop the actions described in paragraph (1) in coordination with the Secretary of Transportation.

(c) FORFEITURE.— Any unmanned aircraft system or unmanned aircraft described in subsection (a) that is seized by the Secretary of Energy is subject to forfeiture to the United States.

(d) REGULATIONS.— The Secretary of Energy and the Secretary of Transportation may prescribe regulations and shall issue guidance in the respective areas of each Secretary to carry out this section.

(e) DEFINITIONS.— In this section:

(1) The term "covered facility or asset" means any facility or asset that is—

(A) identified by the Secretary of Energy for purposes of this section;

(B) located in the United States (including the territories and possessions of the United States); and

(C) owned by the United States or contracted to the United States, to store or use special nuclear material.

(2) The terms "unmanned aircraft" and "unmanned aircraft system" have the meanings given those terms in section 331 of

the FAA Modernization and Reform Act of 2012 (Public Law 112–95; 49 U.S.C. 40101 note).

SECTION 210G OF THE HOMELAND

SECURITY ACT OF 2002
PUBLIC LAW 107-296

PUBLIC LAW 107-296

HOMELAND SECURITY ACT OF 2002

[Public Law 107–296; Approved November 25, 2002]

[As Amended Through P.L. 118–103, Enacted October 1, 2024]

AN ACT To establish the Department of Homeland Security, and for other purposes.

Be it enacted by the Senate and House of Representatives of the United States of America in Congress assembled,

SECTION 1. SHORT TITLE; TABLE OF CONTENTS.

(a) [6 U.S.C. 101 note] SHORT TITLE.—This Act may be cited as the "Homeland Security Act of 2002".

(b) TABLE OF CONTENTS.—The table of contents for this Act is as follows:

TITLE II—INFORMATION ANALYSIS

Subtitle A—Information and Analysis; Access to Information

* * * * * * *

SEC. 210G. [6 U.S.C. 124n] PROTECTION OF CERTAIN FACILITIES AND ASSETS FROM UNMANNED AIRCRAFT.

(a) AUTHORITY.—Notwithstanding section 46502 of title 49, United States Code, or sections 32, 1030, 1367 and chapters 119 and 206 of title 18, United States Code, the Secretary and the Attorney General may, for their respective Departments, take, and may authorize personnel with assigned duties that include the security or protection of people, facilities, or assets, to take such actions as are described in subsection (b)(1) that are necessary to mitigate a credible threat (as defined by the Secretary or the Attorney General, in consultation with the Secretary of Transportation) that an unmanned aircraft system or unmanned aircraft poses to the safety or security of a covered facility or asset.

(b) ACTIONS DESCRIBED.—

(1) IN GENERAL.—The actions authorized in subsection (a) are the following:

(A) During the operation of the unmanned aircraft system, detect, identify, monitor, and track the unmanned aircraft system or unmanned aircraft, without prior consent, including by means of intercept or other access of a wire communication, an oral communication, or an electronic communication used to control the unmanned aircraft system or unmanned aircraft.

(B) Warn the operator of the unmanned aircraft system or unmanned aircraft, including by passive or active, and direct or indirect physical, electronic, radio, and electromagnetic means.

(C) Disrupt control of the unmanned aircraft system or unmanned aircraft, without prior consent, including by disabling the unmanned aircraft system or unmanned aircraft by intercepting, interfering, or causing interference with wire, oral, electronic, or radio communications used to control the unmanned aircraft system or unmanned aircraft.

(D) Seize or exercise control of the unmanned aircraft system or unmanned aircraft.

(E) Seize or otherwise confiscate the unmanned

aircraft system or unmanned aircraft.

(F) Use reasonable force, if necessary, to disable, damage, or destroy the unmanned aircraft system or unmanned aircraft.

(2) REQUIRED COORDINATION.—The Secretary and the Attorney General shall develop for their respective Departments the actions described in paragraph (1) in coordination with the Secretary of Transportation.

(3) RESEARCH, TESTING, TRAINING, AND EVALUATION.—The Secretary and the Attorney General shall conduct research, testing, training on, and evaluation of any equipment, including any electronic equipment, to determine its capability and utility prior to the use of any such technology for any action described in subsection (b)(1).

(4) COORDINATION.—The Secretary and the Attorney General shall coordinate with the Administrator of the Federal Aviation Administration when any action authorized by this section might affect aviation safety, civilian aviation and aerospace operations, aircraft airworthiness, or the use of the airspace.

(c) FORFEITURE.—Any unmanned aircraft system or unmanned aircraft described in subsection (a) that is seized by the Secretary or the Attorney General is subject to forfeiture to the United States.

(d) REGULATIONS AND GUIDANCE.—

(1) IN GENERAL.—The Secretary, the Attorney General, and the Secretary of Transportation may prescribe regulations and shall issue guidance in the respective areas of each Secretary or the Attorney General to carry out this section.

(2) COORDINATION.—

(A) COORDINATION WITH DEPARTMENT OF TRANSPORTATION.—The Secretary and the Attorney General shall coordinate the development of their respective guidance under paragraph (1) with the Secretary of Transportation.

(B) EFFECT ON AVIATION SAFETY.—The Secretary and the Attorney General shall respectively coordinate with the Secretary of Transportation and the Administrator of the Federal Aviation Administration before issuing any guidance, or otherwise implementing this section, if such guidance or implementation might affect aviation safety, civilian aviation and aerospace operations, aircraft airworthiness, or the use of airspace.

(e) PRIVACY PROTECTION.—The regulations or guidance issued to carry out actions authorized under subsection (b) by each Secretary or the Attorney General, as the case may be, shall ensure that—

(1) the interception or acquisition of, or access to, or maintenance or use of, communications to or from an unmanned aircraft system under this section is conducted in a manner consistent with the First and Fourth Amendments to the Constitution of the United States and applicable provisions of Federal law;

(2) communications to or from an unmanned aircraft system are intercepted or acquired only to the extent necessary to support an action described in subsection (b)(1);

(3) records of such communications are maintained only for as long as necessary, and in no event for more than 180 days, unless the Secretary of Homeland Security or the Attorney General determine that maintenance of such records is necessary to investigate or prosecute a violation of law, directly support an ongoing security operation, is required under Federal law, or for the purpose of any litigation;

(4) such communications are not disclosed outside the Department of Homeland Security or the Department of Justice unless the disclosure—

(A) is necessary to investigate or prosecute a violation of law;

(B) would support the Department of Defense, a Federal law enforcement agency, or the enforcement activities of a regulatory agency of the Federal Government in connection with a criminal or civil investigation of, or any regulatory, statutory, or other enforcement action relating to an action described in subsection (b)(1);

(C) is between the Department of Homeland Security and the Department of Justice in the course of a security or protection operation of either agency or a joint operation of such agencies; or

(D) is otherwise required by law; and

(5) to the extent necessary, the Department of Homeland Security and the Department of Justice are authorized to share threat information, which shall not include communications referred to in subsection (b), with State, local, territorial, or tribal law enforcement agencies in the course of a security or protection operation.

(f) BUDGET.—The Secretary and the Attorney General shall submit to Congress, as a part of the homeland security or justice budget materials for each fiscal year after fiscal year 2019, a consolidated funding display that identifies the funding source for the actions described in subsection (b)(1) within the Department of Homeland Security or the Department of Justice. The funding display shall be in unclassified form, but may contain a classified annex.

(g) SEMIANNUAL BRIEFINGS AND NOTIFICATIONS.—

(1) IN GENERAL.—On a semiannual basis during the period beginning 6 months after the date of enactment of this section and ending on the date specified in subsection (i), the Secretary and the Attorney General shall, respectively, provide a briefing to the appropriate congressional committees on the activities carried out pursuant to this section.

(2) REQUIREMENT.—Each briefing required under paragraph (1) shall be conducted jointly with the Secretary of Transportation.

(3) CONTENT.—Each briefing required under paragraph (1) shall include—

(A) policies, programs, and procedures to mitigate or eliminate impacts of such activities to the National Airspace System;

(B) a description of instances in which actions described in subsection (b)(1) have been taken, including all such instances that may have resulted in harm, damage, or loss to a person or to private property;

(C) a description of the guidance, policies, or procedures established to address privacy, civil rights, and civil liberties issues implicated by the actions allowed under this section, as well as any changes or subsequent efforts that would significantly affect privacy, civil rights or civil liberties;

(D) a description of options considered and steps taken to mitigate any identified impacts to the national airspace system related to the use of any system or technology, including the minimization of the use of any technology that disrupts the transmission of radio or electronic signals, for carrying out the actions described in subsection (b)(1);

(E) a description of instances in which communications intercepted or acquired during the course of operations of an unmanned aircraft system were held for more than 180 days or shared outside of the Department of Justice or the Department of Homeland Security;

(F) how the Secretary, the Attorney General, and the Secretary of Transportation have informed the public as to the possible use of authorities under this section;

(G) how the Secretary, the Attorney General, and the Secretary of Transportation have engaged with Federal, State, and local law enforcement agencies to implement and use such authorities.

(4) UNCLASSIFIED FORM.—Each briefing required under paragraph (1) shall be in unclassified form, but may be accompanied by an additional classified briefing.

(5) NOTIFICATION.—Within 30 days of deploying any new technology to carry out the actions described in subsection (b)(1), the Secretary and the Attorney General shall, respectively, submit a notification to the appropriate congressional committees. Such notification shall include a description of options considered to mitigate any identified impacts to the national airspace system related to the use of any system or technology, including the minimization of the use of any technology that disrupts the transmission of radio or electronic signals, for carrying out the actions described in subsection (b)(1).

(h) RULE OF CONSTRUCTION.—Nothing in this section may be construed to—

(1) vest in the Secretary or the Attorney General any authority of the Secretary of Transportation or the Administrator of the Federal Aviation Administration;

(2) vest in the Secretary of Transportation or the

Administrator of the Federal Aviation Administration any authority of the Secretary or the Attorney General;

(3) vest in the Secretary of Homeland Security any authority of the Attorney General;

(4) vest in the Attorney General any authority of the Secretary of Homeland Security; or

(5) provide a new basis of liability for any State, local, territorial, or tribal law enforcement officers who participate in the protection of a mass gathering identified by the Secretary or Attorney General under subsection (k)(3)(C)(iii)(II), act within the scope of their authority, and do not exercise the authority granted to the Secretary and Attorney General by this section.

(i) TERMINATION.—The authority to carry out this section with respect to a covered facility or asset specified in subsection (k)(3) shall terminate on December 20, 2024.

(j) SCOPE OF AUTHORITY.—Nothing in this section shall be construed to provide the Secretary or the Attorney General with additional authorities beyond those described in subsections (a) and (k)(3)(C)(iii).

(k) DEFINITIONS.—In this section:

(1) The term "appropriate congressional committees" means—

(A) the Committee on Homeland Security and Governmental Affairs, the Committee on Commerce, Science, and Transportation, and the Committee on the Judiciary of the Senate; and

(B) the Committee on Homeland Security, the Committee on Transportation and Infrastructure, the Committee on Energy and Commerce, and the Committee on the Judiciary of the House of Representatives.

(2) The term "budget", with respect to a fiscal year, means the budget for that fiscal year that is submitted to Congress by the President under section 1105(a) of title 31.

(3) The term "covered facility or asset" means any facility or asset that—

(A) is identified as high-risk and a potential target for unlawful unmanned aircraft activity by the Secretary or the Attorney General, in coordination with the Secretary of Transportation with respect to potentially impacted airspace, through a risk-based assessment for purposes of this section (except that in the case of the missions described in subparagraph (C)(i)(II) and (C)(iii)(I), such missions shall be presumed to be for the protection of a facility or asset that is assessed to be high-risk and a potential target for unlawful unmanned aircraft activity);

(B) is located in the United States (including the territories and possessions, territorial seas or navigable waters of the United States); and

(C) directly relates to one or more—

(i) missions authorized to be performed by the Department of Homeland Security, consistent with governing statutes, regulations, and orders issued by the Secretary, pertaining to—

(I) security or protection functions of the U.S. Customs and Border Protection, including securing or protecting facilities, aircraft, and vessels, whether moored or underway;

(II) United States Secret Service protection operations pursuant to sections 3056(a) and 3056A(a) of title 18, United States Code, and the Presidential Protection Assistance Act of 1976 (18 U.S.C. 3056 note); or

(III) protection of facilities pursuant to section 1315(a) of title 40, United States Code;

(ii) missions authorized to be performed by the Department of Justice, consistent with governing statutes, regulations, and orders issued by the Attorney General, pertaining to—

(I) personal protection operations by—

(aa) the Federal Bureau of Investigation as specified in section 533 of title 28, United States Code; and

(bb) the United States Marshals Service of Federal jurists, court officers, witnesses, and other threatened persons in the interests of justice, as specified in section 566(e)(1)(A) of title 28, United States Code;

(II) protection of penal, detention, and correctional facilities and operations conducted by the Federal Bureau of Prisons; or

(III) protection of the buildings and grounds leased, owned, or operated by or for the Department of Justice, and the provision of security for Federal courts, as specified in section 566(a) of title 28, United States Code;

(iii) missions authorized to be performed by the Department of Homeland Security or the Department of Justice, acting together or separately, consistent with governing statutes, regulations, and orders issued by the Secretary or the Attorney General, respectively, pertaining to—

(I) protection of a National Special Security Event and Special Event Assessment Rating event;

(II) the provision of support to State, local, territorial, or tribal law enforcement, upon request of the chief executive officer of the State or territory, to ensure protection of people and property at mass gatherings, that is limited to a specified timeframe and location, within available resources, and without delegating any authority under this section to State, local, territorial, or tribal law enforcement; or

(III) protection of an active Federal law enforcement investigation, emergency response, or security function, that is limited to a specified timeframe and location; and

(iv) missions authorized to be performed by the United States Coast Guard, including those described in clause (iii) as directed by the Secretary, and as further set forth in section 104 of title 14, United States Code, and consistent with governing statutes, regulations, and orders issued by the Secretary of the Department in which the Coast Guard is operating.

(4) The terms "electronic communication", "intercept", "oral communication", and "wire communication" have the meaning

given those terms in section 2510 of title 18, United States Code.

(5) The term "homeland security or justice budget materials", with respect to a fiscal year, means the materials submitted to Congress by the Secretary and the Attorney General in support of the budget for that fiscal year.

(6) For purposes of subsection (a), the term "personnel" means officers and employees of the Department of Homeland Security or the Department of Justice.

(7) The terms "unmanned aircraft" and "unmanned aircraft system" have the meanings given those terms in section 44801, of title 49, United States Code.

(8) For purposes of this section, the term "risk-based assessment" includes an evaluation of threat information specific to a covered facility or asset and, with respect to potential impacts on the safety and efficiency of the national airspace system and the needs of law enforcement and national security at each covered facility or asset identified by the Secretary or the Attorney General, respectively, of each of the following factors:

(A) Potential impacts to safety, efficiency, and use of the national airspace system, including potential effects on manned aircraft and unmanned aircraft systems, aviation safety, airport operations, infrastructure, and air navigation services related to the use of any system or technology for carrying out the actions described in subsection (b)(1).

(B) Options for mitigating any identified impacts to the national airspace system related to the use of any system or technology, including minimizing when possible the use of any technology which disrupts the transmission of radio or electronic signals, for carrying out the actions described in subsection (b)(1).

(C) Potential consequences of the impacts of any actions taken under subsection (b)(1) to the national airspace system and infrastructure if not mitigated.

(D) The ability to provide reasonable advance notice to aircraft operators consistent with the safety of the national airspace system and the needs of law enforcement and national security.

(E) The setting and character of any covered facility or asset, including whether it is located in a populated area or near other structures, whether the facility is open to the public, whether the facility is also used for nongovernmental functions, and any potential for interference with wireless communications or for injury or damage to persons or property.

(F) The setting, character, timeframe, and national airspace system impacts of National Special Security Event and Special Event Assessment Rating events.

(G) Potential consequences to national security, public safety, or law enforcement if threats posed by unmanned aircraft systems are not mitigated or defeated.

(l) DEPARTMENT OF HOMELAND SECURITY ASSESSMENT.—

(1) REPORT.—Not later than 1 year after the date of the enactment of this section, the Secretary shall conduct, in coordination with the Attorney General and the Secretary of Transportation, an assessment to the appropriate congressional committees, including—

(A) an evaluation of the threat from unmanned aircraft systems to United States critical infrastructure (as defined in this Act) and to domestic large hub airports (as defined in section 40102 of title 49, United States Code);

(B) an evaluation of current Federal and State, local, territorial, or tribal law enforcement authorities to counter the threat identified in subparagraph (A), and recommendations, if any, for potential changes to existing authorities to allow State, local, territorial, and tribal law enforcement to assist Federal law enforcement to counter the threat where appropriate;

(C) an evaluation of the knowledge of, efficiency of, and effectiveness of current procedures and resources available to owners of critical infrastructure and domestic large hub airports when they believe a threat from unmanned aircraft systems is present and what additional actions, if any, the Department of Homeland Security or the Department of Transportation could implement under existing authorities to assist these entities to counter the threat identified in subparagraph (A);

(D) an assessment of what, if any, additional authorities are needed by each Department and law enforcement to counter the threat identified in subparagraph (A); and

(E) an assessment of what, if any, additional research and development the Department needs to counter the threat identified in subparagraph (A).

(2) UNCLASSIFIED FORM.—The report required under paragraph (1) shall be submitted in unclassified form, but may contain a classified annex.

* * * * * * *

AMERICAN SECURITY DRONE ACT OF 2023

PUBLIC LAW 118-31

National Defense Authorization Act for Fiscal Year 2024

[(Public Law 118–31)]

[As Amended Through P.L. 118–78, Enacted July 30, 2024]

AN ACT To authorize appropriations for fiscal year 2024 for military activities of the Department of Defense and for military construction, and for defense activities of the Department of Energy, to prescribe military personnel strengths for such fiscal year, and for other purposes.

Be it enacted by the Senate and House of Representatives of the United States of America in Congress assembled,

SECTION 1. SHORT TITLE.

This Act may be cited as the "National Defense Authorization Act for Fiscal Year 2024".

SEC. 2. ORGANIZATION OF ACT INTO DIVISIONS; TABLE OF CONTENTS.

* * * * * * *

(b) TABLE OF CONTENTS.—The table of contents for this Act is as follows:

* * * * * * *

DIVISION A—DEPARTMENT OF DEFENSE AUTHORIZATIONS

* * * * * * *

TITLE XVIII—OTHER DEFENSE MATTERS

* * * * * * *

Subtitle B—Drone Security

* * * * * * *

Subtitle B—Drone Security

SEC. 1821. SHORT TITLE.

This subtitle may be cited as the "American Security Drone Act of 2023".

SEC. 1822. DEFINITIONS.

In this subtitle:

(1) COVERED FOREIGN ENTITY.—The term ""covered foreign entity"" means an entity included on a list developed and maintained by the Federal Acquisition Security Council and published in the System for Award Management (SAM). This list will include entities in the following categories:

(A) An entity included on the Consolidated Screening List.

(B) Any entity that is subject to extrajudicial direction from a foreign government, as determined by the Secretary of Homeland Security.

(C) Any entity the Secretary of Homeland Security, in coordination with the Attorney General, Director of National Intelligence, and the Secretary of Defense, determines poses a national security risk.

(D) Any entity domiciled in the People's Republic of China or subject to influence or control by the Government of the People's Republic of China or the Communist Party of the People's Republic of China, as determined by the Secretary of Homeland Security.

(E) Any subsidiary or affiliate of an entity described in subparagraphs (A) through (D).

(2) COVERED UNMANNED AIRCRAFT SYSTEM.—The term
""covered unmanned aircraft system"" has the meaning given
the term ""unmanned aircraft system"" in section 44801 of title
49, United States Code.

(3) INTELLIGENCE; INTELLIGENCE COMMUNITY.—The terms
"intelligence" and "intelligence community" have the meanings
given those terms in section 3 of the National Security Act of
1947 (50 U.S.C. 3003).

SEC. 1823. PROHIBITION ON PROCUREMENT OF COVERED UNMANNED AIRCRAFT SYSTEMS FROM COVERED FOREIGN ENTITIES.

(a) IN GENERAL.—Except as provided under subsections (b)
through (f), the head of an executive agency may not procure any
covered unmanned aircraft system that is manufactured or
assembled by a covered foreign entity, which includes associated
elements related to the collection and transmission of sensitive
information (consisting of communication links and the components
that control the unmanned aircraft) that enable the operator to
operate the aircraft in the National Airspace System. The Federal
Acquisition Security Council, in coordination with the Secretary
of Transportation, shall develop and update a list of associated
elements.

(b) EXEMPTION.—The Secretary of Homeland Security, the
Secretary of Defense, the Secretary of State, and the Attorney
General are exempt from the restriction under subsection (a) if
the procurement is required in the national interest of the United
States and—

(1) is for the sole purposes of research, evaluation, training,
testing, or analysis for electronic warfare, information warfare
operations, cybersecurity, or development of unmanned aircraft
system or counter-unmanned aircraft system technology;

(2) is for the sole purposes of conducting counterterrorism
or counterintelligence activities, protective missions, or Federal
criminal or national security investigations, including forensic
examinations, or for electronic warfare, information warfare
operations, cybersecurity, or development of an unmanned
aircraft system or counter-unmanned aircraft system
technology; or

(3) is an unmanned aircraft system that, as procured or
as modified after procurement but before operational use, can

no longer transfer to, or download data from, a covered foreign
entity and otherwise poses no national security cybersecurity
risks as determined by the exempting official.

(c) DEPARTMENT OF TRANSPORTATION AND FEDERAL AVIATION
ADMINISTRATION EXEMPTION.—The Secretary of Transportation is
exempt from the restriction under subsection (a) if the operation
or procurement is deemed to support the safe, secure, or efficient
operation of the National Airspace System or maintenance of public
safety, including activities carried out under the Federal Aviation
Administration's Alliance for System Safety of UAS through
Research Excellence (ASSURE) Center of Excellence (COE) and
any other activity deemed to support the safe, secure, or efficient
operation of the National Airspace System or maintenance of public
safety, as determined by the Secretary or the Secretary's designee.

(d) NATIONAL TRANSPORTATION SAFETY BOARD
EXEMPTION.—The National Transportation Safety Board, in
consultation with the Secretary of Homeland Security, is exempt
from the restriction under subsection (a) if the operation or
procurement is necessary for the sole purpose of conducting safety
investigations.

(e) NATIONAL OCEANIC AND ATMOSPHERIC ADMINISTRATION
EXEMPTION.—The Administrator of the National Oceanic and
Atmospheric Administration (NOAA), in consultation with the
Secretary of Homeland Security, is exempt from the restriction
under subsection (a) if the procurement is necessary for the purpose
of meeting NOAA's science or management objectives or operational
mission.

(f) WAIVER.—The head of an executive agency may waive the
prohibition under subsection (a) on a case-by-case basis—

(1) with the approval of the Director of the Office of
Management and Budget, after consultation with the Federal
Acquisition Security Council; and

(2) upon notification to—

(A) the Committee on Homeland Security and
Governmental Affairs of the Senate;

(B) the Committee on Oversight and Accountability in
the House of Representatives; and

(C) other appropriate congressional committees of
jurisdiction.

SEC. 1824. PROHIBITION ON OPERATION OF COVERED UNMANNED AIRCRAFT SYSTEMS FROM COVERED FOREIGN ENTITIES.

(a) PROHIBITION.—

(1) IN GENERAL.—Beginning on the date that is two years after the date of the enactment of this Act, no Federal department or agency may operate a covered unmanned aircraft system manufactured or assembled by a covered foreign entity.

(2) APPLICABILITY TO CONTRACTED SERVICES.—The prohibition under paragraph (1) applies to any covered unmanned aircraft systems that are being used by any executive agency through the method of contracting for the services of covered unmanned aircraft systems.

(b) EXEMPTION.—The Secretary of Homeland Security, the Secretary of Defense, the Secretary of State, and the Attorney General are exempt from the restriction under subsection (a) if the operation is required in the national interest of the United States and—

(1) is for the sole purposes of research, evaluation, training, testing, or analysis for electronic warfare, information warfare operations, cybersecurity, or development of unmanned aircraft system or counter-unmanned aircraft system technology;

(2) is for the sole purposes of conducting counterterrorism or counterintelligence activities, protective missions, or Federal criminal or national security investigations, including forensic examinations, or for electronic warfare, information warfare operations, cybersecurity, or development of an unmanned aircraft system or counter-unmanned aircraft system technology; or

(3) is an unmanned aircraft system that, as procured or as modified after procurement but before operational use, can no longer transfer to, or download data from, a covered foreign entity and otherwise poses no national security cybersecurity risks as determined by the exempting official.

(c) DEPARTMENT OF TRANSPORTATION AND FEDERAL AVIATION ADMINISTRATION EXEMPTION. The Secretary of Transportation is exempt from the restriction under subsection (a) if the operation is deemed to support the safe, secure, or efficient operation of the National Airspace System or maintenance of public safety, including activities carried out under the Federal Aviation Administration's Alliance for System Safety of UAS through Research Excellence (ASSURE) Center of Excellence (COE) and any other activity deemed to support the safe, secure, or efficient operation of the National Airspace System or maintenance of public safety, as determined by the Secretary or the Secretary's designee.

(d) NATIONAL TRANSPORTATION SAFETY BOARD EXEMPTION.—The National Transportation Safety Board, in consultation with the Secretary of Homeland Security, is exempt from the restriction under subsection (a) if the operation is necessary for the sole purpose of conducting safety investigations.

(e) NATIONAL OCEANIC AND ATMOSPHERIC ADMINISTRATION EXEMPTION.—The Administrator of the National Oceanic and Atmospheric Administration (NOAA), in consultation with the Secretary of Homeland Security, is exempt from the restriction under subsection (a) if the procurement is necessary for the purpose of meeting NOAA's science or management objectives or operational mission.

(f) WAIVER.—The head of an executive agency may waive the prohibition under subsection (a) on a case-by-case basis—

(1) with the approval of the Director of the Office of Management and Budget, after consultation with the Federal Acquisition Security Council; and

(2) upon notification to—

(A) the Committee on Homeland Security and Governmental Affairs of the Senate;

(B) the Committee on Oversight and Accountability in the House of Representatives; and

(C) other appropriate congressional committees of jurisdiction.

(g) REGULATIONS AND GUIDANCE.—Not later than 180 days after the date of the enactment of this Act, the Secretary of Homeland Security, in consultation with the Attorney General and the Secretary of Transportation, shall prescribe regulations or guidance to implement this section.

SEC. 1825. PROHIBITION ON USE OF FEDERAL FUNDS FOR PROCUREMENT AND OPERATION OF COVERED UNMANNED AIRCRAFT SYSTEMS FROM COVERED FOREIGN ENTITIES.

(a) IN GENERAL.—Beginning on the date that is two years after the date of the enactment of this Act, except as provided in subsection (b), no Federal funds awarded through a contract, grant, or cooperative agreement, or otherwise made available may be used—

(1) to procure a covered unmanned aircraft system that is manufactured or assembled by a covered foreign entity; or

(2) in connection with the operation of such a drone or unmanned aircraft system.

(b) EXEMPTION.—The Secretary of Homeland Security, the Secretary of Defense, the Secretary of State, and the Attorney General are exempt from the restriction under subsection (a) if the procurement or operation is required in the national interest of the United States and—

(1) is for the sole purposes of research, evaluation, training, testing, or analysis for electronic warfare, information warfare operations, cybersecurity, or development of unmanned aircraft system or counter-unmanned aircraft system technology;

(2) is for the sole purposes of conducting counterterrorism or counterintelligence activities, protective missions, or Federal criminal or national security investigations, including forensic examinations, or for electronic warfare, information warfare operations, cybersecurity, or development of an unmanned aircraft system or counter-unmanned aircraft system technology; or

(3) is an unmanned aircraft system that, as procured or as modified after procurement but before operational use, can no longer transfer to, or download data from, a covered foreign entity and otherwise poses no national security cybersecurity risks as determined by the exempting official.

(c) DEPARTMENT OF TRANSPORTATION AND FEDERAL AVIATION ADMINISTRATION EXEMPTION. The Secretary of Transportation is exempt from the restriction under subsection (a) if the operation or procurement is deemed to support the safe, secure, or efficient operation of the National Airspace System or maintenance of public safety, including activities carried out under the Federal Aviation Administration's Alliance for System Safety of UAS through Research Excellence (ASSURE) Center of Excellence (COE) and any other activity deemed to support the safe, secure, or efficient operation of the National Airspace System or maintenance of public safety, as determined by the Secretary or the Secretary's designee.

(d) NATIONAL OCEANIC AND ATMOSPHERIC ADMINISTRATION EXEMPTION.—The Administrator of the National Oceanic and Atmospheric Administration (NOAA), in consultation with the Secretary of Homeland Security, is exempt from the restriction under subsection (a) if the operation or procurement is necessary for the purpose of meeting NOAA's science or management objectives or operational mission.

(e) WAIVER.—The head of an executive agency may waive the prohibition under subsection (a) on a case-by-case basis—

(1) with the approval of the Director of the Office of Management and Budget, after consultation with the Federal Acquisition Security Council; and

(2) upon notification to—

(A) the Committee on Homeland Security and Governmental Affairs of the Senate;

(B) the Committee on Oversight and Accountability in the House of Representatives; and

(C) other appropriate congressional committees of jurisdiction.

(f) REGULATIONS.—Not later than 180 days after the date of the enactment of this Act, the Federal Acquisition Regulatory Council shall prescribe regulations or guidance, as necessary, to implement the requirements of this section pertaining to Federal contracts.

SEC. 1826. PROHIBITION ON USE OF GOVERNMENT-ISSUED PURCHASE CARDS TO PURCHASE COVERED UNMANNED AIRCRAFT SYSTEMS FROM COVERED FOREIGN ENTITIES.

Effective immediately, Government-issued Purchase Cards may not be used to procure any covered unmanned aircraft system from a covered foreign entity.

SEC. 1827. MANAGEMENT OF EXISTING INVENTORIES OF COVERED UNMANNED AIRCRAFT SYSTEMS FROM COVERED FOREIGN ENTITIES.

(a) IN GENERAL.—All executive agencies must account for existing inventories of covered unmanned aircraft systems manufactured or assembled by a covered foreign entity in their personal property accounting systems, within one year of the date of enactment of this Act, regardless of the original procurement cost, or the purpose of procurement due to the special monitoring and accounting measures necessary to track the items' capabilities.

(b) CLASSIFIED TRACKING.—Due to the sensitive nature of missions and operations conducted by the United States Government, inventory data related to covered unmanned aircraft systems manufactured or assembled by a covered foreign entity may be tracked at a classified level, as determined by the Secretary of Homeland Security or the Secretary's designee.

(c) EXCEPTIONS.—The Department of Defense, the Department of Homeland Security, the Department of Justice, the Department of Transportation, and the National Oceanic and Atmospheric Administration may exclude from the full inventory process, covered unmanned aircraft systems that are deemed expendable due to mission risk such as recovery issues, or that are one-time-use covered unmanned aircraft due to requirements and low cost.

(d) INTELLIGENCE COMMUNITY EXCEPTION.—Nothing in this section shall apply to any element of the intelligence community.

SEC. 1828. COMPTROLLER GENERAL REPORT.

Not later than 275 days after the date of the enactment of this Act, the Comptroller General of the United States shall submit to Congress a report on the amount of commercial off-the-shelf drones and covered unmanned aircraft systems procured by Federal departments and agencies from covered foreign entities, except that nothing in this section shall apply to any element of the intelligence community.

SEC. 1829. GOVERNMENT-WIDE POLICY FOR PROCUREMENT OF UNMANNED AIRCRAFT SYSTEMS.

(a) IN GENERAL.—Not later than 180 days after the date of the enactment of this Act, the Director of the Office of Management and Budget, in coordination with the Department of Homeland Security, Department of Transportation, the Department of Justice, and other Departments as determined by the Director of the Office of Management and Budget, and in consultation with the National Institute of Standards and Technology, shall establish a government-wide policy for the procurement of an unmanned aircraft system—

(1) for non-Department of Defense and non-intelligence community operations; and

(2) through grants and cooperative agreements entered into with non-Federal entities.

(b) INFORMATION SECURITY.—The policy developed under subsection (a) shall include the following specifications, which to the extent practicable, shall be based on industry standards and technical guidance from the National Institute of Standards and Technology, to address the risks associated with processing, storing, and transmitting Federal information in an unmanned aircraft system:

(1) Protections to ensure controlled access to an unmanned aircraft system.

(2) Protecting software, firmware, and hardware by ensuring changes to an unmanned aircraft system are properly managed, including by ensuring an unmanned aircraft system can be updated using a secure, controlled, and configurable mechanism.

(3) Cryptographically securing sensitive collected, stored, and transmitted data, including proper handling of privacy data and other controlled unclassified information.

(4) Appropriate safeguards necessary to protect sensitive information, including during and after use of an unmanned aircraft system.

(5) Appropriate data security to ensure that data is not transmitted to or stored in non-approved locations.

(6) The ability to opt out of the uploading, downloading, or transmitting of data that is not required by law or regulation and an ability to choose with whom and where information is shared when it is required.

(c) REQUIREMENT.—The policy developed under subsection (a) shall reflect an appropriate risk-based approach to information security related to use of an unmanned aircraft system.

(d) REVISION OF ACQUISITION REGULATIONS.—Not later than 180 days after the date on which the policy required under subsection (a) is issued—

(1) the Federal Acquisition Regulatory Council shall revise the Federal Acquisition Regulation, as necessary, to implement

the policy; and

(2) any Federal department or agency or other Federal entity not subject to, or not subject solely to, the Federal Acquisition Regulation shall revise applicable policy, guidance, or regulations, as necessary, to implement the policy.

(e) EXEMPTION.—In developing the policy required under subsection (a), the Director of the Office of Management and Budget shall—

(1) incorporate policies to implement the exemptions contained in this subtitle; and

(2) incorporate an exemption to the policy in the case of a head of the procuring department or agency determining, in writing, that no product that complies with the information security requirements described in subsection (b) is capable of fulfilling mission critical performance requirements, and such determination—

(A) may not be delegated below the level of the Deputy Secretary, or Administrator, of the procuring department or agency;

(B) shall specify—

(i) the quantity of end items to which the waiver applies and the procurement value of those items; and

(ii) the time period over which the waiver applies, which shall not exceed three years;

(C) shall be reported to the Office of Management and Budget following issuance of such a determination; and

(D) not later than 30 days after the date on which the determination is made, shall be provided to the Committee on Homeland Security and Governmental Affairs of the Senate and the Committee on Oversight and Accountability of the House of Representatives.

SEC. 1830. STATE, LOCAL, AND TERRITORIAL LAW ENFORCEMENT AND EMERGENCY SERVICE EXEMPTION.

(a) RULE OF CONSTRUCTION.—Nothing in this subtitle shall prevent a State, local, or territorial law enforcement or emergency service agency from procuring or operating a covered unmanned aircraft system purchased with non-Federal dollars.

(b) CONTINUITY OF ARRANGEMENTS.—The Federal Government
may continue entering into contracts, grants, and cooperative
agreements or other Federal funding instruments with State, local,
or territorial law enforcement or emergency service agencies under
which a covered unmanned aircraft system will be purchased or
operated if the agency has received approval or waiver to purchase
or operate a covered unmanned aircraft system pursuant to section
1825.

SEC. 1831. STUDY.

(a) STUDY ON THE SUPPLY CHAIN FOR UNMANNED AIRCRAFT
SYSTEMS AND COMPONENTS.—

(1) REPORT REQUIRED.—Not later than one year after the
date of the enactment of this Act, the Under Secretary of
Defense for Acquisition and Sustainment shall provide to the
appropriate congressional committees a report on the supply
chain for covered unmanned aircraft systems, including a
discussion of current and projected future demand for covered
unmanned aircraft systems.

(2) ELEMENTS.—The report under paragraph (1) shall
include the following:

(A) A description of the current and future global and
domestic market for covered unmanned aircraft systems
that are not widely commercially available except from a
covered foreign entity.

(B) A description of the sustainability, availability,
cost, and quality of secure sources of covered unmanned
aircraft systems domestically and from sources in allied
and partner countries.

(C) The plan of the Secretary of Defense to address
any gaps or deficiencies identified in subparagraph (B),
including through the use of funds available under the
Defense Production Act of 1950 (50 U.S.C. 4501 et seq.)
and partnerships with the National Aeronautics and Space
Administration and other interested persons.

(D) Such other information as the Under Secretary of
Defense for Acquisition and Sustainment determines to be
appropriate.

(3) APPROPRIATE CONGRESSIONAL COMMITTEES

DEFINED.—In this section, the term "appropriate congressional committees" means the following:

(A) The Committees on Armed Services of the Senate and the House of Representatives.

(B) The Committee on Homeland Security and Governmental Affairs of the Senate and the Committee on Oversight and Accountability of the House of Representatives.

(C) The Committee on Commerce, Science, and Transportation of the Senate and the Committee on Science, Space, and Technology of the House of Representatives.

(D) The Select Committee on Intelligence of the Senate and the Permanent Select Committee on Intelligence of the House of Representatives.

(E) The Committee on Transportation and Infrastructure of the House of Representatives.

(F) The Committee on Homeland Security of the House of Representatives.

(G) The Committee on Foreign Relations of the Senate and the Committee on Foreign Affairs of the House of Representatives.

SEC. 1832. EXCEPTIONS.

(a) EXCEPTION FOR WILDFIRE MANAGEMENT OPERATIONS AND SEARCH AND RESCUE OPERATIONS.—The appropriate Federal agencies, in consultation with the Secretary of Homeland Security, are exempt from the procurement and operation restrictions under sections 1823, 1824, and 1825 to the extent the procurement or operation is necessary for the purpose of supporting the full range of wildfire management operations or search and rescue operations.

(b) EXCEPTION FOR INTELLIGENCE ACTIVITIES.—Sections 1823, 1824, and 1825 shall not apply to any activity subject to the reporting requirements under title V of the National Security Act of 1947 (50 U.S.C. 3091 et seq.), any authorized intelligence activities of the United States, or any activity or procurement that supports an authorized intelligence activity.

(c) EXCEPTION FOR TRIBAL LAW ENFORCEMENT OR EMERGENCY SERVICE AGENCY.—Tribal law enforcement or Tribal emergency service agencies, in consultation with the Secretary of Homeland Security, are exempt from the procurement, operation, and purchase restrictions under sections 1823, 1824, and 1825 to the extent the procurement or operation is necessary for the purpose of supporting the full range of law enforcement operations or search and rescue operations on Indian lands.

SEC. 1833. SUNSET.

Sections 1823, 1824, and 1825 shall cease to have effect on the date that is five years after the date of the enactment of this Act.

* * * * * * *

Selected Provisions of Title VII

of the Trade Act
Public Law 93-618

Public Law 93-618

PROVISIONS OF THE TRADE ACT OF 1974

(Title VIII - Narcotics Control Trade Act)

[(Public Law 93–618, as amended)]

[As Amended Through P.L. 118–31, Enacted December 22, 2023]

AN ACT To promote the development of an open, nondiscriminatory, and fair world economic system, to stimulate fair and free competition between the United States and foreign nations, to foster the economic growth of, and full employment in, the United States, and for other purposes.

Be it enacted by the Senate and House of Representatives of the United States of America in Congress assembled,

That this Act, with the following table of contents, may be cited as the "Trade Act of 1974".

TABLE OF CONTENTS

* * * * * * *

[19 U.S.C. 2101]

* * * * * * *

TITLE VIII— TARIFF TREATMENT OF

PRODUCTS OF, AND OTHER SANCTIONS AGAINST, UNCOOPERATIVE MAJOR DRUG PRODUCING OR DRUG-TRANSIT COUNTRIES

SEC. 801. SHORT TITLE.

This title may be cited as the " Narcotics Control Trade Act ".
[19 U.S.C. 2491]

SEC. 802. TARIFF TREATMENT OF PRODUCTS OF UNCOOPERATIVE MAJOR DRUG PRODUCING OR DRUG-TRANSIT COUNTRIES.

(a) REQUIRED ACTION BY PRESIDENT.— Subject to subsection (b), for every major drug producing country and every major drug-transit country, the President shall, on or after March 1, 1987, and March 1 of each succeeding year, to the extent considered necessary by the President to achieve the purposes of this title—

(1) deny to any or all of the products of that country tariff treatment under the Generalized System of Preferences, the Caribbean Basin Economic Recovery Act, or any other law providing preferential tariff treatment.

(2) apply to any or all of the dutiable products of that country an additional duty at a rate not to exceed 50 percent ad valorem or the specific rate equivalent;

(3) apply to one or more duty-free products of that country a duty at a rate not to exceed 50 percent a valorem;

(4) take the steps described in subsection (d)(1) or (d)(2), or both, to curtail air transportation between the United States and that country;

(5) withdraw the personnel and resources of the United States from participation in any arrangement with that country for the pre-clearance of customs by visitors between the United States and that country; or

(6) take any combination of the actions described in paragraphs (1) through (5).

(b) (1) (A) Subject to paragraph (3), subsection (a) shall not apply with respect to a country if the President determines and certifies to the Congress, at the time of the submission of the report required by section 489 of the Foreign Assistance Act of 1961 (22 U.S.C. 2291h), that—

(i) during the previous year the country has cooperated fully with the United States, or has taken adequate steps on its own—

(I) in satisfying the goals agreed to in an applicable bilateral narcotics agreement with the United States (as described in paragraph (B)) or a multilateral agreement which achieves the objectives of paragraph (B),

(II) in preventing narcotic and psychotropic drugs and other controlled substances produced or processed, in whole or in part, in such country or transported through such country, from being sold illegally within the jurisdiction of such country to United States Government personnel or their dependents or from being transported, directly or indirectly, into the United States,

(III) in preventing and punishing the laundering in that country of drug-related profits or drug-related moneys, and

(IV) in preventing and punishing bribery and other forms of public corruption which facilitate the illicit production, processing, or shipment of narcotic and psychotropic drugs and other controlled substances, or which discourage the investigation and prosecution of such acts; or

(ii) for a country that would not otherwise qualify for certification under clause (i), the vital national interests of the United States require that subsection (a) not be applied with respect to that country.

(B) A bilateral narcotics agreement referred to in subparagraph (A)(i)(I) is an agreement between the United States and a foreign country in which the foreign country agrees to take specific activities, including, where applicable, efforts to—

(i) reduce drug production, drug consumption, and drug trafficking within its territory, including activities to address illicit crop eradication and crop substitution;

(ii) increase drug interdiction and enforcement;

(iii) increase drug education and treatment programs;

(iv) increase the identification of and elimination of illicit drug laboratories;

(v) increase the identification and elimination of the trafficking of essential precursor chemicals for the use in production of illegal drugs;

(vi) increase cooperation with United States drug enforcement officials; and

(vii) where applicable, increase participation in extradition treaties, mutual legal assistance provisions directed at money laundering, sharing of evidence, and other initiatives for cooperative drug enforcement.

(C) A country which in the previous year was designated as a major drug producing country or a major drug-transit country may not be determined to be cooperating fully under subparagraph (A)(i) unless it has in place a bilateral narcotics agreement with the United States or a multilateral agreement which achieves the objectives of subparagraph (B).

(D) If the President makes a certification with respect to a country pursuant to subparagraph (A)(ii), he shall include in such certification—

(i) a full and complete description of the vital national interests placed at risk if action is taken pursuant to subsection (a) with respect to that country; and

(ii) a statement weighing the risk described in clause (i) against the risks posed to the vital national interests of the United States by the failure of such country to cooperate fully with the United States in combating narcotics or to take adequate steps to combat narcotics on its own.

(E) The President may make a certification under subparagraph (A)(i) with respect to a major drug producing country or drug-transit country which is also a producer of licit opium only if the President determines that such country has taken steps to prevent significant diversion of its licit cultivation and production into the illicit market, maintains production and stockpiles at levels no higher than those consistent with licit market demand, and prevents illicit cultivation and production.

(2) In determining whether to make the certification

required by paragraph (1) with respect to a country, the President shall consider the following:

(A) Have the actions of the government of that country resulted in the maximum reductions in illicit drug production which were determined to be achievable pursuant to section 481(e)(4) of the Foreign Assistance Act of 1961? In the case of a major drug producing country, the President shall give foremost consideration, in determining whether to make the certification required by paragraph (1), to whether the government of that country has taken actions which have resulted in such reductions.

(B) Has that government taken the legal and law enforcement measures to enforce in its territory, to the maximum extent possible, the elimination of illicit cultivation and the suppression of illicit manufacturing of and trafficking in narcotic and psychotropic drugs and other controlled substances, as evidenced by seizures of such drugs and substances and of illicit laboratories and the arrest and prosecution of violators involved in the traffic in such drugs and substances significantly affecting the United States?

(C) Has that government taken the legal and law enforcement steps necessary to eliminate, to the maximum extent possible, the laundering in that country of drug-related profits or drug-related moneys, as evidenced by—

(i) the enactment and enforcement by that government of laws prohibiting such conduct,

(ii) that government entering into, and cooperating under the terms of, mutual legal assistance agreements with the United States governing (but not limited to) money laundering, and

(iii) the degree to which that government otherwise cooperates with United States law enforcement authorities on anti-money laundering efforts?

(D) Has that government taken the legal and law enforcement steps necessary to eliminate, to the maximum extent possible, bribery and other forms of public corruption which facilitate the illicit production, processing, or shipment of narcotic and psychotropic drugs and other controlled substances, or which discourage the investigation and prosecution of such acts, as evidenced by the enactment and enforcement of laws prohibiting such conduct?

(E) Has that government, as a matter of government policy, encouraged or facilitated the production or distribution of illicit narcotic and psychotropic drugs and other controlled substances?

(F) Does any senior official of that government engage in, encourage, or facilitate the production or distribution of illicit narcotic and psychotropic drugs and other controlled substances?

(G) Has that government investigated aggressively all cases in which any member of an agency of the United States Government engaged in drug enforcement activities since January 1, 1985, has been the victim of acts or threats of violence, inflicted by or with the complicity of any law enforcement or other officer of such country or any political subdivision thereof, and has energetically sought to bring the perpetrators of such offense or offenses to justice?

(H) Having been requested to do so by the United States Government, does that government fail to provide reasonable cooperation to lawful activities of United States drug enforcement agents, including the refusal of permission to such agents engaged in interdiction of aerial smuggling into the United States to pursue suspected aerial smugglers a reasonable distance into the airspace of the requested country?

(I) Has that government made necessary changes in legal codes in order to enable law enforcement officials to move more effectively against narcotics traffickers, such as new conspiracy laws and new asset seizure laws?

(J) Has that government expeditiously processed United States extradition requests relating to narcotics trafficking?

(K) Has that government refused to protect or give haven to any known drug traffickers, and has it expeditiously processed extradition requests relating to narcotics trafficking made by other countries?

(3) Subsection (a) shall apply to a country without regard to paragraph (1) of this subsection if the Congress enacts, within 45 days of continuous session after receipt of a certification under paragraph (1), a joint resolution disapproving the determination of the President contained in that certification.

(4) If the President takes action under subsection (a), that action shall remain in effect until—

(A) the President makes the certification under paragraph (1), a period of 45 days of continuous session of Congress elapses, and during that period the Congress does not enact a joint resolution of disapproval; or

(B) the President submits at any other time a certification of the matters discribed in paragraph (1) with respect to that country, a period of 45 days of continuous session of Congress elapses, and during that period the Congress does not enact a joint resolution of disapproving the determination contained in that certification.

(5) For the purpose of expediting the consideration and enactment of joint resolutions under paragraphs (3) and (4)—

(A) a motion to proceed to the consideration of any such joint resolution after it has been reported by the Committee on Ways and Means shall be treated as highly privileged in the House of Representatives; and

(B) a motion to proceed to the consideration of any such joint resolution after it has been reported by the Committee on Finance shall be treated as privileged in the Senate.

(c) DURATION OF ACTION.— The action taken by the President under paragraph (1), (2), or (3) of subsection (a) shall apply to the products of a foreign country that are entered, or withdrawn from warehouse for consumption, during the period that such action is in effect.

(d) PRESIDENTIAL ACTION REGARDING AVIATION.—

(1) (A) The President is authorized to notify the government of a country against which is imposed the sanction described in subsection (a)(4) of his intention to suspend the authority of foreign air carriers owned or controlled by the government or nationals of that country to engage in foreign air

transportation to or from the United States.

(B) Within 10 days after the date of notification of a government under subparagraph (A), the Secretary of Transportation shall take all steps necessary to suspend at the earliest possible date the authority of any foreign air carrier owned or controlled, directly or indirectly, by the government or nationals of that country to engage in foreign air transportation to or from the United States, notwithstanding any agreement relating to air services.

(C) The President may also direct the Secretary of Transportation to take such steps as may be necessary to suspend the authority of any air carrier to engage in foreign air transportation between the United States and that country.

(2) (A) The President may direct the Secretary of State to terminate any air service agreement between the United States and a country against which the sanction described in subsection (a)(4) is imposed in accordance with the provisions of that agreement.

(B) Upon termination of an agreement under this paragraph, the Secretary of Transportation shall take such steps as may be necessary to revoke at the earliest possible date the right of any foreign air carrier owned, or controlled, directly or indirectly, by the government or nationals of that country to engage in foreign air transportation to or from the United States.

(C) Upon termination of an agreement under this paragraph, the Secretary of Transportation may also revoke the authority of any air carrier to engage in foreign air transportation between the United States and that country.

(3) The Secretary of Transportation may provide for such exceptions from paragraphs (1) and (2) as the Secretary considers necessary to provide for emergencies in which the safety of an aircraft or its crew or passengers is threatened.

(4) For purposes of this subsection, the terms "air transportation", "air carrier", "foreign air carrier" and "foreign air transportation" have the meanings such terms have under section 101 of the Federal Aviation Act of 1958 (49 U.S.C. App.

1301).

(e) For each calendar year, the Secretary of State, after consultation with the appropriate committees of the Congress, shall establish numerical standards and other guidelines for determining which countries will be considered to be major drug-transit countries under section 805(3)(A) and (B).

[19 U.S.C. 2492]

* * * * * * *

SEC. 805. DEFINITIONS.

For purposes of this title—

(1) continuity of a session of Congress is broken only by an adjournment of the Congress sine die, and the days on which either House is not in session because of an adjournment of more than three days to a day certain are excluded in the computation of the period indicated;

(2) the term "major drug producing country" means a country that illicitly produces during a fiscal year 5 metric tons or more of opium or opium derivative, 500 metric tons or more of coca, or 500 metric tons or more of marijuana;

(3) the term "major drug-transit country" means a country—

(A) that is a significant direct source of illicit narcotic or psychotropic drugs or other controlled substances significantly affecting the United States;

(B) through which are transported such drugs or substances; or

(C) through which significant sums of drug-related profits or monies are laundered with the knowledge or complicity of the government; and

(4) the term "narcotic and psychotropic drugs and other controlled substances" has the same meaning as is given by any applicable international narcotics control agreement or domestic law of the country or countries concerned.

[19 U.S.C. 2495]

Selected Provisions of the International Security and Development Cooperation Act of 1985

Title V, Part B —Foreign Airport Security

Public Law 99-83

INTERNATIONAL SECURITY AND DEVELOPMENT COOPERATION ACT OF 1985

(Provisions of Title V - International Terrorism and Foreign Airport Security)

[(Public Law 99–83; 99 Stat. 222–227)]

[As Amended Through P.L. 117–81, Enacted December 27, 2021]

* * * * * * *

TITLE V—INTERNATIONAL TERRORISM AND FOREIGN AIRPORT SECURITY

* * * * * * *

Part B—Foreign Airport Security

SEC. 551. SECURITY STANDARDS FOR FOREIGN AIR TRANSPORTATION. [Subsections (a) and (b) repealed by Public Law 103–272]

(c) CLOSING OF BEIRUT INTERNATIONAL AIRPORT.— It is the sense of the Congress that the President is urged and encouraged to take all appropriate steps to carry forward his announced policy of seeking the effective closing of the international airport in Beirut, Lebanon, at least until such time as the Government of Lebanon has instituted measures and procedures designed to prevent the use of that airport by aircraft hijackers and other terrorists in attacking civilian airlines or their passengers, hijacking their aircraft, or taking or holding their passengers hostage.

[Sections 552 and 553 repealed by Public Law 103–272]

SEC. 554. ENFORCEMENT OF INTERNATIONAL CIVIL AVIATION

ORGANIZATION STANDARDS.

The Secretary of State and the Secretary of Transportation, jointly, shall call on the member countries of the International Civil Aviation Organization to enforce that Organization's existing standards and to support United States actions enforcing such standards.

SEC. 555. INTERNATIONAL CIVIL AVIATION BOYCOTT OF COUNTRIES SUPPORTING INTERNATIONAL TERRORISM.

It is the sense of the Congress that the President—

(1) should call for an international civil aviation boycott with respect to those countries which the President determines—

(A) grant sanctuary from prosecution to any individual or group which has committed an act of international terrorism, or

(B) otherwise support international terrorism; and

(2) should take steps, both bilateral and multilateral, to achieve a total international civil aviation boycott with respect to those countries.

[Section 556 repealed by Public Law 103–272]

SEC. 557. RESEARCH ON AIRPORT SECURITY TECHNIQUES FOR DETECTING EXPLOSIVES.

In order to improve security at international airports, there are authorized to be appropriated to the Secretary of Transportation from the Airport and Airway Trust Fund (in addition to amounts otherwise available for such purpose) $5,000,000, without fiscal year limitation, to be used for research on and the development of airport security devices or techniques for detecting explosives.

SEC. 558. HIJACKING OF TWA FLIGHT 847 AND OTHER ACTS OF TERRORISM.

The Congress joins with all Americans in celebrating the release of the hostages taken from Trans World Airlines flight 847. It is the sense of the Congress that—

(1) purser Uli Derickson, pilot John Testrake, co-pilot Philip Maresca, flight engineer Benjamin Zimmermann, and the rest of the crew of Trans World Airlines flight 847 displayed extraordinary valor and heroism during the hostages' ordeal

and therefore should be commended;

(2) the hijackers who murdered United States Navy Petty Officer Stethem should be immediately brought to justice;

(3) all diplomatic means should continue to be employed to obtain the release of the 7 United States citizens previously kidnapped and still held in Lebanon;

(4) acts of international terrorism should be universally condemned; and

(5) the Secretary of State should be supported in his efforts to gain international cooperation to prevent future acts of terrorism.

SEC. 559. EFFECTIVE DATE.
This part shall take effect on the date of enactment of this Act.

* * * * * * *

RAILWAY LABOR ACT

45 U.S.C. 151-163; 181-188

RAILWAY LABOR ACT

[Chapter 8 of Title 45—RAILROADS]

CHAPTER 8—RAILWAY LABOR

SUBCHAPTER I—GENERAL PROVISIONS

SUBCHAPTER II—CARRIERS BY AIR

SUBCHAPTER I—GENERAL PROVISIONS

§151. DEFINITIONS; SHORT TITLE

When used in this chapter and for the purposes of this chapter—

First. The term "carrier" includes any railroad subject to the jurisdiction of the Surface Transportation Board, any express company that would have been subject to subtitle IV of title 49, as of December 31, 1995,,[1] and any company which is directly or indirectly owned or controlled by or under common control with any carrier by railroad and which operates any equipment or facilities or performs any service (other than trucking service) in connection with the transportation, receipt, delivery, elevation, transfer in transit, refrigeration or icing, storage, and handling of property transported by railroad, and any receiver, trustee, or other individual or body, judicial or otherwise, when in the possession of the business of any such "carrier": *Provided, however*, That the term "carrier" shall not include any street, interurban, or suburban electric railway, unless such railway is operating as a part of a general steam-railroad system of transportation, but shall not exclude any part of the general steam-railroad system of transportation now or hereafter operated by any other motive power. The Surface Transportation Board is authorized and directed upon request of the Mediation Board or upon complaint of any party interested to determine after hearing whether any line operated by electric power falls within the terms of this proviso. The term "carrier" shall not include any company by reason of its being engaged in the mining of coal, the supplying of coal to a carrier where delivery is not beyond the mine tipple, and the operation of equipment or facilities therefor, or in any of such activities.

Second. The term "Adjustment Board" means the National Railroad Adjustment Board created by this chapter.

Third. The term "Mediation Board" means the National Mediation Board created by this chapter.

Fourth. The term "commerce" means commerce among the several States or between any State, Territory, or the District of Columbia and any foreign nation, or between any Territory or the District of Columbia and any State, or between any Territory and any other Territory, or between any Territory and the District of Columbia, or within any Territory or the District of Columbia, or between points in the same State but through any other State or any Territory or the District of Columbia or any foreign nation.

Fifth. The term "employee" as used herein includes every person in the service of a carrier (subject to its continuing authority to supervise and direct the manner of rendition of his service) who performs any work defined as that of an employee or subordinate official in the orders of the Surface Transportation Board now in effect, and as the same may be amended or interpreted by orders hereafter entered by the Board pursuant to the authority which is conferred upon it to enter orders amending or interpreting such existing orders: *Provided, however*, That no occupational classification made by order of the Surface Transportation Board shall be construed to define the crafts according to which railway employees may be organized by their voluntary action, nor shall the jurisdiction or powers of such employee organizations be regarded as in any way limited or defined by the provisions of this chapter or by the orders of the Board.

The term "employee" shall not include any individual while such individual is engaged in the physical operations consisting of the mining of coal, the preparation of coal, the handling (other than movement by rail with standard railroad locomotives) of coal not beyond the mine tipple, or the loading of coal at the tipple.

Sixth. The term "representative" means any person or persons, labor union, organization, or corporation designated either by a carrier or group of carriers or by its or their employees, to act for it or them.

Seventh. The term "district court" includes the United States District Court for the District of Columbia; and the term "court of appeals" includes the United States Court of Appeals for the District of Columbia.

This chapter may be cited as the "Railway Labor Act."

(May 20, 1926, ch. 347, §1, 44 Stat. 577; June 7, 1934, ch. 426, 48 Stat. 926; June 21, 1934, ch. 691, §1, 48 Stat. 1185; June 25, 1936, ch. 804, 49 Stat. 1921; Aug. 13, 1940, ch. 664, §§2, 3, 54 Stat. 785, 786; June 25, 1948, ch. 646, §32(a), (b), 62 Stat. 991; May 24, 1949, ch. 139, §127, 63 Stat. 107; Pub. L. 104–88, title III, §322, Dec. 29, 1995, 109 Stat. 950; Pub. L. 104–264, title XII, §1223, Oct. 9, 1996, 110 Stat. 3287.)

[1] *So in original.*

§151a. GENERAL PURPOSES

The purposes of the chapter are: (1) To avoid any interruption to commerce or to the operation of any carrier engaged therein; (2) to forbid any limitation upon freedom of association among employees or any denial, as a condition of employment or otherwise, of the right of employees to join a labor organization; (3) to provide for the complete independence of carriers and of employees in the matter of self-organization to carry out the purposes of this chapter; (4) to provide for the prompt and orderly settlement of all disputes concerning rates of pay, rules, or working conditions; (5) to provide for the prompt and orderly settlement of all disputes growing out of grievances or out of the interpretation or application of agreements covering rates of pay, rules, or working conditions.

(May 20, 1926, ch. 347, §2, 44 Stat. 577; June 21, 1934, ch. 691, §2, 48 Stat. 1186.)

§152. GENERAL DUTIES

FIRST. DUTY OF CARRIERS AND EMPLOYEES TO SETTLE DISPUTES.—

It shall be the duty of all carriers, their officers, agents, and employees to exert every reasonable effort to make and maintain agreements concerning rates of pay, rules, and working conditions, and to settle all disputes, whether arising out of the application of such agreements or otherwise, in order to avoid any interruption to commerce or to the operation of any carrier growing out of any dispute between the carrier and the employees thereof.

SECOND. CONSIDERATION OF DISPUTES BY REPRESENTATIVES.—

All disputes between a carrier or carriers and its or their employees shall be considered, and, if possible, decided, with all expedition, in conference between representatives designated and authorized so to confer, respectively, by the carrier or carriers and by the employees thereof interested in the dispute.

Third. Designation of representatives.—

Representatives, for the purposes of this chapter, shall be designated by the respective parties without interference, influence, or coercion by either party over the designation of representatives by the other; and neither party shall in any way interfere with, influence, or coerce the other in its choice of representatives. Representatives of employees for the purposes of this chapter need not be persons in the employ of the carrier, and no carrier shall, by interference, influence, or coercion seek in any manner to prevent the designation by its employees as their representatives of those who or which are not employees of the carrier.

Fourth. Organization and collective bargaining; freedom from interference by carrier; assistance in organizing or maintaining organization by carrier forbidden; deduction of dues from wages forbidden.—

Employees shall have the right to organize and bargain collectively through representatives of their own choosing. The majority of any craft or class of employees shall have the right to determine who shall be the representative of the craft or class for the purposes of this chapter. No carrier, its officers, or agents shall deny or in any way question the right of its employees to join, organize, or assist in organizing the labor organization of their choice, and it shall be unlawful for any carrier to interfere in any way with the organization of its employees, or to use the funds of the carrier in maintaining or assisting or contributing to any labor organization, labor representative, or other agency of collective bargaining, or in performing any work therefor, or to influence or coerce employees in an effort to induce them to join or remain or not to join or remain members of any labor organization, or to deduct from the wages of employees any dues, fees, assessments, or other contributions payable to labor organizations, or to collect or to assist in the collection of any such dues, fees, assessments, or other contributions: *Provided*, That nothing in this chapter shall be construed to prohibit a carrier from permitting an employee, individually, or local representatives of employees from conferring with management during working hours without loss of time, or to prohibit a carrier from furnishing free transportation to its employees while engaged in the business of a labor organization.

Fifth. Agreements to join or not to join labor organizations forbidden.—

No carrier, its officers, or agents shall require any person seeking employment to sign any contract or agreement promising to join or not to join a labor organization; and if any such contract has been enforced prior to the effective date of this chapter, then such carrier shall notify the employees by an appropriate order that such contract has been discarded and is no longer binding on them in any way.

Sixth. Conference of representatives; time; place; private agreements.—

In case of a dispute between a carrier or carriers and its or their employees, arising out of grievances or out of the interpretation or application of agreements concerning rates of pay, rules, or working conditions, it shall be the duty of the designated representative or representatives of such carrier or carriers and of such employees, within ten days after the receipt of notice of a desire on the part of either party to confer in respect to such dispute, to specify a time and place at which such conference shall be held: *Provided*, (1) That the place so specified shall be situated upon the line of the carrier involved or as otherwise mutually agreed upon; and (2) that the time so specified shall allow the designated conferees reasonable opportunity to reach such place of conference, but shall not exceed twenty days from the receipt of such notice: *And provided further*, That nothing in this chapter shall be construed to supersede the provisions of any agreement (as to conferences) then in effect between the parties.

SEVENTH. CHANGE IN PAY, RULES, OR WORKING CONDITIONS CONTRARY TO AGREEMENT OR TO SECTION 156 FORBIDDEN.—

No carrier, its officers, or agents shall change the rates of pay, rules, or working conditions of its employees, as a class, as embodied in agreements except in the manner prescribed in such agreements or in section 156 of this title.

EIGHTH. NOTICES OF MANNER OF SETTLEMENT OF DISPUTES; POSTING.—

Every carrier shall notify its employees by printed notices in such form and posted at such times and places as shall be specified by the Mediation Board that all disputes between the carrier and its employees will be handled in accordance with the requirements of this chapter, and in such notices there shall be printed verbatim, in large type, the third, fourth, and fifth paragraphs of this section. The provisions of said paragraphs are made a part of the contract of employment between the carrier and each employee, and shall be held binding upon the parties, regardless of any other express or implied agreements between them.

NINTH. DISPUTES AS TO IDENTITY OF REPRESENTATIVES; DESIGNATION BY MEDIATION BOARD; SECRET ELECTIONS.—

If any dispute shall arise among a carrier's employees as to who are the representatives of such employees designated and authorized in accordance with the requirements of this chapter, it shall be the duty of the Mediation Board, upon request of either party to the dispute, to investigate such dispute and to certify to both parties, in writing, within thirty days after the receipt of the invocation of its services, the name or names of the individuals or organizations that have been designated and authorized to represent the employees involved in the dispute, and certify the same to the carrier. Upon receipt of such certification the carrier shall treat with the representative so certified as the representative of the craft or class for the purposes of this chapter. In such an investigation, the Mediation Board shall be authorized to take a secret ballot of the employees involved, or to utilize any other appropriate method of ascertaining the names of their duly designated and authorized representatives in such manner as shall insure the choice of representatives by the employees without interference, influence, or coercion exercised by the carrier. In the conduct of any election for the purposes herein indicated the Board shall designate who may participate in the election and establish the rules to govern the election, or may appoint a committee of three neutral persons who after hearing shall within ten days designate the employees who may participate in the election. In any such election for which there are 3 or more options (including the option of not being represented by any labor organization) on the ballot and no such option receives a majority of the valid votes cast, the Mediation Board shall arrange for a second election between the options receiving the largest and the second largest number of votes. The Board shall have access to and have power to make copies of the books and records of the carriers to obtain and utilize such information as may be deemed necessary by it to carry out the purposes and provisions of this paragraph.

TENTH. VIOLATIONS; PROSECUTION AND PENALTIES.—

The willful failure or refusal of any carrier, its officers or agents, to comply with the terms of the third, fourth, fifth, seventh, or eighth paragraph of this section shall be a misdemeanor, and upon conviction thereof the carrier, officer, or agent offending shall be subject to a fine of not less than $1,000, nor more than $20,000, or imprisonment for not more than six months, or both fine and imprisonment, for each offense, and each day during which such carrier, officer, or agent shall willfully fail or refuse to comply with the terms of the said paragraphs of this section shall constitute a separate offense. It shall be the duty of any United States attorney to whom any duly designated representative of a carrier's employees may apply to institute in the proper court and to prosecute under the direction of the Attorney General of the United States, all necessary proceedings for the enforcement of the provisions of this section, and for the punishment of all violations thereof and the costs and expenses of such prosecution shall be paid out of the appropriation for the expenses of the courts of the United States: *Provided*, That nothing in this chapter shall be construed to require an individual employee to render labor or service without his consent, nor shall anything in this chapter be construed to make the quitting of his labor by an individual employee an illegal act; nor shall any court issue any process to compel the performance by an individual employee of such labor or service, without his consent.

ELEVENTH. UNION SECURITY AGREEMENTS; CHECK-OFF.—

Notwithstanding any other provisions of this chapter, or of any other statute or law of the United States, or Territory thereof, or of any State, any carrier or carriers as defined in this chapter and a labor organization or labor organizations duly designated and authorized to represent employees in accordance with the requirements of this chapter shall be permitted—

(a) to make agreements, requiring, as a condition of continued employment, that within sixty days following the beginning of such employment, or the effective date of such agreements, whichever is the later, all employees shall become members of the labor organization representing their craft or class: *Provided*, That no such agreement shall require such condition of employment with respect to employees to whom membership is not available upon the same terms and conditions as are generally applicable to any other member or with respect to employees to whom membership was denied or terminated for any reason other than the failure of the employee to tender the periodic dues, initiation fees, and assessments (not including fines and penalties) uniformly required as a condition of acquiring or retaining membership.

(b) to make agreements providing for the deduction by such carrier or carriers from the wages of its or their employees in a craft or class and payment to the labor organization representing the craft or class of such employees, of any periodic dues, initiation fees, and assessments (not including fines and penalties) uniformly required as a condition of acquiring or retaining membership: *Provided*, That no such agreement shall be effective with respect to any individual employee until he shall have furnished the employer with a written assignment to the labor organization of such membership dues, initiation fees, and assessments, which shall be revocable in writing after the expiration of one year or upon the termination date of the applicable collective agreement, whichever occurs sooner.

(c) The requirement of membership in a labor organization in an agreement made pursuant to subparagraph (a) of this paragraph shall be satisfied, as to both a present or future employee in engine, train, yard, or hostling service, that is, an employee engaged in any of the services or capacities covered in the First division of paragraph (h) of section 153 of this title defining the jurisdictional scope of the First Division of the National Railroad Adjustment Board, if said employee shall hold or acquire membership in any one of the labor organizations, national in scope, organized in accordance with this chapter and admitting to membership employees of a craft or class in any of said services; and no agreement made pursuant to subparagraph (b) of this paragraph shall provide for deductions from his wages for periodic dues, initiation fees, or assessments payable to any labor organization other than that in which he holds membership: *Provided, however*, That as to an employee in any of said services on a particular carrier at the effective date of any such agreement on a carrier, who is not a member of any one of the labor organizations, national in scope, organized in accordance with this chapter and admitting to membership employees of a craft or class in any of said services, such employee, as a condition of continuing his employment, may be required to become a member of the organization representing the craft in which he is employed on the effective date of the first agreement applicable to him: *Provided, further*, That nothing herein or in any such agreement or agreements shall prevent an employee from changing membership from one organization to another organization admitting to membership employees of a craft or class in any of said services.

(d) Any provisions in paragraphs Fourth and Fifth of this section in conflict herewith are to the extent of such conflict amended.

TWELFTH. SHOWING OF INTEREST FOR REPRESENTATION ELECTIONS.—

The Mediation Board, upon receipt of an application requesting that an organization or individual be certified as the representative of any craft or class of employees, shall not direct an election or use any other method to determine who shall be the representative of such craft or class unless the Mediation Board determines that the application is supported by a showing of interest from not less than 50 percent of the employees in the craft or class.

(May 20, 1926, ch. 347, §2, 44 Stat. 577; June 21, 1934, ch. 691, §2, 48 Stat. 1186; June 25, 1948, ch. 646, §1, 62 Stat. 909; Jan. 10, 1951, ch. 1220, 64 Stat. 1238; Pub. L. 112–95, title X, §§1002, 1003, Feb. 14, 2012, 126 Stat. 146, 147.)

§153. NATIONAL RAILROAD ADJUSTMENT BOARD

FIRST. ESTABLISHMENT; COMPOSITION; POWERS AND DUTIES;

DIVISIONS; HEARINGS AND AWARDS; JUDICIAL REVIEW.—

There is established a Board, to be known as the "National Railroad Adjustment Board", the members of which shall be selected within thirty days after June 21, 1934, and it is provided—

(a) That the said Adjustment Board shall consist of thirty-four members, seventeen of whom shall be selected by the carriers and seventeen by such labor organizations of the employees, national in scope, as have been or may be organized in accordance with the provisions of sections 151a and 152 of this title.

(b) The carriers, acting each through its board of directors or its receiver or receivers, trustee or trustees, or through an officer or officers designated for that purpose by such board, trustee or trustees, or receiver or receivers, shall prescribe the rules under which its representatives shall be selected and shall select the representatives of the carriers on the Adjustment Board and designate the division on which each such representative shall serve, but no carrier or system of carriers shall have more than one voting representative on any division of the Board.

(c) Except as provided in the second paragraph of subsection (h) of this section, the national labor organizations, as defined in paragraph (a) of this section, acting each through the chief executive or other medium designated by the organization or association thereof, shall prescribe the rules under which the labor members of the Adjustment Board shall be selected and shall select such members and designate the division on which each member shall serve; but no labor organization shall have more than one voting representative on any division of the Board.

(d) In case of a permanent or temporary vacancy on the Adjustment Board, the vacancy shall be filled by selection in the same manner as in the original selection.

(e) If either the carriers or the labor organizations of the employees fail to select and designate representatives to the Adjustment Board, as provided in paragraphs (b) and (c) of this section, respectively, within sixty days after June 21, 1934, in case of any original appointment to office of a member of the Adjustment Board, or in case of a vacancy in any such office within thirty days after such vacancy occurs, the Mediation Board shall thereupon directly make the appointment and shall select an individual associated in interest with the carriers or the group of labor organizations of employees, whichever he is to represent.

(f) In the event a dispute arises as to the right of any national labor organization to participate as per paragraph (c) of this section in the selection and designation of the labor members of the Adjustment Board, the Secretary of Labor shall investigate the claim of such labor organization to participate, and if such claim in the judgment of the Secretary of Labor has merit, the Secretary shall notify the Mediation Board accordingly, and within ten days after receipt of such advice the Mediation Board shall request those national labor organizations duly qualified as per paragraph (c) of this section to participate in the selection and designation of the labor members of the Adjustment Board to select a representative. Such representative, together with a representative likewise designated by the claimant, and a third or neutral party designated by the Mediation Board, constituting a board of three, shall within thirty days after the appointment of the neutral member, investigate the claims of the labor organization desiring participation and decide whether or not it was organized in accordance with sections 151a and 152 of this title and is otherwise properly qualified to participate in the selection of the labor members of the Adjustment Board, and the findings of such boards of three shall be final and binding.

(g) Each member of the Adjustment Board shall be compensated by the party or parties he is to represent. Each third or neutral party selected under the provisions of paragraph (f) of this section shall receive from the Mediation Board such compensation as the Mediation Board may fix, together with his necessary traveling expenses and expenses actually incurred for subsistence, or per diem allowance in lieu thereof, subject to the provisions of law applicable thereto, while serving as such third or neutral party.

(h) The said Adjustment Board shall be composed of four divisions, whose proceedings shall be independent of one another, and the said divisions as well as the number of their members shall be as follows:

First division: To have jurisdiction over disputes involving train- and yard-service employees of carriers; that is, engineers, firemen, hostlers, and outside hostler helpers, conductors, trainmen, and yard-service employees. This division shall consist of eight members, four of whom shall be selected and designated by the carriers and four of whom shall be selected and designated by the labor organizations, national in scope and organized in accordance with sections 151a and 152 of this title and which represent employees in engine, train, yard, or hostling service: *Provided, however,* That each labor organization shall select and designate two members on the First Division and that no labor organization shall have more than one vote in any proceedings of the First Division or in the adoption of any award with respect to any dispute submitted to the First Division: *Provided further, however,* That the carrier members of the First Division shall cast no more than two votes in any proceedings of the division or in the adoption of any award with respect to any dispute submitted to the First Division.

Second division: To have jurisdiction over disputes involving machinists, boilermakers, blacksmiths, sheet-metal workers, electrical workers, carmen, the helpers and apprentices of all the foregoing, coach cleaners, power-house employees, and railroad-shop laborers. This division shall consist of ten members, five of whom shall be selected by the carriers and five by the national labor organizations of the employees.

Third division: To have jurisdiction over disputes involving station, tower, and telegraph employees, train dispatchers, maintenance-of-way men, clerical employees, freight handlers, express, station, and store employees, signal men, sleeping-car conductors, sleeping-car porters, and maids and dining-car employees. This division shall consist of ten members, five of whom shall be selected by the carriers and five by the national labor organizations of employees.

Fourth division: To have jurisdiction over disputes involving employees of carriers directly or indirectly engaged in transportation of passengers or property by water, and all other employees of carriers over which jurisdiction is not given to the first, second, and third divisions. This division shall consist of six members, three of whom shall be selected by the carriers and three by the national labor organizations of the employees.

(i) The disputes between an employee or group of employees and a carrier or carriers growing out of grievances or out of the interpretation or application of agreements concerning rates of pay, rules, or working conditions, including cases pending and unadjusted on June 21, 1934, shall be handled in the usual manner up to and including the chief operating officer of the carrier designated to handle such disputes; but, failing to reach an adjustment in this manner, the disputes may be referred by petition of the parties or by either party to the appropriate division of the Adjustment Board with a full statement of the facts and all supporting data bearing upon the disputes.

(j) Parties may be heard either in person, by counsel, or by other representatives, as they may respectively elect, and the several divisions of the Adjustment Board shall give due notice of all hearings to the employee or employees and the carrier or carriers involved in any disputes submitted to them.

(k) Any division of the Adjustment Board shall have authority to empower two or more of its members to conduct hearings and make findings upon disputes, when properly submitted, at any place designated by the division: *Provided, however,* That except as provided in paragraph (h) of this section, final awards as to any such dispute must be made by the entire division as hereinafter provided.

(l) Upon failure of any division to agree upon an award because of a deadlock or inability to secure a majority vote of the division members, as provided in paragraph (n) of this section, then such division shall forthwith agree upon and select a neutral person, to be known as "referee", to sit with the division as a member thereof, and make an award. Should the division fail to agree upon and select a referee within ten days of the date of the deadlock or inability to secure a majority vote, then the division, or any member thereof, or the parties or either party to the dispute may certify that fact to the Mediation Board, which Board shall, within ten days from the date of receiving such certificate, select and name the referee to sit with the division as a member thereof and make an award. The Mediation Board shall be bound by the same provisions in the appointment of these neutral referees as are provided elsewhere in this chapter for the appointment of arbitrators and shall fix and pay the compensation of such referees.

(m) The awards of the several divisions of the Adjustment Board shall be stated in writing. A copy of the awards shall be furnished to the respective parties to the controversy, and the awards shall be final and binding upon both parties to the dispute. In case a dispute arises involving an interpretation of the award, the division of the board upon request of either party shall interpret the award in the light of the dispute.

(n) A majority vote of all members of the division of the Adjustment Board eligible to vote shall be competent to make an award with respect to any dispute submitted to it.

(o) In case of an award by any division of the Adjustment Board in favor of petitioner, the division of the Board shall make an order, directed to the carrier, to make the award effective and, if the award includes a requirement for the payment of money, to pay to the employee the sum to which he is entitled under the award on or before a day named. In the event any division determines that an award favorable to the petitioner should not be made in any dispute referred to it, the division shall make an order to the petitioner stating such determination.

(p) If a carrier does not comply with an order of a division of the Adjustment Board within the time limit in such order, the petitioner, or any person for whose benefit such order was made, may file in the District Court of the United States for the district in which he resides or in which is located the principal operating office of the carrier, or through which the carrier operates, a petition setting forth briefly the causes for which he claims relief, and the order of the division of the Adjustment Board in the premises. Such suit in the District Court of the United States shall proceed in all respects as other civil suits, except that on the trial of such suit the findings and order of the division of the Adjustment Board shall be conclusive on the parties, and except that the petitioner shall not be liable for costs in the district court nor for costs at any subsequent stage of the proceedings, unless they accrue upon his appeal, and such costs shall be paid out of the appropriation for the expenses of the courts of the United States. If the petitioner shall finally prevail he shall be allowed a reasonable attorney's fee, to be taxed and collected as a part of the costs of the suit. The district courts are empowered, under the rules of the court governing actions at law, to make such order and enter such judgment, by writ of mandamus or otherwise, as may be appropriate to enforce or set aside the order of the division of the Adjustment Board: *Provided, however*, That such order may not be set aside except for failure of the division to comply with the requirements of this chapter, for failure of the order to conform, or confine itself, to matters within the scope of the division's jurisdiction, or for fraud or corruption by a member of the division making the order.

(q) If any employee or group of employees, or any carrier, is aggrieved by the failure of any division of the Adjustment Board to make an award in a dispute referred to it, or is aggrieved by any of the terms of an award or by the failure of the division to include certain terms in such award, then such employee or group of employees or carrier may file in any United States district court in which a petition under paragraph (p) could be filed, a petition for review of the division's order. A copy of the petition shall be forthwith transmitted by the clerk of the court to the Adjustment Board. The Adjustment Board shall file in the court the record of the proceedings on which it based its action. The court shall have jurisdiction to affirm the order of the division, or to set it aside, in whole or in part, or it may remand the proceedings to the division for such further action as it may direct. On such review, the findings and order of the division shall be conclusive on the parties, except that the order of the division may be set aside, in whole or in part, or remanded to the division, for failure of the division to comply with the requirements of this chapter, for failure of the order to conform, or confine itself, to matters within the scope of the division's jurisdiction, or for fraud or corruption by a member of the division making the order. The judgment of the court shall be subject to review as provided in sections 1291 and 1254 of title 28.

(r) All actions at law based upon the provisions of this section shall be begun within two years from the time the cause of action accrues under the award of the division of the Adjustment Board, and not after.

(s) The several divisions of the Adjustment Board shall maintain headquarters in Chicago, Illinois, meet regularly, and continue in session so long as there is pending before the division any matter within its jurisdiction which has been submitted for its consideration and which has not been disposed of.

(t) Whenever practicable, the several divisions or subdivisions of the Adjustment Board shall be supplied with suitable quarters in any Federal building located at its place of meeting.

(u) The Adjustment Board may, subject to the approval of the Mediation Board, employ and fix the compensations of such assistants as it deems necessary in carrying on its proceedings. The compensation of such employees shall be paid by the Mediation Board.

(v) The Adjustment Board shall meet within forty days after June 21, 1934, and adopt such rules as it deems necessary to control proceedings before the respective divisions and not in conflict with the provisions of this section. Immediately following the meeting of the entire Board and the adoption of such rules, the respective divisions shall meet and organize by the selection of a chairman, a vice chairman, and a secretary. Thereafter each division shall annually designate one of its members to act as chairman and one of its members to act as vice chairman: *Provided, however,* That the chairmanship and vice-chairmanship of any division shall alternate as between the groups, so that both the chairmanship and vice-chairmanship shall be held alternately by a representative of the carriers and a representative of the employees. In case of a vacancy, such vacancy shall be filled for the unexpired term by the selection of a successor from the same group.

(w) Each division of the Adjustment Board shall annually prepare and submit a report of its activities to the Mediation Board, and the substance of such report shall be included in the annual report of the Mediation Board to the Congress of the United States. The reports of each division of the Adjustment Board and the annual report of the Mediation Board shall state in detail all cases heard, all actions taken, the names, salaries, and duties of all agencies, employees, and officers receiving compensation from the United States under the authority of this chapter, and an account of all moneys appropriated by Congress pursuant to the authority conferred by this chapter and disbursed by such agencies, employees, and officers.

(x) Any division of the Adjustment Board shall have authority, in its discretion, to establish regional adjustment boards to act in its place and stead for such limited period as such division may determine to be necessary. Carrier members of such regional boards shall be designated in keeping with rules devised for this purpose by the carrier members of the Adjustment Board and the labor members shall be designated in keeping with rules devised for this purpose by the labor members of the Adjustment Board. Any such regional board shall, during the time for which it is appointed, have the same authority to conduct hearings, make findings upon disputes and adopt the same procedure as the division of the Adjustment Board appointing it, and its decisions shall be enforceable to the same extent and under the same processes. A neutral person, as referee, shall be appointed for service in connection with any such regional adjustment board in the same circumstances and manner as provided in paragraph (l) hereof, with respect to a division of the Adjustment Board.

SECOND. SYSTEM, GROUP, OR REGIONAL BOARDS: ESTABLISHMENT BY
   VOLUNTARY AGREEMENT; SPECIAL ADJUSTMENT BOARDS:
   ESTABLISHMENT, COMPOSITION, DESIGNATION OF REPRESENTATIVES
   BY MEDIATION BOARD, NEUTRAL MEMBER, COMPENSATION,
   QUORUM, FINALITY AND ENFORCEMENT OF AWARDS.—

Nothing in this section shall be construed to prevent any individual carrier, system, or group of carriers and any class or classes of its or their employees, all acting through their representatives, selected in accordance with the provisions of this chapter, from mutually agreeing to the establishment of system, group, or regional boards of adjustment for the purpose of adjusting and deciding disputes of the character specified in this section. In the event that either party to such a system, group, or regional board of adjustment is dissatisfied with such arrangement, it may upon ninety days' notice to the other party elect to come under the jurisdiction of the Adjustment Board.

If written request is made upon any individual carrier by the representative of any craft or class of employees of such carrier for the establishment of a special board of adjustment to resolve disputes otherwise referable to the Adjustment Board, or any dispute which has been pending before the Adjustment Board for twelve months from the date the dispute (claim) is received by the Board, or if any carrier makes such a request upon any such representative, the carrier or the representative upon whom such request is made shall join in an agreement establishing such a board within thirty days from the date such request is made. The cases which may be considered by such board shall be defined in the agreement establishing it. Such board shall consist of one person designated by the carrier and one person designated by the representative of the employees. If such carrier or such representative fails to agree upon the establishment of such a board as provided herein, or to exercise its rights to designate a member of the board, the carrier or representative making the request for the establishment of the special board may request the Mediation Board to designate a member of the special board on behalf of the carrier or representative upon whom such request was made. Upon receipt of a request for such designation the Mediation Board shall promptly make such designation and shall select an individual associated in interest with the carrier or representative he is to represent, who, with the member appointed by the carrier or representative requesting the establishment of the special board, shall constitute the board. Each member of the board shall be compensated by the party he is to represent. The members of the board so designated shall determine all matters not previously agreed upon by the carrier and the representative of the employees with respect to the establishment and jurisdiction of the board. If they are unable to agree such matters shall be determined by a neutral member of the board selected or appointed and compensated in the same manner as is hereinafter provided with respect to situations where the members of the board are unable to agree upon an award. Such neutral member shall cease to be a member of the board when he has determined such matters. If with respect to any dispute or group of disputes the members of the board designated by the carrier and the representative are unable to agree upon an award disposing of the dispute or group of disputes they shall by mutual agreement select a neutral person to be a member of the board for the consideration and disposition of such dispute or group of disputes. In the event the members of the board designated by the parties are unable, within ten days after their failure to agree upon an award, to agree upon the selection of such neutral person, either member of the board may request the Mediation Board to appoint such neutral person and upon receipt of such request the Mediation Board shall promptly make such appointment. The neutral person so selected or appointed shall be compensated and reimbursed for expenses by the Mediation Board. Any two members of the board shall be competent to render an award. Such awards shall be final and binding upon both parties to the dispute and if in favor of the petitioner, shall direct the other party to comply therewith on or before the day named. Compliance with such awards shall be enforcible by proceedings in the United States district courts in the same manner and subject to the same provisions that apply to proceedings for enforcement of compliance with awards of the Adjustment Board.

(May 20, 1926, ch. 347, §3, 44 Stat. 578; June 21, 1934, ch. 691, §3, 48 Stat. 1189; Pub. L. 89–456, §§1, 2, June 20, 1966, 80 Stat. 208, 209; Pub. L. 91–234, §§1–6, Apr. 23, 1970, 84 Stat. 199, 200.)

§154. NATIONAL MEDIATION BOARD

FIRST. BOARD OF MEDIATION ABOLISHED; NATIONAL MEDIATION BOARD ESTABLISHED; COMPOSITION; TERM OF OFFICE; QUALIFICATIONS; SALARIES; REMOVAL.—

The Board of Mediation is abolished, effective thirty days from June 21, 1934, and the members, secretary, officers, assistants, employees, and agents thereof, in office upon June 21, 1934, shall continue to function and receive their salaries for a period of thirty days from such date in the same manner as though this chapter had not been passed. There is established, as an independent agency in the executive branch of the Government, a board to be known as the "National Mediation Board", to be composed of three members appointed by the President, by and with the advice and consent of the Senate, not more than two of whom shall be of the same political party. Each member of the Mediation Board in office on January 1, 1965, shall be deemed to have been appointed for a term of office which shall expire on July 1 of the year his term would have otherwise expired. The terms of office of all successors shall expire three years after the expiration of the terms for which their predecessors were appointed; but any member appointed to fill a vacancy occurring prior to the expiration of the term for which his predecessor was appointed shall be appointed only for the unexpired term of his predecessor. Vacancies in the Board shall not impair the powers nor affect the duties of the Board nor of the remaining members of the Board. Two of the members in office shall constitute a quorum for the transaction of the business of the Board. Each member of the Board shall receive necessary traveling and subsistence expenses, or per diem allowance in lieu thereof, subject to the provisions of law applicable thereto, while away from the principal office of the Board on business required by this chapter. No person in the employment of or who is pecuniarily or otherwise interested in any organization of employees or any carrier shall enter upon the duties of or continue to be a member of the Board. Upon the expiration of his term of office a member shall continue to serve until his successor is appointed and shall have qualified.

All cases referred to the Board of Mediation and unsettled on June 21, 1934, shall be handled to conclusion by the Mediation Board.

A member of the Board may be removed by the President for inefficiency, neglect of duty, malfeasance in office, or ineligibility, but for no other cause.

SECOND. CHAIRMAN; PRINCIPAL OFFICE; DELEGATION OF POWERS; OATHS; SEAL; REPORT.—

The Mediation Board shall annually designate a member to act as chairman. The Board shall maintain its principal office in the District of Columbia, but it may meet at any other place whenever it deems it necessary so to do. The Board may designate one or more of its members to exercise the functions of the Board in mediation proceedings. Each member of the Board shall have power to administer oaths and affirmations. The Board shall have a seal which shall be judicially noticed. The Board shall make an annual report to Congress.

THIRD. APPOINTMENT OF EXPERTS AND OTHER EMPLOYEES; SALARIES OF EMPLOYEES; EXPENDITURES.—

The Mediation Board may (1) subject to the provisions of the civil service laws, appoint such experts and assistants to act in a confidential capacity and such other officers and employees as are essential to the effective transaction of the work of the Board; (2) in accordance with chapter 51 and subchapter III of chapter 53 of title 5, fix the salaries of such experts, assistants, officers, and employees; and (3) make such expenditures (including expenditures for rent and personal services at the seat of government and elsewhere, for law books, periodicals, and books of reference, and for printing and binding, and including expenditures for salaries and compensation, necessary traveling expenses and expenses actually incurred for subsistence, and other necessary expenses of the Mediation Board, Adjustment Board, Regional Adjustment Boards established under paragraph (w) of section 153 of this title, and boards of arbitration, in accordance with the provisions of this section and sections 153 and 157 of this title, respectively), as may be necessary for the execution of the functions vested in the Board, in the Adjustment Board and in the boards of arbitration, and as may be provided for by the Congress from time to time. All expenditures of the Board shall be allowed and paid on the presentation of itemized vouchers therefor approved by the chairman.

FOURTH. DELEGATION OF POWERS AND DUTIES.—

The Mediation Board is authorized by its order to assign, or refer, any portion of its work, business, or functions arising under this chapter or any other Act of Congress, or referred to it by Congress or either branch thereof, to an individual member of the Board or to an employee or employees of the Board to be designated by such order for action thereon, and by its order at any time to amend, modify, supplement, or rescind any such assignment or reference. All such orders shall take effect forthwith and remain in effect until otherwise ordered by the Board. In conformity with and subject to the order or orders of the Mediation Board in the premises, [and] such individual member of the Board or employee designated shall have power and authority to act as to any of said work, business, or functions so assigned or referred to him for action by the Board.

FIFTH. TRANSFER OF OFFICERS AND EMPLOYEES OF BOARD OF MEDIATION; TRANSFER OF APPROPRIATION.—

All officers and employees of the Board of Mediation (except the members thereof, whose offices are abolished) whose services in the judgment of the Mediation Board are necessary to the efficient operation of the Board are transferred to the Board, without change in classification or compensation; except that the Board may provide for the adjustment of such classification or compensation to conform to the duties to which such officers and employees may be assigned.

All unexpended appropriations for the operation of the Board of Mediation that are available at the time of the abolition of the Board of Mediation shall be transferred to the Mediation Board and shall be available for its use for salaries and other authorized expenditures.

(May 20, 1926, ch. 347, §4, 44 Stat. 579; June 21, 1934, ch. 691, §4, 48 Stat. 1193; Oct. 28, 1949, ch. 782, title XI, §1106(a), 63 Stat. 972; Pub. L. 88–542, Aug. 31, 1964, 78 Stat. 748.)

§155. Functions of Mediation Board

First. Disputes within jurisdiction of Mediation Board.—

The parties, or either party, to a dispute between an employee or group of employees and a carrier may invoke the services of the Mediation Board in any of the following cases:

(a) A dispute concerning changes in rates of pay, rules, or working conditions not adjusted by the parties in conference.

(b) Any other dispute not referable to the National Railroad Adjustment Board and not adjusted in conference between the parties or where conferences are refused.

The Mediation Board may proffer its services in case any labor emergency is found by it to exist at any time.

In either event the said Board shall promptly put itself in communication with the parties to such controversy, and shall use its best efforts, by mediation, to bring them to agreement. If such efforts to bring about an amicable settlement through mediation shall be unsuccessful, the said Board shall at once endeavor as its final required action (except as provided in paragraph third of this section and in section 160 of this title) to induce the parties to submit their controversy to arbitration, in accordance with the provisions of this chapter.

If arbitration at the request of the Board shall be refused by one or both parties, the Board shall at once notify both parties in writing that its mediatory efforts have failed and for thirty days thereafter, unless in the intervening period the parties agree to arbitration, or an emergency board shall be created under section 160 of this title, no change shall be made in the rates of pay, rules, or working conditions or established practices in effect prior to the time the dispute arose.

Second. Interpretation of agreement.—

In any case in which a controversy arises over the meaning or the application of any agreement reached through mediation under the provisions of this chapter, either party to the said agreement, or both, may apply to the Mediation Board for an interpretation of the meaning or application of such agreement. The said Board shall upon receipt of such request notify the parties to the controversy, and after a hearing of both sides give its interpretation within thirty days.

Third. Duties of Board with respect to arbitration of disputes; arbitrators; acknowledgment of agreement; notice to arbitrators; reconvening of arbitrators; filing contracts with Board; custody of records and documents.—

The Mediation Board shall have the following duties with respect to the arbitration of disputes under section 157 of this title:

(a) On failure of the arbitrators named by the parties to agree on the remaining arbitrator or arbitrators within the time set by section 157 of this title, it shall be the duty of the

Mediation Board to name such remaining arbitrator or arbitrators. It shall be the duty of the Board in naming such arbitrator or arbitrators to appoint only those whom the Board shall deem wholly disinterested in the controversy to be arbitrated and impartial and without bias as between the parties to such arbitration. Should, however, the Board name an arbitrator or arbitrators not so disinterested and impartial, then, upon proper investigation and presentation of the facts, the Board shall promptly remove such arbitrator.

If an arbitrator named by the Mediation Board, in accordance with the provisions of this chapter, shall be removed by such Board as provided by this chapter, or if such an arbitrator refuses or is unable to serve, it shall be the duty of the Mediation Board, promptly, to select another arbitrator, in the same manner as provided in this chapter for an original appointment by the Mediation Board.

(b) Any member of the Mediation Board is authorized to take the acknowledgement of an agreement to arbitrate under this chapter. When so acknowledged, or when acknowledged by the parties before a notary public or the clerk of a district court or a court of appeals of the United States, such agreement to arbitrate shall be delivered to a member of said Board or transmitted to said Board, to be filed in its office.

(c) When an agreement to arbitrate has been filed with the Mediation Board, or with one of its members, as provided by this section, and when the said Board has been furnished the names of the arbitrators chosen by the parties to the controversy it shall be the duty of the Board to cause a notice in writing to be served upon said arbitrators, notifying them of their appointment, requesting them to meet promptly to name the remaining arbitrator or arbitrators necessary to complete the Board of Arbitration, and advising them of the period within which, as provided by the agreement to arbitrate, they are empowered to name such arbitrator or arbitrators.

(d) Either party to an arbitration desiring the reconvening of a board of arbitration to pass upon any controversy arising over the meaning or application of an award may so notify the Mediation Board in writing, stating in such notice the question or questions to be submitted to such reconvened Board. The Mediation Board shall thereupon promptly communicate with the members of the Board of Arbitration, or a subcommittee of such Board appointed for such purpose pursuant to a provision in the agreement to arbitrate, and arrange for the reconvening of said Board of Arbitration or subcommittee, and shall notify the respective parties to the controversy of the time and place at which the Board, or the subcommittee, will meet for hearings upon the matters in controversy to be submitted to it. No evidence other than that contained in the record filed with the original award shall be received or considered by such reconvened Board or subcommittee, except such evidence as may be necessary to illustrate the interpretations suggested by the parties. If any member of the original Board is unable or unwilling to serve on such reconvened Board or subcommittee thereof, another arbitrator shall be named in the same manner and with the same powers and duties as such original arbitrator.

(e) Within sixty days after June 21, 1934, every carrier shall file with the Mediation Board a copy of each contract with its employees in effect on the 1st day of April 1934, covering rates of pay, rules, and working conditions. If no contract with any craft or class of its employees has been entered into, the carrier shall file with the Mediation Board a statement of that fact, including also a statement of the rates of pay, rules, and working conditions applicable in dealing with such craft or class. When any new contract is executed or change is made in an existing contract with any class or craft of its employees covering rates of pay, rules, or working conditions, or in those rates of pay, rules, and working conditions of employees not covered by contract, the carrier shall file the same with the Mediation Board within thirty days after such new contract or change in existing contract has been executed or rates of pay, rules, and working conditions have been made effective.

(f) The Mediation Board shall be the custodian of all papers and documents heretofore filed with or transferred to the Board of Mediation bearing upon the settlement, adjustment, or determination of disputes between carriers and their employees or upon mediation or arbitration proceedings held under or pursuant to the provisions of any Act of Congress in respect thereto; and the President is authorized to designate a custodian of the records and property of the Board of Mediation until the transfer and delivery of such records to the Mediation Board and to require the transfer and delivery to the Mediation Board of any and all such papers and documents filed with it or in its possession.

(May 20, 1926, ch. 347, §5, 44 Stat. 580; June 21, 1934, ch. 691, §5, 48 Stat. 1195; June 25, 1948, ch. 646, §32(a), 62 Stat. 991; May 24, 1949, ch. 139, §127, 63 Stat. 107.)

§156. PROCEDURE IN CHANGING RATES OF PAY, RULES, AND WORKING CONDITIONS

Carriers and representatives of the employees shall give at least thirty days' written notice of an intended change in agreements affecting rates of pay, rules, or working conditions, and the time and place for the beginning of conference between the representatives of the parties interested in such intended changes shall be agreed upon within ten days after the receipt of said notice, and said time shall be within the thirty days provided in the notice. In every case where such notice of intended change has been given, or conferences are being held with reference thereto, or the services of the Mediation Board have been requested by either party, or said Board has proffered its services, rates of pay, rules, or working conditions shall not be altered by the carrier until the controversy has been finally acted upon, as required by section 155 of this title, by the Mediation Board, unless a period of ten days has elapsed after termination of conferences without request for or proffer of the services of the Mediation Board.

(May 20, 1926, ch. 347, §6, 44 Stat. 582; June 21, 1934, ch. 691, §6, 48 Stat. 1197.)

§157. ARBITRATION

FIRST. SUBMISSION OF CONTROVERSY TO ARBITRATION.—

Whenever a controversy shall arise between a carrier or carriers and its or their employees which is not settled either in conference between representatives of the parties or by the appropriate adjustment board or through mediation, in the manner provided in sections 151—156 of this title such controversy may, by agreement of the parties to such controversy, be submitted to the arbitration of a board of three (or, if the parties to the controversy so stipulate, of six) persons: *Provided, however*, That the failure or refusal of either party to submit a controversy to arbitration shall not be construed as a violation of any legal obligation imposed upon such party by the terms of this chapter or otherwise.

SECOND. MANNER OF SELECTING BOARD OF ARBITRATION.—

Such board of arbitration shall be chosen in the following manner:

(a) In the case of a board of three the carrier or carriers and the representatives of the employees, parties respectively to the agreement to arbitrate, shall each name one arbitrator; the two arbitrators thus chosen shall select a third arbitrator. If the arbitrators chosen by the parties shall fail to name the third arbitrator within five days after their first meeting, such third arbitrator shall be named by the Mediation Board.

(b) In the case of a board of six the carrier or carriers and the representatives of the employees, parties respectively to the agreement to arbitrate, shall each name two arbitrators; the four arbitrators thus chosen shall, by a majority vote, select the remaining two arbitrators. If the arbitrators chosen by the parties shall fail to name the two arbitrators within fifteen days after their first meeting, the said two arbitrators, or as many of them as have not been named, shall be named by the Mediation Board.

THIRD. BOARD OF ARBITRATION; ORGANIZATION; COMPENSATION; PROCEDURE.—

(a) NOTICE OF SELECTION OR FAILURE TO SELECT ARBITRATORS.—

When the arbitrators selected by the respective parties have agreed upon the remaining arbitrator or arbitrators, they shall notify the Mediation Board; and, in the event of their failure to agree upon any or upon all of the necessary arbitrators within the period fixed by this chapter, they shall, at the expiration of such period, notify the Mediation Board of the arbitrators selected, if any, or of their failure to make or to complete such selection.

(b) ORGANIZATION OF BOARD; PROCEDURE.—

The board of arbitration shall organize and select its own chairman and make all necessary rules for conducting its hearings: *Provided, however,* That the board of arbitration shall be bound to give the parties to the controversy a full and fair hearing, which shall include an opportunity to present evidence in support of their claims, and an opportunity to present their case in person, by counsel, or by other representative as they may respectively elect.

(c) DUTY TO RECONVENE; QUESTIONS CONSIDERED.—

Upon notice from the Mediation Board that the parties, or either party, to an arbitration desire the reconvening of the board of arbitration (or a subcommittee of such board of arbitration appointed for such purpose pursuant to the agreement to arbitrate) to pass upon any controversy over the meaning or application of their award, the board, or its subcommittee, shall at once reconvene. No question other than, or in addition to, the questions relating to the meaning or application of the award, submitted by the party or parties in writing, shall be considered by the reconvened board of arbitration or its subcommittee.

Such rulings shall be acknowledged by such board or subcommittee thereof in the same manner, and filed in the same district court clerk's office, as the original award and become a part thereof.

(d) Competency of arbitrators.—

No arbitrator, except those chosen by the Mediation Board, shall be incompetent to act as an arbitrator because of his interest in the controversy to be arbitrated, or because of his connection with or partiality to either of the parties to the arbitration.

(e) Compensation and expenses.—

Each member of any board of arbitration created under the provisions of this chapter named by either party to the arbitration shall be compensated by the party naming him. Each arbitrator selected by the arbitrators or named by the Mediation Board shall receive from the Mediation Board such compensation as the Mediation Board may fix, together with his necessary traveling expenses and expenses actually incurred for subsistence, while serving as an arbitrator.

(f) Award; disposition of original and copies.—

The board of arbitration shall furnish a certified copy of its award to the respective parties to the controversy, and shall transmit the original, together with the papers and proceedings and a transcript of the evidence taken at the hearings, certified under the hands of at least a majority of the arbitrators, to the clerk of the district court of the United States for the district wherein the controversy arose or the arbitration is entered into, to be filed in said clerk's office as hereinafter provided. The said board shall also furnish a certified copy of its award, and the papers and proceedings, including testimony relating thereto, to the Mediation Board to be filed in its office; and in addition a certified copy of its award shall be filed in the office of the Interstate Commerce Commission: *Provided, however*, That such award shall not be construed to diminish or extinguish any of the powers or duties of the Interstate Commerce Commission, under subtitle IV of title 49.

(g) Compensation of assistants to board of arbitration; expenses; quarters.—

A board of arbitration may, subject to the approval of the Mediation Board, employ and fix the compensation of such assistants as it deems necessary in carrying on the arbitration proceedings. The compensation of such employees, together with their necessary traveling expenses and expenses actually incurred for subsistence, while so employed, and the necessary expenses of boards of arbitration, shall be paid by the Mediation Board.

Whenever practicable, the board shall be supplied with suitable quarters in any Federal building located at its place of meeting or at any place where the board may conduct its proceedings or deliberations.

(h) Testimony before board; oaths; attendance of witnesses; production of documents; subpoenas; fees.—

All testimony before said board shall be given under oath or affirmation, and any member of the board shall have the power to administer oaths or affirmations. The board of arbitration, or any member thereof, shall have the power to require the attendance of witnesses and the production of such books, papers, contracts, agreements, and documents as may be deemed by the board of arbitration material to a just determination of the matters submitted to its arbitration, and may for that purpose request the clerk of the district court of the United States for the district wherein said arbitration is being conducted to issue the necessary subpoenas, and upon such request the said clerk or his duly authorized deputy shall be, and he is, authorized, and it shall be his duty, to issue such subpoenas.

Any witness appearing before a board of arbitration shall receive the same fees and mileage as witnesses in courts of the United States, to be paid by the party securing the subpoena.

(May 20, 1926, ch. 347, §7, 44 Stat. 582; June 21, 1934, ch. 691, §7, 48 Stat. 1197; Pub. L. 91–452, title II, §238, Oct. 15, 1970, 84 Stat. 930.)

§158. AGREEMENT TO ARBITRATE; FORM AND CONTENTS; SIGNATURES AND ACKNOWLEDGMENT; REVOCATION

The agreement to arbitrate—

(a) Shall be in writing;

(b) Shall stipulate that the arbitration is had under the provisions of this chapter;

(c) Shall state whether the board of arbitration is to consist of three or of six members;

(d) Shall be signed by the duly accredited representatives of the carrier or carriers and the employees, parties respectively to the agreement to arbitrate, and shall be acknowledged by said parties before a notary public, the clerk of a district court or court of appeals of the United States, or before a member of the Mediation Board, and, when so acknowledged, shall be filed in the office of the Mediation Board;

(e) Shall state specifically the questions to be submitted to the said board for decision; and that, in its award or awards, the said board shall confine itself strictly to decisions as to the questions so specifically submitted to it;

(f) Shall provide that the questions, or any one or more of them, submitted by the parties to the board of arbitration may be withdrawn from arbitration on notice to that effect signed by the duly accredited representatives of all the parties and served on the board of arbitration;

(g) Shall stipulate that the signatures of a majority of said board of arbitration affixed to their award shall be competent to constitute a valid and binding award;

(h) Shall fix a period from the date of the appointment of the arbitrator or arbitrators necessary to complete the board (as provided for in the agreement) within which the said board shall commence its hearings;

(i) Shall fix a period from the beginning of the hearings within which the said board shall make and file its award: *Provided*, That the parties may agree at any time upon an extension of this period;

(j) Shall provide for the date from which the award shall become effective and shall fix the period during which the award shall continue in force;

(k) Shall provide that the award of the board of arbitration and the evidence of the proceedings before the board relating thereto, when certified under the hands of at least a majority of the arbitrators, shall be filed in the clerk's office of the district court of the United States for the district wherein the controversy arose or the arbitration was entered into, which district shall be designated in the agreement; and, when so filed, such award and proceedings shall constitute the full and complete record of the arbitration;

(l) Shall provide that the award, when so filed, shall be final and conclusive upon the parties as to the facts determined by said award and as to the merits of the controversy decided;

(m) Shall provide that any difference arising as to the meaning, or the application of the provisions, of an award made by a board of arbitration shall be referred back for a ruling to the same board, or, by agreement, to a subcommittee of such board; and that such ruling, when acknowledged in the same manner, and filed in the same district court clerk's office, as the original award, shall be a part of and shall have the same force and effect as such original award; and

(n) Shall provide that the respective parties to the award will each faithfully execute the same.

The said agreement to arbitrate, when properly signed and acknowledged as herein provided, shall not be revoked by a party to such agreement: *Provided, however,* That such agreement to arbitrate may at any time be revoked and canceled by the written agreement of both parties, signed by their duly accredited representatives, and (if no board of arbitration has yet been constituted under the agreement) delivered to the Mediation Board or any member thereof; or, if the board of arbitration has been constituted as provided by this chapter, delivered to such board of arbitration.

(May 20, 1926, ch. 347, §8, 44 Stat. 584; June 21, 1934, ch. 691, §7, 48 Stat. 1197; June 25, 1948, ch. 646, §32(a), 62 Stat. 991; May 24, 1949, ch. 139, §127, 63 Stat. 107.)

§159. Award and judgment thereon; effect of chapter on individual employee

First. Filing of award.—

The award of a board of arbitration, having been acknowledged as herein provided, shall be filed in the clerk's office of the district court designated in the agreement to arbitrate.

Second. Conclusiveness of award; judgment.—

An award acknowledged and filed as herein provided shall be conclusive on the parties as to the merits and facts of the controversy submitted to arbitration, and unless, within ten days after the filing of the award, a petition to impeach the award, on the grounds hereinafter set forth, shall be filed in the clerk's office of the court in which the award has been filed, the court shall enter judgment on the award, which judgment shall be final and conclusive on the parties.

Third. Impeachment of award; grounds.—

Such petition for the impeachment or contesting of any award so filed shall be entertained by the court only on one or more of the following grounds:

(a) That the award plainly does not conform to the substantive requirements laid down by this chapter for such awards, or that the proceedings were not substantially in conformity with this chapter;

(b) That the award does not conform, nor confine itself, to the stipulations of the agreement to arbitrate; or

(c) That a member of the board of arbitration rendering the award was guilty of fraud or corruption; or that a party to the arbitration practiced fraud or corruption which fraud or corruption affected the result of the arbitration: *Provided, however*, That no court shall entertain any such petition on the ground that an award is invalid for uncertainty; in such case the proper remedy shall be a submission of such award to a reconvened board, or subcommittee thereof, for interpretation, as provided by this chapter: *Provided further*, That an award contested as herein provided shall be construed liberally by the court, with a view to favoring its validity, and that no award shall be set aside for trivial irregularity or clerical error, going only to form and not to substance.

FOURTH. EFFECT OF PARTIAL INVALIDITY OF AWARD.—

If the court shall determine that a part of the award is invalid on some ground or grounds designated in this section as a ground of invalidity, but shall determine that a part of the award is valid, the court shall set aside the entire award: *Provided, however*, That, if the parties shall agree thereto, and if such valid and invalid parts are separable, the court shall set aside the invalid part, and order judgment to stand as to the valid part.

FIFTH. APPEAL; RECORD.—

At the expiration of 10 days from the decision of the district court upon the petition filed as aforesaid, final judgment shall be entered in accordance with said decision, unless during said 10 days either party shall appeal therefrom to the court of appeals. In such case only such portion of the record shall be transmitted to the appellate court as is necessary to the proper understanding and consideration of the questions of law presented by said petition and to be decided.

SIXTH. FINALITY OF DECISION OF COURT OF APPEALS.—

The determination of said court of appeals upon said questions shall be final, and, being certified by the clerk thereof to said district court, judgment pursuant thereto shall thereupon be entered by said district court.

SEVENTH. JUDGMENT WHERE PETITIONER'S CONTENTIONS ARE SUSTAINED.—

If the petitioner's contentions are finally sustained, judgment shall be entered setting aside the award in whole or, if the parties so agree, in part; but in such case the parties may agree upon a judgment to be entered disposing of the subject matter of the controversy, which judgment when entered shall have the same force and effect as judgment entered upon an award.

EIGHTH. DUTY OF EMPLOYEE TO RENDER SERVICE WITHOUT CONSENT; RIGHT TO QUIT.—

Nothing in this chapter shall be construed to require an individual employee to render labor or service without his consent, nor shall anything in this chapter be construed to make the quitting of his labor or service by an individual employee an illegal act; nor shall any court issue any process to compel the performance by an individual employee of such labor or service, without his consent.

(May 20, 1926, ch. 347, §9, 44 Stat. 585; June 25, 1948, ch. 646, §32(a), 62 Stat. 991; May 24, 1949, ch. 139, §127, 63 Stat. 107.)

§159A. SPECIAL PROCEDURE FOR COMMUTER SERVICE

(a) APPLICABILITY OF PROVISIONS.—

Except as provided in section 590(h) of this title, the provisions of this section shall apply to any dispute subject to this chapter between a publicly funded and publicly operated carrier providing rail commuter service (including the Amtrak Commuter Services Corporation) and its employees.

(b) REQUEST FOR ESTABLISHMENT OF EMERGENCY BOARD.—

If a dispute between the parties described in subsection (a) is not adjusted under the foregoing provisions of this chapter and the President does not, under section 160 of this title, create an emergency board to investigate and report on such dispute, then any party to the dispute or the Governor of any State through which the service that is the subject of the dispute is operated may request the President to establish such an emergency board.

(c) ESTABLISHMENT OF EMERGENCY BOARD.—

(1) Upon the request of a party or a Governor under subsection (b), the President shall create an emergency board to investigate and report on the dispute in accordance with section 160 of this title. For purposes of this subsection, the period during which no change, except by agreement, shall be made by the parties in the conditions out of which the dispute arose shall be 120 days from the day of the creation of such emergency board.

(2) If the President, in his discretion, creates a board to investigate and report on a dispute between the parties described in subsection (a), the provisions of this section shall apply to the same extent as if such board had been created pursuant to paragraph (1) of this subsection.

(d) PUBLIC HEARING BY NATIONAL MEDIATION BOARD UPON FAILURE OF EMERGENCY BOARD TO EFFECTUATE SETTLEMENT OF DISPUTE.—

Within 60 days after the creation of an emergency board under this section, if there has been no settlement between the parties, the National Mediation Board shall conduct a public hearing on the dispute at which each party shall appear and provide testimony setting forth the reasons it has not accepted the recommendations of the emergency board for settlement of the dispute.

(e) ESTABLISHMENT OF SECOND EMERGENCY BOARD.—

If no settlement in the dispute is reached at the end of the 120-day period beginning on the date of the creation of the emergency board, any party to the dispute or the Governor of any State through which the service that is the subject of the dispute is operated may request the President to establish another emergency board, in which case the President shall establish such emergency board.

(f) SUBMISSION OF FINAL OFFERS TO SECOND EMERGENCY BOARD BY PARTIES.—

Within 30 days after creation of a board under subsection (e), the parties to the dispute shall submit to the board final offers for settlement of the dispute.

(g) Report of second emergency board.—

Within 30 days after the submission of final offers under subsection (f), the emergency board shall submit a report to the President setting forth its selection of the most reasonable offer.

(h) Maintenance of status quo during dispute period.—

From the time a request to establish a board is made under subsection (e) until 60 days after such board makes its report under subsection (g), no change, except by agreement, shall be made by the parties in the conditions out of which the dispute arose.

(i) Work stoppages by employees subsequent to carrier offer selected; eligibility of employees for benefits.—

If the emergency board selects the final offer submitted by the carrier and, after the expiration of the 60-day period described in subsection (h), the employees of such carrier engage in any work stoppage arising out of the dispute, such employees shall not be eligible during the period of such work stoppage for benefits under the Railroad Unemployment Insurance Act [45 U.S.C. 351 et seq.].

(j) Work stoppages by employees subsequent to employees offer selected; eligibility of employer for benefits.—

If the emergency board selects the final offer submitted by the employees and, after the expiration of the 60-day period described in subsection (h), the carrier refuses to accept the final offer submitted by the employees and the employees of such carrier engage in any work stoppage arising out of the dispute, the carrier shall not participate in any benefits of any agreement between carriers which is designed to provide benefits to such carriers during a work stoppage.

(May 20, 1926, ch. 347, §9A, as added Pub. L. 97–35, title XI, §1157, Aug. 13, 1981, 95 Stat. 681.)

§160. Emergency board

If a dispute between a carrier and its employees be not adjusted under the foregoing provisions of this chapter and should, in the judgment of the Mediation Board, threaten substantially to interrupt interstate commerce to a degree such as to deprive any section of the country of essential transportation service, the Mediation Board shall notify the President, who may thereupon, in his discretion, create a board to investigate and report respecting such dispute. Such board shall be composed of such number of persons as to the President may seem desirable: *Provided, however*, That no member appointed shall be pecuniarily or otherwise interested in any organization of employees or any carrier. The compensation of the members of any such board shall be fixed by the President. Such board shall be created separately in each instance and it shall investigate promptly the facts as to the dispute and make a report thereon to the President within thirty days from the date of its creation.

There is authorized to be appropriated such sums as may be necessary for the expenses of such board, including the compensation and the necessary traveling expenses and expenses actually incurred for subsistence, of the members of the board. All expenditures of the board shall be allowed and paid on the presentation of itemized vouchers therefor approved by the chairman.

After the creation of such board and for thirty days after such board has made its report to the President, no change, except by agreement, shall be made by the parties to the controversy in the conditions out of which the dispute arose.

(May 20, 1926, ch. 347, §10, 44 Stat. 586; June 21, 1934, ch. 691, §7, 48 Stat. 1197.)

§160A. RULES AND REGULATIONS

(a) IN GENERAL.—

The Mediation Board shall have the authority from time to time to make, amend, and rescind, in the manner prescribed by section 553 of title 5, and after opportunity for a public hearing, such rules and regulations as may be necessary to carry out the provisions of this chapter.

(b) APPLICATION.—

The requirements of subsection (a) shall not apply to any rule or proposed rule to which the third sentence of section 553(b) of title 5 applies.

(May 20, 1926, ch. 347, §10A, as added Pub. L. 112–95, title X, §1001, Feb. 14, 2012, 126 Stat. 146.)

§161. EFFECT OF PARTIAL INVALIDITY OF CHAPTER

If any provision of this chapter, or the application thereof to any person or circumstance, is held invalid, the remainder of the chapter, and the application of such provision to other persons or circumstances, shall not be affected thereby.

(May 20, 1926, ch. 347, §11, 44 Stat. 587.)

§162. AUTHORIZATION OF APPROPRIATIONS

There is authorized to be appropriated such sums as may be necessary for expenditure by the Mediation Board in carrying out the provisions of this chapter.

(May 20, 1926, ch. 347, §12, 44 Stat. 587; June 21, 1934, ch. 691, §7, 48 Stat. 1197.)

§163. REPEAL OF PRIOR LEGISLATION; EXCEPTION

Chapters 6 and 7 of this title, providing for mediation, conciliation, and arbitration, and all Acts and parts of Acts in conflict with the provisions of this chapter are repealed, except that the members, secretary, officers, employees, and agents of the Railroad Labor Board, in office on May 20, 1926, shall receive their salaries for a period of 30 days from such date, in the same manner as though this chapter had not been passed.

(May 20, 1926, ch. 347, §14, 44 Stat. 587.)

§164. REPEALED. OCT. 10, 1940, CH. 851, §4, 54 STAT. 1111

Section, act Feb. 11, 1927, ch. 104, §1, 44 Stat. 1072, related to advertisements for proposals for purchases or services rendered for Board of Mediation, including arbitration boards.

§165. EVALUATION AND AUDIT OF MEDIATION BOARD

(a) EVALUATION AND AUDIT OF MEDIATION BOARD.—

(1) IN GENERAL.—

In order to promote economy, efficiency, and effectiveness in the administration of the programs, operations, and activities of the Mediation Board, the Comptroller General of the United States shall evaluate and audit the programs and expenditures of the Mediation Board. Such an evaluation and audit shall be conducted not less frequently than every 2 years, but may be conducted as determined necessary by the Comptroller General or the appropriate congressional committees.

(2) RESPONSIBILITY OF COMPTROLLER GENERAL.—

In carrying out the evaluation and audit required under paragraph (1), the Comptroller General shall evaluate and audit the programs, operations, and activities of the Mediation Board, including, at a minimum—

(A) information management and security, including privacy protection of personally identifiable information;

(B) resource management;

(C) workforce development;

(D) procurement and contracting planning, practices, and policies;

(E) the extent to which the Mediation Board follows leading practices in selected management areas; and

(F) the processes the Mediation Board follows to address challenges in—

(i) initial investigations of applications requesting that an organization or individual be certified as the representative of any craft or class of employees;

(ii) determining and certifying representatives of employees; and

(iii) ensuring that the process occurs without interference, influence, or coercion.

(b) IMMEDIATE REVIEW OF CERTIFICATION PROCEDURES.—

Not later than 180 days after February 14, 2012, the Comptroller General shall review the processes applied by the Mediation Board to certify or decertify representation of employees by a labor organization and make recommendations to the Board and appropriate congressional committees regarding actions that may be taken by the Board or Congress to ensure that the processes are fair and reasonable for all parties. Such review shall be conducted separately from any evaluation and audit under subsection (a) and shall include, at a minimum—

(1) an evaluation of the existing processes and changes to such processes that have occurred since the establishment of the Mediation Board and whether those changes are consistent with congressional intent; and

(2) a description of the extent to which such processes are consistent with similar processes applied to other Federal or State agencies with jurisdiction over labor relations, and an evaluation of any justifications for any discrepancies between the processes of the Mediation Board and such similar Federal or State processes.

(c) Appropriate congressional committee defined.—

In this section, the term "appropriate congressional committees" means the Committee on Transportation and Infrastructure of the House of Representatives, the Committee on Commerce, Science, and Transportation of the Senate, and the Committee on Health, Education, Labor, and Pensions of the Senate.

(May 20, 1926, ch. 347, §15, as added Pub. L. 112–95, title X, §1004, Feb. 14, 2012, 126 Stat. 147.)

SUBCHAPTER II—CARRIERS BY AIR

§181. Application of subchapter I to carriers by air

All of the provisions of subchapter I of this chapter except section 153 of this title are extended to and shall cover every common carrier by air engaged in interstate or foreign commerce, and every carrier by air transporting mail for or under contract with the United States Government, and every air pilot or other person who performs any work as an employee or subordinate official of such carrier or carriers, subject to its or their continuing authority to supervise and direct the manner of rendition of his service.

(May 20, 1926, ch. 347, §201, as added Apr. 10, 1936, ch. 166, 49 Stat. 1189.)

§182. Duties, penalties, benefits, and privileges of subchapter I applicable

The duties, requirements, penalties, benefits, and privileges prescribed and established by the provisions of subchapter I of this chapter except section 153 of this title shall apply to said carriers by air and their employees in the same manner and to the same extent as though such carriers and their employees were specifically included within the definition of "carrier" and "employee", respectively, in section 151 of this title.

(May 20, 1926, ch. 347, §202, as added Apr. 10, 1936, ch. 166, 49 Stat. 1189.)

§183. Disputes within jurisdiction of Mediation Board

The parties or either party to a dispute between an employee or a group of employees and a carrier or carriers by air may invoke the services of the National Mediation Board and the jurisdiction of said Mediation Board is extended to any of the following cases:

(a) A dispute concerning changes in rates of pay, rules, or working conditions not adjusted by the parties in conference.

(b) Any other dispute not referable to an adjustment board, as hereinafter provided, and not adjusted in conference between the parties, or where conferences are refused.

The National Mediation Board may proffer its services in case any labor emergency is found by it to exist at any time.

The services of the Mediation Board may be invoked in a case under this subchapter in the same manner and to the same extent as are the disputes covered by section 155 of this title.

(May 20, 1926, ch. 347, §203, as added Apr. 10, 1936, ch. 166, 49 Stat. 1189.)

§184. System, group, or regional boards of adjustment

The disputes between an employee or group of employees and a carrier or carriers by air growing out of grievances, or out of the interpretation or application of agreements concerning rates of pay, rules, or working conditions, including cases pending and unadjusted on April 10, 1936 before the National Labor Relations Board, shall be handled in the usual manner up to and including the chief operating officer of the carrier designated to handle such disputes; but, failing to reach an adjustment in this manner, the disputes may be referred by petition of the parties or by either party to an appropriate adjustment board, as hereinafter provided, with a full statement of the facts and supporting data bearing upon the disputes.

It shall be the duty of every carrier and of its employees, acting through their representatives, selected in accordance with the provisions of this subchapter, to establish a board of adjustment of jurisdiction not exceeding the jurisdiction which may be lawfully exercised by system, group, or regional boards of adjustment, under the authority of section 153 of this title.

Such boards of adjustment may be established by agreement between employees and carriers either on any individual carrier, or system, or group of carriers by air and any class or classes of its or their employees; or pending the establishment of a permanent National Board of Adjustment as hereinafter provided. Nothing in this chapter shall prevent said carriers by air, or any class or classes of their employees, both acting through their representatives selected in accordance with provisions of this subchapter, from mutually agreeing to the establishment of a National Board of Adjustment of temporary duration and of similarly limited jurisdiction.

(May 20, 1926, ch. 347, §204, as added Apr. 10, 1936, ch. 166, 49 Stat. 1189.)

§185. National Air Transport Adjustment Board

When, in the judgment of the National Mediation Board, it shall be necessary to have a permanent national board of adjustment in order to provide for the prompt and orderly settlement of disputes between said carriers by air, or any of them, and its or their employees, growing out of grievances or out of the interpretation or application of agreements between said carriers by air or any of them, and any class or classes of its or their employees, covering rates of pay, rules, or working conditions, the National Mediation Board is empowered and directed, by its order duly made, published, and served, to direct the said carriers by air and such labor organizations of their employees, national in scope, as have been or may be recognized in accordance with the provisions of this chapter, to select and designate four representatives who shall constitute a board which shall be known as the "National Air Transport Adjustment Board." Two members of said National Air Transport Adjustment Board shall be selected by said carriers by air and two members by the said labor organizations of the employees, within thirty days after the date of the order of the National Mediation Board, in the manner and by the procedure prescribed by section 153 of this title for the selection and designation of members of the National Railroad Adjustment Board. The National Air Transport Adjustment Board shall meet within forty days after the date of the order of the National Mediation Board directing the selection and designation of its members and shall organize and adopt rules for conducting its proceedings, in the manner prescribed in section 153 of this title. Vacancies in membership or office shall be filled, members shall be appointed in case of failure of the carriers or of labor organizations of the employees to select and designate representatives, members of the National Air Transport Adjustment Board shall be compensated, hearings shall be held, findings and awards made, stated, served, and enforced, and the number and compensation of any necessary assistants shall be determined and the compensation of such employees shall be paid, all in the same manner and to the same extent as provided with reference to the National Railroad Adjustment Board by section 153 of this title. The powers and duties prescribed and established by the provisions of section 153 of this title with reference to the National Railroad Adjustment Board and the several divisions thereof are conferred upon and shall be exercised and performed in like manner and to the same extent by the said National Air Transport Adjustment Board, not exceeding, however, the jurisdiction conferred upon said National Air Transport Adjustment Board by the provisions of this subchapter. From and after the organization of the National Air Transport Adjustment Board, if any system, group, or regional board of adjustment established by any carrier or carriers by air and any class or classes of its or their employees is not satisfactory to either party thereto, the said party, upon ninety days' notice to the other party, may elect to come under the jurisdiction of the National Air Transport Adjustment Board.

(May 20, 1926, ch. 347, §205, as added Apr. 10, 1936, ch. 166, 49 Stat. 1190.)

§186. OMITTED

§187. SEPARABILITY

If any provision of this subchapter or application thereof to any person or circumstance is held invalid, the remainder of such sections and the application of such provision to other persons or circumstances shall not be affected thereby.

(May 20, 1926, ch. 347, §207, as added Apr. 10, 1936, ch. 166, 49 Stat. 1191.)

§188. AUTHORIZATION OF APPROPRIATIONS

There is authorized to be appropriated such sums as may be necessary for expenditure by the Mediation Board in carrying out the provisions of this chapter.

(May 20, 1926, ch. 347, §208, as added Apr. 10, 1936, ch. 166, 49 Stat. 1191.)

SELECTED PROVISIONS OF THE FAA REAUTHORIZATION ACT OF 2018

PUBLIC LAW 115-254

FAA REAUTHORIZATION ACT OF 2018

[(Public Law 115–254)]

[As Amended Through P.L. 118–63, Enacted May 16, 2024]

AN ACT To provide protections for certain sports medicine professionals, to reauthorize Federal aviation programs, to improve aircraft safety certification processes, and for other purposes.

Be it enacted by the Senate and House of Representatives of the United States of America in Congress assembled,

SECTION 1. SHORT TITLE; TABLE OF CONTENTS.

(a) **[49 U.S.C. 40101 note]** SHORT TITLE.—This Act may be cited as the "FAA Reauthorization Act of 2018".

(b) TABLE OF CONTENTS.—The table of contents for this Act is as follows:

TITLE II—FAA SAFETY CERTIFICATION REFORM

* * * * * * *

DIVISION B— FAA REAUTHORIZATION ACT OF 2018

SEC. 101. [49 U.S.C. 40101 note] DEFINITION OF APPROPRIATE COMMITTEES OF CONGRESS.

In this division, the term "appropriate committees of Congress" means the Committee on Commerce, Science, and Transportation of the Senate and the Committee on Transportation and Infrastructure of the House of Representatives.

TITLE I— AUTHORIZATIONS

* * * * * * *

Subtitle B—Passenger Facility Charges

* * * * * * *

SEC. 122. FUTURE AVIATION INFRASTRUCTURE AND FINANCING STUDY.

(a) FUTURE AVIATION INFRASTRUCTURE AND FINANCING STUDY.— Not later than 60 days after the date of enactment of this Act, the Secretary of Transportation shall enter into an agreement with a qualified organization to conduct a study assessing the infrastructure needs of airports and existing financial resources for commercial service airports and make recommendations on the actions needed to upgrade the national aviation infrastructure system to meet the growing and shifting demands of the 21st century.

(b) CONSULTATION.— In carrying out the study, the qualified organization shall convene and consult with a panel of national experts, including representatives of—

> (1) nonhub airports;

> (2) small hub airports;

> (3) medium hub airports;

> (4) large hub airports;

> (5) airports with international service;

> (6) nonprimary airports;

> (7) local elected officials;

> (8) relevant labor organizations;

> (9) passengers;

> (10) air carriers;

> (11) the tourism industry; and

> (12) the business travel industry.

(c) CONSIDERATIONS.—In carrying out the study, the qualified organization shall consider—

> (1) the ability of airport infrastructure to meet current and projected passenger volumes;

> (2) the available financial tools and resources for airports of different sizes;

> (3) the available financing tools and resources for airports in rural areas;

> (4) the current debt held by airports, and its impact on future construction and capacity needs;

(5) the impact of capacity constraints on passengers and ticket prices;

(6) the purchasing power of the passenger facility charge from the last increase in 2000 to the year of enactment of this Act;

(7) the impact to passengers and airports of indexing the passenger facility charge for inflation;

(8) how long airports are constrained with current passenger facility charge collections;

(9) the impact of passenger facility charges on promoting competition;

(10) the additional resources or options to fund terminal construction projects;

(11) the resources eligible for use toward noise reduction and emission reduction projects;

(12) the gap between the cost of projects eligible for the airport improvement program and the annual Federal funding provided;

(13) the impact of regulatory requirements on airport infrastructure financing needs;

(14) airline competition;

(15) airline ancillary fees and their impact on ticket pricing and taxable revenue; and

(16) the ability of airports to finance necessary safety, security, capacity, and environmental projects identified in capital improvement plans.

(d) LARGE HUB AIRPORTS.—The study shall, to the extent not considered under subsection (c), separately evaluate the infrastructure requirements of the large hub airports identified in the National Plan of Integrated Airport Systems (NPIAS). The evaluation shall—

(1) analyze the current and future capacity constraints of large hub airports;

(2) quantify large hub airports' infrastructure requirements, including terminal, landside, and airside infrastructure;

(3) quantify the percentage growth in infrastructure

requirements of the large hub airports relative to other commercial service airports;

(4) analyze how much funding from the airport improvement program (AIP) has gone to meet the requirements of large hub airports over the past 10 years; and

(5) project how much AIP funding would be available to meet the requirements of large hub airports in the next 5 years if funding levels are held constant.

(e) REPORT.—Not later than 15 months after the date of enactment of this Act, the qualified organization shall submit to the Secretary and the appropriate committees of Congress a report on the results of the study described in subsection (a), including its findings and recommendations related to each item in subsections (c) and (d).

(f) DEFINITION OF QUALIFIED ORGANIZATION.—In this section, the term "qualified organization" means an independent nonprofit organization that recommends solutions to public policy challenges through objective analysis.

SEC. 123. INTERMODAL ACCESS PROJECTS.

Not later than 6 months after the date of enactment of this Act, the Administrator of the Federal Aviation Administration shall, after consideration of all public comments, publish in the Federal Register a final policy amendment consistent with the notice published in the Federal Register on May 3, 2016 (81 Fed. Reg. 26611).

Subtitle C—Airport Improvement Program Modifications

* * * * * * *

SEC. 133. CONTRACT TOWER PROGRAM.

* * * * * * *

(d) [49 U.S.C. 47124 note] APPROVAL OF CERTAIN APPLICATIONS FOR THE CONTRACT TOWER PROGRAM.—

(1) IN GENERAL.—If the Administrator of the Federal Aviation Administration has not implemented a revised cost-

benefit methodology for purposes of determining eligibility for the Contract Tower Program before the date that is 30 days after the date of enactment of this Act, any airport with an application for participation in the Contract Tower Program pending as of January 1, 2017, shall be approved for participation in the Contract Tower Program if the Administrator determines the tower is eligible under the criteria set forth in the Federal Aviation Administration report entitled "Establishment and Discontinuance Criteria for Airport Traffic Control Towers", and dated August 1990 (FAA-APO-90-7).

(2) REQUESTS FOR ADDITIONAL AUTHORITY.—The Administrator shall respond not later than 60 days after the date the Administrator receives a formal request from an airport and air traffic control contractor for additional authority to expand contract tower operational hours and staff to accommodate flight traffic outside of current tower operational hours.

(3) DEFINITION OF CONTRACT TOWER PROGRAM.—In this section, the term "Contract Tower Program" has the meaning given the term in section 47124(e) of title 49, United States Code, as added by this Act.

* * * * * * *

SEC. 156. [49 U.S.C. 47112 note] PRIORITY REVIEW OF CONSTRUCTION PROJECTS IN COLD WEATHER STATES.

(a) IN GENERAL.—The Administrator of the Federal Aviation Administration, to the extent practicable, shall schedule the Administrator's review of construction projects so that projects to be carried out in the States in which the weather during a typical calendar year prevents major construction projects from being carried out before May 1 are reviewed as early as possible.

(b) TECHNICAL AMENDMENT.—Section 154 of the FAA Modernization and Reform Act of 2012 (49 U.S.C. 47112 note) and the item relating to that section in the table of contents under section 1(b) of that Act (126 Stat. 13) are repealed.

SEC. 157. [49 U.S.C. 47113 note] MINORITY AND DISADVANTAGED BUSINESS PARTICIPATION.

(a) FINDINGS.—Congress finds the following:

(1) While significant progress has occurred due to the establishment of the airport disadvantaged business enterprise program (sections 47107(e) and 47113 of title 49, United States Code), discrimination and related barriers continue to pose significant obstacles for minority- and women-owned businesses seeking to do business in airport-related markets across the Nation. These continuing barriers merit the continuation of the airport disadvantaged business enterprise program.

(2) Congress has received and reviewed testimony and documentation of race and gender discrimination from numerous sources, including congressional hearings and roundtables, scientific reports, reports issued by public and private agencies, news stories, reports of discrimination by organizations and individuals, and discrimination lawsuits. This testimony and documentation shows that race- and gender-neutral efforts alone are insufficient to address the problem.

(3) This testimony and documentation demonstrates that discrimination across the Nation poses a barrier to full and fair participation in airport-related businesses of women business owners and minority business owners in the racial groups detailed in parts 23 and 26 of title 49, Code of Federal Regulations, and has impacted firm development and many aspects of airport-related business in the public and private markets.

(4) This testimony and documentation provides a strong basis that there is a compelling need for the continuation of the airport disadvantaged business enterprise program and the airport concessions disadvantaged business enterprise program to address race and gender discrimination in airport-related business.

(b) PROMPT PAYMENTS.—

(1) REPORTING OF COMPLAINTS.—Not later than 120 days after the date of enactment of this Act, the Administrator of the Federal Aviation Administration shall ensure that each airport that participates in the Program tracks, and reports to the Administrator, the number of covered complaints made in relation to activities at that airport.

(2) IMPROVING COMPLIANCE.—

(A) IN GENERAL.—The Administrator shall take actions to assess and improve compliance with prompt payment requirements under part 26 of title 49, Code of Federal Regulations.

(B) CONTENTS OF ASSESSMENT.—In carrying out subparagraph (A), the Administrator shall assess—

(i) whether requirements relating to the inclusion of prompt payment language in contracts are being satisfied;

(ii) whether and how airports are enforcing prompt payment requirements;

(iii) the processes by which covered complaints are received and resolved by airports;

(iv) whether improvements need to be made to—

(I) better track covered complaints received by airports; and

(II) assist the resolution of covered complaints in a timely manner;

(v) whether changes to prime contractor specifications need to be made to ensure prompt payments to subcontractors; and,

(vi) whether changes to prime contractor specifications need to be made to ensure prompt payment of retainage to subcontractors.

(C) REPORTING.—The Administrator shall make available to the public on an appropriate website operated by the Administrator a report describing the results of the assessment completed under this paragraph, including a plan to respond to such results.

(D) PUBLISHING DATA.—The Secretary of Transportation shall report on a publicly accessible website the uniform report of DBE awards/commitments and payments specified in part 26 of title 49, Code of Federal Regulations, and the uniform report of ACDBE Participation for non-car rental and car rental concessions, for each airport sponsor beginning with fiscal year 2025.

(3) DEFINITIONS.—In this subsection, the following

definitions apply:

(A) COVERED COMPLAINT.—The term "covered complaint" means a complaint relating to an alleged failure to satisfy a prompt payment requirement under part 26 of title 49, Code of Federal Regulations.

(B) PROGRAM.—The term "Program" means the airport disadvantaged business enterprise program referenced in subsection (a)(1) of the FAA Modernization and Reform Act of 2012 (49 U.S.C. 47113 note).

* * * * * * *

SEC. 159. STATE TAXATION.

* * * * * * *

(b) [49 U.S.C. 40116 note] RULE OF CONSTRUCTION.— Nothing in this section or an amendment made by this section shall affect a change to a rate or other provision of a tax, fee, or charge under section 40116 of title 49, United States Code, that was enacted prior to the date of enactment of this Act. Such provision of a tax, fee, or charge shall continue to be subject to the requirements to which such provision was subject under that section as in effect on the day before the date of enactment of this Act.

* * * * * * *

SEC. 161. [49 U.S.C. 47104 note] REMOTE TOWER PILOT PROGRAM FOR RURAL AND SMALL COMMUNITIES.

(a) PILOT PROGRAM.—

(1) ESTABLISHMENT.— The Administrator of the Federal Aviation Administration shall establish—

(A) in consultation with airport operators and other aviation stakeholders, a pilot program at public-use airports to construct and operate remote towers in order to assess their operational benefits;

(B) a selection process for participation in the pilot program; and

(C) a clear process for the safety and operational certification of the remote towers.

(2) SAFETY CONSIDERATIONS.—

(A) SAFETY RISK MANAGEMENT PANEL.— Prior to the operational use of a remote tower under the pilot program established in subsection (a), the Administrator shall convene a safety risk management panel for the tower to address any safety issues with respect to the tower. The panels shall be created and utilized in a manner similar to that of the safety risk management panels previously convened for remote towers and shall take into account existing best practices and operational data from existing remote towers in the United States.

(B) CONSULTATION.— In establishing the pilot program, the Administrator shall consult with operators of remote towers in the United States and foreign countries to design the pilot program in a manner that leverages as many safety and airspace efficiency benefits as possible.

(3) APPLICATIONS.— The operator of an airport seeking to participate in the pilot program shall submit to the Administrator an application that is in such form and contains such information as the Administrator may require.

(4) PROGRAM DESIGN.— In designing the pilot program, the Administrator shall—

(A) to the maximum extent practicable, ensure that at least 2 different vendors of remote tower systems participate;

(B) identify which air traffic control information and data will assist the Administrator in evaluating the feasibility, safety, costs, and benefits of remote towers;

(C) implement processes necessary to collect the information and data identified in subparagraph (B);

(D) develop criteria, in addition to considering possible selection criteria in paragraph (5), for the selection of airports that will best assist the Administrator in evaluating the feasibility, safety, costs, and benefits of remote towers, including the amount and variety of air traffic at an airport; and

(E) prioritize the selection of airports that can best demonstrate the capabilities and benefits of remote towers, including applicants proposing to operate multiple remote towers from a single facility.

(5) SELECTION CRITERIA FOR CONSIDERATION.—In selecting airports for participation in the pilot program, the Administrator, after consultation with representatives of labor organizations representing operators and employees of the air traffic control system, shall consider for participation in the pilot program—

(A) 1 nonhub airport;

(B) 3 airports that are not primary airports and that do not have existing air traffic control towers;

(C) 1 airport that participates in the Contract Tower Program; and

(D) 1 airport selected at the discretion of the Administrator.

(6) DATA.—The Administrator shall clearly identify and collect air traffic control information and data from participating airports that will assist the Administrator in evaluating the feasibility, safety, costs, and benefits of remote towers.

(7) REPORT.—Not later than 1 year after the date the first remote tower is operational, and annually thereafter, the Administrator shall submit to the appropriate committees of Congress a report—

(A) detailing any benefits, costs, or safety improvements associated with the use of the remote towers; and

(B) evaluating the feasibility of using remote towers, particularly in the Contract Tower Program, for airports without an air traffic control tower, to improve safety at airports with towers, or to reduce costs without impacting safety at airports with or without existing towers.

(8) DEADLINE.—Not later than 1 year after the date of enactment of this Act, the Administrator shall select airports for participation in the pilot program.

(9) DEFINITIONS.—In this subsection:

(A) CONTRACT TOWER PROGRAM.—The term "Contract Tower Program" has the meaning given the term in section 47124(e) of title 49, United States Code, as added by this Act.

(B) REMOTE TOWER.—The term "remote tower" means a remotely operated air navigation facility, including all necessary system components, that provides the functions and capabilities of an air traffic control tower whereby air traffic services are provided to operators at an airport from a location that may not be on or near the airport.

(C) OTHER DEFINITIONS.—The terms "nonhub airport", "primary airport", and "public-use airport" have the meanings given such terms in section 47102 of title 49, United States Code.

(10) SUNSET.—This subsection, including the report required under paragraph (8), shall not be in effect after September 30, 2028.

(b) REMOTE TOWER PROGRAM.—Concurrent with the establishment of the process for safety and operational certification of remote towers under subsection (a)(1)(C), the Administrator shall establish a process to authorize the construction and commissioning of additional remote towers that are certificated under subsection (a)(1)(C) at other airports.

(c) AIP FUNDING ELIGIBILITY.—For purposes of the pilot program under subsection (a), and after certificated remote towers are available under subsection (b), constructing a remote tower or acquiring and installing air traffic control, communications, or related equipment specifically for a remote tower shall be considered airport development (as defined in section 47102 of title 49, United States Code) for purposes of subchapter I of chapter 471 of that title if the components are installed and used at the airport, except, as needed, for off-airport sensors installed on leased towers.

SEC. 162. [49 U.S.C. 47102 note] AIRPORT ACCESS ROADS IN REMOTE LOCATIONS.

Notwithstanding section 47102 of title 49, United States Code, for fiscal years 2024 through 2028—

(1) the definition of the term "airport development" under that section includes the construction of a storage facility to shelter snow removal equipment or aircraft rescue and firefighting equipment that is owned by an airport sponsor and used exclusively to maintain safe airfield operations, up to the facility size necessary to accommodate the types and quantities of equipment prescribed by the FAA, regardless of whether

EC. 162. [49 U.S.C. 47102 note] AIRPORT
CCESS ROADS IN REMOTE LOCATIONS.

FAA Reauthorization Act of 2018

Federal funding was used to acquire the equipment;

(2) a storage facility to shelter snow removal equipment may exceed the facility size limitation described in paragraph (1) if the airport sponsor certifies to the Secretary that the following conditions are met:

(A) The storage facility to be constructed will be used to store snow removal equipment exclusively used for clearing airfield pavement of snow and ice following a weather event.

(B) The airport is categorized as a local general aviation airport in the Federal Aviation Administration's 2017-2021 National Plan of Integrated Airport Systems (NPIAS) report.

(C) The 30-year annual snowfall normal of the nearest weather station based on the National Oceanic and Atmospheric Administration Summary of Monthly Normals 1981-2010 exceeds 26 inches.

(D) The airport serves as a base for a medical air ambulance transport aircraft.

(E) The airport master record (Form 5010-1) effective on September 14, 2017 for the airport indicates 45 based aircraft consisting of single engine, multiple engine, and jet engine aircraft.

(F) No funding under this section will be used for any portion of the storage facility designed to shelter maintenance and operations equipment that are not required for clearing airfield pavement of snow and ice.

(G) The airport sponsor will complete design of the storage building not later than September 30, 2019, and will initiate construction of the storage building not later than September 30, 2020.

(H) The area of the storage facility, or portion thereof, to be funded under this subsection does not exceed 6,000 square feet; and

(3) the definition of the term "terminal development" under that section includes the development of an airport access road that—

(A) is located in a noncontiguous State;

(B) is not more than 5 miles in length;

(C) connects to the nearest public roadways of not more than the 2 closest census designated places; and

(D) may provide incidental access to public or private property that is adjacent to the road and is not otherwise connected to a public road.

SEC. 163. LIMITED REGULATION OF NON-FEDERALLY SPONSORED PROPERTY.

(a) [Reserved].

(b) [Reserved].

(c) [49 U.S.C. 47107 note] RULE OF CONSTRUCTION.—Nothing in this section shall be construed to affect the applicability of sections 47107(b) or 47133 of title 49, United States Code, to revenues generated by the use, lease, encumbrance, transfer, or disposal of land under subsection (a), facilities upon such land, or any portion of such land or facilities.

* * * * * * *

SEC. 167. [49 U.S.C. 50101 note] BUY AMERICA REQUIREMENTS.

(a) NOTICE OF WAIVERS.—If the Secretary of Transportation determines that it is necessary to waive the application of section 50101(a) of title 49, United States Code, based on a finding under section 50101(b) of that title, the Secretary, at least 10 days before the date on which the waiver takes effect, shall—

(1) make publicly available, in an easily identifiable location on the website of the Department of Transportation, a detailed written justification of the waiver determination; and

(2) provide an informal public notice and comment opportunity on the waiver determination.

(b) ANNUAL REPORT.—For each fiscal year, the Secretary shall submit to the appropriate committees of Congress a report on waivers issued under section 50101 of title 49, United States Code, during the fiscal year.

Subtitle D—Airport Noise and Environmental Streamlining

* * * * * * *

SEC. 172. [49 U.S.C. 47521 note] AUTHORIZATION OF CERTAIN FLIGHTS BY STAGE 2 AIRCRAFT.

(a) IN GENERAL.—Notwithstanding chapter 475 of title 49, United States Code, not later than 180 days after the date of enactment of this Act, the Administrator of the Federal Aviation Administration shall initiate a pilot program to permit an operator of a stage 2 aircraft to operate that aircraft in nonrevenue service into not more than 4 medium hub airports or nonhub airports if—

(1) the airport—

(A) is certified under part 139 of title 14, Code of Federal Regulations;

(B) has a runway that—

(i) is longer than 8,000 feet and not less than 200 feet wide; and

(ii) is load bearing with a pavement classification number of not less than 38; and

(C) has a maintenance facility with a maintenance certificate issued under part 145 of such title; and

(2) the operator of the stage 2 aircraft operates not more than 10 flights per month using that aircraft.

(b) TERMINATION.—The pilot program shall terminate on the earlier of—

(1) the date that is 10 years after the date of the enactment of this Act; or

(2) the date on which the Administrator determines that no stage 2 aircraft remain in service.

(c) DEFINITIONS.—In this section:

(1) MEDIUM HUB AIRPORT; NONHUB AIRPORT.—The terms "medium hub airport" and "nonhub airport" have the meanings given those terms in section 40102 of title 49, United States Code.

(2) STAGE 2 AIRCRAFT.—The term "stage 2 aircraft" has the meaning given the term "stage 2 airplane" in section 91.851 of title 14, Code of Federal Regulations (as in effect on the day before the date of the enactment of this Act).

SEC. 173. [49 U.S.C. 47501 note] ADDRESSING
COMMUNITY NOISE CONCERNS.

FAA Reauthorization Act (

SEC. 173. ALTERNATIVE AIRPLANE NOISE METRIC EVALUATION DEADLINE.

Not later than 1 year after the date of enactment of this Act, the Administrator of the Federal Aviation Administration shall complete the ongoing evaluation of alternative metrics to the current Day Night Level (DNL) 65 standard.

* * * * * * *

SEC. 175. [49 U.S.C. 47501 note] ADDRESSING COMMUNITY NOISE CONCERNS.

When proposing a new area navigation departure procedure, or amending an existing procedure that would direct aircraft between the surface and 6,000 feet above ground level over noise sensitive areas, the Administrator of the Federal Aviation Administration shall consider the feasibility of dispersal headings or other lateral track variations to address community noise concerns, if—

(1) the affected airport operator, in consultation with the affected community, submits a request to the Administrator for such a consideration;

(2) the airport operator's request would not, in the judgment of the Administrator, conflict with the safe and efficient operation of the national airspace system; and

(3) the effect of a modified departure procedure would not significantly increase noise over noise sensitive areas, as determined by the Administrator.

SEC. 176. COMMUNITY INVOLVEMENT IN FAA NEXTGEN PROJECTS LOCATED IN METROPLEXES.

(a) COMMUNITY INVOLVEMENT POLICY.—Not later than 180 days after the date of enactment of this Act, the Administrator of the Federal Aviation Administration shall complete a review of the Federal Aviation Administration's community involvement practices for Next Generation Air Transportation System (NextGen) projects located in metroplexes identified by the Administration. The review shall include, at a minimum, a determination of how and when to engage airports and communities in performance-based navigation proposals.

(b) REPORT.—Not later than 60 days after completion of the review, the Administrator shall submit to the appropriate committees of Congress a report on—

(1) how the Administration will improve community involvement practices for NextGen projects located in metroplexes;

(2) how and when the Administration will engage airports and communities in performance-based navigation proposals; and

(3) lessons learned from NextGen projects and pilot programs and how those lessons learned are being integrated into community involvement practices for future NextGen projects located in metroplexes.

SEC. 177. LEAD EMISSIONS.

(a) STUDY.—The Secretary of Transportation shall enter into appropriate arrangements with the National Academies of Sciences, Engineering, and Medicine under which the National Research Council will study aviation gasoline.

(b) CONTENTS.—The study shall include an assessment of—

(1) existing non-leaded fuel alternatives to the aviation gasoline used by piston-powered general aviation aircraft;

(2) ambient lead concentrations at and around airports where piston-powered general aviation aircraft are used; and

(3) mitigation measures to reduce ambient lead concentrations, including increasing the size of run-up areas, relocating run-up areas, imposing restrictions on aircraft using aviation gasoline, and increasing the use of motor gasoline in piston-powered general aviation aircraft.

(c) REPORT TO CONGRESS.—Not later than 1 year after the date of enactment of this Act, the Secretary shall submit to the appropriate committees of Congress the study developed by the National Research Council pursuant to this section.

* * * * * * *

SEC. 179. AIRPORT NOISE MITIGATION AND SAFETY STUDY.

(a) STUDY.—Not later than 1 year after the date of enactment of this Act, the Administrator of the Federal Aviation Administration shall initiate a study to review and evaluate existing studies and analyses of the relationship between jet aircraft approach and takeoff speeds and corresponding noise impacts on communities surrounding airports.

(b) CONSIDERATIONS.—In conducting the study initiated under subsection (a), the Administrator shall determine—

(1) whether a decrease in jet aircraft approach or takeoff speeds results in significant aircraft noise reductions;

(2) whether the jet aircraft approach or takeoff speed reduction necessary to achieve significant noise reductions—

(A) jeopardizes aviation safety; or

(B) decreases the efficiency of the National Airspace System, including lowering airport capacity, increasing travel times, or increasing fuel burn;

(3) the advisability of using jet aircraft approach or takeoff speeds as a noise mitigation technique; and

(4) if the Administrator determines that using jet aircraft approach or takeoff speeds as a noise mitigation technique is advisable, whether any of the metropolitan areas specifically identified in section 189(b)(2) would benefit from such a noise mitigation technique without a significant impact to aviation safety or the efficiency of the National Airspace System.

(c) REPORT.—Not later than 2 years after the date of enactment of this Act, the Administrator shall submit to the appropriate committees of Congress a report on the results of the study initiated under subsection (a).

SEC. 180. [49 U.S.C. 106 note] REGIONAL OMBUDSMEN.

(a) IN GENERAL.—Not later than 1 year after the date of enactment of this Act, with respect to each region of the Federal Aviation Administration, the Regional Administrator for that region shall designate an individual to be the Regional Ombudsman for the region.

(b) REQUIREMENTS.—Each Regional Ombudsman shall—

(1) serve as a regional liaison with the public, including community groups, on issues regarding aircraft noise, pollution, and safety;

(2) make recommendations to the Administrator for the region to address concerns raised by the public and improve the consideration of public comments in decision-making processes;

and

(3) be consulted on proposed changes in aircraft operations affecting the region, including arrival and departure routes, in order to minimize environmental impacts, including noise.

SEC. 181. [49 U.S.C. 40101 note] FAA LEADERSHIP ON CIVIL SUPERSONIC AIRCRAFT.

(a) IN GENERAL.—The Administrator of the Federal Aviation Administration shall exercise leadership in the creation of Federal and international policies, regulations, standards, and recommended practices relating to the certification and safe and efficient operation of civil supersonic aircraft.

(b) EXERCISE OF LEADERSHIP.—In carrying out subsection (a), the Administrator shall—

(1) consider the needs of the aerospace industry and other stakeholders when creating policies, regulations, and standards that enable the safe commercial deployment of civil supersonic aircraft technology and the safe and efficient operation of civil supersonic aircraft; and

(2) obtain the input of aerospace industry stakeholders regarding—

(A) the appropriate regulatory framework and timeline for permitting the safe and efficient operation of civil supersonic aircraft within United States airspace, including updating or modifying existing regulations on such operation;

(B) issues related to standards and regulations for the type certification and safe operation of civil supersonic aircraft, including noise certification, including—

(i) the operational differences between subsonic aircraft and supersonic aircraft;

(ii) costs and benefits associated with landing and takeoff noise requirements for civil supersonic aircraft, including impacts on aircraft emissions;

(iii) public and economic benefits of the operation of civil supersonic aircraft and associated aerospace industry activity; and

(iv) challenges relating to ensuring that standards

and regulations aimed at relieving and protecting the public health and welfare from aircraft noise and sonic booms are economically reasonable, technologically practicable, and appropriate for civil supersonic aircraft; and

(C) other issues identified by the Administrator or the aerospace industry that must be addressed to enable the safe commercial deployment and safe and efficient operation of civil supersonic aircraft.

(c) INTERNATIONAL LEADERSHIP.—The Administrator, in the appropriate international forums, shall take actions that—

(1) demonstrate global leadership under subsection (a);

(2) address the needs of the aerospace industry identified under subsection (b); and

(3) protect the public health and welfare.

(d) REPORT TO CONGRESS.—Not later than 1 year after the date of enactment of this Act, the Administrator shall submit to the appropriate committees of Congress a report detailing—

(1) the Administrator's actions to exercise leadership in the creation of Federal and international policies, regulations, and standards relating to the certification and safe and efficient operation of civil supersonic aircraft;

(2) planned, proposed, and anticipated actions to update or modify existing policies and regulations related to civil supersonic aircraft, including those identified as a result of industry consultation and feedback; and

(3) a timeline for any actions to be taken to update or modify existing policies and regulations related to civil supersonic aircraft.

(e) LONG-TERM REGULATORY REFORM.—

(1) NOISE STANDARDS.—Not later than March 31, 2020, the Administrator shall issue a notice of proposed rulemaking to revise part 36 of title 14, Code of Federal Regulations, to include supersonic aircraft in the applicability of such part. The proposed rule shall include necessary definitions, noise standards for landing and takeoff, and noise test requirements that would apply to a civil supersonic aircraft.

(2) SPECIAL FLIGHT AUTHORIZATIONS.—Not later than

December 31, 2019, the Administrator shall issue a notice of proposed rulemaking to revise appendix B of part 91 of title 14, Code of Federal Regulations, to modernize the application process for a person applying to operate a civil aircraft at supersonic speeds for the purposes stated in that rule.

(f) NEAR-TERM CERTIFICATION OF SUPERSONIC CIVIL AIRCRAFT.—

(1) IN GENERAL.—If a person submits an application requesting type certification of a civil supersonic aircraft pursuant to part 21 of title 14, Code of Federal Regulations, before the Administrator promulgates a final rule amendingpart 36 of title 14, Code of Federal Regulations, in accordance with subsection (e)(1), the Administrator shall, not later than 18 months after having received such application, issue a notice of proposed rulemaking applicable solely for the type certification, inclusive of the aircraft engines, of the supersonic aircraft design for which such application was made.

(2) CONTENTS.—A notice of proposed rulemaking described in paragraph (1) shall—

(A) address safe operation of the aircraft type, including development and flight testing prior to type certification;

(B) address manufacturing of the aircraft;

(C) address continuing airworthiness of the aircraft;

(D) specify landing and takeoff noise standards for that aircraft type that the Administrator considers appropriate, practicable, and consistent with section 44715 of title 49, United States Code; and

(E) consider differences between subsonic and supersonic aircraft including differences in thrust requirements at equivalent gross weight, engine requirements, aerodynamic characteristics, operational characteristics, and other physical properties.

(3) NOISE AND PERFORMANCE DATA.—The requirement of the Administrator to issue a notice of proposed rulemaking under paragraph (1) shall apply only if an application contains sufficient aircraft noise and performance data as the Administrator finds necessary to determine appropriate noise standards and operating limitations for the aircraft type

consistent with section 44715 of title 49, United States Code.

(4) FINAL RULE.—Not later than 18 months after the end of the public comment period provided in the notice of proposed rulemaking required under paragraph (1), the Administrator shall publish in the Federal Register a final rule applying solely to the aircraft model submitted for type certification.

(5) REVIEW OF RULES OF CIVIL SUPERSONIC FLIGHTS.—Beginning December 31, 2020, and every 2 years thereafter, the Administrator shall review available aircraft noise and performance data, and consult with heads of appropriate Federal agencies, to determine whether section 91.817 of title 14, Code of Federal Regulations, and Appendix B of part 91 of title 14, Code of Federal Regulations, may be amended, consistent with section 44715 of title 49, United States Code, to permit supersonic flight of civil aircraft over land in the United States.

(6) IMPLEMENTATION OF NOISE STANDARDS.—The portion of the regulation issued by the Administrator of the Federal Aviation Administration titled "Revision of General Operating and Flight Rules" and published in the Federal Register on August 18, 1989 (54 Fed. Reg. 34284) that restricts operation of civil aircraft at a true flight Mach number greater than 1 shall have no force or effect beginning on the date on which the Administrator publishes in the Federal Register a final rule specifying sonic boom noise standards for civil supersonic aircraft.

(g) ADDITIONAL REPORTS.—

(1) INITIAL PROGRESS REPORT.—Not later than 1 year after the date of enactment of this subsection, the Administrator shall submit to the appropriate committees of Congress a report describing—

(A) the progress of the actions described in subsection (d)(1);

(B) any planned, proposed, or anticipated action to update or modify existing policies and regulations related to civil supersonic aircraft, including such actions identified as a result of stakeholder consultation and feedback (such as landing and takeoff noise); and

(C) any other information determined appropriate by

the Administrator.

(2) SUBSEQUENT REPORT.—Not later than 2 years after the date on which the Administrator submits the initial progress report under paragraph (1), the Administrator shall update the report described in paragraph (1) and submit to the appropriate committees of Congress such report.

SEC. 182. MANDATORY USE OF THE NEW YORK NORTH SHORE HELICOPTER ROUTE.

(a) PUBLIC COMMENT PERIOD.—

(1) IN GENERAL.—The Administrator of the Federal Aviation Administration shall provide notice of, and an opportunity for, at least 60 days of public comment with respect to the regulations in subpart H of part 93 of title 14, Code of Federal Regulations.

(2) TIMING.—The public comment period required under paragraph (1) shall begin not later than 30 days after the date of enactment of this Act.

(b) PUBLIC HEARING.—Not later than 30 days after the date of enactment of this Act, the Administrator shall hold a public hearing in the communities impacted by the regulations described in subsection (a)(1) to solicit feedback with respect to the regulations.

(c) REVIEW.—Not later than 30 days after the date of enactment of this Act, the Administrator shall initiate a review of the regulations described in subsection (a)(1) that assesses the—

(1) noise impacts of the regulations for communities, including communities in locations where aircraft are transitioning to or from a destination or point of landing;

(2) enforcement of applicable flight standards, including requirements for helicopters operating on the relevant route to remain at or above 2,500 feet mean sea level; and

(3) availability of alternative or supplemental routes to reduce the noise impacts of the regulations, including the institution of an all water route over the Atlantic Ocean.

* * * * * * *

SEC. 187. AIRCRAFT NOISE EXPOSURE.

(a) REVIEW.—The Administrator of the Federal Aviation Administration shall conclude the Administrator's ongoing review of the relationship between aircraft noise exposure and its effects on communities around airports.

(b) REPORT.—

(1) IN GENERAL.—Not later than 2 years after the date of enactment of this Act, the Administrator shall submit to Congress a report containing the results of the review.

(2) PRELIMINARY RECOMMENDATIONS.—The report shall contain such preliminary recommendations as the Administrator determines appropriate for revising the land use compatibility guidelines in part 150 of title 14, Code of Federal Regulations, based on the results of the review and in coordination with other agencies.

SEC. 188. STUDY REGARDING DAY-NIGHT AVERAGE SOUND LEVELS.

(a) STUDY.—The Administrator of the Federal Aviation Administration shall evaluate alternative metrics to the current average day-night level standard, such as the use of actual noise sampling and other methods, to address community airplane noise concerns.

(b) REPORT.—Not later than 1 year after the date of enactment of this Act, the Administrator shall submit to the appropriate committees of Congress a report on the results of the study under subsection (a).

SEC. 189. STUDY ON POTENTIAL HEALTH AND ECONOMIC IMPACTS OF OVERFLIGHT NOISE.

(a) IN GENERAL.—Not later than 180 days after the date of enactment of this Act, the Administrator of the Federal Aviation Administration shall enter into an agreement with an eligible institution of higher education to conduct a study on the health impacts of noise from aircraft flights on residents exposed to a range of noise levels from such flights.

(b) SCOPE OF STUDY.—The study conducted under subsection (a) shall—

(1) include an examination of the incremental health impacts attributable to noise exposure that result from aircraft

flights, including sleep disturbance and elevated blood pressure;

(2) be focused on residents in the metropolitan area of—

(A) Boston;

(B) Chicago;

(C) the District of Columbia;

(D) New York;

(E) the Northern California Metroplex;

(F) Phoenix;

(G) the Southern California Metroplex;

(H) Seattle; or

(I) such other area as may be identified by the Administrator;

(3) consider, in particular, the incremental health impacts on residents living partly or wholly underneath flight paths most frequently used by aircraft flying at an altitude lower than 10,000 feet, including during takeoff or landing;

(4) include an assessment of the relationship between a perceived increase in aircraft noise, including as a result of a change in flight paths that increases the visibility of aircraft from a certain location, and an actual increase in aircraft noise, particularly in areas with high or variable levels of nonaircraft-related ambient noise; and

(5) consider the economic harm or benefits to businesses located party or wholly underneath flight paths most frequently used by aircraft flying at an altitude lower than 10,000 feet, including during takeoff or landing.

(c) ELIGIBILITY.—An institution of higher education is eligible to conduct the study if the institution—

(1) has—

(A) a school of public health that has participated in the Center of Excellence for Aircraft Noise and Aviation Emissions Mitigation of the Federal Aviation Administration; or

(B) a center for environmental health that receives funding from the National Institute of Environmental Health Sciences;

(2) is located in one of the areas identified in subsection (b);

(3) applies to the Administrator in a timely fashion;

(4) demonstrates to the satisfaction of the Administrator that the institution is qualified to conduct the study;

(5) agrees to submit to the Administrator, not later than 3 years after entering into an agreement under subsection (a), the results of the study, including any source materials used; and

(6) meets such other requirements as the Administrator determines necessary.

(d) SUBMISSION OF STUDY.—Not later than 90 days after the Administrator receives the results of the study, the Administrator shall submit to the appropriate committees of Congress the study and a summary of the results.

SEC. 190. [49 U.S.C. 47104 note] ENVIRONMENTAL MITIGATION PILOT PROGRAM.

(a) IN GENERAL.—The Secretary of Transportation may carry out a pilot program involving not more than 6 projects in each fiscal year at public-use airports in accordance with this section.

(b) GRANTS.—In carrying out the program, the Secretary may make grants to sponsors of public-use airports from funds apportioned under section 47117(e)(1)(A) of title 49, United States Code.

(c) USE OF FUNDS.—Amounts from a grant received by the sponsor of a public-use airport under the program shall be used for environmental mitigation projects that will measurably reduce or mitigate aviation impacts on noise, air quality, or water quality at the airport or within 5 miles of the airport.

(d) ELIGIBILITY.—Notwithstanding any other provision of chapter 471 of title 49, United States Code, an environmental mitigation project approved under this section shall be treated as eligible for assistance under that chapter.

(e) SELECTION CRITERIA.—In selecting from among applicants for participation in the program, the Secretary may give priority consideration to projects that—

(1) will achieve the greatest reductions in aircraft noise, airport emissions, or airport water quality impacts either on an absolute basis or on a per dollar of funds expended basis; and

(2) will be implemented by an eligible consortium.

(f) FEDERAL SHARE.—The Federal share of the cost of a project carried out under the program shall be 50 percent.

(g) MAXIMUM AMOUNT.—Not more than $2,500,000 may be made available by the Secretary in grants under the program for any single project.

(h) IDENTIFYING BEST PRACTICES.—The Secretary may establish and publish information identifying best practices for reducing or mitigating aviation impacts on noise, air quality, and water quality at airports or in the vicinity of airports based on the projects carried out under the program.

(i) SUNSET.—The program shall terminate on October 1, 2028.

(j) DEFINITIONS.—In this section, the following definitions apply:

(1) ELIGIBLE CONSORTIUM.—The term "eligible consortium" means a consortium that is composed of 2 or more of the following entities:

(A) Businesses incorporated in the United States.

(B) Public or private educational or research organizations located in the United States.

(C) Entities of State or local governments in the United States.

(D) Federal laboratories.

(2) ENVIRONMENTAL MITIGATION PROJECT.—The term "environmental mitigation project" means a project that—

(A) introduces new environmental mitigation techniques or technologies that have been proven in laboratory demonstrations;

(B) proposes methods for efficient adaptation or integration of new concepts into airport operations; and

(C) will demonstrate whether new techniques or technologies for environmental mitigation are—

(i) practical to implement at or near multiple public-use airports; and

(ii) capable of reducing noise, airport emissions, or water quality impacts in measurably significant amounts.

(k) AUTHORIZATION FOR THE TRANSFER OF FUNDS FROM
DEPARTMENT OF DEFENSE.—

(1) IN GENERAL.—The Administrator of the Federal
Aviation Administration may accept funds from the Secretary
of Defense to increase the authorized funding for this section by
the amount of such transfer only to carry out projects designed
for environmental mitigation at a site previously, but not
currently, managed by the Department of Defense.

(2) ADDITIONAL GRANTEES.—If additional funds are made
available by the Secretary of Defense under paragraph (1),
the Administrator may increase the number of grantees under
subsection (a).

* * * * * * *

SEC. 192. ZERO-EMISSION VEHICLES AND TECHNOLOGY.

* * * * * * *

(c) [49 U.S.C. 47136 note] DEPLOYMENT OF ZERO EMISSION
VEHICLE TECHNOLOGY.—

(1) ESTABLISHMENT.—The Secretary of Transportation may
establish a zero-emission airport technology program—

(A) to facilitate the deployment of commercially viable
zero-emission airport vehicles, technology, and related
infrastructure; and

(B) to minimize the risk of deploying such vehicles,
technology, and infrastructure.

(2) GENERAL AUTHORITY.—

(A) ASSISTANCE TO NONPROFIT ORGANIZATIONS.—The
Secretary may provide assistance under the program to not
more than 3 geographically diverse, eligible organizations
to conduct zero-emission airport technology and
infrastructure projects.

(B) FORMS OF ASSISTANCE.—The Secretary may
provide assistance under the program in the form of grants,
contracts, and cooperative agreements.

(3) SELECTION OF PARTICIPANTS.—

(A) NATIONAL SOLICITATION.—In selecting
participants, the Secretary shall—

(i) conduct a national solicitation for applications for assistance under the program; and

(ii) select the recipients of assistance under the program on a competitive basis.

(B) CONSIDERATIONS.—In selecting from among applicants for assistance under the program, the Secretary shall consider—

(i) the ability of an applicant to contribute significantly to deploying zero-emission technology as the technology relates to airport operations;

(ii) the financing plan and cost-share potential of the applicant; and

(iii) other factors, as the Secretary determines appropriate.

(C) PRIORITY.—In selecting from among applicants for assistance under the program, the Secretary shall give priority consideration to an applicant that has successfully managed advanced transportation technology projects, including projects related to zero-emission transportation operations.

(4) ELIGIBLE PROJECTS.—A recipient of assistance under the program shall use the assistance—

(A) to review and conduct demonstrations of zero-emission technologies and related infrastructure at airports;

(B) to evaluate the credibility of new, unproven vehicle and energy-efficient technologies in various aspects of airport operations prior to widespread investment in the technologies by airports and the aviation industry;

(C) to collect data and make the recipient's findings available to airports, so that airports can evaluate the applicability of new technologies to their facilities; and

(D) to report the recipient's findings to the Secretary.

(5) ADMINISTRATIVE PROVISIONS.—

(A) FEDERAL SHARE.—The Federal share of the cost of a project carried out under the program may not exceed 80 percent.

(B) TERMS AND CONDITIONS.—A grant, contract, or

cooperative agreement under this section shall be subject to such terms and conditions as the Secretary determines appropriate.

(6) DEFINITIONS.—In this subsection, the following definitions apply:

(A) ELIGIBLE ORGANIZATION.—The term "eligible organization" means an organization that has expertise in zero-emission technology.

(B) ORGANIZATION.—The term "organization" means—

(i) described in section 501(c)(3) of the Internal Revenue Code of 1986 and exempt from tax under section 501(a) of the Internal Revenue Code of 1986;

(ii) a university transportation center receiving grants under section 5505 of title 49, United States Code; or

(iii) any other Federal or non-Federal entity as the Secretary considers appropriate.

TITLE II—FAA SAFETY CERTIFICATION REFORM

Subtitle A—General Provisions

SEC. 201. [49 U.S.C. 44701 note] DEFINITIONS.

In this title, the following definitions apply:

(1) ADMINISTRATOR.—The term "Administrator" means the Administrator of the FAA.

(2) ADVISORY COMMITTEE.—The term "Advisory Committee" means the Safety Oversight and Certification Advisory Committee established under section 202.

(3) FAA.—The term "FAA" means the Federal Aviation Administration.

(4) SECRETARY.—The term "Secretary" means the Secretary of Transportation.

(5) SYSTEMS SAFETY APPROACH.—The term "systems safety approach" means the application of specialized technical and managerial skills to the systematic, forward-looking

identification and control of hazards throughout the lifecycle of a project, program, or activity.

SEC. 202. [49 U.S.C. 44701 note] SAFETY OVERSIGHT AND CERTIFICATION ADVISORY COMMITTEE.

(a) ESTABLISHMENT.—Not later than 60 days after the date of enactment of this Act, the Secretary shall establish a Safety Oversight and Certification Advisory Committee.

(b) DUTIES.—The Advisory Committee shall provide advice to the Secretary on policy-level issues facing the aviation community that are related to FAA safety oversight and certification programs and activities, including, at a minimum, the following:

(1) Aircraft and flight standards certification processes, including efforts to streamline those processes.

(2) Implementation and oversight of safety management systems.

(3) Risk-based oversight efforts.

(4) Utilization of delegation and designation authorities, including organization designation authorization.

(5) Regulatory interpretation standardization efforts.

(6) Training programs.

(7) Expediting the rulemaking process and giving priority to rules related to safety.

(8) Enhancing global competitiveness of United States manufactured and United States certificated aerospace and aviation products and services throughout the world.

(c) FUNCTIONS.—In carrying out its duties under subsection (b), the Advisory Committee shall:

(1) Foster industry collaboration in an open and transparent manner.

(2) Consult with, and ensure participation by—

(A) the private sector, including representatives of—

(i) general aviation;

(ii) commercial aviation;

(iii) aviation labor;

(iv) aviation maintenance, repair, and overhaul;

(v) aviation, aerospace, and avionics manufacturing;

(vi) unmanned aircraft systems operators and manufacturers; and

(vii) the commercial space transportation industry;

(B) members of the public; and

(C) other interested parties.

(3) Recommend consensus national goals, strategic objectives, and priorities for the most efficient, streamlined, and cost-effective certification and safety oversight processes in order to maintain the safety of the aviation system and, at the same time, allow the FAA to meet future needs and ensure that aviation stakeholders remain competitive in the global marketplace.

(4) Provide policy guidance recommendations for the FAA's certification and safety oversight efforts.

(5) On a regular basis, review and provide recommendations on the FAA's certification and safety oversight efforts.

(6) Periodically review and evaluate registration, certification, and related fees.

(7) Provide appropriate legislative, regulatory, and guidance recommendations for the air transportation system and the aviation safety regulatory environment.

[Paragraphs (8) and (9) of section 202(c) were repealed by section 129(b) of division V of Public Law 116-260.]

(10) Provide a venue for tracking progress toward national goals and sustaining joint commitments.

(11) Recommend recruiting, hiring, training, and continuing education objectives for FAA aviation safety engineers and aviation safety inspectors.

(12) Provide advice and recommendations to the FAA on how to prioritize safety rulemaking projects.

(13) Improve the development of FAA regulations by providing information, advice, and recommendations related to aviation issues.

(14) Facilitate the validation and acceptance of United States manufactured and United States certificated products and services throughout the world.

(d) MEMBERSHIP.—

(1) IN GENERAL.—The Advisory Committee shall be composed of the following members:

(A) The Administrator (or the Administrator's designee).

(B) At least 11 individuals, appointed by the Secretary, each of whom represents at least 1 of the following interests:

(i) Transport aircraft and engine manufacturers.

(ii) General aviation aircraft and engine manufacturers.

(iii) Avionics and equipment manufacturers.

(iv) Aviation labor organizations, including collective bargaining representatives of FAA aviation safety inspectors and aviation safety engineers.

(v) General aviation operators.

(vi) Air carriers.

(vii) Business aviation operators.

(viii) Unmanned aircraft systems manufacturers and operators.

(ix) Aviation safety management experts.

(x) Aviation maintenance, repair, and overhaul.

(xi) Airport owners and operators.

(2) NONVOTING MEMBERS.—

(A) IN GENERAL.—In addition to the members appointed under paragraph (1), the Advisory Committee shall be composed of nonvoting members appointed by the Secretary from among individuals representing FAA safety oversight program offices.

(B) DUTIES.—The nonvoting members may—

(i) take part in deliberations of the Advisory Committee; and

(ii) provide input with respect to any final reports

or recommendations of the Advisory Committee.

(C) LIMITATION.—The nonvoting members may not represent any stakeholder interest other than that of an FAA safety oversight program office.

(3) TERMS.—Each voting member and nonvoting member of the Advisory Committee appointed by the Secretary shall be appointed for a term of 2 years.

(4) COMMITTEE CHARACTERISTICS.—The Advisory Committee shall have the following characteristics:

(A) Each voting member under paragraph (1)(B) shall be an executive officer of the organization who has decisionmaking authority within the member's organization and can represent and enter into commitments on behalf of such organization.

(B) The ability to obtain necessary information from experts in the aviation and aerospace communities.

(C) A membership size that enables the Advisory Committee to have substantive discussions and reach consensus on issues in a timely manner.

(D) Appropriate expertise, including expertise in certification and risked-based safety oversight processes, operations, policy, technology, labor relations, training, and finance.

(5) LIMITATION ON STATUTORY CONSTRUCTION.— Public Law 104-65 (2 U.S.C. 1601 et seq.) may not be construed to prohibit or otherwise limit the appointment of any individual as a member of the Advisory Committee.

(e) CHAIRPERSON.—

(1) IN GENERAL.—The Chairperson of the Advisory Committee shall be appointed by the Secretary from among those members of the Advisory Committee that are voting members under subsection (d)(1)(B).

(2) TERM.—Each member appointed under paragraph (1) shall serve a term of 2 years as Chairperson.

(f) MEETINGS.—

(1) FREQUENCY.—The Advisory Committee shall meet at least twice each year at the call of the Chairperson.

(2) PUBLIC ATTENDANCE.—The meetings of the Advisory

Committee shall be open and accessible to the public.

(g) SPECIAL COMMITTEES.—

(1) ESTABLISHMENT.—The Advisory Committee may establish special committees composed of private sector representatives, members of the public, labor representatives, and other relevant parties in complying with consultation and participation requirements under this section.

(2) RULEMAKING ADVICE.—A special committee established by the Advisory Committee may—

(A) provide rulemaking advice and recommendations to the Advisory Committee with respect to aviation-related issues;

(B) provide the FAA additional opportunities to obtain firsthand information and insight from those parties that are most affected by existing and proposed regulations; and

(C) assist in expediting the development, revision, or elimination of rules without circumventing public rulemaking processes and procedures.

(3) APPLICABLE LAW.— Public Law 92-463 shall not apply to a special committee established by the Advisory Committee.

(h) SUNSET.—The Advisory Committee shall terminate on October 1, 2028.

(i) TERMINATION OF AIR TRAFFIC PROCEDURES ADVISORY COMMITTEE.—The Air Traffic Procedures Advisory Committee established by the FAA shall terminate on the date of the initial appointment of the members of the Advisory Committee.

Subtitle B—Aircraft Certification Reform

SEC. 212. ORGANIZATION DESIGNATION AUTHORIZATIONS.

(a) IN GENERAL.—Chapter 447 of title 49, United States Code, is amended by adding at the end the following:

"SEC. 44736. [49 U.S.C. 44736] Organization designation authorizations

"(a) DELEGATIONS OF FUNCTIONS.—

"(1) IN GENERAL.—Except as provided in paragraph (3),

when overseeing an ODA holder, the Administrator of the FAA shall—

"(A) require, based on an application submitted by the ODA holder and approved by the Administrator (or the Administrator's designee), a procedures manual that addresses all procedures and limitations regarding the functions to be performed by the ODA holder;

"(B) delegate fully to the ODA holder each of the functions to be performed as specified in the procedures manual, unless the Administrator determines, after the date of the delegation and as a result of an inspection or other investigation, that the public interest and safety of air commerce requires a limitation with respect to 1 or more of the functions;

"(C) conduct regular oversight activities by inspecting the ODA holder's delegated functions and taking action based on validated inspection findings; and

"(D) for each function that is limited under subparagraph (B), work with the ODA holder to develop the ODA holder's capability to execute that function safely and effectively and return to full authority status.

"(2) DUTIES OF ODA HOLDERS.—An ODA holder shall—

"(A) perform each specified function delegated to the ODA holder in accordance with the approved procedures manual for the delegation;

"(B) make the procedures manual available to each member of the appropriate ODA unit; and

"(C) cooperate fully with oversight activities conducted by the Administrator in connection with the delegation.

"(3) EXISTING ODA HOLDERS.—With regard to an ODA holder operating under a procedures manual approved by the Administrator before the date of enactment of the FAA Reauthorization Act of 2018, the Administrator shall—

"(A) at the request of the ODA holder and in an expeditious manner, approve revisions to the ODA holder's procedures manual;

"(B) delegate fully to the ODA holder each of the functions to be performed as specified in the procedures manual, unless the Administrator determines, after the date of the delegation and as a result of an inspection or other investigation, that the public interest and safety of air commerce requires a limitation with respect to one or more of the functions;

"(C) conduct regular oversight activities by inspecting the ODA holder's delegated functions and taking action based on validated inspection findings; and

"(D) for each function that is limited under subparagraph (B), work with the ODA holder to develop the ODA holder's capability to execute that function safely and effectively and return to full authority status.

"(b) ODA OFFICE.—

"(1) ESTABLISHMENT.—Not later than 120 days after the date of enactment of this section, the Administrator of the FAA shall identify, within the FAA Office of Aviation Safety, a centralized policy office to be known as the Organization Designation Authorization Office or the ODA Office.

"(2) PURPOSE.—The purpose of the ODA Office shall be to provide oversight and ensure the consistency of the FAA's audit functions under the ODA program across the FAA.

"(3) FUNCTIONS.—The ODA Office shall—

"(A)(i) at the request of an ODA holder, eliminate all limitations specified in a procedures manual in place on the day before the date of enactment of the FAA Reauthorization Act of 2018 that are low and medium risk as determined by a risk analysis using criteria established by the ODA Office and disclosed to the ODA holder, except where an ODA holder's performance warrants the retention of a specific limitation due to documented concerns about inadequate current performance in carrying out that authorized function;

"(ii) require an ODA holder to establish a corrective action plan to regain authority for any retained limitations;

"(iii) require an ODA holder to notify the ODA Office when all corrective actions have been accomplished; and

"(iv) make a reassessment to determine if

subsequent performance in carrying out any retained limitation warrants continued retention and, if such reassessment determines performance meets objectives, lift such limitation immediately;

"(B) improve FAA and ODA holder performance and ensure full utilization of the authorities delegated under the ODA program;

"(C) develop a more consistent approach to audit priorities, procedures, and training under the ODA program;

"(D) review, in a timely fashion, a random sample of limitations on delegated authorities under the ODA program to determine if the limitations are appropriate;

"(E) ensure national consistency in the interpretation and application of the requirements of the ODA program, including any limitations, and in the performance of the ODA program; and

"(F) at the request of an ODA holder, review and approve new limitations to ODA functions.

"(c) DEFINITIONS.—In this section, the following definitions apply:

"(1) FAA.—The term 'FAA' means the Federal Aviation Administration.

"(2) ODA HOLDER.—The term 'ODA holder' means an entity authorized to perform functions pursuant to a delegation made by the Administrator of the FAA under section 44702(d).

"(3) ODA UNIT.—The term 'ODA unit' means a group of 2 or more individuals who perform, under the supervision of an ODA holder, authorized functions under an ODA.

"(4) ORGANIZATION.—The term 'organization' means a firm, partnership, corporation, company, association, joint-stock association, or governmental entity.

"(5) ORGANIZATION DESIGNATION AUTHORIZATION; ODA.—The term 'Organization Designation Authorization' or 'ODA' means an authorization by the FAA under section 44702(d) for an organization composed of 1 or more ODA units to perform approved functions on behalf of the FAA."

(b) **[49 U.S.C. 44701]** CLERICAL AMENDMENT.—The analysis for chapter 447 of title 49, United States Code,is amended by adding at the end the following:

"44736.   Organization designation authorizations."

.

SEC. 213. ODA REVIEW.

(a) ESTABLISHMENT OF EXPERT REVIEW PANEL.—

(1) EXPERT PANEL.—Not later than 120 days after the date of enactment of this Act, the Administrator shall convene a multidisciplinary expert review panel (in this section referred to as the "Panel").

(2) COMPOSITION OF PANEL.—

(A) APPOINTMENT OF MEMBERS.—The Panel shall be composed of not more than 20 members appointed by the Administrator.

(B) QUALIFICATIONS.—The members appointed to the Panel shall—

(i) each have a minimum of 5 years of experience in processes and procedures under the ODA program; and

(ii) represent, at a minimum, ODA holders, aviation manufacturers, safety experts, and FAA labor organizations, including labor representatives of FAA aviation safety inspectors and aviation safety engineers.

(b) SURVEY.—The Panel shall conduct a survey of ODA holders and ODA program applicants to document and assess FAA certification and oversight activities, including use of the ODA program and the timeliness and efficiency of the certification process. In carrying out this subsection, the Panel shall consult with appropriate survey experts to best design and conduct the survey.

(c) BEST PRACTICES REVIEW.—In addition to conducting the survey required under subsection (b), the Panel shall conduct a review of a sampling of ODA holders to identify and develop best practices. At a minimum, the best practices shall address preventing and deterring instances of undue pressure on or by an ODA unit member, within an ODA, or by an ODA holder, or failures to maintain independence between the FAA and an ODA holder or an ODA unit member. In carrying out such review, the Panel shall—

(1) examine other government regulated industries to gather lessons learned, procedures, or processes that address undue pressure of employees, perceived regulatory coziness, or other failures to maintain independence;

(2) identify ways to improve communications between an ODA Administrator, ODA unit members, and FAA engineers and inspectors, consistent with section 44736(g) of title 49, United States Code, in order to enable direct communication of technical concerns that arise during a certification project without fear of reprisal to the ODA Administrator or ODA unit member; and

(3) examine FAA designee programs, including the assignment of FAA advisors to designees, to determine which components of the program may improve the FAA's oversight of ODA units, ODA unit members, and the ODA program.

(d) ASSESSMENT AND RECOMMENDATIONS.—The Panel shall assess and make recommendations concerning—

(1) the FAA's processes and procedures under the ODA program and whether the processes and procedures function as intended;

(2) the best practices of and lessons learned by ODA holders and FAA personnel who provide oversight of ODA holders;

(3) training activities related to the ODA program for FAA personnel and ODA holders;

(4) the impact, if any, that oversight of the ODA program has on FAA resources and the FAA's ability to process applications for certifications outside of the ODA program;

(5) the results of the survey conducted under subsection (b); and

(6) the results of the review conducted under subsection (c).

(e) REPORT.—Not later than 180 days after the date the Panel is convened under subsection (a), the Panel shall submit to the Administrator, the Advisory Committee, and the appropriate committees of Congress a report on the findings and recommendations of the Panel.

(f) DEFINITIONS.—The definitions contained in section 44736 of title 49, United States Code, as added by this Act, apply to this section.

(g) APPLICABLE LAW.— Public Law 92-463 shall not apply to the Panel.

(h) BEST PRACTICES ADOPTION.—

(1) IN GENERAL.—Not later than 180 days after the date on which the Administrator receives the report required under subsection (e), the Administrator shall establish best practices that are generally applicable to all ODA holders and require such practices to be incorporated, as appropriate, into each ODA holder's approved procedures manual.

(2) NOTICE AND COMMENT PERIOD.—The Administrator shall publish the established best practices for public notice and comment for not fewer than 60 days prior to requiring the practices, as appropriate, be incorporated into each ODA holder's approved procedures manual.

(i) SUNSET.—The Panel shall terminate on the earlier of—

(1) the date of submission of the report under subsection (e); or

(2) the date that is 2 years after the date on which the Panel is first convened under subsection (a).

* * * * * * *

SEC. 215. REVIEW OF CERTIFICATION PROCESS FOR SMALL GENERAL AVIATION AIRPLANES.

(a) IN GENERAL.—Not later than 1 year after the date of enactment of this Act, the Comptroller General of the United States shall initiate a review of the Federal Aviation Administration's implementation of the final rule titled "Revision of Airworthiness Standards for Normal, Utility, Acrobatic, and Commuter Category Airplanes" (81 Fed. Reg. 96572).

(b) CONSIDERATIONS.—In carrying out the review, the Comptroller General shall assess—

(1) how the rule puts into practice the Administration's efforts to implement performance and risk-based safety standards;

(2) the extent to which the rule has resulted in the implementation of a streamlined regulatory regime to improve safety, reduce regulatory burden, and decrease costs;

(3) whether the rule and its implementation have spurred innovation and technological adoption;

(4) how consensus standards accepted by the FAA facilitate the development of new safety equipment and aircraft capabilities; and

(5) whether lessons learned from the rule and its implementation have resulted in best practices that could be applied to airworthiness standards for other categories of aircraft.

(c) REPORT.—Not later than 180 days after the date of initiation of the review, the Comptroller General shall submit to the appropriate committees of Congress a report on the results of the review, including findings and recommendations.

SEC. 216. ODA STAFFING AND OVERSIGHT.

(a) REPORT TO CONGRESS.—Not later than 270 days after the date of enactment of this Act, the Administrator shall submit to the appropriate committees of Congress a report on the Administration's progress with respect to—

(1) determining what additional model inputs and labor distribution codes are needed to identify ODA oversight staffing needs;

(2) developing and implementing system-based evaluation criteria and risk-based tools to aid ODA team members in targeting their oversight activities;

(3) developing agreements and processes for sharing resources to ensure adequate oversight of ODA personnel performing certification and inspection work at supplier and company facilities; and

(4) ensuring full utilization of ODA authority.

(b) ODA DEFINED.—In this section, the term "ODA" has the meaning given that term in section 44736 of title 49, United States Code, as added by this Act.

Subtitle C—Flight Standards Reform

SEC. 222. FAA TASK FORCE ON FLIGHT STANDARDS REFORM.

(a) ESTABLISHMENT.—Not later than 90 days after the date of enactment of this Act, the Administrator shall establish the FAA Task Force on Flight Standards Reform (in this section referred to as the "Task Force").

(b) MEMBERSHIP.—

(1) APPOINTMENT.—The membership of the Task Force shall be appointed by the Administrator.

(2) NUMBER.—The Task Force shall be composed of not more than 20 members.

(3) REPRESENTATION REQUIREMENTS.—The membership of the Task Force shall include representatives, with knowledge of flight standards regulatory processes and requirements, of—

(A) air carriers;

(B) general aviation;

(C) business aviation;

(D) repair stations;

(E) unmanned aircraft systems operators;

(F) flight schools;

(G) labor unions, including those representing FAA aviation safety inspectors and those representing FAA aviation safety engineers;

(H) aviation and aerospace manufacturers; and

(I) aviation safety experts.

(c) DUTIES.—The duties of the Task Force shall include, at a minimum, identifying best practices and providing recommendations, for current and anticipated budgetary environments, with respect to—

(1) simplifying and streamlining flight standards regulatory processes, including issuance and oversight of certificates;

(2) reorganizing Flight Standards Services to establish an entity organized by function rather than geographic region, if appropriate;

(3) FAA aviation safety inspector training opportunities;

(4) ensuring adequate and timely provision of Flight

SEC. 223. [49 U.S.C. 44701 note] CENTRALIZED
SAFETY GUIDANCE DATABASE.

FAA Reauthorization Act of

Standards activities and responses necessary for type certification, operational evaluation, and entry into service of newly manufactured aircraft;

(5) FAA aviation safety inspector standards and performance; and

(6) achieving, across the FAA, consistent—

(A) regulatory interpretations; and

(B) application of oversight activities.

(d) REPORT.—Not later than 1 year after the date of the establishment of the Task Force, the Task Force shall submit to the appropriate committees of Congress a report detailing—

(1) the best practices identified and recommendations provided by the Task Force under subsection (c); and

(2) any recommendations of the Task Force for additional regulatory, policy, or cost-effective legislative action to improve the efficiency of agency activities.

(e) APPLICABLE LAW.— Public Law 92-463 shall not apply to the Task Force.

(f) SUNSET.—The Task Force shall terminate on the earlier of—

(1) the date on which the Task Force submits the report required under subsection (d); or

(2) the date that is 18 months after the date on which the Task Force is established under subsection (a).

SEC. 223. [49 U.S.C. 44701 note] CENTRALIZED SAFETY GUIDANCE DATABASE.

(a) ESTABLISHMENT.—Not later than 1 year after the date of enactment of this Act, the Administrator shall establish a centralized safety guidance database that will—

(1) encompass all of the regulatory guidance documents of the FAA Office of Aviation Safety;

(2) contain, for each such guidance document, a link to the Code of Federal Regulations provision to which the document relates; and

(3) be publicly available in a manner that—

(A) protects from disclosure identifying information regarding an individual or entity; and

(B) prevents inappropriate disclosure proprietary information.

(b) DATA ENTRY TIMING.—

(1) EXISTING DOCUMENTS.—Not later than 14 months after the date of enactment of this Act, the Administrator shall begin entering into the database established under subsection (a) all of the regulatory guidance documents of the Office of Aviation Safety that are in effect and were issued before the date on which the Administrator begins such entry process.

(2) NEW DOCUMENTS AND CHANGES.—On and after the date on which the Administrator begins the document entry process under paragraph (1), the Administrator shall ensure that all new regulatory guidance documents of the Office of Aviation Safety and any changes to existing documents are included in the database established under subsection (a) as such documents or changes to existing documents are issued.

(c) CONSULTATION REQUIREMENT.—In establishing the database under subsection (a), the Administrator shall consult and collaborate with appropriate stakeholders, including labor organizations (including those representing aviation workers, FAA aviation safety engineers and FAA aviation safety inspectors) and aviation industry stakeholders.

(d) REGULATORY GUIDANCE DOCUMENTS DEFINED.—In this section, the term "regulatory guidance documents" means all forms of written information issued by the FAA that an individual or entity may use to interpret or apply FAA regulations and requirements, including information an individual or entity may use to determine acceptable means of compliance with such regulations and requirements, such as an order, manual, circular, policy statement, legal interpretation memorandum, or rulemaking document.

SEC. 224. [49 U.S.C. 44701 note] REGULATORY CONSISTENCY COMMUNICATIONS BOARD.

(a) ESTABLISHMENT.—Not later than 180 days after the date of enactment of this Act, the Administrator shall establish a Regulatory Consistency Communications Board (in this section referred to as the "Board").

(b) CONSULTATION REQUIREMENT.—In establishing the Board,

the Administrator shall consult and collaborate with appropriate stakeholders, including FAA labor organizations (including labor organizations representing FAA aviation safety inspectors) and industry stakeholders.

(c) MEMBERSHIP.—The Board shall be composed of FAA representatives, appointed by the Administrator, from—

(1) the Flight Standards Service;

(2) the Aircraft Certification Service;

(3) the Office of the Chief Counsel;

(4) the Office of Airports;

(5) the Office of Security and Hazardous Materials Safety;

(6) the Office of Rulemaking and Regulatory Improvement; and

(7) such other offices as the Administrator determines appropriate.

(d) FUNCTIONS.—The Board shall carry out the following functions:

(1) Establish, at a minimum, processes by which—

(A) FAA personnel and persons regulated by the FAA may submit regulatory interpretation questions, including anonymously, without fear of retaliation;

(B) FAA personnel may submit written questions, and receive written responses, as to whether a previous approval or regulatory interpretation issued by FAA personnel in another office or region is correct or incorrect; and

(C) any other person may submit written regulatory interpretation questions, including anonymously.

(2) Meet on a regular basis to discuss and resolve questions submitted pursuant to paragraph (1) and the appropriate application of regulations and policy with respect to each question.

(3) Provide to a person that submitted a question pursuant to subparagraph (A) or (B) of paragraph (1) a timely written response to the question.

(4) Establish a process to make resolutions of common regulatory interpretation questions publicly available to FAA

SEC. 231. [49 U.S.C. 44701 note] REGULATORY CONSISTENCY COMMUNICATIONS BOARD.

FAA Reauthorization Act of 2018

personnel, persons regulated by the FAA, and the public without revealing any identifying data of the person that submitted the question and in a manner that protects any proprietary information.

(5) Ensure the incorporation of resolutions of questions submitted pursuant to paragraph (1) into regulatory guidance documents, as such term is defined in section 223(d).

(6)[6] Submit recommendations, as needed, to the Assistant Administrator for Rulemaking and Regulatory Improvement for consideration.

---

[6] The placement of paragraph (6) at the end of subsection (d) reflects the probable intent of Congress. Section 823(2)(C) of Public Law 118–63 adds paragraph (6) to the end of paragraph (1).

(e) PERFORMANCE METRICS, TIMELINES, AND GOALS.—Not later than 180 days after the date on which the Advisory Committee recommends performance objectives and performance metrics for the FAA and the regulated aviation industry under section 202, the Administrator, in collaboration with the Advisory Committee, shall—

(1) establish performance metrics, timelines, and goals to measure the progress of the Board in resolving regulatory interpretation questions submitted pursuant to subsection (d)(1); and

(2) implement a process for tracking the progress of the Board in meeting the performance metrics, timelines, and goals established under paragraph (1).

Subtitle D—Safety Workforce

SEC. 231. SAFETY WORKFORCE TRAINING STRATEGY.

(a) SAFETY WORKFORCE TRAINING STRATEGY.—Not later than 60 days after the date of enactment of this Act, the Administrator shall review and revise its safety workforce training strategy to ensure that such strategy—

(1) aligns with an effective risk-based approach to safety oversight;

(2) best uses available resources;

SEC. 231. [49 U.S.C. 44701 note] REGULATORY CONSISTENCY COMMUNICATIONS BOARD.

FAA Reauthorization Act of

(3) allows FAA employees participating in organization management teams or conducting ODA program audits to complete, in a timely fashion, appropriate training, including recurrent training, in auditing and a systems safety approach to oversight;

(4) seeks knowledge-sharing opportunities between the FAA and the aviation industry in new technologies, equipment and systems, best practices, and other areas of interest related to safety oversight;

(5) functions within the current and anticipated budgetary environments;

(6) fosters an inspector and engineer workforce that has the skills and training necessary to improve risk-based approaches that focus on requirements management and auditing skills; and

(7) includes, as appropriate, milestones and metrics for meeting the requirements of paragraphs (1) through (5).

(b) REPORT.—Not later than 270 days after the date of the revision of the strategy required under subsection (a), the Administrator shall submit to the appropriate committees of Congress a report on the implementation of the strategy and progress in meeting any milestones and metrics included in the strategy.

(c) DEFINITIONS.—In this section, the following definitions apply:

(1) ODA; ODA HOLDER.—The terms "ODA" and "ODA holder" have the meanings given those terms in section 44736 of title 49, United States Code, as added by this Act.

(2) ODA PROGRAM.—The term "ODA program" means the program to standardize FAA management and oversight of the organizations that are approved to perform certain functions on behalf of the Administration under section 44702(d) of title 49, United States Code.

(3) ORGANIZATION MANAGEMENT TEAM.—The term "organization management team" means a team consisting of FAA aviation safety engineers, flight test pilots, and aviation safety inspectors overseeing an ODA holder and its certification activity.

SEC. 232. WORKFORCE REVIEW.

(a) WORKFORCE REVIEW.—Not later than 90 days after the date of enactment of this Act, the Comptroller General of the United States shall conduct a review to assess the workforce and training needs of the FAA Office of Aviation Safety in the anticipated budgetary environment.

(b) CONTENTS.—The review required under subsection (a) shall include—

(1) a review of current aviation safety inspector and aviation safety engineer hiring, training, and recurrent training requirements;

(2) an analysis of the skills and qualifications required of aviation safety inspectors and aviation safety engineers for successful performance in the current and future projected aviation safety regulatory environment, including the need for a systems engineering discipline within the FAA to guide the engineering of complex systems, with an emphasis on auditing designated authorities;

(3) a review of current performance incentive policies of the FAA, as applied to the Office of Aviation Safety, including awards for performance;

(4) an analysis of ways the FAA can work with industry and labor, including labor groups representing FAA aviation safety inspectors and aviation safety engineers, to establish knowledge-sharing opportunities between the FAA and the aviation industry regarding new equipment and systems, best practices, and other areas of interest; and

(5) recommendations on the most effective qualifications, training programs (including e-learning training), and performance incentive approaches to address the needs of the future projected aviation safety regulatory system in the anticipated budgetary environment.

(c) REPORT.—Not later than 270 days after the date of enactment of this Act, the Comptroller General shall submit to the appropriate committees of Congress a report on the results of the review required under subsection (a).

Subtitle E—International Aviation

* * * * * * *

SEC. 243. [49 U.S.C. 44701 note] FAA LEADERSHIP ABROAD.

(a) IN GENERAL.— To promote United States aerospace safety standards, reduce redundant regulatory activity, and facilitate acceptance of FAA design and production approvals abroad, the Administrator shall—

(1) attain greater expertise in issues related to dispute resolution, intellectual property, and export control laws to better support FAA certification and other aerospace regulatory activities abroad;

(2) work with United States companies to more accurately track the amount of time it takes foreign authorities, including bilateral partners, to validate United States certificated aeronautical products;

(3) provide assistance to United States companies that have experienced significantly long foreign validation wait times;

(4) work with foreign authorities, including bilateral partners, to collect and analyze data to determine the timeliness of the acceptance and validation of FAA design and production approvals by foreign authorities and the acceptance and validation of foreign-certified products by the FAA;

(5) establish appropriate benchmarks and metrics to measure the success of bilateral aviation safety agreements and to reduce the validation time for United States certificated aeronautical products abroad; and

(6) work with foreign authorities, including bilateral partners, to improve the timeliness of the acceptance and validation of FAA design and production approvals by foreign authorities and the acceptance and validation of foreign-certified products by the FAA.

(b) REPORT.— Not later than 1 year after the date of enactment of this Act, the Administrator shall submit to the appropriate committees of Congress a report that—

(1) describes the FAA's strategic plan for international engagement;

(2) describes the structure and responsibilities of all FAA offices that have international responsibilities, including the

Aircraft Certification Office, and all the activities conducted by those offices related to certification and production;

(3) describes current and forecasted staffing and travel needs for the FAA's international engagement activities, including the needs of the Aircraft Certification Office in the current and forecasted budgetary environment;

(4) provides recommendations, if appropriate, to improve the existing structure and personnel and travel policies supporting the FAA's international engagement activities, including the activities of the Aviation Certification Office, to better support the growth of United States aerospace exports; and

(5) identifies cost-effective policy initiatives, regulatory initiatives, or legislative initiatives needed to improve and enhance the timely acceptance of United States aerospace products abroad.

(c) INTERNATIONAL TRAVEL.— The Administrator, or the Administrator's designee, may authorize international travel for any FAA employee, without the approval of any other person or entity, if the Administrator determines that the travel is necessary—

(1) to promote United States aerospace safety standards; or

(2) to support expedited acceptance of FAA design and production approvals.

* * * * * * *

SELECTED PROVISIONS OF THE FAA EXTENSION, SAFETY, AND SECURITY ACT OF 2016

PUBLIC LAW 114-190

FAA EXTENSION, SAFETY, AND SECURITY ACT OF 2016

[(Public Law 114–190)]

[As Amended Through P.L. 118–63, Enacted May 16, 2024]

AN ACT To amend title 49, United States Code, to extend authorizations for the airport improvement program, to amend the Internal Revenue Code of 1986 to extend the funding and expenditure authority of the Airport and Airway Trust Fund, and for other purposes.

Be it enacted by the Senate and House of Representatives of the United States of America in Congress assembled,

SECTION 1. [49 U.S.C. 40101 note] SHORT TITLE; TABLE OF CONTENTS.

(a) SHORT TITLE.—This Act may be cited as the "FAA Extension, Safety, and Security Act of 2016".

(b) TABLE OF CONTENTS.—The table of contents for this Act is as follows:

SEC. 2. [49 U.S.C. 40101 note] APPROPRIATE
COMMITTEES OF CONGRESS DEFINED.

FAA Extension, Safety, and Security Act of

**SEC. 2. [49 U.S.C. 40101 note] APPROPRIATE COMMITTEES OF
CONGRESS DEFINED.**

In this Act, unless expressly provided otherwise, the term
"appropriate committees of Congress" means the Committee on
Commerce, Science, and Transportation of the Senate and the
Committee on Transportation and Infrastructure of the House of
Representatives.

* * * * * * *

TITLE II—AVIATION SAFETY CRITICAL REFORMS

Subtitle A—Safety

* * * * * * *

SEC. 2104. [49 U.S.C. 46301 note] LASER POINTER INCIDENTS.

(a) IN GENERAL.—Beginning 90 days after the date of
enactment of this Act, the Administrator of the Federal Aviation
Administration, in coordination with appropriate Federal law
enforcement agencies, shall provide annually an annual briefing to
the appropriate committees of Congress regarding—

(1) the number of incidents involving the beam from a laser
pointer (as defined in section 39A of title 18, United States
Code) being aimed at, or in the flight path of, an aircraft in the
airspace jurisdiction of the United States;

(2) the number of civil or criminal enforcement actions
taken by the Federal Aviation Administration, the Department
of Transportation, or another Federal agency with regard to the

EC. 2109. [49 U.S.C. 44701 note] ADDITIONAL
ERTIFICATION RESOURCES.

FAA Extension, Safety, and Security Act of 2016

incidents described in paragraph (1), including the amount of
the civil or criminal penalties imposed on violators;

(3) the resolution of any incidents described in paragraph
(1) that did not result in a civil or criminal enforcement action;
and

(4) any actions the Department of Transportation or
another Federal agency has taken on its own, or in conjunction
with other Federal agencies or local law enforcement agencies,
to deter the type of activity described in paragraph (1).

(b) CIVIL PENALTIES.—The Administrator shall revise the
maximum civil penalty that may be imposed on an individual who
aims the beam of a laser pointer at an aircraft in the airspace
jurisdiction of the United States, or at the flight path of such an
aircraft, to be $25,000.

(c) REPORT SUNSET.—Subsection (a) shall cease to be effective
after September 30, 2028.

* * * * * * *

SEC. 2109. [49 U.S.C. 44701 note] ADDITIONAL CERTIFICATION
RESOURCES.

(a) IN GENERAL.—Notwithstanding any other provision of law,
and subject to the requirements of subsection (b), the Administrator
of the FAA may enter into a reimbursable agreement with an
applicant or certificate-holder for the reasonable travel and per
diem expenses of the FAA associated with official travel to expedite
the acceptance or validation by a foreign authority of an FAA
certificate or design approval or the acceptance or validation by the
FAA of a foreign authority certificate or design approval.

(b) CONDITIONS.—The Administrator may enter into an
agreement under subsection (a) only if—

(1) the travel covered under the agreement is deemed
necessary, by both the Administrator and the applicant or
certificate-holder, to expedite the acceptance or validation of
the relevant certificate or approval;

(2) the travel is conducted at the request of the applicant or
certificate-holder;

(3) travel plans and expenses are approved by the applicant
or certificate-holder prior to travel; and

(4) the agreement requires payment in advance of FAA services and is consistent with the processes under section 106(l)(6) of title 49, United States Code.

(c) REPORT.—Not later than 2 years after the date of enactment of this Act, the Administrator shall submit to the appropriate committees of Congress a report on—

(1) the number of occasions on which the Administrator entered into reimbursable agreements under this section;

(2) the number of occasions on which the Administrator declined a request by an applicant or certificate-holder to enter into a reimbursable agreement under this section;

(3) the amount of reimbursements collected in accordance with agreements under this section; and

(4) the extent to which reimbursable agreements under this section assisted in reducing the amount of time necessary for validations of certificates and design approvals.

(d) DEFINITIONS.—In this section, the following definitions apply:

(1) APPLICANT.—The term "applicant" means a person that has—

(A) applied to a foreign authority for the acceptance or validation of an FAA certificate or design approval; or

(B) applied to the FAA for the acceptance or validation of a foreign authority certificate or design approval.

(2) CERTIFICATE-HOLDER.—The term "certificate-holder" means a person that holds a certificate issued by the Administrator under part 21 of title 14, Code of Federal Regulations.

(3) FAA.—The term "FAA" means the Federal Aviation Administration.

SEC. 2110. [49 U.S.C. 44718 note] TOWER MARKING.

(a) APPLICATION.—

(1) IN GENERAL.—Except as provided by paragraph (2), not later than 18 months after the date of enactment of the FAA Reauthorization Act of 2018 or the date of availability of the database developed by the Administrator pursuant to subsection (c), whichever is later, all covered towers shall be

either—

(A) clearly marked consistent with applicable guidance in the advisory circular of the FAA issued December 4, 2015 (AC 70/7460-IL); or

(B) included in the database described in subsection (c).

(2) METEOROLOGICAL EVALUATION TOWER.—A covered tower that is a meteorological evaluation tower shall be subject to the requirements of subparagraphs (A) and (B) of paragraph (1).

(b) DEFINITIONS.—

(1) IN GENERAL.—In this section, the following definitions apply:

(A) COVERED TOWER.—

(i) IN GENERAL.—The term "covered tower" means a structure that—

(I) is a meteorological evaluation tower, a self-standing tower, or tower supported by guy wires and ground anchors;

(II) is 10 feet or less in diameter at the above-ground base, excluding concrete footing;

(III) at the highest point of the structure is at least 50 feet above ground level;

(IV) at the highest point of the structure is not more than 200 feet above ground level;

(V) has accessory facilities on which an antenna, sensor, camera, meteorological instrument, or other equipment is mounted; and

(VI) is located on land that is—

(aa) in a rural area; and

(bb) used for agricultural purposes or immediately adjacent to such land.

(ii) EXCLUSIONS.—The term "covered tower" does not include any structure that—

(I) is adjacent to a house, barn, electric utility station, or other building;

(II) is within the curtilage of a farmstead or

adjacent to another building or visible structure;

(III) supports electric utility transmission or distribution lines;

(IV) is a wind-powered electrical generator with a rotor blade radius that exceeds 6 feet;

(V) is a street light erected or maintained by a Federal, State, local, or tribal entity;

(VI) is designed and constructed to resemble a tree or visible structure other than a tower;

(VII) is an advertising billboard;

(VIII) is located within the right-of-way of a rail carrier, including within the boundaries of a rail yard, and is used for a railroad purpose;

(IX)(aa) is registered with the Federal Communications Commission under the Antenna Structure Registration program set forth under part 17 of title 47, Code of Federal Regulations; and

(bb) is determined by the Administrator to pose no hazard to air navigation; or

(X) has already mitigated any hazard to aviation safety in accordance with Federal Aviation Administration guidance or as otherwise approved by the Administrator.

(B) RURAL AREA.—The term "rural area" has the meaning given the term in section 609(a)(5) of the Public Utility Regulatory Policies Act of 1978 (7 U.S.C. 918c(a)(5)).

(C) AGRICULTURAL PURPOSES.—The term "agricultural purposes" means farming in all its branches and the cultivation and tillage of the soil, the production, cultivation, growing, and harvesting of any agricultural or horticultural commodities performed by a farmer or on a farm, or on pasture land or rangeland.

(2) OTHER DEFINITIONS.—The Administrator shall define such other terms as may be necessary to carry out this section.

(c) DATABASE.—The Administrator shall—

(1) develop a new database, or if appropriate use an existing database that meets the requirements under this

section, that contains the location and height of each covered tower that, pursuant to subsection (a), the owner or operator of such tower elects not to mark (unless the Administrator has determined that there is a significant safety risk requiring that the tower be marked), except that meteorological evaluation towers shall be marked and contained in the database;

(2) keep the database current to the extent practicable;

(3) ensure that any proprietary information in the database is protected from disclosure in accordance with law;

(4) ensure that, by virtue of accessing the database, users agree and acknowledge that information in the database—

(A) may only be used for aviation safety purposes; and

(B) may not be disclosed for purposes other than aviation safety, regardless of whether or not the information is marked or labeled as proprietary or with a similar designation;

(5) ensure that the tower information in the database is de-identified and that the information only includes the location and height of covered towers and whether the tower has guy wires;

(6) ensure that information in the dataset is encrypted at rest and in transit and is protected from unauthorized access and acquisition;

(7) ensure that towers excluded from the definition of covered tower under subsection (d)(1)(B)(ii)(VIII) must be registered by its owner in the database;

(8) ensure that a tower to be included in the database pursuant to subsection (c)(1) and constructed after the date on which the database is fully operational is submitted by its owner to the FAA for inclusion in the database before its construction;

(9) ensure that pilots who intend to conduct low-altitude operations in locations described in subsection (b)(1)(A)(i)(VI) consult the relevant parts of the database before conducting such operations; and

(10) make the database available for use not later than 1 year after the date of enactment of the FAA Reauthorization Act of 2018.

(d) EXCLUSION AND WAIVER AUTHORITIES.—As part of a rulemaking conducted pursuant to this section, the Administrator—

(1) may exclude a class, category, or type of tower that is determined by the Administrator, after public notice and comment, to not pose a hazard to aviation safety;

(2) shall establish a process to waive specific covered towers from the marking requirements under this section as required under the rulemaking if the Administrator later determines such tower or towers do not pose a hazard to aviation safety;

(3) shall consider, in establishing exclusions and granting waivers under this subsection, factors that may sufficiently mitigate risks to aviation safety, such as the length of time the tower has been in existence or alternative marking methods or technologies that maintains a tower's level of conspicuousness to a degree which adequately maintains the safety of the airspace; and

(4) shall consider excluding towers located in a State that has enacted tower marking requirements according to the Federal Aviation Administration's recommended guidance for the voluntary marking of meteorological evaluation towers erected in remote and rural areas that are less than 200 feet above ground level to enhance the conspicuity of the towers for low level agricultural operations in the vicinity of those towers.

(e) PERIODIC REVIEW.—The Administrator shall, in consultation with the Federal Communications Commission, periodically review any regulations or guidance regarding the marking of covered towers issued pursuant to this section and update them as necessary, consistent with this section, and in the interest of safety of low-altitude aircraft operations.

(f) FCC REGULATIONS.—The Federal Communications Commission shall amend section 17.7 of title 47, Code of Federal Regulations, to require a notification to the Federal Aviation Administration for any construction or alteration of an antenna structure, as defined in section 17.2(a) of title 47, Code of Federal Regulations, that is a covered tower as defined by this section.

SEC. 2111. [49 U.S.C. 44903 note] AVIATION CYBERSECURITY.

(a) COMPREHENSIVE AND STRATEGIC AVIATION FRAMEWORK.—

(1) IN GENERAL.—Not later than 240 days after the date

of enactment of this Act, the Administrator of the Federal Aviation Administration shall facilitate and support the development of a comprehensive and strategic framework of principles and policies to reduce cybersecurity risks to the national airspace system, civil aviation, and agency information systems using a total systems approach that takes into consideration the interactions and interdependence of different components of aircraft systems and the national airspace system.

(2) SCOPE.—In carrying out paragraph (1), the Administrator shall—

(A) identify and address the cybersecurity risks associated with—

(i) the modernization of the national airspace system;

(ii) the automation of aircraft, equipment, and technology; and

(iii) aircraft systems, including by—

(I) directing the Aircraft Systems Information Security Protection Working Group—

(aa) to assess cybersecurity risks to aircraft systems;

(bb) to review the extent to which existing rulemaking, policy, and guidance to promote safety also promote aircraft systems information security protection; and

(cc) to provide appropriate recommendations to the Administrator if separate or additional rulemaking, policy, or guidance is needed to address cybersecurity risks to aircraft systems; and

(II) identifying and addressing—

(aa) cybersecurity risks associated with in-flight entertainment systems; and

(bb) whether in-flight entertainment systems can and should be isolated and separate, such as through an air gap, under existing rulemaking, policy, and guidance;

(B) clarify cybersecurity roles and responsibilities of offices and employees of the Federal Aviation Administration, as the roles and responsibilities relate to cybersecurity at the Federal Aviation Administration;

(C) identify and implement objectives and actions to reduce cybersecurity risks to air traffic control information systems, including actions to improve implementation of information security standards, such as those of the National Institute of Standards and Technology;

(D) support voluntary efforts by industry, RTCA, Inc., and other standards-setting organizations to develop and identify consensus standards and best practices relating to guidance on aviation systems information security protection, consistent, to the extent appropriate, with the cybersecurity risk management activities described in section 2(e) of the National Institute of Standards and Technology Act (15 U.S.C. 272(e));

(E) establish guidelines for the voluntary exchange of information between and among aviation stakeholders pertaining to aviation-related cybersecurity incidents, threats, and vulnerabilities;

(F) identify short- and long-term objectives and actions that can be taken in response to cybersecurity risks to the national airspace system; and

(G) identify research and development activities to inform actions in response to cybersecurity risks.

(3) IMPLEMENTATION REQUIREMENTS.—In carrying out the activities under this subsection, the Administrator shall—

(A) coordinate with aviation stakeholders, including, at a minimum, representatives of industry, airlines, manufacturers, airports, RTCA, Inc., and unions;

(B) consult with the heads of relevant agencies and with international regulatory authorities;

(C) if determined appropriate, convene an expert panel or working group to identify and address cybersecurity risks; and

(D) evaluate, on a periodic basis, the effectiveness of the principles established under this subsection.

(b) UPDATE ON CYBERSECURITY IMPLEMENTATION PROGRESS.—Not later than 90 days after the date of enactment of this Act, the Administrator shall provide to the appropriate committees of Congress an update on progress made toward the implementation of this section.

(c) CYBERSECURITY THREAT MODEL.—Not later than 1 year after the date of enactment of this Act, the Administrator, in consultation with the Director of the National Institute of Standards and Technology, shall implement the open recommendation issued in 2015 by the Government Accountability Office to assess and research the potential cost and timetable of developing and maintaining an agencywide threat model, which shall be updated regularly, to strengthen the cybersecurity of agency systems across the Federal Aviation Administration. The Administrator shall brief the Committee on Science, Space, and Technology and the Committee on Transportation and Infrastructure of the House of Representatives and the Committee on Commerce, Science, and Transportation of the Senate on the status, results, and composition of the threat model.

(d) NATIONAL INSTITUTE OF STANDARDS AND TECHNOLOGY INFORMATION SECURITY STANDARDS.—Not later than 180 days after the date of enactment of this Act, the Administrator of the Federal Aviation Administration, after consultation with the Director of the National Institute of Standards and Technology, shall transmit to the Committee on Science, Space, and Technology and the Committee on Transportation and Infrastructure of the House of Representatives and the Committee on Commerce, Science, and Transportation of the Senate a report on—

(1) a cybersecurity standards plan to improve implementation of the National Institute of Standards and Technology's latest revisions to information security guidance for Federal Aviation Administration information and Federal Aviation Administration information systems within set timeframes; and

(2) an explanation of why any such revisions are not incorporated in the plan or are not incorporated within set timeframes.

(e) CYBERSECURITY RESEARCH AND DEVELOPMENT.—Not later than 1 year after the date of enactment of this Act, the Administrator, in consultation with other agencies as appropriate, shall establish a cybersecurity research and development plan for the national airspace system, including—

(1) any proposal for research and development cooperation with international partners;

(2) an evaluation and determination of research and development needs to determine any cybersecurity risks of cabin communications and cabin information technology systems on board in the passenger domain; and

(3) objectives, proposed tasks, milestones, and a 5-year budgetary profile.

* * * * * * *

Subtitle C—Time Sensitive Aviation Reforms

* * * * * * *

SEC. 2303. WORKING GROUP ON IMPROVING AIR SERVICE TO SMALL COMMUNITIES.

(a) IN GENERAL.—Not later than 120 days after the date of enactment of this Act, the Secretary of Transportation shall establish a working group—

(1) to identify obstacles to attracting and maintaining air transportation service to and from small communities; and

(2) to develop recommendations for maintaining and improving air transportation service to and from small communities.

(b) OUTREACH.—In carrying out subsection (a), the working group shall consult with—

(1) interested Governors;

(2) representatives of State and local agencies, and other officials and groups, representing rural States and other rural areas;

(3) other representatives of relevant State and local agencies; and

(4) members of the public with experience in aviation safety, pilot training, economic development, and related

issues.

(c) CONSIDERATIONS.—In carrying out subsection (a), the working group shall—

(1) consider whether funding for, and the terms of, current or potential new programs are sufficient to help ensure continuation of or improvement to air transportation service to small communities, including the essential air service program and the small community air service development program;

(2) identify initiatives to help support pilot training and aviation safety to maintain air transportation service to small communities;

(3) consider whether Federal funding for airports serving small communities, including airports that have lost air transportation services or had decreased enplanements in recent years, is adequate to ensure that small communities have access to quality, affordable air transportation service;

(4) identify innovative State or local efforts that have established public-private partnerships that are successful in attracting and retaining air transportation service in small communities; and

(5) consider such other issues as the Secretary considers appropriate.

(d) COMPOSITION.—

(1) IN GENERAL.—The working group shall be facilitated through the Secretary or the Secretary's designee.

(2) MEMBERSHIP.—Members of the working group shall be appointed by the Secretary and shall include representatives of—

(A) State and local government, including State and local aviation officials;

(B) State Governors;

(C) aviation safety experts;

(D) economic development officials; and

(E) the traveling public from small communities.

(e) REPORT AND RECOMMENDATIONS.—Not later than 1 year after the date of enactment of this Act, the Secretary shall submit to the appropriate committees of Congress a report, including—

SEC. 2305. [49 U.S.C. 41704 note] REFUNDS
FOR DELAYED BAGGAGE.

FAA Extension, Safety, and Security Act of

(1) a summary of the views expressed by the participants in the outreach under subsection (b);

(2) a description of the working group's findings, including the identification of any areas of general consensus among the non-Federal participants in the outreach under subsection (b); and

(3) any recommendations for legislative or regulatory action that would assist in maintaining and improving air transportation service to and from small communities.

* * * * * * *

SEC. 2305. [49 U.S.C. 41704 note] REFUNDS FOR DELAYED BAGGAGE.

(a) IN GENERAL.—Not later than 1 year after the date of enactment of this Act, the Secretary of Transportation shall issue final regulations to require an air carrier or foreign air carrier to promptly provide to a passenger an automated refund for any ancillary fees paid by the passenger for checked baggage if—

(1) the air carrier or foreign air carrier fails to deliver the checked baggage to the passenger—

(A) not later than 12 hours after the arrival of a domestic flight; or

(B) not later than 15 hours after the arrival of an international flight; and

(2) the passenger has notified the air carrier or foreign air carrier of the lost or delayed checked baggage.

(b) EXCEPTION.—If, as part of the rulemaking, the Secretary makes a determination on the record that a requirement under subsection (a) is not feasible and would adversely affect consumers in certain cases, the Secretary may modify 1 or both of the deadlines specified in subsection (a)(1) for such cases, except that—

(1) the deadline relating to a domestic flight may not exceed 18 hours after the arrival of the domestic flight; and

(2) the deadline relating to an international flight may not exceed 30 hours after the arrival of the international flight.

SEC. 2306. CONTRACT WEATHER OBSERVERS.

(a) IN GENERAL.—Not later than 1 year after the date of

enactment of this Act, the Administrator of the Federal Aviation Administration shall submit to the appropriate committees of Congress a report, which includes public and stakeholder input—

(1) examining the safety risks, hazard effects, and efficiency and operational effects for airports, airlines, and other stakeholders that could result from a loss of contract weather observer service at the 57 airports targeted for the loss of the service;

(2) detailing how the Federal Aviation Administration will accurately report rapidly changing severe weather conditions at the airports, including thunderstorms, lightning, fog, visibility, smoke, dust, haze, cloud layers and ceilings, ice pellets, and freezing rain or drizzle, without contract weather observers;

(3) indicating how airports can comply with applicable Federal Aviation Administration orders governing weather observations given the current documented limitations of automated surface observing systems; and

(4) identifying the process through which the Federal Aviation Administration analyzed the safety hazards associated with the elimination of the contract weather observer program.

(b) CONTINUED USE OF CONTRACT WEATHER OBSERVERS.—The Administrator may not discontinue or diminish the contract weather observer program at any airport until September 30, 2028.

SEC. 2307. [49 U.S.C. 44703 note] MEDICAL CERTIFICATION OF CERTAIN SMALL AIRCRAFT PILOTS.

(a) IN GENERAL.—Not later than 180 days after the date of enactment of this Act, the Administrator of the Federal Aviation Administration shall issue or revise regulations to ensure that an individual may operate as pilot in command of a covered aircraft if—

(1) the individual possesses a valid driver's license issued by a State, territory, or possession of the United States and complies with all medical requirements or restrictions associated with that license;

(2) the individual holds a medical certificate issued by the Federal Aviation Administration or has held such a certificate at any time after July 14, 2006;

(3) the most recent medical certificate issued by the Federal Aviation Administration to the individual—

(A) indicates whether the certificate is first, second, or third class;

(B) may include authorization for special issuance;

(C) may be expired;

(D) cannot have been revoked or suspended; and

(E) cannot have been withdrawn;

(4) the most recent application for airman medical certification submitted to the Federal Aviation Administration by the individual cannot have been completed and denied;

(5) the individual has completed a medical education course described in subsection (c) during the 24 calendar months before acting as pilot in command of a covered aircraft and demonstrates proof of completion of the course;

(6) the individual, when serving as a pilot in command, is under the care and treatment of a physician if the individual has been diagnosed with any medical condition that may impact the ability of the individual to fly;

(7) the individual has received a comprehensive medical examination from a State-licensed physician during the previous 48 calendar months and—

(A) prior to the examination, the individual—

(i) completed the individual's section of the checklist described in subsection (b); and

(ii) provided the completed checklist to the physician performing the examination; and

(B) the physician conducted the comprehensive medical examination in accordance with the checklist described in subsection (b), checking each item specified during the examination and addressing, as medically appropriate, every medical condition listed, and any medications the individual is taking; and

(8) the individual is operating in accordance with the following conditions:

(A) The covered aircraft is carrying not more than 6 passengers.

(B) The individual is operating the covered aircraft under visual flight rules or instrument flight rules.

(C) The flight, including each portion of that flight, is not carried out—

(i) for compensation or hire, including that no passenger or property on the flight is being carried for compensation or hire;

(ii) at an altitude that is more than 18,000 feet above mean sea level;

(iii) outside the United States, unless authorized by the country in which the flight is conducted; or

(iv) at an indicated air speed exceeding 250 knots.

(b) COMPREHENSIVE MEDICAL EXAMINATION.—

(1) IN GENERAL.—Not later than 180 days after the date of enactment of this Act, the Administrator shall develop a checklist for an individual to complete and provide to the physician performing the comprehensive medical examination required in subsection (a)(7).

(2) REQUIREMENTS.—The checklist shall contain—

(A) a section, for the individual to complete that contains—

(i) boxes 3 through 13 and boxes 16 through 19 of the Federal Aviation Administration Form 8500-8 (3-99) (or any successor form) ; and

(ii) a signature line for the individual to affirm that—

(I) the answers provided by the individual on that checklist, including the individual's answers regarding medical history, are true and complete;

(II) the individual understands that he or she is prohibited under Federal Aviation Administration regulations from acting as pilot in command, or any other capacity as a required flight crew member, if he or she knows or has reason to know of any medical deficiency or medically disqualifying condition that would make the individual unable to operate the aircraft in a safe manner; and

(III) the individual is aware of the regulations pertaining to the prohibition on operations during medical deficiency and has no medically disqualifying conditions in accordance with applicable law;

(B) a section with instructions for the individual to provide the completed checklist to the physician performing the comprehensive medical examination required in subsection (a)(7); and

(C) a section, for the physician to complete, that instructs the physician—

(i) to perform a clinical examination of—

(I) head, face, neck, and scalp;

(II) nose, sinuses, mouth, and throat;

(III) ears, general (internal and external canals), and eardrums (perforation);

(IV) eyes (general), ophthalmoscopic, pupils (equality and reaction), and ocular motility (associated parallel movement, nystagmus);

(V) lungs and chest (not including breast examination);

(VI) heart (precordial activity, rhythm, sounds, and murmurs);

(VII) vascular system (pulse, amplitude, and character, and arms, legs, and others);

(VIII) abdomen and viscera (including hernia);

(IX) anus (not including digital examination);

(X) skin;

(XI) G-U system (not including pelvic examination);

(XII) upper and lower extremities (strength and range of motion);

(XIII) spine and other musculoskeletal;

(XIV) identifying body marks, scars, and tattoos (size and location);

(XV) lymphatics;

(XVI) neurologic (tendon reflexes, equilibrium, senses, cranial nerves, and coordination, etc.);

(XVII) psychiatric (appearance, behavior, mood, communication, and memory);

(XVIII) general systemic;

(XIX) hearing;

(XX) vision (distant, near, and intermediate vision, field of vision, color vision, and ocular alignment);

(XXI) blood pressure and pulse; and

(XXII) anything else the physician, in his or her medical judgment, considers necessary;

(ii) to exercise medical discretion to address, as medically appropriate, any medical conditions identified, and to exercise medical discretion in determining whether any medical tests are warranted as part of the comprehensive medical examination;

(iii) to discuss all drugs the individual reports taking (prescription and nonprescription) and their potential to interfere with the safe operation of an aircraft or motor vehicle;

(iv) to sign the checklist, stating: "I certify that I discussed all items on this checklist with the individual during my examination, discussed any medications the individual is taking that could interfere with their ability to safely operate an aircraft or motor vehicle, and performed an examination that included all of the items on this checklist. I certify that I am not aware of any medical condition that, as presently treated, could interfere with the individual's ability to safely operate an aircraft."; and

(v) to provide the date the comprehensive medical examination was completed, and the physician's full name, address, telephone number, and State medical license number.

(3) LOGBOOK.—The completed checklist shall be retained in the individual's logbook and made available on request.

(c) MEDICAL EDUCATION COURSE REQUIREMENTS.—The medical education course described in this subsection shall—

(1) be available on the Internet free of charge;

(2) be developed and periodically updated in coordination with representatives of relevant nonprofit and not-for-profit general aviation stakeholder groups;

(3) educate pilots on conducting medical self-assessments;

(4) advise pilots on identifying warning signs of potential serious medical conditions;

(5) identify risk mitigation strategies for medical conditions;

(6) increase awareness of the impacts of potentially impairing over-the-counter and prescription drug medications;

(7) encourage regular medical examinations and consultations with primary care physicians;

(8) inform pilots of the regulations pertaining to the prohibition on operations during medical deficiency and medically disqualifying conditions;

(9) provide the checklist developed by the Federal Aviation Administration in accordance with subsection (b); and

(10) upon successful completion of the course, electronically provide to the individual and transmit to the Federal Aviation Administration—

(A) a certification of completion of the medical education course, which shall be printed and retained in the individual's logbook and made available upon request, and shall contain the individual's name, address, and airman certificate number;

(B) subject to subsection (d), a release authorizing the National Driver Register through a designated State Department of Motor Vehicles to furnish to the Federal Aviation Administration information pertaining to the individual's driving record;

(C) a certification by the individual that the individual is under the care and treatment of a physician if the individual has been diagnosed with any medical condition that may impact the ability of the individual to fly, as required under subsection (a)(6);

(D) a form that includes—

(i) the name, address, telephone number, and airman certificate number of the individual;

(ii) the name, address, telephone number, and State medical license number of the physician performing the comprehensive medical examination required in subsection (a)(7);

(iii) the date of the comprehensive medical examination required in subsection (a)(7); and

(iv) a certification by the individual that the checklist described in subsection (b) was followed and signed by the physician in the comprehensive medical examination required in subsection (a)(7); and

(E) a statement, which shall be printed, and signed by the individual certifying that the individual understands the existing prohibition on operations during medical deficiency by stating: "I understand that I cannot act as pilot in command, or any other capacity as a required flight crew member, if I know or have reason to know of any medical condition that would make me unable to operate the aircraft in a safe manner.".

(d) NATIONAL DRIVER REGISTER.—The authorization under subsection (c)(10)(B) shall be an authorization for a single access to the information contained in the National Driver Register.

(e) SPECIAL ISSUANCE PROCESS.—

(1) IN GENERAL.—An individual who has qualified for the third-class medical certificate exemption under subsection (a) and is seeking to serve as a pilot in command of a covered aircraft shall be required to have completed the process for obtaining an Authorization for Special Issuance of a Medical Certificate for each of the following:

(A) A mental health disorder, limited to an established medical history or clinical diagnosis of—

(i) personality disorder that is severe enough to have repeatedly manifested itself by overt acts;

(ii) psychosis, defined as a case in which an individual—

(I) has manifested delusions, hallucinations,

283

grossly bizarre or disorganized behavior, or other commonly accepted symptoms of psychosis; or

(II) may reasonably be expected to manifest delusions, hallucinations, grossly bizarre or disorganized behavior, or other commonly accepted symptoms of psychosis;

(iii) bipolar disorder; or

(iv) substance dependence within the previous 2 years, as defined in section 67.307(a)(4) of title 14, Code of Federal Regulations.

(B) A neurological disorder, limited to an established medical history or clinical diagnosis of any of the following:

(i) Epilepsy.

(ii) Disturbance of consciousness without satisfactory medical explanation of the cause.

(iii) A transient loss of control of nervous system functions without satisfactory medical explanation of the cause.

(C) A cardiovascular condition, limited to a one-time special issuance for each diagnosis of the following:

(i) Myocardial infraction.

(ii) Coronary heart disease that has required treatment.

(iii) Cardiac valve replacement.

(iv) Heart replacement.

(2) SPECIAL RULE FOR CARDIOVASCULAR CONDITIONS.—In the case of an individual with a cardiovascular condition, the process for obtaining an Authorization for Special Issuance of a Medical Certificate shall be satisfied with the successful completion of an appropriate clinical evaluation without a mandatory wait period.

(3) SPECIAL RULE FOR MENTAL HEALTH CONDITIONS.—

(A) IN GENERAL.—In the case of an individual with a clinically diagnosed mental health condition, the third-class medical certificate exemption under subsection (a) shall not apply if—

(i) in the judgment of the individual's State-licensed medical specialist, the condition—

(I) renders the individual unable to safely perform the duties or exercise the airman privileges described in subsection (a)(8); or

(II) may reasonably be expected to make the individual unable to perform the duties or exercise the privileges described in subsection (a)(8); or

(ii) the individual's driver's license is revoked by the issuing agency as a result of a clinically diagnosed mental health condition.

(B) CERTIFICATION.—Subject to subparagraph (A), an individual clinically diagnosed with a mental health condition shall certify every 2 years, in conjunction with the certification under subsection (c)(10)(C), that the individual is under the care of a State-licensed medical specialist for that mental health condition.

(4) SPECIAL RULE FOR NEUROLOGICAL CONDITIONS.—

(A) IN GENERAL.—In the case of an individual with a clinically diagnosed neurological condition, the third-class medical certificate exemption under subsection (a) shall not apply if—

(i) in the judgment of the individual's State-licensed medical specialist, the condition—

(I) renders the individual unable to safely perform the duties or exercise the airman privileges described in subsection (a)(8); or

(II) may reasonably be expected to make the individual unable to perform the duties or exercise the privileges described in subsection (a)(8); or

(ii) the individual's driver's license is revoked by the issuing agency as a result of a clinically diagnosed neurological condition.

(B) CERTIFICATION.—Subject to subparagraph (A), an individual clinically diagnosed with a neurological condition shall certify every 2 years, in conjunction with the certification under subsection (c)(10)(C), that the individual is under the care of a State-licensed medical specialist for that neurological condition.

(f) IDENTIFICATION OF ADDITIONAL MEDICAL CONDITIONS FOR CACI PROGRAM.—

(1) IN GENERAL.—Not later than 180 days after the date of enactment of this Act, the Administrator shall review and identify additional medical conditions that could be added to the program known as the Conditions AMEs Can Issue (CACI) program.

(2) CONSULTATIONS.—In carrying out paragraph (1), the Administrator shall consult with aviation, medical, and union stakeholders.

(3) REPORT REQUIRED.—Not later than 180 days after the date of enactment of this Act, the Administrator shall submit to the appropriate committees of Congress a report listing the medical conditions that have been added to the CACI program under paragraph (1).

(g) EXPEDITED AUTHORIZATION FOR SPECIAL ISSUANCE OF A MEDICAL CERTIFICATE.—

(1) IN GENERAL.—The Administrator shall implement procedures to expedite the process for obtaining an Authorization for Special Issuance of a Medical Certificate under section 67.401 of title 14, Code of Federal Regulations.

(2) CONSULTATIONS.—In carrying out paragraph (1), the Administrator shall consult with aviation, medical, and union stakeholders.

(3) REPORT REQUIRED.—Not later than 1 year after the date of enactment of this Act, the Administrator shall submit to the appropriate committees of Congress a report describing how the procedures implemented under paragraph (1) will streamline the process for obtaining an Authorization for Special Issuance of a Medical Certificate and reduce the amount of time needed to review and decide special issuance cases.

(h) REPORT REQUIRED.—Not later than 4 years after the date of enactment of the FAA Reauthorization Act of 2024, the Administrator, in coordination with the National Transportation Safety Board, shall submit to the Committee on Transportation and Infrastructure of the House of Representatives and the Committee on Commerce, Science, and Transportation of the Senate a report that describes the effect of the regulations issued or revised under subsection (a) and includes statistics with respect to changes in small aircraft activity and safety incidents.

(i) PROHIBITION ON ENFORCEMENT ACTIONS.—Beginning on the date that is 1 year after the date of enactment of this Act, the Administrator may not take an enforcement action for not holding a valid third-class medical certificate against a pilot of a covered aircraft for a flight if the pilot and the flight meet, through a good faith effort, the applicable requirements under subsection (a), except paragraph (5) of that subsection, unless the Administrator has published final regulations in the Federal Register under that subsection.

(j) COVERED AIRCRAFT DEFINED.—In this section, the term "covered aircraft" means an aircraft that—

(1) is authorized under Federal law to carry not more than 7 occupants;

(2) has a maximum certificated takeoff weight of not more than 12,500 pounds; and

(3) is not a transport category rotorcraft certified to airworthiness standards under part 29 of title 14, Code of Federal Regulations.

(k) OPERATIONS COVERED.—The provisions and requirements covered in this section do not apply to pilots who elect to operate under the medical requirements under subsection (b) or subsection (c) of section 61.23 of title 14, Code of Federal Regulations.

(l) AUTHORITY TO REQUIRE ADDITIONAL INFORMATION.—

(1) IN GENERAL.—If the Administrator receives credible or urgent information, including from the National Driver Register or the Administrator's Safety Hotline, that reflects on an individual's ability to safely operate a covered aircraft under the third-class medical certificate exemption in subsection (a), the Administrator may require the individual to provide additional information or history so that the Administrator may determine whether the individual is safe to continue operating a covered aircraft.

(2) USE OF INFORMATION.—The Administrator may use credible or urgent information received under paragraph (1) to request an individual to provide additional information or to take actions under section 44709(b) of title 49, United States Code.

* * * * * * *

SEC. 2309. [49 U.S.C. 42301note] FAMILY SEATING.

(a) IN GENERAL.—Not later than 1 year after the date of enactment of this Act, the Secretary of Transportation shall review and, if appropriate, establish a policy directing all air carriers providing scheduled passenger interstate or intrastate air transportation to establish policies that enable a child, who is age 13 or under on the date an applicable flight is scheduled to occur, to be seated in a seat adjacent to the seat of an accompanying family member over the age of 13, to the maximum extent practicable and at no additional cost, except when assignment to an adjacent seat would require an upgrade to another cabin class or a seat with extra legroom or seat pitch for which additional payment is normally required.

(b) EFFECT ON AIRLINE BOARDING AND SEATING POLICIES.—When considering any new policy under this section, the Secretary shall consider the traditional seating and boarding policies of air carriers providing scheduled passenger interstate or intrastate air transportation and whether those policies generally allow families to sit together.

(c) STATUTORY CONSTRUCTION.—Notwithstanding the requirement in subsection (a), nothing in this section may be construed to allow the Secretary to impose a significant change in the overall seating or boarding policy of an air carrier providing scheduled passenger interstate or intrastate air transportation that has an open or flexible seating policy in place that generally allows adjacent family seating as described in subsection (a).

* * * * * * *

SELECTED PROVISIONS OF THE FAA MODERNIZATION AND REFORM ACT OF 2012

PUBLIC LAW 112-95

FAA MODERNIZATION AND REFORM ACT OF 2012

[(Public Law 112–95)]

[As Amended Through P.L. 118–63, Enacted May 16, 2024]

AN ACT To amend title 49, United States Code, to authorize appropriations for the Federal Aviation Administration for fiscal years 2011 through 2014, to streamline programs, create efficiencies, reduce waste, and improve aviation safety and capacity, to provide stable funding for the national aviation system, and for other purposes.

Be it enacted by the Senate and House of Representatives of the United States of America in Congress assembled,

SECTION 1. [49 U.S.C. 40101 note] SHORT TITLE; TABLE OF CONTENTS.

(a) SHORT TITLE.—This Act may be cited as the "FAA Modernization and Reform Act of 2012".

(b) TABLE OF CONTENTS.—The table of contents for this Act is as follows:

SECTION 1. [49 U.S.C. 40101 note] SHORT TITLE; TABLE OF CONTENTS.

FAA Modernization and Reform Act of

SECTION 1. [49 U.S.C. 40101 note] SHORT
TITLE; TABLE OF CONTENTS.

FAA Modernization and Reform Act of 2012

SECTION 1. [49 U.S.C. 40101 note] SHORT
TITLE; TABLE OF CONTENTS.

FAA Modernization and Reform Act of

SEC. 3. [49 U.S.C. 40101 note] EFFECTIVE DATE.

Except as otherwise expressly provided, this Act and the amendments made by this Act shall take effect on the date of enactment of this Act.

TITLE I—AUTHORIZATIONS

* * * * * * *

Subtitle B—Passenger Facility Charges

* * * * * * *

SEC. 112. GAO STUDY OF ALTERNATIVE MEANS OF COLLECTING PFCS.

(a) IN GENERAL.—The Comptroller General of the United States shall conduct a study of alternative means of collecting passenger facility charges imposed under section 40117 of title 49, United States Code, that would permit such charges to be collected without being included in the ticket price. In conducting the study, the Comptroller General shall consider, at a minimum—

(1) collection options for arriving, connecting, and departing passengers at airports;

(2) cost sharing or allocation methods based on passenger travel to address connecting traffic; and

(3) examples of airport charges collected by domestic and international airports that are not included in ticket prices.

(b) REPORT.—Not later than 1 year after the date of enactment of this Act, the Comptroller General shall submit to the Committee on Commerce, Science, and Transportation of the Senate and the Committee on Transportation and Infrastructure of the House of Representatives a report on the study, including the Comptroller General's findings, conclusions, and recommendations.

SEC. 113. QUALIFICATIONS-BASED SELECTION.

It is the sense of Congress that airports should consider the use of qualifications-based selection in carrying out capital improvement projects funded using passenger facility charges collected under section 40117 of title 49, United States Code, with the goal of serving the needs of all stakeholders.

* * * * * * *

TITLE II—NEXTGEN AIR TRANSPORTATION SYSTEM AND AIR TRAFFIC CONTROL MODERNIZATION

SEC. 201. [49 U.S.C. 40101 note] DEFINITIONS.

In this title, the following definitions apply:

(1) NEXTGEN.—The term "NextGen" means the Next Generation Air Transportation System.

(2) ADS-B.—The term "ADS-B" means automatic dependent surveillance-broadcast.

(3) ADS-B OUT.—The term "ADS-B Out" means automatic dependent surveillance-broadcast with the ability to transmit information from the aircraft to ground stations and to other equipped aircraft.

(4) ADS-B IN.—The term "ADS-B In" means automatic dependent surveillance-broadcast with the ability to transmit information from the aircraft to ground stations and to other equipped aircraft as well as the ability of the aircraft to receive information from other transmitting aircraft and the ground infrastructure.

(5) RNAV.—The term "RNAV" means area navigation.

(6) RNP.—The term "RNP" means required navigation performance.[Section 202 was repealed by section 503(e) of division B of Public Law 115–254.]

* * * * * * *

SEC. 208. NEXT GENERATION AIR TRANSPORTATION SYSTEM JOINT PLANNING AND DEVELOPMENT OFFICE.

(a) [49 U.S.C. 40101 note] REDESIGNATION OF JPDO DIRECTOR TO ASSOCIATE ADMINISTRATOR.—

(1) ASSOCIATE ADMINISTRATOR FOR NEXT GENERATION AIR TRANSPORTATION SYSTEM PLANNING, DEVELOPMENT, AND INTERAGENCY COORDINATION.—Section 709(a) of the Vision 100—Century of Aviation Reauthorization Act (49 U.S.C. 40101 note; 117 Stat. 2582) is amended—

(A) by redesignating paragraphs (2), (3), and (4) as paragraphs (3), (4), and (5), respectively; and

(B) by inserting after paragraph (1) the following:

"(2) The head of the Office shall be the Associate Administrator for Next Generation Air Transportation System Planning, Development, and Interagency Coordination, who shall be appointed by the Administrator of the Federal Aviation Administration, with the approval of the Secretary. The Administrator shall appoint the Associate Administrator after consulting with the Chairman of the Next Generation Senior Policy Committee and providing advanced notice to the other members of that Committee.".

(2) RESPONSIBILITIES.—Section 709(a)(3) of such Act (as redesignated by paragraph (1) of this subsection) is amended—

(A) in subparagraph (G) by striking "; and" and inserting a semicolon;

(B) in subparagraph (H) by striking the period at the end and inserting a semicolon; and

(C) by adding at the end the following:

"(I) establishing specific quantitative goals for the safety, capacity, efficiency, performance, and environmental impacts of each phase of Next Generation Air Transportation System planning and development activities and measuring actual operational experience against those goals, taking into account noise pollution reduction concerns of affected communities to the extent practicable in establishing the environmental goals;

"(J) working to ensure global interoperability of the Next Generation Air Transportation System;

"(K) working to ensure the use of weather information and space weather information in the Next Generation Air Transportation System as soon as possible;

"(L) overseeing, with the Administrator and in consultation with the Chief NextGen Officer, the selection of products or outcomes of research and development activities that should be moved to a demonstration phase; and

"(M) maintaining a baseline modeling and simulation environment for testing and evaluating alternative concepts to satisfy Next Generation Air Transportation System enterprise architecture requirements.".

(3) COOPERATION WITH OTHER FEDERAL AGENCIES.—Section 709(a)(4) of such Act (as redesignated by paragraph (1) of this subsection) is amended—

(A) by striking "(4)" and inserting "(4)(A)"; and

(B) by adding at the end the following:

"(B) The Secretary of Defense, the Administrator of the National Aeronautics and Space Administration, the Secretary of Commerce, the Secretary of Homeland Security, and the head of any other Federal agency from which the Secretary of Transportation requests assistance under subparagraph (A) shall designate a senior official in the agency to be responsible for—

"(i) carrying out the activities of the agency relating to the Next Generation Air Transportation System in coordination with the Office, including the execution of all aspects of the work of the agency in developing and implementing the integrated work plan described in subsection (b)(5);

"(ii) serving as a liaison for the agency in activities of the agency relating to the Next Generation Air Transportation System and coordinating with other Federal agencies involved in activities relating to the System; and

"(iii) ensuring that the agency meets its obligations as set forth in any memorandum of understanding executed by or on behalf of the agency relating to the Next Generation Air Transportation System.

"(C) The head of a Federal agency referred to in subparagraph (B) shall—

"(i) ensure that the responsibilities of the agency relating to the Next Generation Air Transportation System are clearly communicated to the senior official of the agency designated under subparagraph (B);

"(ii) ensure that the performance of the senior official in carrying out the responsibilities of the agency relating to the Next Generation Air Transportation System is reflected in the official's annual performance evaluations and compensation;

"(iii) establish or designate an office within the agency to carry out its responsibilities under the memorandum of understanding under the supervision of the designated official; and

"(iv) ensure that the designated official has sufficient budgetary authority and staff resources to carry out the agency's Next Generation Air Transportation System responsibilities as set forth in the integrated plan under subsection (b).

"(D) Not later than 6 months after the date of enactment of this subparagraph, the head of each Federal agency that has responsibility for carrying out any activity under the integrated plan under subsection (b) shall execute a memorandum of understanding with the Office obligating that agency to carry out the activity.".

(4) COORDINATION WITH OMB.—Section 709(a) of such Act (117 Stat. 2582) is further amended by adding at the end the following:

"(6)(A) The Office shall work with the Director of the Office of Management and Budget to develop a process whereby the Director will identify projects related to the Next Generation Air Transportation System across the agencies referred to in paragraph (4)(A) and consider the Next Generation Air Transportation System as a unified, cross-agency program.

"(B) The Director of the Office of Management and Budget, to the extent practicable, shall—

"(i) ensure that—

"(I) each Federal agency covered by the plan has sufficient funds requested in the President's budget, as submitted under section 1105(a) of title 31, United States Code, for each fiscal year covered by the plan to carry out its responsibilities under the plan; and

"(II) the development and implementation of the Next Generation Air Transportation System remains on schedule;

"(ii) include, in the President's budget, a statement of the portion of the estimated budget of each Federal agency covered by the plan that relates to the activities of the agency under the Next Generation Air Transportation System; and

"(iii) identify and justify as part of the President's budget submission any inconsistencies between the plan and amounts requested in the budget.

"(7) The Associate Administrator for Next Generation Air Transportation System Planning, Development, and Interagency Coordination shall be a voting member of the Joint Resources Council of the Federal Aviation Administration.".

(b) [49 U.S.C. 40101 note] INTEGRATED PLAN.—Section 709(b) of such Act (117 Stat. 2583) is amended—

(1) in the matter preceding paragraph (1)—

(A) by striking "meets air" and inserting "meets anticipated future air"; and

(B) by striking "beyond those currently included in the Federal Aviation Administration's operational evolution plan";

(2) at the end of paragraph (3) by striking "and";

(3) at the end of paragraph (4) by striking the period and inserting "; and"; and

(4) by adding at the end the following:

"(5) a multiagency integrated work plan for the Next Generation Air Transportation System that includes—

"(A) an outline of the activities required to achieve the end-state architecture, as expressed in the concept of operations and enterprise architecture documents, that identifies each Federal agency or other entity responsible for each activity in the outline;

"(B) details on a year-by-year basis of specific accomplishments, activities, research requirements, rulemakings, policy decisions, and other milestones of progress for each Federal agency or entity conducting activities relating to the Next Generation Air Transportation System;

"(C) for each element of the Next Generation Air Transportation System, an outline, on a year-by-year basis, of what is to be accomplished in that year toward meeting the Next Generation Air Transportation System's end-state architecture, as expressed in the concept of operations and enterprise architecture documents, as well as identifying each Federal agency or other entity that will be responsible for each component of any research, development, or implementation program;

"(D) an estimate of all necessary expenditures on a year-by-year basis, including a statement of each Federal agency or entity's responsibility for costs and available resources, for each stage of development from the basic research stage through the demonstration and implementation phase;

"(E) a clear explanation of how each step in the development of the Next Generation Air Transportation System will lead to the following step and of the implications of not successfully completing a step in the time period described in the integrated work plan;

"(F) a transition plan for the implementation of the Next Generation Air Transportation System that includes date-specific milestones for the implementation of new capabilities into the national airspace system;

"(G) date-specific timetables for meeting the environmental goals identified in subsection (a)(3)(I); and

"(H) a description of potentially significant operational or workforce changes resulting from deployment of the Next Generation Air Transportation System.".

(c) [49 U.S.C. 40101 note] NextGen Implementation Plan.—Section 709(d) of such Act (117 Stat. 2584) is amended to read as follows:

"(d) NextGen Implementation Plan. The Administrator shall develop and publish annually the document known as the NextGen Implementation Plan, or any successor document, that provides a detailed description of how the agency is implementing the Next Generation Air Transportation System.".

(d) [49 U.S.C. 40101 note] Contingency Planning.—The Associate Administrator for Next Generation Air Transportation System Planning, Development, and Interagency Coordination shall, as part of the design of the System, develop contingency plans for dealing with the degradation of the System in the event of a natural disaster, major equipment failure, or act of terrorism.

* * * * * * *

SEC. 211. [49 U.S.C. 40101 note] AUTOMATIC DEPENDENT SURVEILLANCE-BROADCAST SERVICES.

(a) Review by DOT Inspector General.—

(1) In General.—The Inspector General of the Department of Transportation shall conduct a review concerning the Federal Aviation Administration's award and oversight of any contracts entered into by the Administration to provide ADS-B

services for the national airspace system.

(2) CONTENTS.—The review shall include, at a minimum—

(A) an examination of how the Administration manages program risks;

(B) an assessment of expected benefits attributable to the deployment of ADS-B services, including the Administration's plans for implementation of advanced operational procedures and air-to-air applications, as well as the extent to which ground radar will be retained;

(C) an assessment of the Administration's analysis of specific operational benefits, and benefit/costs analyses of planned operational benefits conducted by the Administration, for ADS-B In and ADS-B Out avionics equipage for airspace users;

(D) a determination of whether the Administration has established sufficient mechanisms to ensure that all design, acquisition, operation, and maintenance requirements have been met by the contractor;

(E) an assessment of whether the Administration and any contractors are meeting cost, schedule, and performance milestones, as measured against the original baseline of the Administration's program for providing ADS-B services;

(F) an assessment of how security issues are being addressed in the overall design and implementation of the ADS-B system;

(G) identification of any potential operational or workforce changes resulting from deployment of ADS-B; and

(H) any other matters or aspects relating to contract implementation and oversight that the Inspector General determines merit attention.

(3) REPORTS TO CONGRESS.—The Inspector General shall submit, periodically (and on at least an annual basis), to the Committee on Transportation and Infrastructure of the House of Representatives and the Committee on Commerce, Science, and Transportation of the Senate a report on the results of the review conducted under this subsection.

[Subsection (b) of section 211 was repealed by section 522(a) of division B of Public Law 115–254.]

(c) USE OF ADS-B TECHNOLOGY.—

(1) PLANS.—Not later than 18 months after the date of enactment of this Act, the Administrator shall develop, in consultation with appropriate employee and industry groups, a plan for the use of ADS-B technology for surveillance and active air traffic control.

(2) CONTENTS.—The plan shall—

(A) include provisions to test the use of ADS-B technology for surveillance and active air traffic control in specific regions of the United States with the most congested airspace;

(B) identify the equipment required at air traffic control facilities and the training required for air traffic controllers;

(C) identify procedures, to be developed in consultation with appropriate employee and industry groups, to conduct air traffic management in mixed equipage environments; and

(D) establish a policy in test regions referred to in subparagraph (A), in consultation with appropriate employee and industry groups, to provide incentives for equipage with ADS-B technology, including giving priority to aircraft equipped with such technology before the 2020 equipage deadline.

* * * * * * *

SEC. 213. [49 U.S.C. 40101 note] ACCELERATION OF NEXTGEN TECHNOLOGIES.

(a) OPERATIONAL EVOLUTION PARTNERSHIP (OEP) AIRPORT PROCEDURES.—

(1) OEP AIRPORTS REPORT.—Not later than 6 months after the date of enactment of this Act, the Administrator of the Federal Aviation Administration shall publish a report, after consultation with representatives of appropriate Administration employee groups, airport operators, air carriers, general aviation representatives, aircraft and avionics

manufacturers, and third parties that have received letters of qualification from the Administration to design and validate required navigation performance flight paths for public use (in this section referred to as "qualified third parties") that includes the following:

(A) RNP/RNAV OPERATIONS FOR OEP AIRPORTS.—The required navigation performance and area navigation operations, including the procedures to be developed, certified, and published and the air traffic control operational changes, to maximize the fuel efficiency and airspace capacity of NextGen commercial operations at each of the 35 operational evolution partnership airports identified by the Administration and any medium or small hub airport located within the same metroplex area considered appropriate by the Administrator. The Administrator shall, to the maximum extent practicable, avoid overlays of existing flight procedures, but if unavoidable, the Administrator shall clearly identify each required navigation performance and area navigation procedure that is an overlay of an existing instrument flight procedure and the reason why such an overlay was used.

(B) COORDINATION AND IMPLEMENTATION ACTIVITIES FOR OEP AIRPORTS.—A description of the activities and operational changes and approvals required to coordinate and utilize the procedures at OEP airports.

(C) IMPLEMENTATION PLAN FOR OEP AIRPORTS.—A plan for implementing the procedures for OEP airports under subparagraph (A) that establishes—

(i) clearly defined budget, schedule, project organization, and leadership requirements;

(ii) specific implementation and transition steps;

(iii) baseline and performance metrics for—

(I) measuring the Administration's progress in implementing the plan, including the percentage utilization of required navigation performance in the national airspace system; and

(II) achieving measurable fuel burn and carbon dioxide emissions reductions compared to current performance;

(iv) expedited environmental review procedures and processes for timely environmental approval of area navigation and required navigation performance that offer significant efficiency improvements as determined by baseline and performance metrics under clause (iii);

(v) coordination and communication mechanisms with qualified third parties, if applicable;

(vi) plans to address human factors, training, and other issues for air traffic controllers surrounding the adoption of RNP procedures in the en route and terminal environments, including in a mixed operational environment; and

(vii) a lifecycle management strategy for RNP procedures to be developed by qualified third parties, if applicable.

(D) ADDITIONAL PROCEDURES FOR OEP AIRPORTS.—A process for the identification, certification, and publication of additional required navigation performance and area navigation procedures that may provide operational benefits at OEP airports, and any medium or small hub airport located within the same metroplex area as the OEP airport, in the future.

(2) IMPLEMENTATION SCHEDULE FOR OEP AIRPORTS.—The Administrator shall certify, publish, and implement—

(A) not later than 18 months after the date of enactment of this Act, 30 percent of the required procedures at OEP airports;

(B) not later than 36 months after the date of enactment of this Act, 60 percent of the required procedures at OEP airports; and

(C) before June 30, 2015, 100 percent of the required procedures at OEP airports.

(b) NON-OEP AIRPORTS.—

(1) NON-OEP AIRPORTS REPORT.—Not later than 6 months after the date of enactment of this Act, the Administrator of the Federal Aviation Administration shall publish a report,

after consultation with representatives of appropriate Administration employee groups, airport operators, air carriers, general aviation representatives, aircraft and avionics manufacturers, and third parties that have received letters of qualification from the Administration to design and validate required navigation performance flight paths for public use (in this section referred to as "qualified third parties") that includes the following:

(A) RNP OPERATIONS FOR NON-OEP AIRPORTS.—A list of required navigation performance procedures (as defined in FAA order 8260.52(d)) to be developed, certified, and published, and the air traffic control operational changes, to maximize the fuel efficiency and airspace capacity of NextGen commercial operations at 35 non-OEP small, medium, and large hub airports other than those referred to in subsection (a)(1). The Administrator shall choose such non-OEP airports considered appropriate by the Administrator to produce maximum operational benefits, including improved fuel efficiency and emissions reductions that do not have public RNP procedures that produce such benefits on the date of enactment of this Act. The Administrator shall, to the maximum extent practicable, avoid overlays of existing flight procedures, but if unavoidable, the Administrator shall clearly identify each required navigation performance procedure that is an overlay of an existing instrument flight procedure and the reason why such an overlay was used.

(B) COORDINATION AND IMPLEMENTATION ACTIVITIES FOR NON-OEP AIRPORTS.—A description of the activities and operational changes and approvals required to coordinate and to utilize the procedures required by subparagraph (A) at each of the airports described in such subparagraph.

(C) IMPLEMENTATION PLAN FOR NON-OEP AIRPORTS.—A plan for implementation of the procedures required by subparagraph (A) that establishes—

(i) clearly defined budget, schedule, project organization, and leadership requirements;

(ii) specific implementation and transition steps;

(iii) coordination and communications mechanisms with qualified third parties;

(iv) plans to address human factors, training, and other issues for air traffic controllers surrounding the adoption of RNP procedures in the en route and terminal environments, including in a mixed operational environment;

(v) baseline and performance metrics for—

(I) measuring the Administration's progress in implementing the plan, including the percentage utilization of required navigation performance in the national airspace system; and

(II) achieving measurable fuel burn and carbon dioxide emissions reduction compared to current performance;

(vi) expedited environmental review procedures and processes for timely environmental approval of area navigation and required navigation performance that offer significant efficiency improvements as determined by baseline and performance metrics established under clause (v);

(vii) a description of the software and database information, such as a current version of the Noise Integrated Routing System or the Integrated Noise Model that the Administration will need to make available to qualified third parties to enable those third parties to design procedures that will meet the broad range of requirements of the Administration; and

(viii) lifecycle management strategy for RNP procedures to be developed by qualified third parties, if applicable.

(D) ADDITIONAL PROCEDURES FOR NON-OEP AIRPORTS.—A process for the identification, certification, and publication of additional required navigation performance procedures that may provide operational benefits at non-OEP airports in the future.

(2) IMPLEMENTATION SCHEDULE FOR NON-OEP AIRPORTS.—The Administrator shall certify, publish, and implement—

(A) not later than 18 months after the date of

enactment of this Act, 25 percent of the required procedures for non-OEP airports;

(B) not later than 36 months after the date of enactment of this Act, 50 percent of the required procedures for non-OEP airports; and

(C) before June 30, 2016, 100 percent of the required procedures for non-OEP airports.

(c) COORDINATED AND EXPEDITED REVIEW.—

(1) IN GENERAL.—Navigation performance and area navigation procedures developed, certified, published, or implemented under this section shall be presumed to be covered by a categorical exclusion (as defined in section 1508.4 of title 40, Code of Federal Regulations) under chapter 3 of FAA Order 1050.1E unless the Administrator determines that extraordinary circumstances exist with respect to the procedure.

(2) NEXTGEN PROCEDURES.—Any navigation performance or other performance based navigation procedure developed, certified, published, or implemented that, in the determination of the Administrator, would result in measurable reductions in fuel consumption, carbon dioxide emissions, and noise, on a per flight basis, as compared to aircraft operations that follow existing instrument flight rules procedures in the same airspace, shall be presumed to have no significant affect on the quality of the human environment and the Administrator shall issue and file a categorical exclusion for the new procedure.

(3) NOTIFICATIONS AND CONSULTATIONS.—Not later than 90 days before applying a categorical exclusion under this subsection to a new procedure at an OEP airport, the Administrator shall—

(A) notify and consult with the operator of the airport at which the procedure would be implemented; and

(B) consider consultations or other engagement with the community in the which the airport is located to inform the public of the procedure.

(4) REVIEW OF CERTAIN CATEGORICAL EXCLUSIONS.—

(A) IN GENERAL.—The Administrator shall review any decision of the Administrator made on or after February 14, 2012, and before the date of the enactment of this paragraph to grant a categorical exclusion under this subsection with respect to a procedure to be implemented at an OEP airport that was a material change from procedures previously in effect at the airport to determine if the implementation of the procedure had a significant effect on the human environment in the community in which the airport is located.

(B) CONTENT OF REVIEW.—If, in conducting a review under subparagraph (A) with respect to a procedure implemented at an OEP airport, the Administrator, in consultation with the operator of the airport, determines that implementing the procedure had a significant effect on the human environment in the community in which the airport is located, the Administrator shall—

(i) consult with the operator of the airport to identify measures to mitigate the effect of the procedure on the human environment; and

(ii) in conducting such consultations, consider the use of alternative flight paths that do not substantially degrade the efficiencies achieved by the implementation of the procedure being reviewed.

(C) HUMAN ENVIRONMENT DEFINED.—In this paragraph, the term "human environment" has the meaning given such term in section 1508.14 of title 40, Code of Federal Regulations (as in effect on the day before the date of the enactment of this paragraph).

(d) DEPLOYMENT PLAN FOR NATIONWIDE DATA COMMUNICATIONS SYSTEM.—Not later than 1 year after the date of enactment of this Act, the Administrator shall submit to the Committee on Commerce, Science, and Transportation of the Senate and the Committee on Transportation and Infrastructure of the House of Representatives a plan for implementation of a nationwide data communications system. The plan shall include—

(1) clearly defined budget, schedule, project organization, and leadership requirements;

(2) specific implementation and transition steps; and

(3) baseline and performance metrics for measuring the Administration's progress in implementing the plan.

(e) IMPROVED PERFORMANCE STANDARDS.—

(1) ASSESSMENT OF WORK BEING PERFORMED UNDER NEXTGEN IMPLEMENTATION PLAN.—The Administrator shall clearly outline in the NextGen Implementation Plan document of the Administration the work being performed under the plan to determine—

(A) whether utilization of ADS-B, RNP, and other technologies as part of NextGen implementation will display the position of aircraft more accurately and frequently to enable a more efficient use of existing airspace and result in reduced consumption of aviation fuel and aircraft engine emissions; and

(B) the feasibility of reducing aircraft separation standards in a safe manner as a result of the implementation of such technologies.

(2) AIRCRAFT SEPARATION STANDARDS.—If the Administrator determines that the standards referred to in paragraph (1)(B) can be reduced safely, the Administrator shall include in the NextGen Implementation Plan a timetable for implementation of such reduced standards.

(f) THIRD-PARTY USAGE.—The Administration shall establish a program under which the Administrator is authorized to use qualified third parties in the development, testing, and maintenance of flight procedures.

SEC. 214. [49 U.S.C. 40101 note] PERFORMANCE METRICS.

(a) IN GENERAL.—Not later than 180 days after the date of enactment of this Act, the Administrator of the Federal Aviation Administration shall establish and begin tracking national airspace system performance metrics, including, at a minimum, metrics with respect to—

(1) actual arrival and departure rates per hour measured against the currently published aircraft arrival rate and aircraft departure rate for the 35 operational evolution partnership airports;

(2) average gate-to-gate times;

(3) fuel burned between key city pairs;

(4) operations using the advanced navigation procedures, including performance based navigation procedures;

(5) the average distance flown between key city pairs;

(6) the time between pushing back from the gate and taking off;

(7) continuous climb or descent;

(8) average gate arrival delay for all arrivals;

(9) flown versus filed flight times for key city pairs;

(10) implementation of NextGen Implementation Plan, or any successor document, capabilities designed to reduce emissions and fuel consumption;

(11) the Administration's unit cost of providing air traffic control services; and

(12) runway safety, including runway incursions, operational errors, and loss of standard separation events.

(b) BASELINES.—The Administrator, in consultation with aviation industry stakeholders, shall identify baselines for each of the metrics established under subsection (a) and appropriate methods to measure deviations from the baselines.

(c) PUBLICATION.—The Administrator shall make data obtained under subsection (a) available to the public in a searchable, sortable, and downloadable format through the Web site of the Administration and other appropriate media.

(d) REPORT.—Not later than 180 days after the date of enactment of this Act, the Administrator shall submit to the Committee on Commerce, Science, and Transportation of the Senate and the Committee on Transportation and Infrastructure of the House of Representatives a report that contains—

(1) a description of the metrics that will be used to measure the Administration's progress in implementing NextGen capabilities and operational results;

(2) information on any additional metrics developed; and

(3) a process for holding the Administration accountable for meeting or exceeding the metrics baselines identified in subsection (b).

* * * * * * *

SEC. 217. [49 U.S.C. 40101 note] INCLUSION OF STAKEHOLDERS IN AIR TRAFFIC CONTROL MODERNIZATION PROJECTS.

(a) PROCESS FOR EMPLOYEE INCLUSION.—Notwithstanding any

other law or agreement, the Administrator of the Federal Aviation Administration shall establish a process or processes for including qualified employees selected by each exclusive collective bargaining representative of employees of the Administration impacted by the air traffic control modernization process to serve in a collaborative and expert capacity in the planning and development of air traffic control modernization projects, including NextGen.

(b) ADHERENCE TO DEADLINES.—Participants in these processes shall adhere, to the greatest extent possible, to all deadlines and milestones established pursuant to this title.

(c) NO CHANGE IN EMPLOYEE STATUS.—Participation in these processes by an employee shall not—

(1) serve as a waiver of any bargaining obligations or rights;

(2) entitle the employee to any additional compensation or benefits with the exception of a per diem, if appropriate; or

(3) entitle the employee to prevent or unduly delay the exercise of management prerogatives.

(d) WORKING GROUPS.—Except in extraordinary circumstances, the Administrator shall not pay overtime related to work group participation.

(e) REPORT.—Not later than 1 year after the date of enactment of this Act, the Administrator shall report to the Committee on Transportation and Infrastructure of the House of Representatives and the Committee on Commerce, Science, and Transportation of the Senate on the implementation of this section.

* * * * * * *

SEC. 220. [49 U.S.C. 40101 note] NEXTGEN RESEARCH AND DEVELOPMENT CENTER OF EXCELLENCE.

(a) IN GENERAL.—The Administrator of the Federal Aviation Administration may enter into an agreement, on a competitive basis, to assist in the establishment of a center of excellence for the research and development of NextGen technologies.

(b) FUNCTIONS.—The Administrator shall ensure that the center established under subsection (a)—

(1) leverages resources and partnerships, including appropriate programs of the Administration, to enhance the

SEC. 221. [49 U.S.C. 40101 note] PUBLIC-
PRIVATE PARTNERSHIPS.

FAA Modernization and Reform Act o

research and development of NextGen technologies by academia and industry; and

(2) provides educational, technical, and analytical assistance to the Administration and other Federal departments and agencies with responsibilities to research and develop NextGen technologies.

SEC. 221. [49 U.S.C. 40101 note] PUBLIC-PRIVATE PARTNERSHIPS.

(a) IN GENERAL.—The Secretary may establish an avionics equipage incentive program for the purpose of equipping general aviation and commercial aircraft with communications, surveillance, navigation, and other avionics equipment as determined by the Secretary to be in the interest of achieving NextGen capabilities for such aircraft.

(b) NEXTGEN PUBLIC-PRIVATE PARTNERSHIPS.—The incentive program established under subsection (a) shall, at a minimum—

(1) be based on public-private partnership principles; and

(2) leverage and maximize the use of private sector capital.

(c) FINANCIAL INSTRUMENTS.—Subject to the availability of appropriated funds, the Secretary may use financial instruments to facilitate public-private financing for the equipage of general aviation and commercial aircraft registered under section 44103 of title 49, United States Code. To the extent appropriations are not made available, the Secretary may establish the program, provided the costs are covered by the fees and premiums authorized by subsection (d)(2). For purposes of this section, the term "financial instruments" means loan guarantees and other credit assistance designed to leverage and maximize private sector capital.

(d) PROTECTION OF THE TAXPAYER.—

(1) LIMITATION ON PRINCIPAL.—The amount of any guarantee under this program shall be limited to 90 percent of the principal amount of the underlying loan.

(2) COLLATERAL, FEES, AND PREMIUMS.—The Secretary shall require applicants for the incentive program to post collateral and pay such fees and premiums if feasible, as determined by the Secretary, to offset costs to the Government of potential defaults, and agree to performance measures that the Secretary considers necessary and in the best interest of implementing the NextGen program.

(3) USE OF FUNDS.—Applications for this program shall be limited to equipment that is installed on general aviation or commercial aircraft and is necessary for communications, surveillance, navigation, or other purposes determined by the Secretary to be in the interests of achieving NextGen capabilities for commercial and general aviation.

(e) TERMINATION OF AUTHORITY.—The authority of the Secretary to issue such financial instruments under this section shall terminate 5 years after the date of the establishment of the incentive program.

* * * * * * *

SEC. 223. [49 U.S.C. 106 note] EDUCATIONAL REQUIREMENTS.

The Administrator of the Federal Aviation Administration shall make payments to the Department of Defense for the education of dependent children of those Administration employees in Puerto Rico and Guam as they are subject to transfer by policy and practice and meet the eligibility requirements of section 2164(c) of title 10, United States Code.

SEC. 224. [49 U.S.C. 44506 note] AIR TRAFFIC CONTROLLER STAFFING INITIATIVES AND ANALYSIS.

As soon as practicable, and not later than 1 year after the date of enactment of this Act, the Administrator of the Federal Aviation Administration shall—

(1) ensure, to the extent practicable, a sufficient number of contract instructors, classroom space (including off-site locations as needed), and simulators to allow for an increase in the number of air traffic controllers at air traffic control facilities;

(2) distribute, to the extent practicable, the placement of certified professional air traffic controllers-in-training and developmental air traffic controllers at facilities evenly across the calendar year in order to avoid training bottlenecks;

(3) initiate an analysis, to be conducted in consultation with the exclusive bargaining representative of air traffic controllers certified under section 7111 of title 5, United States Code, of scheduling processes and practices, including overtime scheduling practices at those facilities;

(4) provide, to the extent practicable and where appropriate, priority to certified professional air traffic controllers-in-training when filling staffing vacancies at facilities;

(5) assess training programs at air traffic control facilities with below-average success rates to determine if training is being carried out in accordance with Administration standards, and conduct exit interview analyses with all candidates to determine potential weaknesses in training protocols, or in the execution of such training protocols; and

(6) prioritize, to the extent practicable, such efforts to address the recommendations for the facilities identified in the Department of Transportation's Office of the Inspector General Report Number: AV-2009-047.

* * * * * * *

TITLE III—SAFETY

Subtitle A—General Provisions

* * * * * * *

SEC. 304. CABIN CREW COMMUNICATION.

(a) IN GENERAL.—Section 44728 is amended—

(1) by redesignating subsection (f) as subsection (g); and

(2) by inserting after subsection (e) the following:

"(f) MINIMUM LANGUAGE SKILLS.

"(1) IN GENERAL. No person may serve as a flight attendant aboard an aircraft of an air carrier, unless that person has demonstrated to an individual qualified to determine proficiency the ability to read, speak, and write English well enough to—

"(A) read material written in English and comprehend the information;

"(B) speak and understand English sufficiently to provide direction to, and understand and answer questions from, English-speaking individuals;

"(C) write incident reports and statements and log entries and statements; and

"(D) carry out written and oral instructions regarding the proper performance of their duties.

"(2) FOREIGN FLIGHTS. The requirements of paragraph (1) do not apply to a flight attendant serving solely between points outside the United States.".

(b) [49 U.S.C. 44728 note] FACILITATION.—The Administrator of the Federal Aviation Administration shall work with air carriers to facilitate compliance with the requirements of section 44728(f) of title 49, United States Code (as amended by this section).

* * * * * * *

SEC. 312. [49 U.S.C. 44704 note] AIRCRAFT CERTIFICATION PROCESS REVIEW AND REFORM.

(a) IN GENERAL.—The Administrator of the Federal Aviation Administration, in consultation with representatives of the aviation industry, shall conduct an assessment of the certification and approval process under section 44704 of title 49, United States Code.

(b) CONTENTS.—In conducting the assessment, the Administrator shall consider—

(1) the expected number of applications for product certifications and approvals the Administrator will receive under section 44704 of such title in the 1-year, 5-year, and 10-year periods following the date of enactment of this Act;

(2) process reforms and improvements necessary to allow the Administrator to review and approve the applications in a fair and timely fashion;

(3) the status of recommendations made in previous reports on the Administration's certification process;

(4) methods for enhancing the effective use of delegation systems, including organizational designation authorization;

(5) methods for training the Administration's field office employees in the safety management system and auditing; and

(6) the status of updating airworthiness requirements, including implementing recommendations in the Administration's report entitled "Part 23—Small Airplane

SEC. 313. [49 U.S.C. 44701 note] CONSISTENCY OF REGULATORY INTERPRETATION.

FAA Modernization and Reform Act of

Certification Process Study" (OK-09-3468, dated July 2009).

(c) RECOMMENDATIONS.—In conducting the assessment, the Administrator shall make recommendations to improve efficiency and reduce costs through streamlining and reengineering the certification process under section 44704 of such title to ensure that the Administrator can conduct certifications and approvals under such section in a manner that supports and enables the development of new products and technologies and the global competitiveness of the United States aviation industry.

(d) REPORT TO CONGRESS.—Not later than 180 days after the date of enactment of this Act, the Administrator shall submit to the Committee on Transportation and Infrastructure of the House of Representatives and the Committee on Commerce, Science, and Transportation of the Senate a report on the results of the assessment, together with an explanation of how the Administrator will implement recommendations made under subsection (c) and measure the effectiveness of the recommendations.

(e) IMPLEMENTATION OF RECOMMENDATIONS.—Not later than 1 year after the date of enactment of this Act, the Administrator shall begin to implement the recommendations made under subsection (c).

SEC. 313. [49 U.S.C. 44701 note] CONSISTENCY OF REGULATORY INTERPRETATION.

(a) ESTABLISHMENT OF ADVISORY PANEL.—Not later than 90 days after the date of enactment of this Act, the Administrator of the Federal Aviation Administration shall establish an advisory panel comprised of both Government and industry representatives to—

(1) review the October 2010 report by the Government Accountability Office on certification and approval processes (GAO-11-14); and

(2) develop recommendations to address the findings in the report and other concerns raised by interested parties, including representatives of the aviation industry.

(b) MATTERS TO BE CONSIDERED.—The advisory panel shall—

(1) determine the root causes of inconsistent interpretation of regulations by the Administration's Flight Standards Service and Aircraft Certification Service;

(2) develop recommendations to improve the consistency of interpreting regulations by the Administration's Flight Standards Service and Aircraft Certification Service; and

(3) develop recommendations to improve communications between the Administration's Flight Standards Service and Aircraft Certification Service and applicants and certificate and approval holders for the identification and resolution of potentially adverse issues in an expeditious and fair manner.

(c) REPORT TO CONGRESS.—Not later than 1 year after the date of enactment of this Act, the Administrator shall transmit to the Committee on Transportation and Infrastructure of the House of Representatives and the Committee on Commerce, Science, and Transportation of the Senate a report on the findings of the advisory panel, together with an explanation of how the Administrator will implement the recommendations of the advisory panel and measure the effectiveness of the recommendations.

* * * * * * *

SEC. 319. [49 U.S.C. 44713 note] MAINTENANCE PROVIDERS.

(a) REGULATIONS.—Not later than 3 years after the date of enactment of this Act, the Administrator of the Federal Aviation Administration shall issue regulations requiring that covered work on an aircraft used to provide air transportation under part 121 of title 14, Code of Federal Regulations, be performed by persons in accordance with subsection (b).

(b) PERSONS AUTHORIZED TO PERFORM CERTAIN WORK.—A person may perform covered work on aircraft used to provide air transportation under part 121 of title 14, Code of Federal Regulations, only if the person is employed by—

(1) a part 121 air carrier;

(2) a part 145 repair station or a person authorized under section 43.17 of title 14, Code of Federal Regulations (or any successor regulation); or

(3) subject to subsection (c), a person that—

(A) provides contract maintenance workers, services, or maintenance functions to a part 121 air carrier or part 145 repair station; and

(B) meets the requirements of the part 121 air carrier

or the part 145 repair station, as appropriate.

(c) TERMS AND CONDITIONS.—Covered work performed by a person who is employed by a person described in subsection (b)(3) shall be subject to the following terms and conditions:

(1) The applicable part 121 air carrier shall be directly in charge of the covered work being performed.

(2) The covered work shall be carried out in accordance with the part 121 air carrier's maintenance manual.

(3) The person shall carry out the covered work under the supervision and control of the part 121 air carrier directly in charge of the covered work being performed on its aircraft.

(d) DEFINITIONS.—In this section, the following definitions apply:

(1) COVERED WORK.—The term "covered work" means any of the following:

(A) Essential maintenance that could result in a failure, malfunction, or defect endangering the safe operation of an aircraft if not performed properly or if improper parts or materials are used.

(B) Regularly scheduled maintenance.

(C) A required inspection item (as defined by the Administrator).

(2) PART 121 AIR CARRIER.—The term "part 121 air carrier" means an air carrier that holds a certificate issued under part 121 of title 14, Code of Federal Regulations.

(3) PART 145 REPAIR STATION.—The term "part 145 repair station" means a repair station that holds a certificate issued under part 145 of title 14, Code of Federal Regulations.

(4) PERSON.—The term "person" means an individual, firm, partnership, corporation, company, or association that performs maintenance, preventative maintenance, or alterations.

* * * * * * *

[Section 321 was repealed by section 218(j)(2) of Public Law 118–63.]

Subtitle B—Unmanned Aircraft Systems

SEC. 331. [49 U.S.C. 40101 note] DEFINITIONS.

In this subtitle, the following definitions apply:

(1) ARCTIC.—The term "Arctic" means the United States zone of the Chukchi Sea, Beaufort Sea, and Bering Sea north of the Aleutian chain.

(2) CERTIFICATE OF WAIVER; CERTIFICATE OF AUTHORIZATION.—The terms "certificate of waiver" and "certificate of authorization" mean a Federal Aviation Administration grant of approval for a specific flight operation.

(3) PERMANENT AREAS.—The term "permanent areas" means areas on land or water that provide for launch, recovery, and operation of small unmanned aircraft.

(4) PUBLIC UNMANNED AIRCRAFT SYSTEM.—The term "public unmanned aircraft system" means an unmanned aircraft system that meets the qualifications and conditions required for operation of a public aircraft (as defined in section 40102 of title 49, United States Code).

(5) SENSE AND AVOID CAPABILITY.—The term "sense and avoid capability" means the capability of an unmanned aircraft to remain a safe distance from and to avoid collisions with other airborne aircraft.

(6) SMALL UNMANNED AIRCRAFT.—The term "small unmanned aircraft" means an unmanned aircraft weighing less than 55 pounds, including everything that is on board or otherwise attached to the aircraft.

(7) TEST RANGE.—

(A) IN GENERAL.—The term "test range" means a defined geographic area where research and development are conducted as authorized by the Administrator of the Federal Aviation Administration.

(B) INCLUSIONS.—The term "test range" includes any of the 6 test ranges established by the Administrator of the Federal Aviation Administration under section 332(c), as in effect on the day before the date of enactment of this subparagraph, and any public entity authorized by the

Federal Aviation Administration as an unmanned aircraft system flight test center before January 1, 2009.

(8) UNMANNED AIRCRAFT.—The term "unmanned aircraft" means an aircraft that is operated without the possibility of direct human intervention from within or on the aircraft.

(9) UNMANNED AIRCRAFT SYSTEM.—The term "unmanned aircraft system" means an unmanned aircraft and associated elements (including communication links and the components that control the unmanned aircraft) that are required for the pilot in command to operate safely and efficiently in the national airspace system.

[Sections 332—334 were repealed by sections 341(b)(2), 347(b)(2), 346(b)(2), respectively, of division B of Public Law 115–254.]

SEC. 335. [49 U.S.C. 40101 note] SAFETY STUDIES.

The Administrator of the Federal Aviation Administration shall carry out all safety studies necessary to support the integration of unmanned aircraft systems into the national airspace system.
[Section 336 was repealed by section 349(b)(2) of division B of Public Law 115–254.]

Subtitle C—Safety and Protections

* * * * * * *

SEC. 343. [49 U.S.C. 44701 note] REVIEW OF AIR TRANSPORTATION OVERSIGHT SYSTEM DATABASE.

(a) REVIEWS.—The Administrator of the Federal Aviation Administration shall establish a process by which the air transportation oversight system database of the Administration is reviewed by regional teams of employees of the Administration, including at least one employee on each team representing aviation safety inspectors, on a monthly basis to ensure that—

(1) any trends in regulatory compliance are identified; and

(2) appropriate corrective actions are taken in accordance with Administration regulations, advisory directives, policies, and procedures.

(b) MONTHLY TEAM REPORTS.—

(1) IN GENERAL.—A regional team of employees conducting

a monthly review of the air transportation oversight system database under subsection (a) shall submit to the Administrator, the Associate Administrator for Aviation Safety, and the Director of Flight Standards Service a report each month on the results of the review.

(2) CONTENTS.—A report submitted under paragraph (1) shall identify—

(A) any trends in regulatory compliance discovered by the team of employees in conducting the monthly review; and

(B) any corrective actions taken or proposed to be taken in response to the trends.

(c) BIANNUAL REPORTS TO CONGRESS.—The Administrator, on a biannual basis, shall submit to the Committee on Transportation and Infrastructure of the House of Representatives and the Committee on Commerce, Science, and Transportation of the Senate a report on the results of the reviews of the air transportation oversight system database conducted under this section, including copies of reports received under subsection (b).

SEC. 344. [49 U.S.C. 40123 note] IMPROVED VOLUNTARY DISCLOSURE REPORTING SYSTEM.

(a) VOLUNTARY DISCLOSURE REPORTING PROGRAM DEFINED.—In this section, the term "Voluntary Disclosure Reporting Program" means the program established by the Federal Aviation Administration through Advisory Circular 00-58A, dated September 8, 2006, including any subsequent revisions thereto.

(b) VERIFICATION.—The Administrator of the Federal Aviation Administration shall modify the Voluntary Disclosure Reporting Program to require inspectors to—

(1) verify that air carriers are implementing comprehensive solutions to correct the underlying causes of the violations voluntarily disclosed by such air carriers; and

(2) confirm, before approving a final report of a violation, that a violation with the same root causes, has not been previously discovered by an inspector or self-disclosed by the air carrier.

(c) SUPERVISORY REVIEW OF VOLUNTARY SELF-DISCLOSURES.—The Administrator shall establish a process by

323

which voluntary self-disclosures received from air carriers are reviewed and approved by a supervisor after the initial review by an inspector.

(d) INSPECTOR GENERAL STUDY.—

(1) IN GENERAL.—The Inspector General of the Department of Transportation shall conduct a study of the Voluntary Disclosure Reporting Program.

(2) REVIEW.—In conducting the study, the Inspector General shall examine, at a minimum, if the Administration—

(A) conducts comprehensive reviews of voluntary disclosure reports before closing a voluntary disclosure report under the provisions of the program;

(B) evaluates the effectiveness of corrective actions taken by air carriers; and

(C) effectively prevents abuse of the voluntary disclosure reporting program through its secondary review of self-disclosures before they are accepted and closed by the Administration.

(3) REPORT TO CONGRESS.—Not later than 1 year after the date of enactment of this Act, the Inspector General shall submit to the Committee on Transportation and Infrastructure of the House of Representatives and Committee on Commerce, Science, and Transportation of the Senate a report on the results of the study conducted under this section.

[Section 345 was repealed by section 218(l) of Public Law 118–63.]

SEC. 346. CERTAIN EXISTING FLIGHT TIME LIMITATIONS AND REST REQUIREMENTS.

The Administrator of the Federal Aviation Administration may not finalize the interpretation proposed in Docket No. FAA-2010-1259, relating to rest requirements, and published in the Federal Register on December 23, 2010.

SEC. 347. [49 U.S.C. 44712 note] EMERGENCY LOCATOR TRANSMITTERS ON GENERAL AVIATION AIRCRAFT.

(a) INSPECTION.—As part of the annual inspection of general aviation aircraft, the Administrator of the Federal Aviation Administration shall require a detailed inspection of each emergency locator transmitter (in this section referred to as an

SEC. 408. [49 U.S.C. 42302 note] DOT AIRLINE CONSUMER COMPLAINT INVESTIGATIONS.

FAA Modernization and Reform Act of 2012

"ELT") installed in general aviation aircraft operating in the United States to ensure that the ELT is mounted and retained in accordance with the manufacturer's specifications.

(b) MOUNTING AND RETENTION.—

(1) IN GENERAL.—Not later than 90 days after the date of enactment of this Act, the Administrator shall determine if the ELT mounting requirements and retention tests specified by Technical Standard Orders C91a and C126 are adequate to assess retention capabilities in ELT designs.

(2) REVISION.—Based on the determination under paragraph (1), the Administrator shall make any necessary revisions to the requirements and retention tests referred to in paragraph (1) to ensure that ELTs are properly retained in the event of an aircraft accident.

(c) REPORT.—Upon the completion of any revisions under subsection (b)(2), the Administrator shall submit a report on the implementation of this section to—

(1) the Committee on Commerce, Science, and Transportation of the Senate; and

(2) the Committee on Transportation and Infrastructure of the House of Representatives.

TITLE IV—AIR SERVICE IMPROVEMENTS

Subtitle A—Passenger Air Service Improvements

* * * * * * *

SEC. 408. [49 U.S.C. 42302 note] DOT AIRLINE CONSUMER COMPLAINT INVESTIGATIONS.

The Secretary of Transportation may investigate consumer complaints regarding—

(1) flight cancellations;

(2) compliance with Federal regulations concerning overbooking seats on flights;

(3) lost, damaged, or delayed baggage, and difficulties with related airline claims procedures;

(4) problems in obtaining refunds for unused or lost tickets or fare adjustments;

(5) incorrect or incomplete information about fares, discount fare conditions and availability, overcharges, and fare increases;

(6) the rights of passengers who hold frequent flyer miles or equivalent redeemable awards earned through customer-loyalty programs; and

(7) deceptive or misleading advertising.

* * * * * * *

SEC. 411. [49 U.S.C. 42301 prec. note] ESTABLISHMENT OF ADVISORY COMMITTEE FOR AVIATION CONSUMER PROTECTION.

(a) IN GENERAL.—The Secretary of Transportation shall establish an advisory committee for aviation consumer protection to advise the Secretary in carrying out activities relating to airline customer service improvements.

(b) MEMBERSHIP.—The Secretary shall appoint the members of the advisory committee, which shall be comprised of one representative each of—

(1) air carriers;

(2) airport operators;

(3) State or local governments with expertise in consumer protection matters; and

(4) nonprofit public interest groups with expertise in consumer protection matters.

(c) VACANCIES.—A vacancy in the advisory committee shall be filled in the manner in which the original appointment was made.

(d) TRAVEL EXPENSES.—Members of the advisory committee shall serve without pay but shall receive travel expenses, including per diem in lieu of subsistence, in accordance with subchapter I of chapter 57 of title 5, United States Code.

(e) CHAIRPERSON.—The Secretary shall designate, from among the individuals appointed under subsection (b), an individual to serve as chairperson of the advisory committee.

(f) DUTIES.—The duties of the advisory committee shall include—

(1) evaluating existing aviation consumer protection programs and providing recommendations for the improvement of such programs, if needed; and

(2) providing recommendations for establishing additional aviation consumer protection programs, if needed.

(g) REPORT TO CONGRESS.—Not later than February 1 of each of the first 2 calendar years beginning after the date of enactment of this Act, the Secretary shall transmit to Congress a report containing—

(1) the recommendations made by the advisory committee during the preceding calendar year; and

(2) an explanation of how the Secretary has implemented each recommendation and, for each recommendation not implemented, the Secretary's reason for not implementing the recommendation.

(h) TERMINATION.—The advisory committee established under this section shall terminate on September 30, 2028.

(i) CONSULTATION.—The Advisory Committee shall consult, as appropriate, with foreign air carriers, air carriers with an ultra-low-cost business model, nonprofit public interest groups with expertise in disability and accessibility matters, ticket agents, travel management companies, and any other groups as determined by the Secretary.

* * * * * * *

SEC. 413. [49 U.S.C. 41722 note] SCHEDULE REDUCTION.

(a) IN GENERAL.—If the Administrator of the Federal Aviation Administration determines that—

(1) the aircraft operations of air carriers during any hour at an airport exceed the hourly maximum departure and arrival rate established by the Administrator for such operations; and

(2) the operations in excess of the maximum departure and arrival rate for such hour at such airport are likely to have a significant adverse effect on the safe and efficient use of navigable airspace,

the Administrator shall convene a meeting of such carriers to reduce pursuant to section 41722 of title 49, United States Code, on a voluntary basis, the number of such operations so as not to exceed the maximum departure and arrival rate.

(b) NO AGREEMENT.—If the air carriers participating in a meeting with respect to an airport under subsection (a) are not able to agree to a reduction in the number of flights to and from the airport so as not to exceed the maximum departure and arrival rate, the Administrator shall take such action as is necessary to ensure such reduction is implemented.

(c) SUBSEQUENT SCHEDULE INCREASES.—Subsequent to any reduction in operations under subsection (a) or (b) at an airport, if the Administrator determines that the hourly number of aircraft operations at that airport is less than the amount that can be handled safely and efficiently, the Administrator shall ensure that priority is given to United States air carriers in permitting additional aircraft operations with respect to that hour.

* * * * * * *

Subtitle B—Essential Air Service

* * * * * * *

SEC. 426. ADJUSTMENTS TO COMPENSATION FOR SIGNIFICANTLY INCREASED COSTS.[1]

(a) [49 U.S.C. 41737 note] EMERGENCY ACROSS-THE-BOARD ADJUSTMENT.—Subject to the availability of funds, the Secretary of Transportation may increase the rates of compensation payable to air carriers under subchapter II of chapter 417 of title 49, United States Code, to compensate such carriers for increased aviation fuel costs without regard to any agreement or requirement relating to the renegotiation of contracts or any notice requirement under section 41734 of such title.

(b) EXPEDITED PROCESS FOR ADJUSTMENTS TO INDIVIDUAL CONTRACTS.—

(1) IN GENERAL.—Section 41734(d) is amended by striking "continue to pay" and all that follows through "compensation sufficient—" and inserting "provide the carrier with compensation sufficient—".

(2) EFFECTIVE DATE.—The amendment made by paragraph (1) shall apply to compensation to air carriers for air service provided after the 30th day following the date of enactment of this Act.

---

[1] Section 561(a)(4)(B) of Public Law 118–63 amends section 426 by striking subsections (c) and (d). Such amendment neglected to include "of 2012" at the end of the reference to the amended Act but was executed to reflect the probable intent of Congress.

---

* * * * * * *

TITLE V—ENVIRONMENTAL STREAMLINING

* * * * * * *

SEC. 507. [49 U.S.C. 44505 note] AIRCRAFT DEPARTURE QUEUE MANAGEMENT PILOT PROGRAM.

(a) IN GENERAL.—The Secretary of Transportation shall carry out a pilot program at not more than 5 public-use airports under which the Federal Aviation Administration shall use funds made available under section 48101(a) of title 49, United States Code, to test air traffic flow management tools, methodologies, and procedures that will allow air traffic controllers of the Administration to better manage the flow of aircraft on the ground and reduce the length of ground holds and idling time for aircraft.

(b) SELECTION CRITERIA.—In selecting from among airports at which to conduct the pilot program, the Secretary shall give priority consideration to airports at which improvements in ground control efficiencies are likely to achieve the greatest fuel savings or air quality or other environmental benefits, as measured by the amount of reduced fuel, reduced emissions, or other environmental benefits per dollar of funds expended under the pilot program.

(c) MAXIMUM AMOUNT.—Not more than a total of $2,500,000 may be expended under the pilot program at any single public-use airport.

SEC. 508. [49 U.S.C. 44502 note] HIGH PERFORMANCE, SUSTAINABLE, AND COST-EFFECTIVE AIR TRAFFIC CONTROL FACILITIES.

The Administrator of the Federal Aviation Administration may implement, to the extent practicable, sustainable practices for the incorporation of energy-efficient design, equipment, systems, and other measures in the construction and major renovation of air traffic control facilities of the Administration in order to reduce energy consumption at, improve the environmental performance of, and reduce the cost of maintenance for such facilities.

SEC. 509. SENSE OF CONGRESS.

It is the sense of Congress that—

(1) the European Union directive extending the European Union's emissions trading proposal to international civil aviation without working through the International Civil Aviation Organization (in this section referred to as the "ICAO") in a consensus-based fashion is inconsistent with the Convention on International Civil Aviation, completed in Chicago on December 7, 1944 (TIAS 1591; commonly known as the "Chicago Convention"), and other relevant air services agreements and antithetical to building international cooperation to address effectively the problem of greenhouse gas emissions by aircraft engaged in international civil aviation;

(2) the European Union and its member states should instead work with other contracting states of ICAO to develop a consensual approach to addressing aircraft greenhouse gas emissions through ICAO; and

(3) officials of the United States Government, and particularly the Secretary of Transportation and the Administrator of the Federal Aviation Administration, should use all political, diplomatic, and legal tools at the disposal of the United States to ensure that the European Union's emissions trading scheme is not applied to aircraft registered by the United States or the operators of those aircraft, including the mandates that United States carriers provide emissions data to and purchase emissions allowances from or surrender emissions allowances to the European Union Member States.

* * * * * * *

TITLE VIII—MISCELLANEOUS

* * * * * * *

SEC. 804. [49 U.S.C. 44501 note] CONSOLIDATION AND REALIGNMENT OF FAA SERVICES AND FACILITIES.

(a) NATIONAL FACILITIES REALIGNMENT AND CONSOLIDATION REPORT.—

(1) IN GENERAL.—The Administrator of the Federal Aviation Administration shall develop a report, to be known as the National Facilities Realignment and Consolidation Report, in accordance with the requirements of this subsection.

(2) PURPOSE.—The purpose of the report shall be to reduce capital, operating, maintenance, and administrative costs of the FAA where such cost reductions can be implemented without adversely affecting safety.

(3) CONTENTS.—The report shall include—

(A) recommendations of the Administrator on realignment and consolidation of services and facilities (including regional offices) of the FAA; and

(B) for each of the recommendations, a description of—

(i) the Administrator's justification;

(ii) the projected costs and savings; and

(iii) the proposed timing for implementation.

(4)[3] INPUT.—The report shall be prepared by the Administrator (or the Administrator's designee) with the participation of—

(A) representatives of labor organizations representing air traffic control system employees of the FAA; and

(B) industry stakeholders.

---

[3] The amendment to paragraph (4) by section 545(b)(2) of division B of Public Law 115–254 to strike "Chief NextGen Officer" and insert "Chief Technology Officer" could not be carried out as a result of an earlier amendment made by section 510(a)(2) of such Public Law.

---

(5) SUBMISSION TO CONGRESS.—Not later than 120 days after the date of enactment of this Act, the Administrator shall submit the report to the Committee on Transportation and Infrastructure of the House of Representatives and the Committee on Commerce, Science, and Transportation of the

Senate.

(6) PUBLIC NOTICE AND COMMENT.—The Administrator shall publish the report in the Federal Register and allow 45 days for the submission of public comments.

(b) REPORT TO CONGRESS CONTAINING RECOMMENDATIONS OF ADMINISTRATOR.—Not later than 60 days after the last day of the period for public comment under subsection (a)(6), the Administrator shall submit to the committees specified in subsection (a)(5)—

(1) a report containing the recommendations of the Administrator on realignment and consolidation of services and facilities (including regional offices) of the FAA; and

(2) copies of any public comments received by the Administrator under subsection (a)(6).

(c) REALIGNMENT AND CONSOLIDATION OF FAA SERVICES AND FACILITIES.—Except as provided in subsection (d), the Administrator shall realign and consolidate the services and facilities of the FAA in accordance with the recommendations included in the report submitted under subsection (b).

(d) CONGRESSIONAL DISAPPROVAL.—

(1) IN GENERAL.—The Administrator may not carry out a recommendation for realignment or consolidation of services or facilities of the FAA that is included in the report submitted under subsection (b) if a joint resolution of disapproval is enacted disapproving such recommendation before the earlier of—

(A) the last day of the 30-day period beginning on the date of submission of the report; or

(B) the adjournment of Congress sine die for the session during which the report is transmitted.

(2) COMPUTATION OF 30-DAY PERIOD.—For purposes of paragraph (1)(A), the days on which either House of Congress is not in session because of an adjournment of more than 3 days to a day certain shall be excluded in computation of the 30-day period.

(e) MILITARY OPERATIONS EXCLUSION.—

(1) IN GENERAL.—The Administrator may not realign or consolidate a combined TRACON and tower with radar facility

of the FAA under this section if, in 2015, the total annual military operations at the facility comprised at least 40 percent of the total annual TRACON operations at the facility.

(2) TRACON DEFINED.—In this subsection, the term "TRACON" means terminal radar approach control.

(f) DEFINITIONS.—In this section, the following definitions apply:

(1) FAA.—The term "FAA" means the Federal Aviation Administration.

(2) REALIGNMENT; CONSOLIDATION.—

(A) IN GENERAL.—The terms "realignment" and "consolidation" include any action that—

(i) relocates functions, services, or personnel positions;

(ii) discontinues or severs existing facility functions or services; or

(iii) combines the results described in clauses (i) and (ii).

(B) EXCLUSION.—The terms do not include a reduction in personnel resulting from workload adjustments.

SEC. 805. LIMITING ACCESS TO FLIGHT DECKS OF ALL-CARGO AIRCRAFT.

(a) STUDY.—Not later than 180 days after the date of enactment of this Act, the Administrator of the Federal Aviation Administration, in consultation with appropriate air carriers, aircraft manufacturers, and air carrier labor representatives, shall conduct a study to assess the feasibility of developing a physical means, or a combination of physical and procedural means, to prohibit individuals other than authorized flight crewmembers from accessing the flight deck of an all-cargo aircraft.

(b) REPORT.—Not later than 1 year after the date of enactment of this Act, the Administrator shall submit to the Committee on Transportation and Infrastructure of the House of Representatives and the Committee on Commerce, Science, and Transportation of the Senate a report on the results of the study.

SEC. 806. [49 U.S.C. 40114 note] CONSOLIDATION OR ELIMINATION OF OBSOLETE, REDUNDANT, OR OTHERWISE UNNECESSARY

REPORTS; USE OF ELECTRONIC MEDIA FORMAT.

(a) CONSOLIDATION OR ELIMINATION OF REPORTS.—Not later than 2 years after the date of enactment of this Act, and every 2 years thereafter, the Administrator of the Federal Aviation Administration shall submit to the Committee on Commerce, Science, and Transportation of the Senate and the Committee on Transportation and Infrastructure of the House of Representatives a report containing—

(1) a list of obsolete, redundant, or otherwise unnecessary reports the Administration is required by law to submit to Congress or publish that the Administrator recommends eliminating or consolidating with other reports; and

(2) an estimate of the cost savings that would result from the elimination or consolidation of those reports.

(b) USE OF ELECTRONIC MEDIA FOR REPORTS.—

(1) IN GENERAL.—Notwithstanding any other provision of law, the Administration—

(A) may not publish any report required or authorized by law in a printed format; and

(B) shall publish any such report by posting it on the Administration's Internet Web site in an easily accessible and downloadable electronic format.

(2) EXCEPTION.—Paragraph (1) does not apply to any report with respect to which the Administrator determines that—

(A) its publication in a printed format is essential to the mission of the Administration; or

(B) its publication in accordance with the requirements of paragraph (1) would disclose matter—

(i) described in section 552(b) of title 5, United States Code; or

(ii) the disclosure of which would have an adverse impact on aviation safety or security, as determined by the Administrator.

SEC. 807. PROHIBITION ON USE OF CERTAIN FUNDS.

The Secretary of Transportation may not use any funds made available pursuant to this Act (including any amendment made by this Act) to name, rename, designate, or redesignate any project or program authorized by this Act (including any amendment made by this Act) for an individual then serving in Congress as a Member, Delegate, Resident Commissioner, or Senator.

SEC. 808. STUDY ON AVIATION FUEL PRICES.

(a) IN GENERAL.—Not later than 180 days after the date of enactment of this Act, the Comptroller General of the United States shall conduct a study and report to Congress on the impact of increases in aviation fuel prices on the Airport and Airway Trust Fund and the aviation industry in general.

(b) CONTENTS.—The study shall include an assessment of the impact of increases in aviation fuel prices on—

(1) general aviation;

(2) commercial passenger aviation;

(3) piston aircraft purchase and use;

(4) the aviation services industry, including repair and maintenance services;

(5) aviation manufacturing;

(6) aviation exports; and

(7) the use of small airport installations.

(c) ASSUMPTIONS ABOUT AVIATION FUEL PRICES.—In conducting the study required by subsection (a), the Comptroller General shall use the average aviation fuel price for fiscal year 2010 as a baseline and measure the impact of increases in aviation fuel prices that range from 5 percent to 200 percent over the 2010 baseline.

SEC. 809. WIND TURBINE LIGHTING.

(a) STUDY.—The Administrator of the Federal Aviation Administration shall conduct a study on wind turbine lighting systems.

(b) CONTENTS.—In conducting the study, the Administrator shall examine the following:

(1) The aviation safety issues associated with alternative lighting strategies, technologies, and regulations.

(2) The feasibility of implementing alternative lighting strategies or technologies to improve aviation safety.

(3) Any other issue relating to wind turbine lighting.

(c) REPORT.—Not later than 1 year after the date of enactment of this Act, the Administrator shall submit to Congress a report on the results of the study, including information and recommendations concerning the issues examined under subsection (b).

* * * * * * *

SEC. 813. [49 U.S.C. 47133 note] USE OF MINERAL REVENUE AT CERTAIN AIRPORTS.

(a) IN GENERAL.—Notwithstanding any other provision of law, the Administrator of the Federal Aviation Administration may declare certain revenue derived from or generated by mineral extraction, production, lease, or other means at a general aviation airport to be revenue greater than the amount needed to carry out the 5-year projected maintenance needs of the airport in order to comply with the applicable design and safety standards of the Administration.

(b) USE OF REVENUE.—An airport sponsor that is in compliance with the conditions under subsection (c) may allocate revenue identified by the Administrator under subsection (a) for Federal, State, or local transportation infrastructure projects carried out by the airport sponsor or by a governing body within the geographical limits of the airport sponsor's jurisdiction.

(c) CONDITIONS.—An airport sponsor may not allocate revenue identified by the Administrator under subsection (a) unless the airport sponsor—

(1) enters into a written agreement with the Administrator that sets forth a 5-year capital improvement program for the airport, which—

(A) includes the projected costs for the operation, maintenance, and capacity needs of the airport in order to comply with applicable design and safety standards of the Administration; and

(B) appropriately adjusts such costs to account for inflation;

(2) agrees in writing—

(A) to waive all rights to receive entitlement funds or discretionary funds to be used at the airport under section

47114 or 47115 of title 49, United States Code, during the 5-year period of the capital improvement plan described in paragraph (1);

(B) to perpetually comply with sections 47107(b) and 47133 of such title, unless granted specific exceptions by the Administrator in accordance with this section; and

(C) to operate the airport as a public-use airport, unless the Administrator specifically grants a request to allow the airport to close; and

(3) complies with all grant assurance obligations in effect as of the date of the enactment of this Act during the 20-year period beginning on the date of enactment of this Act.

(d) COMPLETION OF DETERMINATION.—Not later than 90 days after receiving an airport sponsor's application and requisite supporting documentation to declare that certain mineral revenue is not needed to carry out the 5-year capital improvement program at such airport, the Administrator shall determine whether the airport sponsor's request should be granted. The Administrator may not unreasonably deny an application under this subsection.

(e) RULEMAKING.—Not later than 90 days after the date of enactment of this Act, the Administrator shall promulgate regulations to carry out this section.

(f) GENERAL AVIATION AIRPORT DEFINED.—In this section, the term "general aviation airport" has the meaning given that term in section 47102 of title 49, United States Code, as amended by this Act.

SEC. 814. [49 U.S.C. 40110 note] CONTRACTING.

When drafting contract proposals for training facilities under the general contracting authority of the Federal Aviation Administration, the Administrator of the Federal Aviation Administration shall ensure—

(1) the proposal is drafted so that all parties can fairly compete; and

(2) the proposal takes into consideration the most cost-effective location, accessibility, and services options.

* * * * * * *

SEC. 816. [49 U.S.C. 44704 note] HISTORICAL AIRCRAFT

SEC. 816. [49 U.S.C. 44704 note] HISTORICAL AIRCRAFT DOCUMENTS.

FAA Modernization and Reform Act o

DOCUMENTS.

(a) PRESERVATION OF DOCUMENTS.—

(1) IN GENERAL.—The Administrator of the Federal Aviation Administration shall take such actions as the Administrator determines necessary to preserve original aircraft type certificate engineering and technical data in the possession of the Federal Aviation Administration related to—

(A) approved aircraft type certificate numbers ATC 1 through ATC 713; and

(B) Group-2 approved aircraft type certificate numbers 2-1 through 2-544.

(2) REVISION OF ORDER.—Not later than 3 years after the date of enactment of this Act, the Administrator shall revise FAA Order 1350.15C, Item Number 8110. Such revision shall prohibit the destruction of the historical aircraft documents identified in paragraph (1).

(3) CONSULTATION.—The Administrator may carry out paragraph (1) in consultation with the Archivist of the United States and the Administrator of General Services.

(b) AVAILABILITY OF DOCUMENTS.—

(1) FREEDOM OF INFORMATION ACT REQUESTS.—The Administrator shall make the documents to be preserved under subsection (a)(1) available to a person—

(A) upon receipt of a request made by the person pursuant to section 552 of title 5, United States Code; and

(B) subject to a prohibition on use of the documents for commercial purposes.

(2) TRADE SECRETS, COMMERCIAL, AND FINANCIAL INFORMATION.—Section 552(b)(4) of such title shall not apply to requests for documents to be made available pursuant to paragraph (1).

(c) HOLDER OF TYPE CERTIFICATE.—

(1) RIGHTS OF HOLDER.—Nothing in this section shall affect the rights of a holder or owner of a type certificate identified in subsection (a)(1), nor require the holder or owner to provide, surrender, or preserve any original or duplicate engineering or technical data to or for the Federal Aviation Administration, a person, or the public.

SEC. 819. [49 U.S.C. 45105 note] HUMAN INTERVENTION MOTIVATION STUDY.

FAA Modernization and Reform Act of 2012

(2) LIABILITY.—There shall be no liability on the part of, and no cause of action of any nature shall arise against, a holder of a type certificate, its authorized representative, its agents, or its employees, or any firm, person, corporation, or insurer related to the type certificate data and documents identified in subsection (a)(1).

(3) AIRWORTHINESS.—Notwithstanding any other provision of law, the holder of a type certificate identified in subsection (a)(1) shall only be responsible for Federal Aviation Administration regulation requirements related to type certificate data and documents identified in subsection (a)(1) for aircraft having a standard airworthiness certificate issued prior to the date the documents are released to a person by the Federal Aviation Administration under subsection (b)(1).

[Section 817 was repealed by section 719(c)(2) of Public Law 118–63.]

* * * * * * *

SEC. 819. [49 U.S.C. 45105 note] HUMAN INTERVENTION MOTIVATION STUDY.

Not later than 180 days after the date of enactment of this Act, the Administrator of the Federal Aviation Administration shall develop a Human Intervention Motivation Study program for cabin crew members employed by commercial air carriers in the United States.

* * * * * * *

SEC. 821. [49 U.S.C. 40101 note] CLARIFICATION OF REQUIREMENTS FOR VOLUNTEER PILOTS OPERATING CHARITABLE MEDICAL FLIGHTS.

(a) REIMBURSEMENT OF FUEL COSTS.—Notwithstanding any other law or regulation, in administering section 61.113(c) of title 14, Code of Federal Regulations (or any successor regulation), the Administrator of the Federal Aviation Administration shall allow an aircraft owner or operator to accept reimbursement from a volunteer pilot organization for the fuel costs associated with a flight operation to provide transportation for an individual or organ for medical purposes (and for other associated individuals), if the aircraft owner or operator has—

(1) volunteered to provide such transportation; and

(2) notified any individual that will be on the flight, at the time of inquiry about the flight, that the flight operation is for charitable purposes and is not subject to the same requirements as a commercial flight.

(b) CONDITIONS TO ENSURE SAFETY.—The Administrator may impose minimum standards with respect to training and flight hours for single-engine, multi-engine, and turbine-engine operations conducted by an aircraft owner or operator that is being reimbursed for fuel costs by a volunteer pilot organization, including mandating that the pilot in command of such aircraft hold an instrument rating and be current and qualified for the aircraft being flown to ensure the safety of flight operations described in subsection (a).

(c) VOLUNTEER PILOT ORGANIZATION.—In this section, the term "volunteer pilot organization" means an organization that—

(1) is described in section 501(c)(3) of the Internal Revenue Code of 1986 and is exempt from taxation under section 501(a) of such Code; and

(2) is organized for the primary purpose of providing, arranging, or otherwise fostering charitable medical transportation.

SEC. 822. [49 U.S.C. 47141 note] PILOT PROGRAM FOR REDEVELOPMENT OF AIRPORT PROPERTIES.

(a) IN GENERAL.—Not later than 1 year after the date of enactment of this Act, the Administrator of the Federal Aviation Administration shall establish a pilot program under which operators of up to 4 public-use airports may receive grants for activities related to the redevelopment of airport properties in accordance with the requirements of this section.

(b) GRANTS.—Under the pilot program, the Administrator may make a grant in a fiscal year, from funds made available for grants under section 47117(e)(1)(A) of title 49, United States Code, to an airport operator for a project—

(1) to support joint planning, engineering, design, and environmental permitting of projects, including the assembly and redevelopment of property purchased with noise mitigation funds made available under section 48103 of such title or

passenger facility revenue collected under section 40117 of such title; and

(2) to encourage airport-compatible land uses and generate economic benefits to the local airport authority and adjacent community.

(c) ELIGIBILITY.—An airport operator shall be eligible to participate in the pilot program if—

(1) the operator has received approval for a noise compatibility program under section 47504 of such title; and

(2) the operator demonstrates, as determined by the Administrator—

(A) a readiness to implement cooperative land use management and redevelopment plans with neighboring local jurisdictions; and

(B) the probability of a clear economic benefit to neighboring local jurisdictions and financial return to the airport through the implementation of those plans.

(d) DISTRIBUTION.—The Administrator shall seek to award grants under the pilot program to airport operators representing different geographic areas of the United States.

(e) PARTNERSHIP WITH NEIGHBORING LOCAL JURISDICTIONS.—An airport operator shall use grant funds made available under the pilot program only in partnership with neighboring local jurisdictions.

(f) GRANT REQUIREMENTS.—The Administrator may not make a grant to an airport operator under the pilot program unless the grant is—

(1) made to enable the airport operator and local jurisdictions undertaking community redevelopment efforts to expedite those efforts;

(2) subject to a requirement that the local jurisdiction governing the property interests subject to the redevelopment efforts has adopted and will continue in effect zoning regulations that permit airport-compatible redevelopment; and

(3) subject to a requirement that, in determining the part of the proceeds from disposing of land that is subject to repayment and reinvestment requirements under section 47107(c)(2)(A) of such title, the total amount of a grant issued under the

pilot program that is attributable to the redevelopment of such land shall be added to other amounts that must be repaid or reinvested under that section upon disposal of such land by the airport operator.

(g) EXCEPTIONS TO REPAYMENT AND REINVESTMENT REQUIREMENTS.—Amounts paid to the Secretary of Transportation under subsection (f)(3)—

(1) shall be available to the Secretary for, giving preference to the actions in descending order—

(A) reinvestment in an approved noise compatibility project at the applicable airport;

(B) reinvestment in another approved project at the airport that is eligible for funding under section 47117(e) of such title;

(C) reinvestment in an approved airport development project at the airport that is eligible for funding under section 47114, 47115, or 47117 of such title;

(D) transfer to an operator of another public airport to be reinvested in an approved noise compatibility project at such airport; and

(E) deposit in the Airport and Airway Trust Fund established under section 9502 of the Internal Revenue Code of 1986 (26 U.S.C. 9502);

(2) shall be available in addition to amounts authorized under section 48103 of such title;

(3) shall not be subject to any limitation on grant obligations for any fiscal year; and

(4) shall remain available until expended.

(h) FEDERAL SHARE.—

(1) IN GENERAL.—Notwithstanding any other provision of law, the Federal share of the allowable costs of a project carried out under the pilot program shall be 80 percent.

(2) ALLOWABLE COSTS.—In determining the allowable costs, the Administrator shall deduct from the total costs of the activities described in subsection (b) that portion of the costs which is equal to that portion of the total property to be redeveloped under this section that is not owned or to be acquired by the airport operator pursuant to the noise

compatibility program or that is not owned by the affected neighboring local jurisdictions or other public entities.

(i) MAXIMUM AMOUNT.—Not more than $5,000,000 of the funds made available for grants under section 47117(e)(1)(A) of such title may be expended under the pilot program for any single public-use airport.

(j) USE OF PASSENGER REVENUE.—An airport operator participating in the pilot program may use passenger facility revenue collected under section 40117 of such title to pay any project cost described in subsection (b) that is not financed by a grant under the pilot program.

(k) SUNSET.—This section shall not be in effect after May 10, 2024.

* * * * * * *

SEC. 824. CYLINDERS OF COMPRESSED OXYGEN OR OTHER OXIDIZING GASES.

(a) IN GENERAL.—Subject to subsections (b) and (c), entities transporting, in the State of Alaska, cylinders of compressed oxygen or other oxidizing gases aboard aircraft shall be exempt from compliance with the regulations described in subsection (d), to the extent that the regulations require that oxidizing gases transported aboard aircraft be enclosed in outer packaging capable of passing the flame penetration resistance test and the thermal resistance test, without regard to the end use of the cylinders.

(b) APPLICABILITY OF EXEMPTION.—The exemption provided under subsection (a) shall apply only if—

(1) transportation of the cylinders by a ground-based or water-based mode of transportation is unavailable and transportation by aircraft is the only practical means for transporting the cylinders to their destination;

(2) each cylinder is fully covered with a fire- or flame-resistant blanket that is secured in place; and

(3) the operator of the aircraft complies with the applicable notification procedures under section 175.33 of title 49, Code of Federal Regulations.

(c) AIRCRAFT RESTRICTION.—The exemption provided under subsection (a) shall apply only to the following types of aircraft:

(1) Cargo-only aircraft transporting the cylinders to a delivery destination that receives cargo-only service at least once a week.

(2) Passenger and cargo-only aircraft transporting the cylinders to a delivery destination that does not receive cargo-only service at least once a week.

(d) DESCRIPTION OF REGULATORY REQUIREMENTS.—The regulations described in this subsection are the regulations of the Pipeline and Hazardous Materials Safety Administration contained in sections 173.302(f)(3), 173.302(f)(4), 173.302(f)(5), 173.304(f)(3), 173.304(f)(4), and 173.304(f)(5) of title 49, Code of Federal Regulations.

SEC. 825. [49 U.S.C. 106 note] ORPHAN AVIATION EARMARKS.

(a) EARMARK DEFINED.—In this section, the term "earmark" means a statutory provision or report language included primarily at the request of a Senator or a Member, Delegate, or Resident Commissioner of the House of Representatives providing, authorizing, or recommending a specific amount of discretionary budget authority, credit authority, or other spending authority for a contract, loan, loan guarantee, grant, or other expenditure with or to an entity or a specific State, locality, or Congressional district, other than through a statutory or administrative formula-driven or competitive award process.

(b) RESCISSION.—If any earmark relating to the Federal Aviation Administration has more than 90 percent of applicable appropriated amounts remaining available for obligation at the end of the 9th fiscal year beginning after the fiscal year in which those amounts were appropriated, the unobligated portion of those amounts is rescinded effective at the end of that 9th fiscal year, except that the Administrator of the Federal Aviation Administration may delay any such rescission if the Administrator determines that an obligation with respect to those amounts is likely to occur during the 12-month period beginning on the last day of that 9th fiscal year.

(c) IDENTIFICATION AND REPORT.—

(1) AGENCY IDENTIFICATION.—At the end of each fiscal year, the Administrator shall identify and report to the Director of the Office of Management and Budget every earmark related to the Administration and with respect to which there is an

344

unobligated balance of appropriated amounts.

(2) ANNUAL REPORT.—Not later than 1 year after the date of enactment of this Act, and annually thereafter, the Director shall submit to Congress and make available to the public on the Internet Web site of the Office a report that includes—

(A) a listing of each earmark related to the Administration and with respect to which there is an unobligated balance of appropriated amounts, which shall include the amount of the original earmark, the amount of the unobligated balance related to that earmark, and the date on which the funding expires, if applicable;

(B) the number of rescissions under subsection (b) and the savings resulting from those rescissions for the previous fiscal year; and

(C) a listing of earmarks related to the Administration with amounts scheduled for rescission at the end of the current fiscal year.

* * * * * * *

SEC. 828. [49 U.S.C. 44701 note] AIR TRANSPORTATION OF LITHIUM CELLS AND BATTERIES.

(a) IN GENERAL.—The Secretary of Transportation, including a designee of the Secretary, may not issue or enforce any regulation or other requirement regarding the transportation by aircraft of lithium metal cells or batteries or lithium ion cells or batteries, whether transported separately or packed with or contained in equipment, if the requirement is more stringent than the requirements of the ICAO Technical Instructions.

(b) EXCEPTIONS.—

(1) PASSENGER CARRYING AIRCRAFT.—Notwithstanding subsection (a), the Secretary may enforce the prohibition on transporting primary (non-rechargeable) lithium batteries and cells aboard passenger carrying aircraft set forth in special provision A100 under section 172.102(c)(2) of title 49, Code of Federal Regulations (as in effect on the date of enactment of this Act).

(2) CREDIBLE REPORTS.—Notwithstanding subsection (a), if the Secretary obtains a credible report with respect to a

safety incident from a national or international governmental regulatory or investigating body that demonstrates that the presence of lithium metal cells or batteries or lithium ion cells or batteries on an aircraft, whether transported separately or packed with or contained in equipment, in accordance with the requirements of the ICAO Technical Instructions, has substantially contributed to the initiation or propagation of an onboard fire, the Secretary—

(A) may issue and enforce an emergency regulation, more stringent than the requirements of the ICAO Technical Instructions, that governs the transportation by aircraft of such cells or batteries, if that regulation—

(i) addresses solely deficiencies referenced in the report; and

(ii) is effective for not more than 1 year; and

(B) may adopt and enforce a permanent regulation, more stringent than the requirements of the ICAO Technical Instructions, that governs the transportation by aircraft of such cells or batteries, if—

(i) the Secretary bases the regulation upon substantial credible evidence that the otherwise permissible presence of such cells or batteries would substantially contribute to the initiation or propagation of an onboard fire;

(ii) the regulation addresses solely the deficiencies in existing regulations; and

(iii) the regulation imposes the least disruptive and least expensive variation from existing requirements while adequately addressing identified deficiencies.

(c) ICAO TECHNICAL INSTRUCTIONS DEFINED.—In this section, the term "ICAO Technical Instructions" means the International Civil Aviation Organization Technical Instructions for the Safe Transport of Dangerous Goods by Air (as amended, including amendments adopted after the date of enactment of this Act).

* * * * * * *

SEC. 830. APPROVAL OF APPLICATIONS FOR THE AIRPORT

SECURITY SCREENING OPT-OUT PROGRAM.

(a) IN GENERAL.—Section 44920(b) is amended to read as follows:

"(b) APPROVAL OF APPLICATIONS.

"(1) IN GENERAL. Not later than 120 days after the date of receipt of an application submitted by an airport operator under subsection (a), the Under Secretary shall approve or deny the application.

"(2) STANDARDS. The Under Secretary shall approve an application submitted by an airport operator under subsection (a) if the Under Secretary determines that the approval would not compromise security or detrimentally affect the cost-efficiency or the effectiveness of the screening of passengers or property at the airport.

"(3) REPORTS ON DENIALS OF APPLICATIONS.

"(A) IN GENERAL. If the Under Secretary denies an application submitted by an airport operator under subsection (a), the Under Secretary shall provide to the airport operator, not later than 60 days following the date of the denial, a written report that sets forth—

"(i) the findings that served as the basis for the denial;

"(ii) the results of any cost or security analysis conducted in considering the application; and

"(iii) recommendations on how the airport operator can address the reasons for the denial.

"(B) SUBMISSION TO CONGRESS. The Under Secretary shall submit to the Committee on Commerce, Science, and Transportation of the Senate and the Committee on Homeland Security of the House of Representatives a copy of any report provided to an airport operator under subparagraph (A).".

(b) WAIVERS.—Section 44920(d) is amended—

(1) by redesignating paragraphs (1) and (2) as subparagraphs (A) and (B), respectively, and moving the subparagraphs 2 ems to the right;

(2) by striking "The Under Secretary" and inserting the following:

"(1) IN GENERAL. The Under Secretary"

; and

(3) by adding at the end the following:

"(2) WAIVERS. The Under Secretary may waive the requirement of paragraph (1)(B) for any company that is a United States subsidiary with a parent company that has implemented a foreign ownership, control, or influence mitigation plan that has been approved by the Defense Security Service of the Department of Defense prior to the submission of the application. The Under Secretary has complete discretion to reject any application from a private screening company to provide screening services at an airport that requires a waiver under this paragraph.".

(c) RECOMMENDATIONS OF AIRPORT OPERATOR.—Section 44920 is amended by adding at the end the following:

"(h) RECOMMENDATIONS OF AIRPORT OPERATOR. As part of any submission of an application for a private screening company to provide screening services at an airport, the airport operator shall provide to the Under Secretary a recommendation as to which company would best serve the security screening and passenger needs of the airport, along with a statement explaining the basis of the operator's recommendation.".

(d) RECONSIDERATION OF APPLICATIONS PENDING AS OF JANUARY 1, 2011.—

(1) IN GENERAL.—Upon the request of an airport operator, the Secretary of Homeland Security shall reconsider any application for the screening of passengers and property that—

(A) was submitted by the operator of an airport pursuant to section 44920(a) of title 49, United States Code;

(B) was pending for final decision by the Secretary on any day between January 1, 2011, and February 3, 2011, and was resubmitted by the applicant in accordance with new guidelines provided by the Secretary after February 3, 2011; and

(C) has not been approved by the Secretary on or before the date of enactment of this Act.

(2) NOTICE TO AIRPORT OPERATORS.—In reconsidering an

application submitted under paragraph (1), the Secretary shall—

    (A) notify the airport operator that submitted the application that the Secretary will reconsider the application;

    (B) if the application was initially denied, advise the operator of the findings that served as the basis for the denial; and

    (C) request the operator to provide the Secretary with such additional information as the Secretary determines necessary to reconsider the application.

(3) DEADLINE; STANDARDS.—The Secretary shall approve or deny an application to be reconsidered under paragraph (1) not later than the 120th day following the date of the request for reconsideration from the airport operator. The Secretary shall apply the standards set forth in section 44920(b) of title 49, United States Code (as amended by this section), in approving and denying such application.

(4) REPORTS ON DENIALS OF APPLICATIONS.—

    (A) IN GENERAL.—If the Secretary denies an application of an airport operator following reconsideration under this subsection, the Secretary shall provide to the airport operator a written report that sets forth—

        (i) the findings that served as the basis for the denial; and

        (ii) the results of any cost or security analysis conducted in considering the application.

    (B) SUBMISSION TO CONGRESS.—The Secretary shall submit to the Committee on Commerce, Science, and Transportation of the Senate and the Committee on Homeland Security of the House of Representatives a copy of any report provided to an airport operator under subparagraph (A).

TITLE IX—FEDERAL AVIATION RESEARCH AND DEVELOPMENT

* * * * * * *

SEC. 902. [49 U.S.C. 40101 note] DEFINITIONS.

In this title, the following definitions apply:

(1) ADMINISTRATOR.—The term "Administrator" means the Administrator of the FAA.

(2) FAA.—The term "FAA" means the Federal Aviation Administration.

(3) INSTITUTION OF HIGHER EDUCATION.—The term "institution of higher education" has the same meaning given the term in section 101(a) of the Higher Education Act of 1965 (20 U.S.C. 1001(a)).

(4) NASA.—The term "NASA" means the National Aeronautics and Space Administration.

(5) NOAA.—The term "NOAA" means the National Oceanic and Atmospheric Administration.

* * * * * * *

SEC. 904. [49 U.S.C. 44505 note] RESEARCH PROGRAM ON RUNWAYS.

Using amounts made available under section 48102(a) of title 49, United States Code, the Administrator shall continue to carry out a research program under which the Administrator may make grants to and enter into cooperative agreements with institutions of higher education and pavement research organizations for research and technology demonstrations related to—

(1) the design, construction, rehabilitation, and repair of airfield pavements to aid in the development of safer, more cost effective, and more durable airfield pavements; and

(2) engineered material restraining systems for runways at both general aviation airports and airports with commercial air carrier operations.

* * * * * * *

SEC. 908. [49 U.S.C. 44513 note] CENTER OF EXCELLENCE FOR AVIATION HUMAN RESOURCE RESEARCH.

(a) ESTABLISHMENT.—Using amounts made available under section 48102(a) of title 49, United States Code, the Administrator may establish a center of excellence to conduct research on—

(1) human performance in the air transportation environment, including among air transportation personnel such as air traffic controllers, pilots, and technicians; and

(2) any other aviation human resource issue pertinent to developing and maintaining a safe and efficient air transportation system.

(b) ACTIVITIES.—Activities conducted under this section may include the following:

(1) Research, development, and evaluation of training programs for air traffic controllers, aviation safety inspectors, airway transportation safety specialists, and engineers.

(2) Research and development of best practices for recruitment of individuals into the aviation field for mission critical positions.

(3) Research, in consultation with other relevant Federal agencies, to develop a baseline of general aviation employment statistics and an analysis of future needs in the aviation field.

(4) Research and the development of a comprehensive assessment of the airframe and power plant technician certification process and its effect on employment trends.

(5) Evaluation of aviation maintenance technician school environments.

(6) Research and an assessment of the ability to develop training programs to allow for the transition of recently unemployed and highly skilled mechanics into the aviation field.

SEC. 909. [49 U.S.C. 40101 note] INTERAGENCY RESEARCH ON AVIATION AND THE ENVIRONMENT.

(a) IN GENERAL.—Using amounts made available under section 48102(a) of title 49, United States Code, the Administrator, in coordination with NASA and after consultation with other relevant agencies, may maintain a research program to assess the potential effect of aviation activities on the environment and, if warranted, to evaluate approaches to address any such effect.

(b) RESEARCH PLAN.—

(1) IN GENERAL.—The Administrator, in coordination with NASA and after consultation with other relevant agencies,

shall jointly develop a plan to carry out the research under subsection (a).

(2) CONTENTS.—The plan shall contain an inventory of current interagency research being undertaken in this area, future research objectives, proposed tasks, milestones, and a 5-year budgetary profile.

(3) REQUIREMENTS.—The plan—

(A) shall be completed not later than 1 year after the date of enactment of this Act;

(B) shall be submitted to Congress for review; and

(C) shall be updated, as appropriate, every 3 years after the initial submission.

SEC. 910. [49 U.S.C. 44504 note] AVIATION FUEL RESEARCH AND DEVELOPMENT PROGRAM.

(a) IN GENERAL.—Using amounts made available under section 48102(a) of title 49, United States Code, the Administrator, in coordination with the Administrator of NASA, shall continue research and development activities into the qualification of an unleaded aviation fuel and safe transition to this fuel for the fleet of piston engine aircraft.

(b) REQUIREMENTS.—In carrying out the program under subsection (a), the Administrator shall, at a minimum—

(1) not later than 120 days after the date of enactment of this Act, develop a research and development plan containing the specific research and development objectives, including consideration of aviation safety, technical feasibility, and other relevant factors, and the anticipated timetable for achieving the objectives;

(2) assess the methods and processes by which the FAA and industry may expeditiously certify and approve new aircraft and recertify existing aircraft with respect to unleaded aviation fuel;

(3) assess technologies that modify existing piston engine aircraft to enable safe operation of the aircraft using unleaded aviation fuel and determine the resources necessary to certify those technologies; and

(4) develop recommendations for appropriate policies and

guidelines to facilitate a transition to unleaded aviation fuel for piston engine aircraft.

(c) COLLABORATION.—In carrying out the program under subsection (a), the Administrator shall collaborate with—

(1) industry groups representing aviation consumers, manufacturers, and fuel producers and distributors; and

(2) other appropriate Federal agencies.

(d) REPORT.—Not later than 270 days after the date of enactment of this Act, the Administrator shall provide to the Committee on Science, Space, and Technology of the House of Representatives and the Committee on Commerce, Science, and Transportation of the Senate a report on the plan, information obtained, and policies and guidelines developed pursuant to subsection (b).

SEC. 911. [49 U.S.C. 44504 note] RESEARCH PROGRAM ON ALTERNATIVE JET FUEL TECHNOLOGY FOR CIVIL AIRCRAFT.

(a) IN GENERAL.—Using amounts made available under section 48102(a) of title 49, United States Code, the Administrator shall establish a research program to assist in the development and qualification of jet fuel from alternative sources (such as natural gas, biomass, ethanol, butanol, and hydrogen) and other renewable sources.

(b) AUTHORITY TO MAKE GRANTS.—The Administrator shall carry out the program through the use of grants or other measures authorized under section 106(l)(6) of such title, including reimbursable agreements with other Federal agencies.

(c) PARTICIPATION IN PROGRAM.—

(1) PARTICIPATION OF EDUCATIONAL AND RESEARCH INSTITUTIONS.—In carrying out the program, the Administrator shall include participation by—

(A) educational and research institutions that have existing facilities and leverage private sector partnerships; and

(B) consortia with experience across the supply chain, including with research, feedstock development and production, small-scale development, testing, and technology evaluation related to the creation, processing, production, and transportation of alternative aviation fuel.

(2) USE OF NASA FACILITIES.—In carrying out the program, the Administrator shall consider utilizing the existing capacity in aeronautics research at Langley Research Center, Glenn Research Center, and other appropriate facilities of NASA.

(d) DESIGNATION OF INSTITUTION AS A CENTER OF EXCELLENCE.—

(1) IN GENERAL.—Not later than 180 days after the date of enactment of this Act, the Administrator may designate an institution described in subsection (c)(1)(A) as a Center of Excellence for Alternative Jet-Fuel Research in Civil Aircraft.

(2) EFFECT OF DESIGNATION.—The center designated under paragraph (1) shall become, upon its designation—

(A) a member of the Consortium for Continuous Low Energy, Emissions, and Noise of the FAA; and

(B) part of a Joint Center of Excellence with the Partnership for Air Transportation Noise and Emission Reduction FAA Center of Excellence.

SEC. 912. REVIEW OF FAA'S ENERGY-RELATED AND ENVIRONMENT-RELATED RESEARCH PROGRAMS.

(a) REVIEW.—Using amounts made available under section 48102(a) of title 49, United States Code, the Administrator shall enter into an arrangement for an independent external review of FAA energy-related and environment-related research programs. The review shall assess whether—

(1) the programs have well-defined, prioritized, and appropriate research objectives;

(2) the programs are properly coordinated with the energy-related and environment-related research programs at NASA, NOAA, and other relevant agencies;

(3) the programs have allocated appropriate resources to each of the research objectives; and

(4) there exist suitable mechanisms for transitioning the research results into the FAA's operational technologies and procedures and certification activities.

(b) REPORT.—Not later than 18 months after the date of enactment of this Act, the Administrator shall submit a report to the Committee on Science, Space, and Technology of the House of Representatives and the Committee on Commerce, Science, and Transportation of the Senate containing the results of the review.

SEC. 913. REVIEW OF FAA'S AVIATION SAFETY-RELATED RESEARCH PROGRAMS.

(a) REVIEW.—Using amounts made available under section 48102(a) of title 49, United States Code, the Administrator shall enter into an arrangement for an independent external review of the FAA's aviation safety-related research programs. The review shall assess whether—

(1) the programs have well-defined, prioritized, and appropriate research objectives;

(2) the programs are properly coordinated with the safety research programs of NASA and other relevant Federal agencies;

(3) the programs have allocated appropriate resources to each of the research objectives;

(4) the programs should include a determination about whether a survey of participants across the air transportation system is an appropriate way to study safety risks within such system; and

(5) there exist suitable mechanisms for transitioning the research results from the programs into the FAA's operational technologies and procedures and certification activities in a timely manner.

(b) AVIATION SAFETY-RELATED RESEARCH PROGRAMS TO BE ASSESSED.—The FAA aviation safety-related research programs to be assessed under the review shall include, at a minimum, the following:

(1) Air traffic control/technical operations human factors.

(2) Runway incursion reduction.

(3) Flightdeck/maintenance system integration human factors.

(4) Airports technology research—safety.

(5) Airport Cooperative Research Program— safety.

(6) Weather Program.

(7) Atmospheric hazards/digital system safety.

(8) Fire research and safety.

(9) Propulsion and fuel systems.

(10) Advanced materials/structural safety.

(11) Aging aircraft.

(12) Aircraft catastrophic failure prevention research.

(13) Aeromedical research.

(14) Aviation safety risk analysis.

(15) Unmanned aircraft systems research.

(c) REPORT.—Not later than 14 months after the date of enactment of this Act, the Administrator shall submit to the Committee on Science, Space, and Technology of the House of Representatives and the Committee on Commerce, Science, and Transportation of the Senate a report on the results of the review.

SEC. 914. [49 U.S.C. 44504 note] PRODUCTION OF CLEAN COAL FUEL TECHNOLOGY FOR CIVILIAN AIRCRAFT.

(a) ESTABLISHMENT OF RESEARCH PROGRAM.—Using amounts made available under section 48102(a) of title 49, United States Code, the Administrator shall establish a research program related to developing jet fuel from clean coal.

(b) AUTHORITY TO MAKE GRANTS.—The Administrator shall carry out the program through grants or other measures authorized under section 106(l)(6) of such title, including reimbursable agreements with other Federal agencies.

(c) PARTICIPATION IN PROGRAM.—In carrying out the program, the Administrator shall include participation by educational and research institutions that have existing facilities and experience in the development and deployment of technology that processes coal into aviation fuel.

(d) DESIGNATION OF INSTITUTION AS A CENTER OF EXCELLENCE.—Not later than 180 days after the date of enactment of this Act, the Administrator may designate an institution described in subsection (c) as a Center of Excellence for Coal-to-Jet-Fuel Research.

* * * * * * *

SEC. 917. [49 U.S.C. 44504 note] RESEARCH AND DEVELOPMENT OF EQUIPMENT TO CLEAN AND MONITOR THE ENGINE AND APU BLEED

AIR SUPPLIED ON PRESSURIZED AIRCRAFT.

(a) IN GENERAL.—Not later than 60 days after the date of enactment of this Act, the Administrator, to the extent practicable, shall implement a research program for the identification or development of appropriate and effective air cleaning technology and sensor technology for the engine and auxiliary power unit bleed air supplied to the passenger cabin and flight deck of a pressurized aircraft.

(b) TECHNOLOGY REQUIREMENTS.—The technology referred to in subsection (a) shall have the capacity, at a minimum—

(1) to remove oil-based contaminants from the bleed air supplied to the passenger cabin and flight deck; and

(2) to detect and record oil-based contaminants in the portion of the total air supplied to the passenger cabin and flight deck from bleed air.

(c) REPORT.—Not later than 1 year after the date of enactment of this Act, the Administrator shall submit to the Committee on Commerce, Science, and Transportation of the Senate and the Committee on Transportation and Infrastructure and the Committee on Science, Space, and Technology of the House of Representatives a report on the results of the research and development work carried out under this section.

* * * * * * *

TITLE XI—AIRPORT AND AIRWAY TRUST FUND PROVISIONS AND RELATED TAXES

* * * * * * *

SEC. 1106. [26 U.S.C. 408 note] ROLLOVER OF AMOUNTS RECEIVED IN AIRLINE CARRIER BANKRUPTCY.

(a) GENERAL RULES.—

(1) ROLLOVER OF AIRLINE PAYMENT AMOUNT.—If a qualified airline employee receives any airline payment amount and transfers any portion of such amount to a traditional IRA within 180 days of receipt of such amount (or, if later, within 180 days of the date of the enactment of this Act), then such

amount (to the extent so transferred) shall be treated as a rollover contribution described in section 402(c) of the Internal Revenue Code of 1986. A qualified airline employee making such a transfer may exclude from gross income the amount transferred, in the taxable year in which the airline payment amount was paid to the qualified airline employee by the commercial passenger airline carrier.

(2) TRANSFER OF AMOUNTS ATTRIBUTABLE TO AIRLINE PAYMENT AMOUNT FOLLOWING ROLLOVER TO ROTH IRA.—A qualified airline employee who has contributed an airline payment amount to a Roth IRA that is treated as a qualified rollover contribution pursuant to section 125 of the Worker, Retiree, and Employer Recovery Act of 2008, may transfer to a traditional IRA, in a trustee-to-trustee transfer, all or any part of the contribution (together with any net income allocable to such contribution), and the transfer to the traditional IRA will be deemed to have been made at the time of the rollover to the Roth IRA, if such transfer is made within 180 days of the date of the enactment of this Act. A qualified airline employee making such a transfer may exclude from gross income the airline payment amount previously rolled over to the Roth IRA, to the extent an amount attributable to the previous rollover was transferred to a traditional IRA, in the taxable year in which the airline payment amount was paid to the qualified airline employee by the commercial passenger airline carrier. No amount so transferred to a traditional IRA may be treated as a qualified rollover contribution with respect to a Roth IRA within the 5-taxable year period beginning with the taxable year in which such transfer was made.

(3) EXTENSION OF TIME TO FILE CLAIM FOR REFUND.—A qualified airline employee who excludes an amount from gross income in a prior taxable year under paragraph (1) or (2) may reflect such exclusion in a claim for refund filed within the period of limitation under section 6511(a) of such Code (or, if later, April 15, 2015).

(4) OVERALL LIMITATION ON AMOUNTS TRANSFERRED TO TRADITIONAL IRAS.—

(A) IN GENERAL.—The aggregate amount of airline payment amounts which may be transferred to 1 or more traditional IRAs under paragraphs (1) and (2) with respect to any qualified employee for any taxable year shall not exceed the excess (if any) of—

(i) 90 percent of the aggregate airline payment amounts received by the qualified airline employee during the taxable year and all preceding taxable years, over

(ii) the aggregate amount of such transfers to which paragraphs (1) and (2) applied for all preceding taxable years.

(B) SPECIAL RULES.—For purposes of applying the limitation under subparagraph (A)—

(i) any airline payment amount received by the surviving spouse of any qualified employee, and any amount transferred to a traditional IRA by such spouse under subsection (d), shall be treated as an amount received or transferred by the qualified employee, and

(ii) any amount transferred to a traditional IRA which is attributable to net income described in paragraph (2) shall not be taken into account.

(5) COVERED EXECUTIVES NOT ELIGIBLE TO MAKE TRANSFERS.—Paragraphs (1) and (2) shall not apply to any transfer by a qualified airline employee (or any transfer authorized under subsection (d) by a surviving spouse of the qualified airline employee) if at any time during the taxable year of the transfer or any preceding taxable year the qualified airline employee held a position described in subparagraph (A) or (B) of section 162(m)(3) with the commercial passenger airline carrier from whom the airline payment amount was received.

(6) SPECIAL RULE FOR CERTAIN AIRLINE PAYMENT AMOUNTS.—In the case of any amount which became an airline payment amount by reason of the amendments made by section 1(b) of Public Law 113–243 (26 U.S.C. 408 note), paragraph (1) shall be applied by substituting "(or, if later, within the period beginning on December 18, 2014, and ending on the date which is 180 days after the date of enactment of the Protecting Americans from Tax Hikes Act of 2015)" for "(or, if later, within 180 days of the date of the enactment of this Act)".

(b) TREATMENT OF AIRLINE PAYMENT AMOUNTS AND TRANSFERS
FOR EMPLOYMENT TAXES.—For purposes of chapter 21 of the
Internal Revenue Code of 1986 and section 209 of the Social
Security Act, an airline payment amount shall not fail to be treated
as a payment of wages by the commercial passenger airline carrier
to the qualified airline employee in the taxable year of payment
because such amount is excluded from the qualified airline
employee's gross income under subsection (a).

(c) DEFINITIONS AND SPECIAL RULES.—For purposes of this
section—

(1) AIRLINE PAYMENT AMOUNT.—

(A) IN GENERAL.—The term "airline payment amount"
means any payment of any money or other property which
is payable by a commercial passenger airline carrier to a
qualified airline employee—

(i) under the approval of an order of a Federal
bankruptcy court in a case filed after September 11,
2001, and before January 1, 2007, or filed on November
29, 2011, and

(ii) in respect of the qualified airline employee's
interest in a bankruptcy claim against the carrier, any
note of the carrier (or amount paid in lieu of a note
being issued), or any other fixed obligation of the
carrier to pay a lump sum amount.

The amount of such payment shall be determined without
regard to any requirement to deduct and withhold tax from
such payment under sections 3102(a) of the Internal
Revenue Code of 1986 and 3402(a) of such Code.

(B) EXCEPTION.—An airline payment amount shall not
include any amount payable on the basis of the carrier's
future earnings or profits.

(2) QUALIFIED AIRLINE EMPLOYEE.—The term "qualified
airline employee" means an employee or former employee of a
commercial passenger airline carrier who was a participant in
a defined benefit plan maintained by the carrier which—

(A) is a plan described in section 401(a) of the Internal
Revenue Code of 1986 which includes a trust exempt from
tax under section 501(a) of such Code, and

(B) was terminated, became subject to the restrictions

contained in paragraphs (2) and (3) of section 402(b) of the Pension Protection Act of 2006, or was frozen effective November 1, 2012.

(3) TRADITIONAL IRA.—The term "traditional IRA" means an individual retirement plan (as defined in section 7701(a)(37) of the Internal Revenue Code of 1986) which is not a Roth IRA.

(4) ROTH IRA.—The term "Roth IRA" has the meaning given such term by section 408A(b) of such Code.

(d) SURVIVING SPOUSE.—If a qualified airline employee died after receiving an airline payment amount, or if an airline payment amount was paid to the surviving spouse of a qualified airline employee in respect of the qualified airline employee, the surviving spouse of the qualified airline employee may take all actions permitted under section 125 of the Worker, Retiree and Employer Recovery Act of 2008, or under this section, to the same extent that the qualified airline employee could have done had the qualified airline employee survived.

(e) [26 U.S.C. 4281 note] EFFECTIVE DATE.—This section shall apply to transfers made after the date of the enactment of this Act with respect to airline payment amounts paid before, on, or after such date.

* * * * * * *

TITLE XII—COMPLIANCE WITH STATUTORY PAY-AS-YOU-GO ACT OF 2010

SEC. 1201. COMPLIANCE PROVISION.

The budgetary effects of this Act, for the purpose of complying with the Statutory Pay-As-You-Go Act of 2010, shall be determined by reference to the latest statement titled "Budgetary Effects of PAYGO Legislation" for this Act, jointly submitted for printing in the Congressional Record by the Chairmen of the House and Senate Budget Committees, provided that such statement has been submitted prior to the vote on passage in the House acting first on this conference report or amendment between the Houses.

EUROPEAN UNION EMISSIONS TRADING SCHEME PROHIBITION ACT OF 2011

PUBLIC LAW 112-200

EUROPEAN UNION EMISSIONS TRADING SCHEME PROHIBITION ACT OF 2011

[(Public Law 112–200)]

[This law has not been amended]

AN ACT To prohibit operators of civil aircraft of the United States from participating in the European Union's emissions trading scheme, and for other purposes.

Be it enacted by the Senate and House of Representatives of the United States of America in Congress assembled,

SECTION 1. SHORT TITLE.

This Act may be cited as the "European Union Emissions Trading Scheme Prohibition Act of 2011".

SEC. 2. [49 U.S.C. 40101 note] PROHIBITION ON PARTICIPATION IN THE EUROPEAN UNION'S EMISSIONS TRADING SCHEME.

(a) IN GENERAL.—The Secretary of Transportation shall prohibit an operator of a civil aircraft of the United States from participating in the emissions trading scheme unilaterally established by the European Union in EU Directive 2003/87/EC of October 13, 2003, as amended, in any case in which the Secretary determines the prohibition to be, and in a manner that is, in the public interest, taking into account—

(1) the impacts on U.S. consumers, U.S. carriers, and U.S. operators;

(2) the impacts on the economic, energy, and environmental security of the United States; and

(3) the impacts on U.S. foreign relations, including existing international commitments.

(b) PUBLIC HEARING.—After determining that a prohibition

under this section may be in the public interest, the Secretary must hold a public hearing at least 30 days before imposing any prohibition.

(c) REASSESSMENT OF DETERMINATION OF PUBLIC INTEREST.—The Secretary—

(1) may reassess a determination under subsection (a) that a prohibition under that subsection is in the public interest at any time after making such a determination; and

(2) shall reassess such a determination after—

(A) any amendment by the European Union to the EU Directive referred to in subsection (a); or

(B) the adoption of any international agreement pursuant to section 3(1).

(C) enactment of a public law or issuance of a final rule after formal agency rulemaking, in the United State to address aircraft emissions.

SEC. 3. [49 U.S.C. 40101 note] NEGOTIATIONS.

(a) IN GENERAL.—The Secretary of Transportation, the Administrator of the Federal Aviation Administration, and other appropriate officials of the United States Government—

(1) should, as appropriate, use their authority to conduct international negotiations, including using their authority to conduct international negotiations to pursue a worldwide approach to address aircraft emissions, including the environmental impact of aircraft emissions; and

(2) shall, as appropriate and except as provided in subsection (b), take other actions under existing authorities that are in the public interest necessary to hold operators of civil aircraft of the United States harmless from the emissions trading scheme referred to under section 2.

(b) EXCLUSION OF PAYMENT OF TAXES AND PENALTIES.—Actions taken under subsection (a)(2) may not include the obligation or expenditure of any amounts in the Airport and Airway Trust Fund established under section 9905 of the Internal Revenue Code of 1986, or amounts otherwise made available to the Department of Transportation or any other Federal agency pursuant to appropriations Acts, for the payment of any tax or penalty imposed on an operator of civil aircraft of the United States pursuant to the

SEC. 4. [49 U.S.C. 40101 note] DEFINITION OF
CIVIL AIRCRAFT OF THE UNITED STATES.

European Union Emissions Trading Scheme
Prohibition Act of 2011

emissions trading scheme referred to under section 2.

SEC. 4. [49 U.S.C. 40101 note] DEFINITION OF CIVIL AIRCRAFT OF THE UNITED STATES.

In this Act, the term "civil aircraft of the United States" has the meaning given the term under section 40102(a) of title 49, United States Code.

Airline Safety and Federal Aviation Administration Extension Act of 2010

Public Law 111-216

AIRLINE SAFETY AND FEDERAL AVIATION ADMINISTRATION EXTENSION ACT OF 2010

[49 U.S.C. 44701 NOTE]

AIRLINE SAFETY AND PILOT TRAINING IMPROVEMENT

Pub. L. 111–216, title II, Aug. 1, 2010, 124 Stat. 2350, as amended by Pub. L. 111–249, §6, Sept. 30, 2010, 124 Stat. 2628; Pub. L. 117–286, §4(a)(315), Dec. 27, 2022, 136 Stat. 4340, provided that:

"SEC. 201. DEFINITIONS.

"(a) [sic] DEFINITIONS.—In this title, the following definitions apply:

"(1) ADVANCED QUALIFICATION PROGRAM.—The term 'advanced qualification program' means the program established by the Federal Aviation Administration in Advisory Circular 120–54A, dated June 23, 2006, including any subsequent revisions thereto.

"(2) AIR CARRIER.—The term 'air carrier' has the meaning given that term in section 40102 of title 49, United States Code.

"(3) AVIATION SAFETY ACTION PROGRAM.—The term 'aviation safety action program' means the program established by the Federal Aviation Administration in Advisory Circular 120–66B, dated November 15, 2002, including any subsequent revisions thereto.

"(4) FLIGHT CREWMEMBER.—The term 'flight crewmember' has the meaning given the term 'flightcrew member' in part 1 of title 14, Code of Federal Regulations.

"(5) FLIGHT OPERATIONAL QUALITY ASSURANCE PROGRAM.—The term 'flight operational quality assurance program' means the program established by the Federal Aviation Administration in Advisory Circular 120–82, dated April 12, 2004, including any subsequent revisions thereto.

"(6) LINE OPERATIONS SAFETY AUDIT.—The term 'line operations safety audit' means the procedure referenced by the Federal Aviation Administration in Advisory Circular 120–90, dated April 27, 2006, including any subsequent revisions thereto.

"(7) PART 121 AIR CARRIER.—The term 'part 121 air carrier' means an air carrier that holds a certificate issued under part 121 of title 14, Code of Federal Regulations.

"(8) PART 135 AIR CARRIER.—The term 'part 135 air carrier' means an air carrier that holds a certificate issued under part 135 of title 14, Code of Federal Regulations.

"SEC. 202. SECRETARY OF TRANSPORTATION RESPONSES TO SAFETY RECOMMENDATIONS.

"[Amended section 1135 of this title.]

"SEC. 203. FAA PILOT RECORDS DATABASE.

"[Amended section 44703 of this title.]

"SEC. 204. FAA TASK FORCE ON AIR CARRIER SAFETY AND PILOT TRAINING.

"(a) ESTABLISHMENT.—The Administrator of the Federal Aviation Administration shall establish a special task force to be known as the FAA Task Force on Air Carrier Safety and Pilot Training (in this section referred to as the 'Task Force').

"(b) COMPOSITION.—The Task Force shall consist of members appointed by the Administrator and shall include air carrier representatives, labor union representatives, and aviation safety experts with knowledge of foreign and domestic regulatory requirements for flight crewmember education and training.

"(c) DUTIES.—The duties of the Task Force shall include, at a minimum, evaluating best practices in the air carrier industry and providing recommendations in the following areas:

"(1) Air carrier management responsibilities for flight crewmember education and support.

"(2) Flight crewmember professional standards.

"(3) Flight crewmember training standards and performance.

"(4) Mentoring and information sharing between air carriers.

"(d) REPORT.—Not later than one year after the date of enactment "of this Act [Aug. 1, 2010], and before the last day of each one-year period thereafter until termination of the Task Force, the Task Force shall submit to the Committee on Transportation and Infrastructure of the House of Representatives and the Committee on Commerce, Science, and Transportation of the Senate a report detailing—

"(1) the progress of the Task Force in identifying best practices in the air carrier industry;

"(2) the progress of air carriers and labor unions in implementing the best practices identified by the Task Force;

"(3) recommendations of the Task Force, if any, for legislative or regulatory actions;

"(4) the progress of air carriers and labor unions in implementing training-related, nonregulatory actions recommended by the Administrator; and

"(5) the progress of air carriers in developing specific programs to share safety data and ensure implementation of the most effective safety practices.

"(e) TERMINATION.—The Task Force shall terminate on September 30, 2012.

"(f) APPLICABILITY OF CHAPTER 10 OF TITLE 5, UNITED STATES CODE.—Chapter 10 of title 5, United States Code, shall not apply to the Task Force.

"SEC. 205. AVIATION SAFETY INSPECTORS AND OPERATIONAL RESEARCH ANALYSTS.

"(a) REVIEW BY DOT INSPECTOR GENERAL.—Not later than 9 months after the date of enactment of this Act [Aug. 1, 2010], the Inspector General of the Department of Transportation shall conduct a review of the aviation safety inspectors and operational research analysts of the Federal Aviation Administration assigned to part 121 air carriers and submit to the Administrator of the Federal Aviation Administration a report on the results of the review.

"(b) PURPOSES.—The purpose of the review shall be, at a minimum—

"(1) to review the level of the Administration's oversight of each part 121 air carrier;

"(2) to make recommendations to ensure that each part 121 air carrier is receiving an equivalent level of oversight;

"(3) to assess the number and level of experience of aviation safety inspectors assigned to each part 121 air carrier;

"(4) to evaluate how the Administration is making assignments of aviation safety inspectors to each part 121 air carrier;

"(5) to review various safety inspector oversight programs, including the geographic inspector program;

"(6) to evaluate the adequacy of the number of operational research analysts assigned to each part 121 air carrier;

"(7) to evaluate the surveillance responsibilities of aviation safety inspectors, including en route inspections;

"(8) to evaluate whether inspectors are able to effectively use data sources, such as the Safety Performance Analysis System and the Air Transportation Oversight System, to assist in targeting oversight of each part 121 air carrier;

"(9) to assess the feasibility of establishment by the Administration of a comprehensive repository of information that encompasses multiple Administration data sources and allows access by aviation safety inspectors and operational research analysts to assist in the oversight of each part 121 air carrier; and

"(10) to conduct such other analyses as the Inspector General considers relevant to the review.

"SEC. 206. FLIGHT CREWMEMBER MENTORING, PROFESSIONAL DEVELOPMENT, AND LEADERSHIP.

"(a) AVIATION RULEMAKING COMMITTEE.—

"(1) IN GENERAL.—The Administrator of the Federal Aviation Administration shall convene an aviation rulemaking committee to develop procedures for each part 121 air carrier to take the following actions:

"(A) Establish flight crewmember mentoring programs under which the air carrier will pair highly experienced flight crewmembers who will serve as mentor pilots and be paired with newly employed flight crewmembers. Mentor pilots should be provided, at a minimum, specific instruction on techniques for instilling and reinforcing the highest standards of technical performance, airmanship, and professionalism in newly employed flight crewmembers.

"(B) Establish flight crewmember professional development committees made up of air carrier management and labor union or professional association representatives to develop, administer, and oversee formal mentoring programs of the carrier to assist flight crewmembers to reach their maximum potential as safe, seasoned, and proficient flight crewmembers.

"(C) Establish or modify training programs to accommodate substantially different levels and types of flight experience by newly employed flight crewmembers.

"(D) Establish or modify training programs for second-in-command flight crewmembers attempting to qualify as pilot-in-command flight crewmembers for the first time in a specific aircraft type and ensure that such programs include leadership and command training.

"(E) Ensure that recurrent training for pilots in command includes leadership and command training.

"(F) Such other actions as the aviation rulemaking committee determines appropriate to enhance flight crewmember professional development.

"(2) COMPLIANCE WITH STERILE COCKPIT RULE.—Leadership and command training described in paragraphs (1)(D) and (1)(E) shall include instruction on compliance with flight crewmember duties under part 121.542 of title 14, Code of Federal Regulations.

"(3) STREAMLINED PROGRAM REVIEW.—

"(A) IN GENERAL.—As part of the rulemaking required by subsection (b), the Administrator shall establish a streamlined review process for part 121 air carriers that have in effect, as of the date of enactment of this Act [Aug. 1, 2010], the programs described in paragraph (1).

"(B) EXPEDITED APPROVALS.—Under the streamlined review process, the Administrator shall—

"(i) review the programs of such part 121 air carriers to determine whether the programs meet the requirements set forth in the final rule referred to in subsection (b)(2); and

"(ii) expedite the approval of the programs that the Administrator determines meet such requirements.

"(b) RULEMAKING.—The Administrator shall issue—

"(1) not later than one year after the date of enactment of this Act, a notice of proposed rulemaking based on the recommendations of the aviation rulemaking committee convened under subsection (a); and

"(2) not later than 36 months after such date of enactment, a final rule based on such recommendations.

"SEC. 207. FLIGHT CREWMEMBER PAIRING AND CREW RESOURCE MANAGEMENT TECHNIQUES.

"(a) STUDY.—The Administrator of the Federal Aviation Administration shall conduct a study on aviation industry best practices with regard to flight crewmember pairing, crew resource management techniques, and pilot commuting.

"(b) REPORT.—Not later than one year after the date of enactment of this Act [Aug. 1, 2010], the Administrator shall submit to the Committee on Transportation and Infrastructure of the House of Representatives and the Committee on Commerce, Science, and Transportation of the Senate a report on the results of the study.

"SEC. 208. IMPLEMENTATION OF NTSB FLIGHT CREWMEMBER TRAINING RECOMMENDATIONS.

"(a) RULEMAKING PROCEEDINGS.—

"(1) STALL AND UPSET RECOGNITION AND RECOVERY TRAINING.—The Administrator of the Federal Aviation Administration shall conduct a rulemaking proceeding to require part 121 air carriers to provide flight crewmembers with ground training and flight training or flight simulator training—

"(A) to recognize and avoid a stall of an aircraft or, if not avoided, to recover from the stall; and

"(B) to recognize and avoid an upset of an aircraft or, if not avoided, to execute such techniques as available data indicate are appropriate to recover from the upset in a given make, model, and series of aircraft.

"(2) REMEDIAL TRAINING PROGRAMS.—The Administrator shall conduct a rulemaking proceeding to require part 121 air carriers to establish remedial training programs for flight crewmembers who have demonstrated performance deficiencies or experienced failures in the training environment.

"(3) DEADLINES.—The Administrator shall—

"(A) not later than one year after the date of enactment of this Act [Aug. 1, 2010], issue a notice of proposed rulemaking under each of paragraphs (1) and (2); and

"(B) not later than 36 months after the date of enactment of this Act, issue a final rule for the rulemaking under each of paragraphs (1) and (2).

"(b) STICK PUSHER TRAINING AND WEATHER EVENT TRAINING.—

"(1) MULTIDISCIPLINARY PANEL.—Not later than 120 days after the date of enactment of this Act, the Administrator shall convene a multidisciplinary panel of specialists in aircraft operations, flight crewmember training, human factors, and aviation safety to study and submit to the Administrator a report on methods to increase the familiarity of flight crewmembers with, and improve the response of flight crewmembers to, stick pusher systems, icing conditions, and microburst and windshear weather events.

"(2) REPORT TO CONGRESS AND NTSB.—Not later than one year after the date on which the Administrator convenes the panel, the Administrator shall—

"(A) submit to the Committee on Transportation and Infrastructure of the House of Representatives, the Committee on Commerce, Science, and Transportation of the Senate, and the National Transportation Safety Board a report based on the findings of the panel; and

"(B) with respect to stick pusher systems, initiate appropriate actions to implement the recommendations of the panel.

"(c) DEFINITIONS.—In this section, the following definitions apply:

"(1) FLIGHT TRAINING AND FLIGHT SIMULATOR.—The terms 'flight training' and 'flight simulator' have the meanings given those terms in part 61.1 of title 14, Code of Federal Regulations (or any successor regulation).

"(2) STALL.—The term 'stall' means an aerodynamic loss of lift caused by exceeding the critical angle of attack.

"(3) STICK PUSHER.—The term 'stick pusher' means a device that, at or near a stall, applies a nose down pitch force to an aircraft's control columns to attempt to decrease the aircraft's angle of attack.

"(4) UPSET.—The term 'upset' means an unusual aircraft attitude.

"SEC. 209. FAA RULEMAKING ON TRAINING PROGRAMS.

"(a) COMPLETION OF RULEMAKING ON TRAINING PROGRAMS.—Not later than 14 months after the date of enactment of this Act [Aug. 1, 2010], the Administrator of the Federal Aviation Administration shall issue a final rule with respect to the notice of proposed rulemaking published in the Federal Register on January 12, 2009 (74 Fed. Reg. 1280; relating to training programs for flight crewmembers and aircraft dispatchers).

"(b) EXPERT PANEL TO REVIEW PART 121 AND PART 135 TRAINING HOURS.—

"(1) ESTABLISHMENT.—Not later than 60 days after the date of enactment of this Act, the Administrator shall convene a multidisciplinary expert panel comprised of, at a minimum, air carrier representatives, training facility representatives, instructional design experts, aircraft manufacturers, safety organization representatives, and labor union representatives.

"(2) ASSESSMENT AND RECOMMENDATIONS.—The panel shall assess and make recommendations concerning—

"(A) the best methods and optimal time needed for flight crewmembers of part 121 air carriers and flight crewmembers of part 135 air carriers to master aircraft systems, maneuvers, procedures, takeoffs and landings, and crew coordination;

"(B) initial and recurrent testing requirements for pilots, including the rigor and consistency of testing programs such as check rides;

"(C) the optimal length of time between training events for such flight crewmembers, including recurrent training events;

"(D) the best methods reliably to evaluate mastery by such flight crewmembers of aircraft systems, maneuvers, procedures, takeoffs and landings, and crew coordination;

"(E) classroom instruction requirements governing curriculum content and hours of instruction;

"(F) the best methods to allow specific academic training courses to be credited toward the total flight hours required to receive an airline transport pilot certificate; and

"(G) crew leadership training.

"(3) BEST PRACTICES.—In making recommendations under subsection (b)(2), the panel shall consider, if appropriate, best practices in the aviation industry with respect to training protocols, methods, and procedures.

"(4) REPORT.—Not later than one year after the date of enactment of this Act, the Administrator shall submit to the Committee on Transportation and Infrastructure of the House of Representatives, the Committee on Commerce, Science, and Transportation of the Senate, and the National Transportation Safety Board a report based on the findings of the panel.

"SEC. 210. DISCLOSURE OF AIR CARRIERS OPERATING FLIGHTS FOR TICKETS SOLD FOR AIR TRANSPORTATION.

"[Amended section 41712 of this title.]

"SEC. 211. SAFETY INSPECTIONS OF REGIONAL AIR CARRIERS.

"The Administrator of the Federal Aviation Administration shall perform, not less frequently than once each year, random, onsite inspections of air carriers that provide air transportation pursuant to a contract with a part 121 air carrier to ensure that such air carriers are complying with all applicable safety standards of the Administration.

"SEC. 212. PILOT FATIGUE.

"(a) FLIGHT AND DUTY TIME REGULATIONS.—

"(1) IN GENERAL.—In accordance with paragraph (3), the Administrator of the Federal Aviation Administration shall issue regulations, based on the best available scientific information, to specify limitations on the hours of flight and duty time allowed for pilots to address problems relating to pilot fatigue.

"(2) MATTERS TO BE ADDRESSED.—In conducting the rulemaking proceeding under this subsection, the Administrator shall consider and review the following:

"(A) Time of day of flights in a duty period.

"(B) Number of takeoff and landings in a duty period.

"(C) Number of time zones crossed in a duty period.

"(D) The impact of functioning in multiple time zones or on different daily schedules.

"(E) Research conducted on fatigue, sleep, and circadian rhythms.

"(F) Sleep and rest requirements recommended by the National Transportation Safety Board and the National Aeronautics and Space Administration.

"(G) International standards regarding flight schedules and duty periods.

"(H) Alternative procedures to facilitate alertness in the cockpit.

"(I) Scheduling and attendance policies and practices, including sick leave.

"(J) The effects of commuting, the means of commuting, and the length of the commute.

"(K) Medical screening and treatment.

"(L) Rest environments.

"(M) Any other matters the Administrator considers appropriate.

"(3) RULEMAKING.—The Administrator shall issue—

"(A) not later than 180 days after the date of enactment of this Act [Aug. 1, 2010], a notice of proposed rulemaking under paragraph (1); and

"(B) not later than one year after the date of enactment of this Act, a final rule under paragraph (1).

"(b) FATIGUE RISK MANAGEMENT PLAN.—

"(1) SUBMISSION OF FATIGUE RISK MANAGEMENT PLAN BY PART 121 AIR CARRIERS.—Not later than 90 days after the date of enactment of this Act, each part 121 air carrier shall submit to the Administrator for review and acceptance a fatigue risk management plan for the carrier's pilots.

"(2) CONTENTS OF PLAN.—A fatigue risk management plan submitted by a part 121 air carrier under paragraph (1) shall include the following:

"(A) Current flight time and duty period limitations.

"(B) A rest scheme consistent with such limitations that enables the management of pilot fatigue, including annual training to increase awareness of—

"(i) fatigue;

"(ii) the effects of fatigue on pilots; and

"(iii) fatigue countermeasures.

"(C) Development and use of a methodology that continually assesses the effectiveness of the program, including the ability of the program—

"(i) to improve alertness; and

"(ii) to mitigate performance errors.

"(3) REVIEW.—Not later than 12 months after the date of enactment of this Act, the Administrator shall review and accept or reject the fatigue risk management plans submitted under this subsection. If the Administrator rejects a plan, the Administrator shall provide suggested modifications for resubmission of the plan.

"(4) PLAN UPDATES.—

"(A) IN GENERAL.—A part 121 air carrier shall update its fatigue risk management plan under paragraph (1) every 2 years and submit the update to the Administrator for review and acceptance.

"(B) REVIEW.—Not later than 12 months after the date of submission of a plan update under subparagraph (A), the Administrator shall review and accept or reject the update. If the Administrator rejects an update, the Administrator shall provide suggested modifications for resubmission of the update.

"(5) COMPLIANCE.—A part 121 air carrier shall comply with the fatigue risk management plan of the air carrier that is accepted by the Administrator under this subsection.

"(6) CIVIL PENALTIES.—A violation of this subsection by a part 121 air carrier shall be treated as a violation of chapter 447 of title 49, United States Code, for purposes of the application of civil penalties under chapter 463 of that title.

"(c) EFFECT OF COMMUTING ON FATIGUE.—

"(1) IN GENERAL.—Not later than 60 days after the date of enactment of this Act, the Administrator shall enter into appropriate arrangements with the National Academy of Sciences to conduct a study of the effects of commuting on pilot fatigue and report its findings to the Administrator.

"(2) STUDY.—In conducting the study, the National Academy of Sciences shall consider—

"(A) the prevalence of pilot commuting in the commercial air carrier industry, including the number and percentage of pilots who commute;

"(B) information relating to commuting by pilots, including distances traveled, time zones crossed, time spent, and methods used;

"(C) research on the impact of commuting on pilot fatigue, sleep, and circadian rhythms;

"(D) commuting policies of commercial air carriers (including passenger and all-cargo air carriers), including pilot check-in requirements and sick leave and fatigue policies;

"(E) postconference materials from the Federal Aviation Administration's June 2008 symposium titled 'Aviation Fatigue Management Symposium: Partnerships for Solutions';

"(F) Federal Aviation Administration and international policies and guidance regarding commuting; and

"(G) any other matters as the Administrator considers appropriate.

"(3) PRELIMINARY FINDINGS.—Not later than 120 days after the date of entering into arrangements under paragraph (1), the National Academy of Sciences shall submit to the Administrator its preliminary findings under the study.

"(4) REPORT.—Not later than 9 months after the date of entering into arrangements under paragraph (1), the National Academy of Sciences shall submit a report to the Administrator containing its findings under the study and any recommendations for regulatory or administrative actions by the Federal Aviation Administration concerning commuting by pilots.

"(5) RULEMAKING.—Following receipt of the report of the National Academy of Sciences under paragraph (4), the Administrator shall—

"(A) consider the findings and recommendations in the report; and

"(B) update, as appropriate based on scientific data, regulations required by subsection (a) on flight and duty time.

"SEC. 213. VOLUNTARY SAFETY PROGRAMS.

"(a) REPORT.—Not later than 180 days after the date of enactment of this Act [Aug. 1, 2010], the Administrator of the Federal Aviation Administration shall submit to the Committee on Transportation and Infrastructure of the House of Representatives and the Committee on Commerce, Science, and Transportation of the Senate a report on the aviation safety action program, the flight operational quality assurance program, the line operations safety audit, and the advanced qualification program.

"(b) CONTENTS.—The report shall include—

"(1) a list of—

"(A) which air carriers are using one or more of the voluntary safety programs referred to in subsection (a); and

"(B) the voluntary safety programs each air carrier is using;

"(2) if an air carrier is not using one or more of the voluntary safety programs—

"(A) a list of such programs the carrier is not using; and

"(B) the reasons the carrier is not using each such program;

"(3) if an air carrier is using one or more of the voluntary safety programs, an explanation of the benefits and challenges of using each such program;

"(4) a detailed analysis of how the Administration is using data derived from each of the voluntary safety programs as safety analysis and accident or incident prevention tools and a detailed plan on how the Administration intends to expand data analysis of such programs;

"(5) an explanation of—

"(A) where the data derived from the voluntary safety programs is stored;

"(B) how the data derived from such programs is protected and secured; and

"(C) what data analysis processes air carriers are implementing to ensure the effective use of the data derived from such programs;

"(6) a description of the extent to which aviation safety inspectors are able to review data derived from the voluntary safety programs to enhance their oversight responsibilities;

"(7) a description of how the Administration plans to incorporate operational trends identified under the voluntary safety programs into the air transport oversight system and other surveillance databases so that such system and databases are more effectively utilized;

"(8) other plans to strengthen the voluntary safety programs, taking into account reviews of such programs by the Inspector General of the Department of Transportation; and

"(9) such other matters as the Administrator determines are appropriate.

"SEC. 214. ASAP AND FOQA IMPLEMENTATION PLAN.

"(a) Development and Implementation Plan.—The Administrator of the Federal Aviation Administration shall develop and implement a plan to facilitate the establishment of an aviation safety action program and a flight operational quality assurance program by all part 121 air carriers.

"(b) Matters To Be Considered.—In developing the plan under subsection (a), the Administrator shall consider—

"(1) how the Administration can assist part 121 air carriers with smaller fleet sizes to derive a benefit from establishing a flight operational quality assurance program;

"(2) how part 121 air carriers with established aviation safety action and flight operational quality assurance programs can quickly begin to report data into the aviation safety information analysis sharing database; and

"(3) how part 121 air carriers and aviation safety inspectors can better utilize data from such database as accident and incident prevention tools.

"(c) Report.—Not later than 180 days after the date of enactment of this Act [Aug. 1, 2010], the Administrator shall submit to the Committee on Transportation and Infrastructure of the House of Representatives and the Committee on Commerce, Science, and Transportation of the Senate a copy of the plan developed under subsection (a) and an explanation of how the Administration will implement the plan.

"(d) Deadline for Beginning Implementation of Plan.—Not later than one year after the date of enactment of this Act, the Administrator shall begin implementation of the plan developed under subsection (a).

"SEC. 215. SAFETY MANAGEMENT SYSTEMS.

"(a) Rulemaking.—The Administrator of the Federal Aviation Administration shall conduct a rulemaking proceeding to require all part 121 air carriers to implement a safety management system.

"(b) Matters To Consider.—In conducting the rulemaking under subsection (a), the Administrator shall consider, at a minimum, including each of the following as a part of the safety management system:

"(1) An aviation safety action program.

"(2) A flight operational quality assurance program.

"(3) A line operations safety audit.

"(4) An advanced qualification program.

"(c) Deadlines.—The Administrator shall issue—

"(1) not later than 90 days after the date of enactment of this Act [Aug. 1, 2010], a notice of proposed rulemaking under subsection (a); and

"(2) not later than 24 months after the date of enactment of this Act, a final rule under subsection (a).

"(d) Safety Management System Defined.—In this section, the term 'safety management system' means the program established by the Federal Aviation Administration in Advisory Circular 120–92, dated June 22, 2006, including any subsequent revisions thereto.

"SEC. 216. FLIGHT CREWMEMBER SCREENING AND QUALIFICATIONS.

"(a) Requirements.—

"(1) RULEMAKING PROCEEDING.—The Administrator of the Federal Aviation Administration shall conduct a rulemaking proceeding to require part 121 air carriers to develop and implement means and methods for ensuring that flight crewmembers have proper qualifications and experience.

"(2) MINIMUM REQUIREMENTS.—

"(A) PROSPECTIVE FLIGHT CREWMEMBERS.—Rules issued under paragraph (1) shall ensure that prospective flight crewmembers undergo comprehensive preemployment screening, including an assessment of the skills, aptitudes, airmanship, and suitability of each applicant for a position as a flight crewmember in terms of functioning effectively in the air carrier's operational environment.

"(B) ALL FLIGHT CREWMEMBERS.—Rules issued under paragraph (1) shall ensure that, after the date that is 3 years after the date of enactment of this Act [Aug. 1, 2010], all flight crewmembers—

"(i) have obtained an airline transport pilot certificate under part 61 of title 14, Code of Federal Regulations; and

"(ii) have appropriate multi-engine aircraft flight experience, as determined by the Administrator.

"(b) DEADLINES.—The Administrator shall issue—

"(1) not later than 180 days after the date of enactment of this Act, a notice of proposed rulemaking under subsection (a); and

"(2) not later than 24 months after such date of enactment, a final rule under subsection (a).

"(c) DEFAULT.—The requirement that each flight crewmember for a part 121 air carrier hold an airline transport pilot certificate under part 61 of title 14, Code of Federal Regulations, shall begin to apply on the date that is 3 years after the date of enactment of this Act even if the Administrator fails to meet a deadline established under this section.

"SEC. 217. AIRLINE TRANSPORT PILOT CERTIFICATION.

"(a) RULEMAKING PROCEEDING.—The Administrator of the Federal Aviation Administration shall conduct a rulemaking proceeding to amend part 61 of title 14, Code of Federal Regulations, to modify requirements for the issuance of an airline transport pilot certificate.

"(b) MINIMUM REQUIREMENTS.—To be qualified to receive an airline transport pilot certificate pursuant to subsection (a), an individual shall—

"(1) have sufficient flight hours, as determined by the Administrator, to enable a pilot to function effectively in an air carrier operational environment; and

"(2) have received flight training, academic training, or operational experience that will prepare a pilot, at a minimum, to—

"(A) function effectively in a multipilot environment;

"(B) function effectively in adverse weather conditions, including icing conditions;

"(C) function effectively during high altitude operations;

"(D) adhere to the highest professional standards; and

"(E) function effectively in an air carrier operational environment.

"(c) FLIGHT HOURS.—

"(1) NUMBERS OF FLIGHT HOURS.—The total flight hours required by the

Administrator under subsection (b)(1) shall be at least 1,500 flight hours.

"(2) FLIGHT HOURS IN DIFFICULT OPERATIONAL CONDITIONS.—The total flight hours required by the Administrator under subsection (b)(1) shall include sufficient flight hours, as determined by the Administrator, in difficult operational conditions that may be encountered by an air carrier to enable a pilot to operate safely in such conditions.

"(d) CREDIT TOWARD FLIGHT HOURS.—The Administrator may allow specific academic training courses, beyond those required under subsection (b)(2), to be credited toward the total flight hours required under subsection (c). The Administrator may allow such credit based on a determination by the Administrator that allowing a pilot to take specific academic training courses will enhance safety more than requiring the pilot to fully comply with the flight hours requirement.

"(e) RECOMMENDATIONS OF EXPERT PANEL.—In conducting the rulemaking proceeding under this section, the Administrator shall review and consider the assessment and recommendations of the expert panel to review part 121 and part 135 training hours established by section 209(b) of this Act.

"(f) DEADLINE.—Not later than 36 months after the date of enactment of this Act [Aug. 1, 2010], the Administrator shall issue a final rule under subsection (a)."

FAA INSPECTOR TRAINING

Pub. L. 108–176, title V, §506, Dec. 12, 2003, 117 Stat. 2560, provided that:

"(a) STUDY.—

"(1) IN GENERAL.—The Comptroller General shall conduct a study of the training of the aviation safety inspectors of the Federal Aviation Administration (in this section referred to as 'FAA inspectors').

"(2) CONTENTS.—The study shall include—

"(A) an analysis of the type of training provided to FAA inspectors;

"(B) actions that the Federal Aviation Administration has undertaken to ensure that FAA inspectors receive up-to-date training on the latest technologies;

"(C) the extent of FAA inspector training provided by the aviation industry and whether such training is provided without charge or on a quid pro quo basis; and

"(D) the amount of travel that is required of FAA inspectors in receiving training.

"(3) REPORT.—Not later than 1 year after the date of enactment of this Act [Dec. 12, 2003], the Comptroller General shall transmit to the Committee on Transportation and Infrastructure of the House of Representatives and the Committee on Commerce, Science, and Transportation of the Senate a report on the results of the study.

"(b) SENSE OF THE HOUSE.—It is the sense of the House of Representatives that—

"(1) FAA inspectors should be encouraged to take the most up-to-date initial and recurrent training on the latest aviation technologies;

"(2) FAA inspector training should have a direct relation to an individual's job requirements; and

"(3) if possible, a FAA inspector should be allowed to take training at the location most convenient for the inspector.

"(c) WORKLOAD OF INSPECTORS.—

"(1) STUDY BY NATIONAL ACADEMY OF SCIENCES.—Not later than 90 days after the date of enactment of this Act [Dec. 12, 2003], the Administrator of the Federal Aviation Administration shall make appropriate arrangements for the National Academy of Sciences to conduct a study of the assumptions and methods used by the Federal Aviation Administration to estimate staffing standards for FAA inspectors to ensure proper oversight over the aviation industry, including the designee program.

"(2) CONTENTS.—The study shall include the following:

"(A) A suggested method of modifying FAA inspectors staffing models for application to current local conditions or applying some other approach to developing an objective staffing standard.

"(B) The approximate cost and length of time for developing such models.

"(3) REPORT.—Not later than 12 months after the initiation of the arrangements under subsection (a), the National Academy of Sciences shall transmit to Congress a report on the results of the study."

AIR TRANSPORTATION OVERSIGHT SYSTEM

Pub. L. 106–181, title V, §513, Apr. 5, 2000, 114 Stat. 144, provided that:

"(a) REPORT.—Not later than August 1, 2000, the Administrator [of the Federal Aviation Administration] shall transmit to the Committee on Transportation and Infrastructure of the House of Representatives and the Committee on Commerce, Science, and Transportation of the Senate a report on the progress of the Federal Aviation Administration in implementing the air transportation oversight system, including in detail the training of inspectors under the system, the number of inspectors using the system, air carriers subject to the system, and the budget for the system.

"(b) REQUIRED CONTENTS.—At a minimum, the report shall indicate—

"(1) any funding or staffing constraints that would adversely impact the Administration's ability to continue to develop and implement the air transportation oversight system;

"(2) progress in integrating the aviation safety data derived from such system's inspections with existing aviation data of the Administration in the safety performance analysis system of the Administration; and

"(3) the Administration's efforts in collaboration with the aviation industry to develop and validate safety performance measures and appropriate risk weightings for such system.

"(c) UPDATE.—Not later than August 1, 2002, the Administrator shall update the report submitted under this section and transmit the updated report to the committees referred to in subsection (a)."

REGULATION OF ALASKA GUIDE PILOTS

Pub. L. 106–181, title VII, §732, Apr. 5, 2000, 114 Stat. 168, as amended by Pub. L. 118–63, title II, §218(h), May 16, 2024, 138 Stat. 1056, provided that:

"(a) IN GENERAL.—Beginning on the date of the enactment of this Act [Apr. 5, 2000], flight operations conducted by Alaska guide pilots shall be regulated under the general operating and flight rules contained in part 91 of title 14, Code of Federal Regulations.

"(b) DEFINITION OF ALASKA GUIDE PILOT.—In this section the term 'Alaska guide pilot' means a pilot who—

"(1) conducts aircraft operations over or within the State of Alaska;

"(2) operates single engine, fixed-wing aircraft on floats, wheels, or skis, providing commercial hunting, fishing, or other guide services and related accommodations in the form of camps or lodges; and

"(3) transports clients by such aircraft incidental to hunting, fishing, or other guide services."

AVIATION MEDICAL ASSISTANCE

Pub. L. 105–170, Apr. 24, 1998, 112 Stat. 47, provided that:

"SECTION 1. SHORT TITLE.

"This Act may be cited as the 'Aviation Medical Assistance Act of 1998'.

"SEC. 2. MEDICAL KIT EQUIPMENT AND TRAINING.

"Not later than 1 year after the date of the enactment of this Act [Apr. 24, 1998], the Administrator of the Federal Aviation Administration shall reevaluate regulations regarding: (1) the equipment required to be carried in medical kits of aircraft operated by air carriers; and (2) the training required of flight attendants in the use of such equipment, and, if the Administrator determines that such regulations should be modified as a result of such reevaluation, shall issue a notice of proposed rulemaking to modify such regulations.

"SEC. 3. REPORTS REGARDING DEATHS ON AIRCRAFT.

"(a) IN GENERAL.—During the 1-year period beginning on the 90th day following the date of the enactment of this Act [Apr. 24, 1998], a major air carrier shall make a good faith effort to obtain, and shall submit quarterly reports to the Administrator of the Federal Aviation Administration on, the following:

"(1) The number of persons who died on aircraft of the air carrier, including any person who was declared dead after being removed from such an aircraft as a result of a medical incident that occurred on such aircraft.

"(2) The age of each such person.

"(3) Any information concerning cause of death that is available at the time such person died on the aircraft or is removed from the aircraft or that subsequently becomes known to the air carrier.

"(4) Whether or not the aircraft was diverted as a result of the death or incident.

"(5) Such other information as the Administrator may request as necessary to aid in a decision as to whether or not to require automatic external defibrillators in airports or on aircraft operated by air carriers, or both.

"(b) FORMAT.—The Administrator may specify a format for reports to be submitted under this section.

"SEC. 4. DECISION ON AUTOMATIC EXTERNAL DEFIBRILLATORS.

"(a) IN GENERAL.—Not later than 120 days after the last day of the 1-year period described in section 3, the Administrator of the Federal Aviation Administration shall make a decision on whether or not to require automatic external defibrillators on passenger aircraft operated by air carriers and whether or not to require automatic external defibrillators at airports.

"(b) FORM OF DECISION.—A decision under this section shall be in the form of a notice of proposed rulemaking requiring automatic external defibrillators in airports or on passenger aircraft operated by air carriers, or both, or a recommendation to Congress for legislation requiring such defibrillators or a notice in the Federal Register that such defibrillators should not be required in airports or on such aircraft. If a decision under this section is in the form of a notice of proposed rulemaking, the Administrator shall make a final decision not later than the 120th day following the date on which comments are due on the notice of proposed rulemaking.

"(c) CONTENTS.—If the Administrator decides that automatic external defibrillators should be required—

"(1) on passenger aircraft operated by air carriers, the proposed rulemaking or recommendation shall include—

"(A) the size of the aircraft on which such defibrillators should be required;

"(B) the class flights (whether interstate, overseas, or foreign air transportation or any combination thereof) on which such defibrillators should be required;

"(C) the training that should be required for air carrier personnel in the use of such defibrillators; and

"(D) the associated equipment and medication that should be required to be carried in the aircraft medical kit; and

"(2) at airports, the proposed rulemaking or recommendation shall include—

"(A) the size of the airport at which such defibrillators should be required;

"(B) the training that should be required for airport personnel in the use of such defibrillators; and

"(C) the associated equipment and medication that should be required at the airport.

"(d) LIMITATION.—The Administrator may not require automatic external defibrillators on helicopters and on aircraft with a maximum payload capacity (as defined in section 119.3 of title 14, Code of Federal Regulations) of 7,500 pounds or less.

"(e) SPECIAL RULE.—If the Administrator decides that automatic external defibrillators should be required at airports, the proposed rulemaking or recommendation shall provide that the airports are responsible for providing the defibrillators.

"SEC. 5. LIMITATIONS ON LIABILITY.

"(a) LIABILITY OF AIR CARRIERS.—An air carrier shall not be liable for damages in any action brought in a Federal or State court arising out of the performance of the air carrier in obtaining or attempting to obtain the assistance of a passenger in an in-flight medical emergency, or out of the acts or omissions of the passenger rendering the assistance, if the passenger is not an employee or agent of the carrier and the carrier in good faith believes that the passenger is a medically qualified individual.

"(b) LIABILITY OF INDIVIDUALS.—An individual shall not be liable for damages in any action brought in a Federal or State court arising out of the acts or omissions of the individual in providing or attempting to provide assistance in the case of an in-flight medical emergency unless the individual, while rendering such assistance, is guilty of gross negligence or willful misconduct.

"SEC. 6. DEFINITIONS.

"In this Act—

"(1) the terms 'air carrier', 'aircraft', 'airport', 'interstate air transportation', 'overseas air transportation', and 'foreign air transportation' have the meanings such terms have under section 40102 of title 49, United States Code;

"(2) the term 'major air carrier' means an air carrier certificated under section 41102 of title 49, United States Code, that accounted for at least 1 percent of domestic scheduled-passenger revenues in the 12 months ending March 31 of the most recent year preceding the date of the enactment of this Act [Apr. 24, 1998], as reported to the Department of Transportation pursuant to part 241 of title 14 of the Code of Federal Regulations; and

"(3) the term 'medically qualified individual' includes any person who is licensed, certified, or otherwise qualified to provide medical care in a State, including a physician, nurse, physician assistant, paramedic, and emergency medical technician."

SELECTED PROVISIONS OF THE INTELLIGENCE REFORM AND TERRORISM PREVENTION ACT OF 2004

PUBLIC LAW 108-458

INTELLIGENCE REFORM AND TERRORISM PREVENTION ACT OF 2004

[(Public Law 108–458; December 17, 2004)]

[As Amended Through P.L. 118–63, Enacted May 16, 2024]

AN ACT To reform the intelligence community and the intelligence and intelligence-related activities of the United States Government, and for other purposes.

Be it enacted by the Senate and House of Representatives of the United States of America in Congress assembled,

SECTION 1. SHORT TITLE; TABLE OF CONTENTS.

(a) **[50 U.S.C. 3001 note]** SHORT TITLE.—This Act may be cited as the "Intelligence Reform and Terrorism Prevention Act of 2004".

(b) TABLE OF CONTENTS.—The table of contents for this Act is as follows:

* * * * * * *

TITLE IV—TRANSPORTATION SECURITY

* * * * * * *

Subtitle B—Aviation Security

SEC. 4011. PROVISION FOR THE USE OF BIOMETRIC OR OTHER TECHNOLOGY.

(a)

* * *

(b) AVIATION SECURITY RESEARCH AND DEVELOPMENT.—There is authorized to be appropriated to the Secretary of Homeland Security for the use of the Transportation Security Administration $20,000,000, in addition to any amounts otherwise authorized by law, for research and development of advanced biometric technology applications to aviation security, including mass identification technology.

(c) SENSE OF CONGRESS ON TRANSFER OF TECHNOLOGY.—It is the sense of Congress that the national intelligence community and the Department of Homeland Security should share information on and technological advancements to biometric systems, biometric technology, and biometric identifier systems obtained through research and development programs conducted by various Federal agencies.

(d) BIOMETRIC CENTER OF EXCELLENCE.—There is authorized to be appropriated $1,000,000, in addition to any amounts otherwise authorized by law, for the establishment of a competitive center of excellence that will develop and expedite the Federal Government's use of biometric identifiers.

SEC. 4012. ADVANCED AIRLINE PASSENGER PRESCREENING.

(a)

* * *

(b) REPORT ON EFFECTS ON PRIVACY AND CIVIL LIBERTIES.—

(1) REQUIREMENT FOR REPORT.—Not later than 180 days after the date of the enactment of this Act, the Security Privacy Officer of the Department of Homeland Security shall submit a report assessing the impact of the automatic selectee and no fly lists on privacy and civil liberties to the Committee on the Judiciary, the Committee on Homeland Security and Governmental Affairs, and the Committee on Commerce, Science, and Transportation of the Senate and the Committee on the Judiciary, the Committee on Government Reform, the Committee on Transportation and Infrastructure, and the Select Committee on Homeland Security of the House of Representatives.

(2) CONTENT.—The report submitted under paragraph (1) shall include—

(A) any recommendations for practices, procedures, regulations, or legislation that the Security Privacy Officer considers necessary to minimize adverse effects of automatic selectee and no fly lists on privacy, discrimination, due process, and other civil liberties;

(B) a discussion of the implications of applying those lists to other modes of transportation; and

(C) the effect that implementation of the recommendations would have on the effectiveness of the use of such lists to protect the United States against terrorist attacks.

(3) FORM.—To the greatest extent consistent with the protection of law enforcement-sensitive information and classified information, and the administration of applicable law, the report shall be submitted in unclassified form and shall be available to the public. The report may contain a classified annex if necessary.

(c) REPORT ON CRITERIA FOR CONSOLIDATED TERRORIST WATCH LIST.—

(1) IN GENERAL.—Within 180 days after the date of enactment of this Act, the Director of National Intelligence, in consultation with the Secretary of Homeland Security, the Secretary of State, and the Attorney General, shall submit to Congress a report on the Terrorist Screening Center consolidated screening watch list.

(2) CONTENTS.—The report shall include—

(A) the criteria for placing the name of an individual on the watch list;

(B) the minimum standards for reliability and accuracy of identifying information;

(C) the degree of information certainty and the range of threat levels that are to be identified for an individual; and

(D) the range of applicable consequences that are to apply to an individual, if located.

(3) FORM.—To the greatest extent consistent with the protection of law enforcement-sensitive information and classified information and the administration of applicable law, the report shall be submitted in unclassified form and shall be available to the public. The report may contain a classified annex if necessary.

* * * * * * *

SEC. 4014. [49 U.S.C. 44925 note] ADVANCED AIRPORT CHECKPOINT SCREENING DEVICES.

(a) ADVANCED INTEGRATED AIRPORT CHECKPOINT SCREENING SYSTEM PILOT PROGRAM.—Not later than March 31, 2005, the Assistant Secretary of Homeland Security (Transportation Security Administration) shall develop and initiate a pilot program to deploy and test advanced airport checkpoint screening devices and technology as an integrated system at not less than 5 airports in the United States.

(b) FUNDING.—Of the amounts appropriated pursuant to section 48301(a) of title 49, United States Code, for each of fiscal years 2005 and 2006, not more than $150,000,000 shall be available to carry out subsection (a).

SEC. 4015. [49 U.S.C. 44935 note] IMPROVEMENT OF SCREENER JOB PERFORMANCE.

(a) REQUIRED ACTION.—The Assistant Secretary of Homeland Security (Transportation Security Administration) shall take such action as may be necessary to improve the job performance of airport screening personnel.

(b) HUMAN FACTORS STUDY.—In carrying out this section, the Assistant Secretary shall provide, not later than 180 days after the date of the enactment of this Act, to the appropriate congressional committees a report on the results of any human factors study conducted by the Department of Homeland Security to better understand problems in screener performance and to improve screener performance.

SEC. 4016. [49 U.S.C. 44917] FEDERAL AIR MARSHALS.

(a) FEDERAL AIR MARSHAL ANONYMITY.—The Director of the Federal Air Marshal Service of the Department of Homeland Security shall continue operational initiatives to protect the anonymity of Federal air marshals.

(b) AUTHORIZATION OF ADDITIONAL APPROPRIATIONS.—There is authorized to be appropriated to the Secretary of Homeland Security for the use of the Bureau of Immigration and Customs Enforcement, in addition to any amounts otherwise authorized by law, for the deployment of Federal air marshals under section 44917 of title 49, United States Code, $83,000,000 for the 3 fiscal-year period beginning with fiscal year 2005. Such sums shall remain

SEC. 4017. [49 U.S.C. 44901 note] IN-LINE
CHECKED BAGGAGE SCREENING.

INTELLIGENCE REFORM AND TERROR
PREVENTION ACT OF

available until expended.

(c) FEDERAL LAW ENFORCEMENT COUNTERTERRORISM
TRAINING.—

(1) AVAILABILITY OF INFORMATION.—The Administrator of
the Transportation Security Administration and the Director of
Federal Air Marshal Service of the Department of Homeland
Security, shall make available, as practicable, appropriate
information on in-flight counterterrorism and weapons
handling procedures and tactics training to Federal law
enforcement officers who fly while in possession of a firearm.

(2) IDENTIFICATION OF FRAUDULENT DOCUMENTS.—The
Administrator of the Transportation Security Administration
and the Director of Federal Air Marshal Service of the
Department of Homeland Security shall ensure that
Transportation Security Administration screeners and Federal
air marshals receive training in identifying fraudulent
identification documents, including fraudulent or expired visas
and passports. Such training shall also be made available to
other Federal law enforcement agencies and local law
enforcement agencies located in a State that borders Canada or
Mexico.

SEC. 4017. INTERNATIONAL AGREEMENTS TO ALLOW MAXIMUM DEPLOYMENT OF FEDERAL AIR MARSHALS.

The President is encouraged to pursue aggressively
international agreements with foreign governments to allow the
maximum deployment of Federal air marshals on international
flights.

* * * * * * *

SEC. 4019. [49 U.S.C. 44901 note] IN-LINE CHECKED BAGGAGE SCREENING.

(a) IN-LINE BAGGAGE SCREENING EQUIPMENT.—The Assistant
Secretary of Homeland Security (Transportation Security
Administration) shall take such action as may be necessary to
expedite the installation and use of in-line baggage screening
equipment at airports at which screening is required by section
44901 of title 49, United States Code.

(b) SCHEDULE.—Not later than 180 days after the date of

SEC. 4019. [49 U.S.C. 44901 note] IN-LINE
CHECKED BAGGAGE SCREENING.

INTELLIGENCE REFORM AND TERRORISM
PREVENTION ACT OF 2004

enactment of this Act, the Assistant Secretary shall submit to the appropriate congressional committees a schedule to expedite the installation and use of in-line baggage screening equipment at such airports, with an estimate of the impact that such equipment, facility modification, and baggage conveyor placement will have on staffing needs and levels related to aviation security.

(c) REPLACEMENT OF TRACE-DETECTION EQUIPMENT.—Not later than 180 days after the date of enactment of this Act, the Assistant Secretary shall establish and submit to the appropriate congressional committees a schedule for replacing trace-detection equipment, as soon as practicable and where appropriate, with explosive detection system equipment.

(d) COST-SHARING STUDY.—The Secretary of Homeland Security, in consultation with representatives of air carriers, airport operators, and other interested parties, shall submit to the appropriate congressional committees, in conjunction with the submission of the budget for fiscal year 2006 to Congress under section 1105(a) of title 31, United States Code—

(1) a proposed formula for cost-sharing among the Federal Government, State and local governments, and the private sector for projects to install in-line baggage screening equipment that reflects the benefits that each of such entities derive from such projects, including national security benefits and labor and other cost savings;

(2) recommendations, including recommended legislation, for an equitable, feasible, and expeditious system for defraying the costs of the in-line baggage screening equipment authorized by this title; and

(3) the results of a review of innovative financing approaches and possible cost savings associated with the installation of in-line baggage screening equipment at airports.

(e) AUTHORIZATION FOR EXPIRING AND NEW LOIs.—

(1) IN GENERAL.—Section 44923(i) of title 49, United States Code, is amended by striking "$250,000,000 for each of fiscal years 2004 through 2007." and inserting "$400,000,000 for each of fiscal years 2005, 2006, and 2007.".

(2) PERIOD OF REIMBURSEMENT.—Notwithstanding any other provision of law, the Secretary may provide that the period of reimbursement under any letter of intent may extend

for a period not to exceed 10 years after the date that the Secretary issues such letter, subject to the availability of appropriations. This paragraph applies to letters of intent issued under section 44923 of title 49, United States Code, and letters of intent issued under section 367 of the Department of Transportation and Related Agencies Appropriation Act, 2003 (49 U.S.C. 47110 note).

SEC. 4020. [49 U.S.C. 44901 note] CHECKED BAGGAGE SCREENING AREA MONITORING.

(a) IN GENERAL.—The Under Secretary for Border and Transportation Security of the Department of Homeland Security shall provide, subject to the availability of funds, assistance to airports at which screening is required by section 44901 of title 49, United States Code, and that have checked baggage screening areas that are not open to public view in the acquisition and installation of security monitoring cameras for surveillance of such areas in order to deter theft from checked baggage and to aid in the speedy resolution of liability claims against the Transportation Security Administration.

(b) AUTHORIZATION OF APPROPRIATIONS.—There is authorized to be appropriated to the Secretary of Homeland Security for fiscal year 2005 such sums as may be necessary to carry out this section. Such sums shall remain available until expended.

SEC. 4021. WIRELESS COMMUNICATION.

(a) STUDY.—The Assistant Secretary of Homeland Security (Transportation Security Administration), in consultation with the Administrator of the Federal Aviation Administration, shall conduct a study to determine the viability of providing devices or methods, including wireless methods, to enable a flight crew to discreetly notify the pilot in the case of a security breach or safety issue occurring in the cabin.

(b) MATTERS TO BE CONSIDERED.—In conducting the study, the Transportation Security Administration and the Federal Aviation Administration shall consider technology that is readily available and can be quickly integrated and customized for use aboard aircraft for flight crew communication.

(c) REPORT.—Not later than 180 days after the date of enactment of this Act, the Transportation Security Administration

SEC. 4023. [49 U.S.C. 44913 note] IMPROVED EXPLOSIVE DETECTION SYSTEMS.

INTELLIGENCE REFORM AND TERRORISM PREVENTION ACT OF 2004

shall submit to the appropriate congressional committees a report on the results of the study.

[Section 4022 was repealed by section 218(j)(1) of Public Law 118–63.]

SEC. 4023. AVIATION SECURITY STAFFING.

(a) AVIATION SECURITY STAFFING.—Not later than 90 days after the date of enactment of this Act, the Assistant Secretary of Homeland Security (Transportation Security Administration) shall develop and submit to the appropriate congressional committees standards for determining the aviation security staffing for all airports at which screening is required under section 44901 of title 49, United States Code, necessary to—

(1) provide necessary levels of aviation security; and

(2) ensure that the average aviation security-related delay experienced by airline passengers is minimized.

(b) GAO ANALYSIS.—As soon as practicable after the date on which the Assistant Secretary has developed standards under subsection (a), the Comptroller General shall conduct an expedited analysis of, and submit a report to the appropriate congressional committees on, the standards for effectiveness, administrability, ease of compliance, and consistency with the requirements of existing law.

(c) INTEGRATION OF FEDERAL AIRPORT WORKFORCE AND AVIATION SECURITY.—The Secretary of Homeland Security shall conduct a study of the feasibility of combining operations of Federal employees involved in screening at commercial airports and aviation security-related functions under the authority of the Department of Homeland Security in order to coordinate security-related activities, increase the efficiency and effectiveness of those activities, and increase commercial air transportation security.

SEC. 4024. [49 U.S.C. 44913 note] IMPROVED EXPLOSIVE DETECTION SYSTEMS.

(a) PLAN AND GUIDELINES.—The Assistant Secretary of Homeland Security (Transportation Security Administration) shall develop a plan and guidelines for implementing improved explosive detection system equipment.

(b) AUTHORIZATION OF APPROPRIATIONS.—There is authorized

to be appropriated to the Secretary of Homeland Security for the use of the Transportation Security Administration $100,000,000, in addition to any amounts otherwise authorized by law, for the purpose of research and development of improved explosive detection systems for aviation security under section 44913 of title 49, United States Code.

SEC. 4025. PROHIBITED ITEMS LIST.

Not later than 60 days after the date of enactment of this Act, the Assistant Secretary for Homeland Security (Transportation Security Administration) shall complete a review of the list of items prohibited from being carried aboard a passenger aircraft operated by an air carrier or foreign air carrier in air transportation or intrastate air transportation set forth in section 1540 of title 49, Code of Federal Regulations, and shall release a revised list that includes—

(1) butane lighters; and

(2) any other modification that the Assistant Secretary considers appropriate.

SEC. 4026. [22 U.S.C. 2751 note] MAN-PORTABLE AIR DEFENSE SYSTEMS (MANPADS).

(a) UNITED STATES POLICY ON NONPROLIFERATION AND EXPORT CONTROL.—

(1) TO LIMIT AVAILABILITY AND TRANSFER OF MANPADS.—The President shall pursue, on an urgent basis, further strong international diplomatic and cooperative efforts, including bilateral and multilateral treaties, in the appropriate forum to limit the availability, transfer, and proliferation of MANPADSs worldwide.

(2) TO LIMIT THE PROLIFERATION OF MANPADS.—The President is encouraged to seek to enter into agreements with the governments of foreign countries that, at a minimum, would—

(A) prohibit the entry into force of a MANPADS manufacturing license agreement and MANPADS co-production agreement, other than the entry into force of a manufacturing license or co-production agreement with a country that is party to such an agreement;

(B) prohibit, except pursuant to transfers between governments, the export of a MANPADS, including any component, part, accessory, or attachment thereof, without an individual validated license; and

(C) prohibit the reexport or retransfer of a MANPADS, including any component, part, accessory, or attachment thereof, to a third person, organization, or government unless the written consent of the government that approved the original export or transfer is first obtained.

(3) TO ACHIEVE DESTRUCTION OF MANPADS.—The President should continue to pursue further strong international diplomatic and cooperative efforts, including bilateral and multilateral treaties, in the appropriate forum to assure the destruction of excess, obsolete, and illicit stocks of MANPADSs worldwide.

(4) REPORTING AND BRIEFING REQUIREMENT.—

(A) PRESIDENT'S REPORT.—Not later than 180 days after the date of enactment of this Act, the President shall transmit to the appropriate congressional committees a report that contains a detailed description of the status of diplomatic efforts under paragraphs (1), (2), and (3) and of efforts by the appropriate United States agencies to comply with the recommendations of the General Accounting Office set forth in its report GAO–04–519, entitled "Nonproliferation: Further Improvements Needed in U.S. Efforts to Counter Threats from Man-Portable Air Defense Systems".

(B) ANNUAL BRIEFINGS.—Annually after the date of submission of the report under subparagraph (A) and until completion of the diplomatic and compliance efforts referred to in subparagraph (A), the Secretary of State shall brief the appropriate congressional committees on the status of such efforts.

(b) FAA AIRWORTHINESS CERTIFICATION OF MISSILE DEFENSE SYSTEMS FOR COMMERCIAL AIRCRAFT.—

(1) IN GENERAL.—As soon as practicable, but not later than the date of completion of Phase II of the Department of Homeland Security's counter-man-portable air defense system (MANPADS) development and demonstration program, the

Administrator of the Federal Aviation Administration shall establish a process for conducting airworthiness and safety certification of missile defense systems for commercial aircraft certified as effective and functional by the Department of Homeland Security. The process shall require a certification by the Administrator that such systems can be safely integrated into aircraft systems and ensure airworthiness and aircraft system integrity.

(2) CERTIFICATION ACCEPTANCE.—Under the process, the Administrator shall accept the certification of the Department of Homeland Security that a missile defense system is effective and functional to defend commercial aircraft against MANPADSs.

(3) EXPEDITIOUS CERTIFICATION.—Under the process, the Administrator shall expedite the airworthiness and safety certification of missile defense systems for commercial aircraft certified by the Department of Homeland Security.

(4) REPORTS.—Not later than 90 days after the first airworthiness and safety certification for a missile defense system for commercial aircraft is issued by the Administrator, and annually thereafter until December 31, 2008, the Federal Aviation Administration shall transmit to the Committee on Transportation and Infrastructure of the House of Representatives and the Committee on Commerce, Science, and Transportation of the Senate a report that contains a detailed description of each airworthiness and safety certification issued for a missile defense system for commercial aircraft.

(c) PROGRAMS TO REDUCE MANPADS.—

(1) IN GENERAL.—The President is encouraged to pursue strong programs to reduce the number of MANPADSs worldwide so that fewer MANPADSs will be available for trade, proliferation, and sale.

(2) REPORTING AND BRIEFING REQUIREMENTS.—Not later than 180 days after the date of enactment of this Act, the President shall transmit to the appropriate congressional committees a report that contains a detailed description of the status of the programs being pursued under subsection (a). Annually thereafter until the programs are no longer needed, the Secretary of State shall brief the appropriate congressional committees on the status of programs.

(3) FUNDING.—There is authorized to be appropriated such sums as may be necessary to carry out this section.

(d) MANPADS VULNERABILITY ASSESSMENTS REPORT.—

(1) IN GENERAL.—Not later than one year after the date of enactment of this Act, the Secretary of Homeland Security shall transmit to the Committee on Transportation and Infrastructure of the House of Representatives and the Committee on Commerce, Science, and Transportation of the Senate a report describing the Department of Homeland Security's plans to secure airports and the aircraft arriving and departing from airports against MANPADSs attacks.

(2) MATTERS TO BE ADDRESSED.—The Secretary's report shall address, at a minimum, the following:

(A) The status of the Department's efforts to conduct MANPADSs vulnerability assessments at United States airports at which the Department is conducting assessments.

(B) How intelligence is shared between the United States intelligence agencies and Federal, State, and local law enforcement to address the MANPADS threat and potential ways to improve such intelligence sharing.

(C) Contingency plans that the Department has developed in the event that it receives intelligence indicating a high threat of a MANPADS attack on aircraft at or near United States airports.

(D) The feasibility and effectiveness of implementing public education and neighborhood watch programs in areas surrounding United States airports in cases in which intelligence reports indicate there is a high risk of MANPADS attacks on aircraft.

(E) Any other issues that the Secretary deems relevant.

(3) FORMAT.—The report required by this subsection may be submitted in a classified format.

(e) DEFINITIONS.—In this section, the following definitions apply:

(1) APPROPRIATE CONGRESSIONAL COMMITTEES.—The term "appropriate congressional committees" means—

(A) the Committee on Armed Services, the Committee on International Relations, and the Committee on Transportation and Infrastructure of the House of Representatives; and

(B) the Committee on Armed Services, the Committee on Foreign Relations, and the Committee on Commerce, Science, and Transportation of the Senate.

(2) MANPADS.—The term "MANPADS" means—

(A) a surface-to-air missile system designed to be man-portable and carried and fired by a single individual; and

(B) any other surface-to-air missile system designed to be operated and fired by more than one individual acting as a crew and portable by several individuals.

* * * * * * *

* * * * * * *

SEC. 4028. REPORT ON SECONDARY FLIGHT DECK BARRIERS.

Not later than 6 months after the date of the enactment of this Act, the Assistant Secretary of Homeland Security (Transportation Security Administration) shall submit to the appropriate congressional committees a report on the costs and benefits associated with the use of secondary flight deck barriers, including the recommendation of the Assistant Secretary whether or not the use of such barriers should be mandated for all air carriers. The report may be submitted in a classified form.

* * * * * * *

Subtitle C—Air Cargo Security

SEC. 4051. [49 U.S.C. 44901 note] PILOT PROGRAM TO EVALUATE USE OF BLAST RESISTANT CARGO AND BAGGAGE CONTAINERS.

(a) IN GENERAL.—Beginning not later than 180 days after the date of enactment of this Act, the Assistant Secretary of Homeland Security (Transportation Security Administration) shall carry out a pilot program to evaluate the use of blast-resistant containers for cargo and baggage on passenger aircraft to minimize the potential effects of detonation of an explosive device.

(b) INCENTIVES FOR PARTICIPATION IN PILOT PROGRAM.—

(1) IN GENERAL.—As part of the pilot program, the Assistant Secretary shall provide incentives to air carriers to volunteer to test the use of blast-resistant containers for cargo and baggage on passenger aircraft.

(2) APPLICATIONS.—To volunteer to participate in the incentive program, an air carrier shall submit to the Assistant Secretary an application that is in such form and contains such information as the Assistant Secretary requires.

(3) TYPES OF INCENTIVES.—Incentives provided by the Assistant Secretary to air carriers that volunteer to participate in the pilot program shall include the use of, and financial assistance to cover increased costs to the carriers associated with the use and maintenance of, blast-resistant containers, including increased fuel costs.

(c) TECHNOLOGICAL IMPROVEMENTS.—The Secretary of Homeland Security, in cooperation with the Secretary of Transportation, shall support efforts to explore alternative technologies for minimizing the potential effects of detonation of an explosive device on cargo and passenger aircraft.

(d) AUTHORIZATION OF APPROPRIATIONS.—There is authorized to be appropriated to carry out subsections (a) and (b) $2,000,000. Such sum shall remain available until expended.

SEC. 4052. [49 U.S.C. 44901 note] AIR CARGO SECURITY.

(a) AIR CARGO SCREENING TECHNOLOGY.—The Assistant Secretary of Homeland Security (Transportation Security Administration) shall develop technology to better identify, track, and screen air cargo.

(b) IMPROVED AIR CARGO AND AIRPORT SECURITY.—There is authorized to be appropriated to the Secretary of Homeland Security for the use of the Transportation Security Administration, in addition to any amounts otherwise authorized by law, for the purpose of improving aviation security related to the transportation of cargo on both passenger aircraft and all-cargo aircraft—

(1) $200,000,000 for fiscal year 2005;

(2) $200,000,000 for fiscal year 2006; and

(3) $200,000,000 for fiscal year 2007.

Such sums shall remain available until expended.

(c) RESEARCH, DEVELOPMENT, AND DEPLOYMENT.—To carry out subsection (a), there is authorized to be appropriated to the Secretary, in addition to any amounts otherwise authorized by law, for research and development related to enhanced air cargo security technology as well as for deployment and installation of enhanced air cargo security technology—

(1) $100,000,000 for fiscal year 2005;

(2) $100,000,000 for fiscal year 2006; and

(3) $100,000,000 for fiscal year 2007.

Such sums shall remain available until expended.

(d) ADVANCED CARGO SECURITY GRANTS.—

(1) IN GENERAL.—The Secretary shall establish and carry out a program to issue competitive grants to encourage the development of advanced air cargo security technology, including use of innovative financing or other means of funding such activities. The Secretary may make available funding for this purpose from amounts appropriated pursuant to subsection (c).

(2) ELIGIBILITY CRITERIA, ETC.—The Secretary shall establish such eligibility criteria, establish such application and administrative procedures, and provide for such matching funding requirements, if any, as may be necessary and appropriate to ensure that the technology is deployed as fully and rapidly as possible.

SEC. 4053. AIR CARGO SECURITY REGULATIONS.

Not later than 240 days after the date of enactment of this Act, the Assistant Secretary of Homeland Security (Transportation Security Administration) shall issue a final rule in Docket Number TSA-2004-19515 to amend transportation security regulations to enhance and improve the security of air cargo transported in both passenger and all-cargo aircraft.

SEC. 4054. REPORT ON INTERNATIONAL AIR CARGO THREATS.

(a) REPORT.—Not later than 180 days after the date of enactment of this Act, the Secretary of Homeland Security, in coordination with the Secretary of Defense and the Administrator of the Federal Aviation Administration, shall submit to the Committee on Commerce, Science, and Transportation and the Committee on Homeland Security and Governmental Affairs of the Senate and the Committee on Transportation and Infrastructure of the House of Representatives a report that contains the following:

(1) A description of the current procedures in place to address the threat of an inbound all-cargo aircraft from outside the United States that intelligence sources indicate could carry explosive, incendiary, chemical, biological, or nuclear devices.

(2) An analysis of the potential for establishing secure facilities along established international aviation routes for the purposes of diverting and securing aircraft described in paragraph (1).

(b) REPORT FORMAT.—The Secretary may submit all, or part, of the report required by this section in such a classified and redacted format as the Secretary determines appropriate or necessary.

* * * * * * *

Subtitle E—General Provisions

SEC. 4081. [49 U.S.C. 44901 note] DEFINITIONS.

In this title (other than in sections 4001 and 4026), the following definitions apply:

(1) APPROPRIATE CONGRESSIONAL COMMITTEES.—The term "appropriate congressional committees" means the Committee on Commerce, Science, and Transportation of the Senate and the Committee on Transportation and Infrastructure of the House of Representatives.

(2) AVIATION DEFINITIONS.—The terms "air carrier", "air transportation", "aircraft", "airport", "cargo", "foreign air carrier", and "intrastate air transportation" have the meanings given such terms in section 40102 of title 49, United States Code.

(3) SECURE AREA OF AN AIRPORT.—The term "secure area of an airport" means the sterile area and the Secure Identification Display Area of an airport (as such terms are defined in section 1540.5 of title 49, Code of Federal Regulations, or any successor regulations).

SEC. 4082. [49 U.S.C. 114 note] EFFECTIVE DATE.

This title shall take effect on the date of enactment of this Act.

* * * * * * *

SELECTED PROVISIONS OF THE VISION 100—CENTURY OF AVIATION REAUTHORIZATION ACT

PUBLIC LAW 108-176

VISION 100–CENTURY OF AVIATION REAUTHORIZATION ACT

[Selected Provisions]

[Public Law 108–176; enacted December 12, 2003]

[As Amended Through P.L. 118–63, Enacted May 16, 2024]

AN ACT To amend title 49, United States Code, to reauthorize programs for the Federal Aviation Administration, and for other purposes.

Be it enacted by the Senate and House of Representatives of the United States of America in Congress assembled,

SECTION 1. SHORT TITLE; TABLE OF CONTENTS.

(a) **[49 U.S.C. 40101 note]** SHORT TITLE.—This Act may be cited as the "Vision 100—Century of Aviation Reauthorization Act".

(b) TABLE OF CONTENTS.—The table of contents for this Act is as follows:

---

[1]   Section 710 and the item relating to such section in the table of sections are repealed by section 218(i) of Public Law 118–63.

TITLE I—AIRPORT AND AIRWAY IMPROVEMENTS

* * * * * * *

Subtitle C—AIP Modifications

* * * * * * *

SEC. 161. [49 U.S.C. 47109 note] TEMPORARY INCREASE IN GOVERNMENT SHARE OF CERTAIN AIP PROJECT COSTS.

Notwithstanding section 47109(a) of title 49, United States Code, the Government's share of allowable project costs for a grant made in any of fiscal years 2009 through 2011, or in the portion of fiscal year 2012 ending before February 18, 2012, under chapter 471 of that title for a project described in paragraph (2) or (3) of that section shall be 95 percent.

* * * * * * *

Subtitle D—Miscellaneous

* * * * * * *

SEC. 182. [49 U.S.C. 44502 note] PILOT PROGRAM FOR INNOVATIVE FINANCING OF AIR TRAFFIC CONTROL EQUIPMENT.

(a) IN GENERAL.—In order to test the cost effectiveness and feasibility of long-term financing of modernization of major air traffic control systems, the Administrator of the Federal Aviation Administration may establish a pilot program to test innovative financing techniques through amending, subject to section 1341 of title 31, United States Code, a contract for more than one, but not more than 20, fiscal years to purchase and install air traffic control equipment for the Administration. Such amendments may be for more than one, but not more than 10, fiscal years.

(b) CANCELLATION.—A contract described in subsection (a) may include a cancellation provision if the Administrator determines that such a provision is necessary and in the best interest of the United States. Any such provision shall include a cancellation liability schedule that covers reasonable and allocable costs incurred by the contractor through the date of cancellation plus reasonable profit, if any, on those costs. Any such provision shall not apply if the contract is terminated by default of the contractor.

(c) CONTRACT PROVISIONS.—If feasible and practicable for the pilot program, the Administrator may make an advance contract provision to achieve economic-lot purchases and more efficient production rates.

(d) LIMITATION.—The Administrator may not amend a contract under this section until the program for the terminal automation replacement systems has been rebaselined in accordance with the acquisition management system of the Administration.

(e) FUNDING.—Out of amounts appropriated under section 48101 for fiscal year 2004, such sums as may be necessary shall be available to carry out this section.

* * * * * * *

SEC. 184. [49 U.S.C. 48101 note] FACILITIES AND EQUIPMENT REPORTS.

SEC. 186. [49 U.S.C. 48101 note] FACILITIES AND EQUIPMENT REPORTS.

Vision 100–Century of Aviation Reauthorization Act

(a) BIANNUAL REPORTS.—Beginning 180 days after the date of enactment of this Act, the Administrator of the Federal Aviation Administration shall transmit a report to the Senate Committee on Commerce, Science, and Transportation and the House of Representatives Committee on Transportation and Infrastructure every 6 months that describes—

(1) the 10 largest programs funded under section 48101(a) of title 49, United States Code;

(2) any changes in the budget for such programs;

(3) the program schedule; and

(4) technical risks associated with the programs.

(b) SUNSET PROVISION.—This section shall cease to be effective beginning on the date that is 4 years after the date of enactment of this Act.

* * * * * * *

SEC. 186. MIDWAY ISLAND AIRPORT.

(a) FINDINGS.—Congress finds that the continued operation of the Midway Island Airport in accordance with the standards of the Federal Aviation Administration applicable to commercial airports is critical to the safety of commercial, military, and general aviation in the mid-Pacific Ocean region.

(b) MEMORANDUM OF UNDERSTANDING ON SALE OF AIRCRAFT FUEL.—The Secretaries of Transportation, Defense, Interior, and Homeland Security shall enter into a memorandum of understanding to facilitate the sale of aircraft fuel on Midway Island at a price that will generate sufficient revenue to improve the ability of the airport to operate on a self-sustaining basis in accordance with the standards of the Federal Aviation Administration applicable to commercial airports. The memorandum shall also address the long-range potential of promoting tourism as a means to generate revenue to operate the airport.

(c) TRANSFER OF NAVIGATION AIDS AT MIDWAY ISLAND AIRPORT.—The Midway Island Airport may transfer, without consideration, to the Administrator the navigation aids at the airport. The Administrator shall accept the navigation aids and operate and maintain the navigation aids under criteria of the

Administrator.

(d) FUNDING TO SECRETARY OF THE INTERIOR FOR MIDWAY ISLAND AIRPORT.—The Secretary of Transportation may enter into a reimbursable agreement with the Secretary of the Interior for the purpose of funding airport development, as defined in section 47102(3) of title 49, United States Code, at Midway Island Airport for for[2] from amounts available in the discretionary fund established by section 47115 of such title. The maximum obligation under the agreement for any such fiscal year shall be $2,500,000.

---

[2] The phrase "for for" in subsection (d) is so in law. See amendment made by section 104(d) of Public Law 118–63.

* * * * * * *

TITLE II—FAA ORGANIZATION

* * * * * * *

Subtitle B—Miscellaneous

SEC. 221. [49 U.S.C. 44506 note] CONTROLLER STAFFING.

(a) ANNUAL REPORT.—Beginning with the submission of the Budget of the United States to the Congress for fiscal year 2005, the Administrator of the Federal Aviation Administration shall transmit a report to the Senate Committee on Commerce, Science, and Transportation and the House of Representatives Committee on Transportation and Infrastructure that describes the overall air traffic controller staffing plan, including strategies to address anticipated retirement and replacement of air traffic controllers.

(b) HUMAN CAPITAL WORKFORCE STRATEGY.—

(1) DEVELOPMENT.—The Administrator shall develop a comprehensive human capital workforce strategy to determine the most effective method for addressing the need for more air traffic controllers that is identified in the June 2002 report of the General Accounting Office.

(2) COMPLETION DATE.—Not later than 1 year after the date of enactment of this Act, the Administrator shall complete development of the strategy.

(3) REPORT.—Not later than 30 days after the date on which the strategy is completed, the Administrator shall transmit to Congress a report describing the strategy.

SEC. 227. DESIGN ORGANIZATION CERTIFICATES.

(a) [49 U.S.C. 44702 note] GENERAL AUTHORITY TO ISSUE CERTIFICATES.—Effective on the last day of the 7-year period beginning on the date of enactment of this Act, section 44702(a) is amended by inserting "design organization certificates," after "airman certificates,".

(b) DESIGN ORGANIZATION CERTIFICATES.—

(1) [49 U.S.C. 44704 note] PLAN.—Not later than 4 years after the date of enactment of this Act, the Administrator of the Federal Aviation Administration shall transmit to the Committee on Transportation and Infrastructure of the House of Representatives and the Committee on Commerce, Science, and Transportation of the Senate a plan for the development and oversight of a system for certification of design organizations to certify compliance with the requirements and minimum standards prescribed under section 44701(a) of title 49, United States Code, for the type certification of aircraft, aircraft engines, propellers, or appliances.

* * * * * * *

SEC. 229. [49 U.S.C. 45301 note] OVERFLIGHT FEES.

(a) ADOPTION AND LEGALIZATION OF CERTAIN RULES.—

(1) APPLICABILITY AND EFFECT OF CERTAIN LAW.—Notwithstanding section 141(d)(1) of the Aviation and Transportation Security Act (49 U.S.C. 44901 note), section 45301(b)(1)(B) of title 49, United States Code, is deemed to apply to and to have effect with respect to the authority of the Administrator of the Federal Aviation Administration with respect to the interim final rule and final rule, relating to overflight fees, issued by the Administrator on May 30, 2000, and August 13, 2001, respectively.

(2) ADOPTION AND LEGALIZATION.—The interim final rule and final rule referred to in subsection (a), including the fees issued pursuant to those rules, are adopted, legalized, and confirmed as fully to all intents and purposes as if the same

had, by prior Act of Congress, been specifically adopted, authorized, and directed as of the date those rules were originally issued.

(3) FEES TO WHICH APPLICABLE.—This subsection applies to fees assessed after November 19, 2001, and before April 8, 2003, and fees collected after the requirements of subsection (b) have been met.

(b) DEFERRED COLLECTION OF FEES.—The Administrator shall defer collecting fees under section 45301(a)(1) of title 49, United States Code, until the Administrator (1) reports to Congress responding to the issues raised by the court in Air Transport Association of Canada v. Federal Aviation Administration and Administrator, FAA, decided on April 8, 2003, and (2) consults with users and other interested parties regarding the consistency of the fees established under such section with the international obligations of the United States.

(c) ENFORCEMENT.—The Administrator shall take an appropriate enforcement action under subtitle VII of title 49, United States Code, against any user that does not pay a fee under section 45301(a)(1) of such title.

TITLE III—ENVIRONMENTAL PROCESS

Subtitle A—Aviation Development Streamlining

* * * * * * *

SEC. 308. [49 U.S.C. 47171 note] LIMITATIONS.

Nothing in this subtitle, including any amendment made by this title, shall preempt or interfere with—

(1) any practice of seeking public comment;

(2) any power, jurisdiction, or authority that a State agency or an airport sponsor has with respect to carrying out an airport capacity enhancement project; and

(3) any obligation to comply with the provisions of the National Environmental Policy Act of 1969 (42 U.S.C. 4371 et seq.) and the regulations issued by the Council on

Environmental Quality to carry out such Act.

SEC. 309. [49 U.S.C. 47171 note] RELATIONSHIP TO OTHER REQUIREMENTS.

The coordinated review process required under the amendments made by this subtitle shall apply to an airport capacity enhancement project at a congested airport whether or not the project is designated by the Secretary of Transportation as a high-priority transportation infrastructure project under Executive Order 13274 (67 Fed. Reg. 59449; relating to environmental stewardship and transportation infrastructure project reviews).

Subtitle B—Miscellaneous

* * * * * * *

SEC. 326. [49 U.S.C. 40101 note] REDUCTION OF NOISE AND EMISSIONS FROM CIVILIAN AIRCRAFT.

(a) ESTABLISHMENT OF RESEARCH PROGRAM.—From amounts made available under section 48102(a) of title 49, United States Code, the Secretary of Transportation shall establish a research program related to reducing community exposure to civilian aircraft noise or emissions through grants or other measures authorized under section 106(l)(6) of such title, including reimbursable agreements with other Federal agencies. The program shall include participation by educational and research institutions that have existing facilities for developing and testing noise reduction engine technology.

(b) DESIGNATION OF INSTITUTE AS A CENTER OF EXCELLENCE.—The Administrator of the Federal Aviation Administration shall designate an institution described in subsection (a) as a Center of Excellence for Noise and Emission Research.

SEC. 327. SPECIAL RULE FOR AIRPORT IN ILLINOIS.

(a) IN GENERAL.—Nothing in this title shall be construed to preclude the application of any provision of this Act to the State of Illinois or any other sponsor of a new airport proposed to be constructed in the State of Illinois.

(b) AUTHORITY OF THE GOVERNOR.—Nothing in this title shall

be construed to preempt the authority of the Governor of the State of Illinois as of August 1, 2001, to approve or disapprove airport development projects.

TITLE IV—AIRLINE SERVICE IMPROVEMENTS

Subtitle A—Small Community Air Service

* * * * * * *

SEC. 406. [49 U.S.C. 41731 note] CODE-SHARING PILOT PROGRAM.

(a) IN GENERAL.—The Secretary of Transportation shall establish a pilot program under which the Secretary may require air carriers providing service with compensation under subchapter II of chapter 417 of title 49, United States Code, and major air carriers (as defined in section 41716(a)(2) of such title) serving large hub airports (as defined in section 40102 of such title) to participate in multiple code-share arrangements consistent with normal industry practice whenever and wherever the Secretary determines that such multiple code-sharing arrangements would improve air transportation services.

(b) LIMITATION.—The Secretary may not require air carriers to participate in the pilot program under this section for more than 10 communities receiving service under subchapter II of chapter 417 of title 49, United States Code.

* * * * * * *

SEC. 409. [49 U.S.C. 41731 note] MEASUREMENT OF HIGHWAY MILES FOR PURPOSES OF DETERMINING ELIGIBILITY OF ESSENTIAL AIR SERVICE SUBSIDIES.

(a) REQUEST FOR SECRETARIAL REVIEW.—An eligible place (as defined in section 41731 of title 49, United States Code) with respect to which the Secretary has, in the 2-year period ending on the date of enactment of this Act, eliminated (or tentatively eliminated) compensation for essential air service to such place, or terminated (or tentatively terminated) the compensation eligibility of such place for essential air service, under section 332 of the Department of Transportation and Related Agencies Appropriations Act, 2000 (49 U.S.C. 41731 note), section 205 of the Wendell H. Ford Aviation Investment and Reform Act for the 21st Century (49 U.S.C. 41731 note), or any prior law of similar effect based on the highway mileage of such place from the nearest hub airport (as defined in section 40102 of such title), may request the Secretary to review such action.

(b) DETERMINATION OF MILEAGE.—In reviewing an action under subsection (a), the highway mileage between an eligible place and the nearest medium hub airport or large hub airport is the highway mileage of the most commonly used route between the place and the medium hub airport or large hub airport. In identifying such route, the Secretary shall identify the most commonly used route for a community by—

(1) consulting with the Governor of a State or the Governor's designee; and

(2) considering the certification of the Governor of a State or the Governor's designee as to the most commonly used route.

(c) ELIGIBILITY DETERMINATION.—Not later than 60 days after receiving a request under subsection (a), the Secretary shall—

(1) determine whether the eligible place would have been subject to an elimination of compensation eligibility for essential air service, or termination of the eligibility of such place for essential air service, under the provisions of law referred to in subsection (a) based on the determination of the highway mileage of such place from the nearest medium hub airport or large hub airport under subsection (b); and

(2) issue a final order with respect to the eligibility of such place for essential air service compensation under subchapter II of chapter 417 of title 49, United States Code.

(d) LIMITATION ON PERIOD OF FINAL ORDER.—A final order issued under subsection (c) shall terminate on May 10, 2024.

* * * * * * *

SEC. 411. NATIONAL COMMISSION ON SMALL COMMUNITY AIR SERVICE.

(a) ESTABLISHMENT.—There is established a commission to be

known as the "National Commission on Small Community Air Service" (in this section referred to as the "Commission").

(b) MEMBERSHIP.—

(1) COMPOSITION.—The Commission shall be composed of nine members of whom—

(A) three members shall be appointed by the Secretary;

(B) two members shall be appointed by the majority leader of the Senate;

(C) one member shall be appointed by the minority leader of the Senate;

(D) two members shall be appointed by the Speaker of the House of Representatives; and

(E) one member shall be appointed by the minority leader of the House of Representatives.

(2) QUALIFICATIONS.—Of the members appointed by the Secretary under paragraph (1)(A)—

(A) one member shall be a representative of a regional airline;

(B) one member shall be a representative of a small hub airport or nonhub airport (as such terms are defined in section 40102 of title 49, United States Code); and

(C) one member shall be a representative of a State aviation agency.

(3) TERMS.—Members shall be appointed for the life of the Commission.

(4) VACANCIES.—A vacancy in the Commission shall be filled in the manner in which the original appointment was made.

(5) TRAVEL EXPENSES.—Members shall serve without pay but shall receive travel expenses, including per diem in lieu of subsistence, in accordance with subchapter I of chapter 57 of title 5, United States Code.

(c) CHAIRPERSON.—The Secretary shall designate, from among the individuals appointed under subsection (b)(1), an individual to serve as chairperson of the Commission.

(d) DUTIES.—

(1) STUDY.—The Commission shall undertake a study of—

(A) the challenges faced by small communities in the United States with respect to retaining and enhancing their scheduled commercial air service; and

(B) whether the existing Federal programs charged with helping small communities are adequate for them to retain and enhance their existing air service.

(2) ESSENTIAL AIR SERVICE COMMUNITIES.—In conducting the study, the Commission shall pay particular attention to the state of scheduled commercial air service in communities currently served by the essential air service program.

(e) RECOMMENDATIONS.—Based on the results of the study under subsection (d), the Commission shall make such recommendations as it considers necessary to—

(1) improve the state of scheduled commercial air service at small communities in the United States, especially communities described in subsection (d)(2); and

(2) improve the ability of small communities to retain and enhance their existing air service.

(f) REPORT.—Not later than 6 months after the date on which initial appointments of members to the Commission are completed, the Commission shall transmit to the President and Congress a report on the activities of the Commission, including recommendations made by the Commission under subsection (e).

(g) COMMISSION PANELS.—The chairperson of the Commission shall establish such panels consisting of members of the Commission as the chairperson determines appropriate to carry out the functions of the Commission.

(h) COMMISSION PERSONNEL MATTERS.—

(1) STAFF.—The Commission may appoint and fix the pay of such personnel as it considers appropriate.

(2) STAFF OF FEDERAL AGENCIES.—Upon request of the chairperson of the Commission, the head of any department or agency of the United States may detail, on a reimbursable basis, any of the personnel of that department or agency to the Commission to assist it in carrying out its duties under this section.

(3) OTHER STAFF AND SUPPORT.—Upon the request of the Commission, or a panel of the Commission, the Secretary shall

provide the Commission or panel with professional and administrative staff and other support, on a reimbursable basis, to assist the Commission or panel in carrying out its responsibilities.

(i) OBTAINING OFFICIAL DATA.—The Commission may secure directly from any department or agency of the United States information (other than information required by any statute of the United States to be kept confidential by such department or agency) necessary for the Commission to carry out its duties under this section. Upon request of the chairperson of the Commission, the head of that department or agency shall furnish such nonconfidential information to the Commission.

(j) TERMINATION.—The Commission shall terminate on the 30th day following the date of transmittal of the report under subsection (f).

(k) APPLICABILITY OF THE FEDERAL ADVISORY COMMITTEE ACT.—The Federal Advisory Committee Act (5 U.S.C. App.) shall not apply to the Commission.

(l) AUTHORIZATION OF APPROPRIATIONS.—There are authorized to be appropriated to the Secretary $250,000 to be used to fund the Commission.

* * * * * * *

TITLE V—AVIATION SAFETY

* * * * * * *

SEC. 504. [49 U.S.C. 44515 note] IMPROVEMENT OF CURRICULUM STANDARDS FOR AVIATION MAINTENANCE TECHNICIANS.

(a) IN GENERAL.—The Administrator of the Federal Aviation Administration shall ensure that the training standards for airframe and powerplant mechanics under part 65 of title 14, Code of Federal Regulations, are updated and revised in accordance with this section. The Administrator may update and revise the training standards through the initiation of a formal rulemaking or by issuing an advisory circular or other agency guidance.

(b) ELEMENTS FOR CONSIDERATION.—The updated and revised standards required under subsection (a) shall include those curriculum adjustments that are necessary to more accurately reflect current technology and maintenance practices.

(c) CERTIFICATION.—Any adjustment or modification of current curriculum standards made pursuant to this section shall be reflected in the certification examinations of airframe and powerplant mechanics.

(d) COMPLETION.—The revised and updated training standards required by subsection (a) shall be completed not later than 12 months after the date of enactment of this Act.

(e) PERIODIC REVIEWS AND UPDATES.—The Administrator shall review the content of the curriculum standards for training airframe and powerplant mechanics referred to in subsection (a) every 3 years after completion of the revised and updated training standards required under subsection (a) as necessary to reflect current technology and maintenance practices.

* * * * * * *

TITLE VII—AVIATION RESEARCH

* * * * * * *

SEC. 704. [49 U.S.C. 44505 note] RESEARCH PROGRAM TO IMPROVE AIRFIELD PAVEMENTS.

(a) CONTINUATION OF PROGRAM.—The Administrator of the Federal Aviation Administration shall continue the program to consider awards to nonprofit concrete and asphalt pavement research foundations to improve the design, construction, rehabilitation, and repair of airfield pavements to aid in the development of safer, more cost effective, and more durable airfield pavements.

(b) USE OF GRANTS OR COOPERATIVE AGREEMENTS.—The Administrator may use grants or cooperative agreements in carrying out this section.

(c) STATUTORY CONSTRUCTION.—Nothing in this section requires the Administrator to prioritize an airfield pavement research program above safety, security, Flight 21, environment, or energy research programs.

* * * * * * *

SEC. 706. [49 U.S.C. 44702 note] DEVELOPMENT OF ANALYTICAL TOOLS AND CERTIFICATION METHODS.

The Federal Aviation Administration shall conduct research to promote the development of analytical tools to improve existing certification methods and to reduce the overall costs for the certification of new products.

* * * * * * *

SEC. 708. [49 U.S.C. 44504 note] FAA CENTER FOR EXCELLENCE FOR APPLIED RESEARCH AND TRAINING IN THE USE OF ADVANCED MATERIALS IN TRANSPORT AIRCRAFT.

(a) IN GENERAL.—The Administrator of the Federal Aviation Administration shall develop a Center for Excellence focused on applied research and training on the durability and maintainability of advanced materials in transport airframe structures. The Center shall—

(1) promote and facilitate collaboration among academia, the Federal Aviation Administration's Transportation Division, and the commercial aircraft industry, including manufacturers, commercial air carriers, and suppliers; and

(2) establish goals set to advance technology, improve engineering practices, and facilitate continuing education in relevant areas of study.

(b) AUTHORIZATION OF APPROPRIATIONS.—There is authorized to be appropriated to the Administrator $500,000 for each of fiscal years 2012 through 2015 to carry out this section.

SEC. 709. [49 U.S.C. 40101 note] AIR TRANSPORTATION SYSTEM JOINT PLANNING AND DEVELOPMENT OFFICE.

(a) ESTABLISHMENT.—(1) The Secretary of Transportation shall establish in the Federal Aviation Administration a joint planning and development office to manage work related to the Next Generation Air Transportation System. The office shall be known as the Next Generation Air Transportation System Joint Planning and Development Office (in this section referred to as the "Office").

(2) The head of the Office shall be the Associate Administrator for Next Generation Air Transportation System Planning, Development, and Interagency Coordination, who shall be appointed by the Administrator of the Federal Aviation

Administration, with the approval of the Secretary. The Administrator shall appoint the Associate Administrator after consulting with the Chairman of the Next Generation Senior Policy Committee and providing advanced notice to the other members of that Committee.

(3) The responsibilities of the Office shall include—

(A) creating and carrying out an integrated plan for a Next Generation Air Transportation System pursuant to subsection (b);

(B) overseeing research and development on that system;

(C) creating a transition plan for the implementation of that system;

(D) coordinating aviation and aeronautics research programs to achieve the goal of more effective and directed programs that will result in applicable research;

(E) coordinating goals and priorities and coordinating research activities within the Federal Government with United States aviation and aeronautical firms;

(F) coordinating the development and utilization of new technologies to ensure that when available, they may be used to their fullest potential in aircraft and in the air traffic control system;

(G) facilitating the transfer of technology from research programs such as the National Aeronautics and Space Administration program and the Department of Defense Advanced Research Projects Agency program to Federal agencies with operational responsibilities and to the private sector;

(H) reviewing activities relating to noise, emissions, fuel consumption, and safety conducted by Federal agencies, including the Federal Aviation Administration, the National Aeronautics and Space Administration, the Department of Commerce, and the Department of Defense;

(I) establishing specific quantitative goals for the safety, capacity, efficiency, performance, and environmental impacts of each phase of Next Generation Air Transportation System planning and development activities and measuring actual operational experience against those goals, taking into account noise pollution reduction concerns of affected communities to the extent practicable in establishing the environmental goals;

(J) working to ensure global interoperability of the Next Generation Air Transportation System;

(K) working to ensure the use of weather information and space weather information in the Next Generation Air Transportation System as soon as possible;

(L) overseeing, with the Administrator and in consultation with the Chief Technology Officer, the selection of products or outcomes of research and development activities that should be moved to a demonstration phase; and

(M) maintaining a baseline modeling and simulation environment for testing and evaluating alternative concepts to satisfy Next Generation Air Transportation System enterprise architecture requirements.

(4)(A) The Office shall operate in conjunction with relevant programs in the Department of Defense, the National Aeronautics and Space Administration, the Department of Commerce and the Department of Homeland Security. The Secretary of Transportation may request assistance from staff from those Departments and other Federal agencies.

(B) The Secretary of Defense, the Administrator of the National Aeronautics and Space Administration, the Secretary of Commerce, the Secretary of Homeland Security, and the head of any other Federal agency from which the Secretary of Transportation requests assistance under subparagraph (A) shall designate a senior official in the agency to be responsible for—

(i) carrying out the activities of the agency relating to the Next Generation Air Transportation System in coordination with the Office, including the execution of all aspects of the work of the agency in developing and implementing the integrated work plan described in subsection (b)(5);

(ii) serving as a liaison for the agency in activities of the agency relating to the Next Generation Air Transportation System and coordinating with other

Federal agencies involved in activities relating to the System; and

(iii) ensuring that the agency meets its obligations as set forth in any memorandum of understanding executed by or on behalf of the agency relating to the Next Generation Air Transportation System.

(C) The head of a Federal agency referred to in subparagraph (B) shall—

(i) ensure that the responsibilities of the agency relating to the Next Generation Air Transportation System are clearly communicated to the senior official of the agency designated under subparagraph (B);

(ii) ensure that the performance of the senior official in carrying out the responsibilities of the agency relating to the Next Generation Air Transportation System is reflected in the official's annual performance evaluations and compensation;

(iii) establish or designate an office within the agency to carry out its responsibilities under the memorandum of understanding under the supervision of the designated official; and

(iv) ensure that the designated official has sufficient budgetary authority and staff resources to carry out the agency's Next Generation Air Transportation System responsibilities as set forth in the integrated plan under subsection (b).

(D) Not later than 6 months after the date of enactment of this subparagraph, the head of each Federal agency that has responsibility for carrying out any activity under the integrated plan under subsection (b) shall execute a memorandum of understanding with the Office obligating that agency to carry out the activity.

(5) In developing and carrying out its plans, the Office shall consult with the public and ensure the participation of experts from the private sector including representatives of commercial aviation, general aviation, aviation labor groups, aviation research and development entities, aircraft and air traffic control suppliers, and the space industry.

(6)(A) The Office shall work with the Director of the Office of Management and Budget to develop a process whereby the Director will identify projects related to the Next Generation Air Transportation System across the agencies referred to in paragraph (4)(A) and consider the Next Generation Air Transportation System as a unified, cross-agency program.

(B) The Director of the Office of Management and Budget, to the extent practicable, shall—

(i) ensure that—

(I) each Federal agency covered by the plan has sufficient funds requested in the President's budget, as submitted under section 1105(a) of title 31, United States Code, for each fiscal year covered by the plan to carry out its responsibilities under the plan; and

(II) the development and implementation of the Next Generation Air Transportation System remains on schedule;

(ii) include, in the President's budget, a statement of the portion of the estimated budget of each Federal agency covered by the plan that relates to the activities of the agency under the Next Generation Air Transportation System; and

(iii) identify and justify as part of the President's budget submission any inconsistencies between the plan and amounts requested in the budget.

(7) The Associate Administrator for Next Generation Air Transportation System Planning, Development, and Interagency Coordination shall be a voting member of the Joint Resources Council of the Federal Aviation Administration.

(b) INTEGRATED PLAN.—The integrated plan shall be designed to ensure that the Next Generation Air Transportation System meets anticipated future air transportation safety, security, mobility, efficiency, and capacity needs and accomplishes the goals under subsection (c). The integrated plan shall include—

(1) a national vision statement for an air transportation system capable of meeting potential air traffic demand by 2025;

(2) a description of the demand and the performance characteristics that will be required of the Nation's future air transportation system, and an explanation of how those

characteristics were derived, including the national goals, objectives, and policies the system is designed to further, and the underlying socioeconomic determinants, and associated models and analyses;

(3) a multiagency research and development roadmap for creating the Next Generation Air Transportation System with the characteristics outlined under clause (ii), including—

(A) the most significant technical obstacles and the research and development activities necessary to overcome them, including for each project, the role of each Federal agency, corporations, and universities;

(B) the annual anticipated cost of carrying out the research and development activities; and

(C) the technical milestones that will be used to evaluate the activities;

(4) a description of the operational concepts to meet the system performance requirements for all system users and a timeline and anticipated expenditures needed to develop and deploy the system to meet the vision for 2025; and

(5) a multiagency integrated work plan for the Next Generation Air Transportation System that includes—

(A) an outline of the activities required to achieve the end-state architecture, as expressed in the concept of operations and enterprise architecture documents, that identifies each Federal agency or other entity responsible for each activity in the outline;

(B) details on a year-by-year basis of specific accomplishments, activities, research requirements, rulemakings, policy decisions, and other milestones of progress for each Federal agency or entity conducting activities relating to the Next Generation Air Transportation System;

(C) for each element of the Next Generation Air Transportation System, an outline, on a year-by-year basis, of what is to be accomplished in that year toward meeting the Next Generation Air Transportation System's end-state architecture, as expressed in the concept of operations and enterprise architecture documents, as well as identifying each Federal agency or other entity that will be responsible for each component of any research, development, or implementation program;

(D) an estimate of all necessary expenditures on a year-by-year basis, including a statement of each Federal agency or entity's responsibility for costs and available resources, for each stage of development from the basic research stage through the demonstration and implementation phase;

(E) a clear explanation of how each step in the development of the Next Generation Air Transportation System will lead to the following step and of the implications of not successfully completing a step in the time period described in the integrated work plan;

(F) a transition plan for the implementation of the Next Generation Air Transportation System that includes date-specific milestones for the implementation of new capabilities into the national airspace system;

(G) date-specific timetables for meeting the environmental goals identified in subsection (a)(3)(I); and

(H) a description of potentially significant operational or workforce changes resulting from deployment of the Next Generation Air Transportation System.

(c) GOALS.—The Next Generation Air Transportation System shall—

(1) improve the level of safety, security, efficiency, quality, and affordability of the National Airspace System and aviation services;

(2) take advantage of data from emerging ground-based and space-based communications, navigation, and surveillance technologies;

(3) integrate data streams from multiple agencies and sources to enable situational awareness and seamless global operations for all appropriate users of the system, including users responsible for civil aviation, homeland security, and national security;

(4) leverage investments in civil aviation, homeland security, and national security and build upon current air traffic management and infrastructure initiatives to meet system performance requirements for all system users;

(5) be scalable to accommodate and encourage substantial growth in domestic and international transportation and anticipate and accommodate continuing technology upgrades and advances;

(6) accommodate a wide range of aircraft operations, including airlines, air taxis, helicopters, general aviation, and unmanned aerial vehicles; and

(7) take into consideration, to the greatest extent practicable, design of airport approach and departure flight paths to reduce exposure of noise and emissions pollution on affected residents.

(d) NEXTGEN IMPLEMENTATION PLAN.—The Administrator shall develop and publish annually the document known as the NextGen Implementation Plan, or any successor document, that provides a detailed description of how the agency is implementing the Next Generation Air Transportation System.

(e) AUTHORIZATION OF APPROPRIATIONS.—There are authorized to be appropriated to the Office $50,000,000 for each of the fiscal years 2004 through 2010.

[Section 710 was repealed by section 218(i) of Public Law 118–63.]

SEC. 711. [49 U.S.C. 44504 note] ROTORCRAFT RESEARCH AND DEVELOPMENT INITIATIVE.

(a) OBJECTIVE.—The Administrator of the Federal Aviation Administration shall establish a rotorcraft initiative with the objective of developing, and demonstrating in a relevant environment, within 10 years after the date of the enactment of this Act, technologies to enable rotorcraft with the following improvements relative to rotorcraft existing as of the date of the enactment of this Act:

(1) 80 percent reduction in noise levels on takeoff and on approach and landing as perceived by a human observer.

(2) Factor of 10 reduction in vibration.

(3) 30 percent reduction in empty weight.

(4) Predicted accident rate equivalent to that of fixed-wing aircraft in commercial service within 10 years after the date of the enactment of this Act.

(5) Capability for zero-ceiling, zero-visibility operations.

(b) IMPLEMENTATION.—Within 180 days after the date of the enactment of this Act, the Administrator of the Federal Aviation Administration, in cooperation with the Administrator of the National Aeronautics and Space Administration, shall provide a plan to the Committee on Science of the House of Representatives and to the Committee on Commerce, Science, and Transportation of the Senate for the implementation of the initiative described in subsection (a).

* * * * * * *

TITLE VIII—MISCELLANEOUS

* * * * * * *

SEC. 805. IMPROVEMENT OF AVIATION INFORMATION COLLECTION.

(a) IN GENERAL.—Section 329(b)(1) is amended by striking "except that in no case" and all that follows through the semicolon at the end and inserting the following: "except that, if the Secretary requires air carriers to provide flight-specific information, the Secretary—

"(A) shall not disseminate fare information for a specific flight to the general public for a period of at least 9 months following the date of the flight; and

"(B) shall give due consideration to and address confidentiality concerns of carriers, including competitive implications, in any rulemaking prior to adoption of a rule requiring the dissemination to the general public of any flight-specific fare;"

(b) [49 U.S.C. 329 note] EFFECTIVE DATE.—The amendment made by subsection (a) shall take effect on the date of the issuance of a final rule to modernize the Origin and Destination Survey of Airline Passenger Traffic, pursuant to the Advance Notice of Proposed Rulemaking published July 15, 1998 (Regulation Identifier Number 2105–AC71), that reduces the reporting burden for air carriers through electronic filing of the survey data collected under section 329(b)(1) of title 49, United States Code.

* * * * * * *

SEC. 812. [49 U.S.C. 40105 note] RECIPROCAL AIRWORTHINESS CERTIFICATION.

Vision 100–Century of Aviation Reauthorization Act

SEC. 812. [49 U.S.C. 40105 note] RECIPROCAL AIRWORTHINESS CERTIFICATION.

(a) IN GENERAL.—As part of their bilateral negotiations with foreign nations and their civil aviation counterparts, the Secretary of State and the Administrator of the Federal Aviation Administration shall facilitate the reciprocal airworthiness certification of aviation products.

(b) RECIPROCAL AIRWORTHINESS DEFINED.—In this section, the term "reciprocal airworthiness certification of aviation products" means that the regulatory authorities of each nation perform a similar review in certifying or validating the certification of aircraft and aircraft components of other nations.

* * * * * * *

SEC. 817. [49 U.S.C. 40101 note] REIMBURSEMENT FOR LOSSES INCURRED BY GENERAL AVIATION ENTITIES.

(a) IN GENERAL.—The Secretary of Transportation may make grants to reimburse the following general aviation entities for the security costs incurred and revenue foregone as a result of the restrictions imposed by the Federal Government following the terrorist attacks on the United States that occurred on September 11, 2001:

(1) General aviation entities that operate at Ronald Reagan Washington National Airport.

(2) Airports that are located within 15 miles of Ronald Reagan Washington National Airport and were operating under security restrictions on the date of enactment of this Act and general aviation entities operating at those airports.

(3) General aviation entities affected by implementation of section 44939 of title 49, United States Code.

(4) General aviation entities that were affected by Federal Aviation Administration Notices to Airmen FDC 2/1099 and 3/1862 or section 352 of the Department of Transportation and Related Agencies Appropriations Act, 2003 (Public Law 108–7, division I), or both.

(5) Sightseeing operations that were not authorized to resume in enhanced class B air space under Federal Aviation Administration notice to airmen 1/1225.

(b) DOCUMENTATION.—Reimbursement under this section shall be made in accordance with sworn financial statements or other appropriate data submitted by each general aviation entity demonstrating the costs incurred and revenue foregone to the satisfaction of the Secretary.

(c) GENERAL AVIATION ENTITY DEFINED.—In this section, the term "general aviation entity" means any person (other than a scheduled air carrier or foreign air carrier, as such terms are defined in section 40102 of title 49, United States Code) that—

(1) operates nonmilitary aircraft under part 91 of title 14, Code of Federal Regulations, for the purpose of conducting its primary business;

(2) manufactures nonmilitary aircraft with a maximum seating capacity of fewer than 20 passengers or aircraft parts to be used in such aircraft;

(3) provides services necessary for nonmilitary operations under such part 91; or

(4) operates an airport, other than a primary airport (as such terms are defined in such section 40102), that—

(A) is listed in the national plan of integrated airport systems developed by the Federal Aviation Administration under section 47103 of such title; or

(B) is normally open to the public, is located within the confines of enhanced class B airspace (as defined by the Federal Aviation Administration in Notice to Airmen FDC 1/0618), and was closed as a result of an order issued by the Federal Aviation Administration in the period beginning September 11, 2001, and ending January 1, 2002, and remained closed as a result of that order on January 1, 2002.

Such term includes fixed based operators, flight schools, manufacturers of general aviation aircraft and products, persons engaged in nonscheduled aviation enterprises, and general aviation independent contractors.

(d) AUTHORIZATION OF APPROPRIATIONS.—There is authorized to be appropriated to carry out this section $100,000,000. Such sums shall remain available until expended.

SEC. 818. INTERNATIONAL AIR SHOW.

If the Secretary of Defense conducts activities necessary to enable the United States to host a major international air show in the United States, the Secretary of Defense shall coordinate such activities with the Secretary of Transportation and the Secretary of Commerce.

* * * * * * *

SEC. 821. [49 U.S.C. 44903 note] REIMBURSEMENT OF AIR CARRIERS FOR CERTAIN SCREENING AND RELATED ACTIVITIES.

The Secretary of Homeland Security, subject to the availability of funds (other than amounts in the Aviation Trust Fund) provided for this purpose, shall reimburse air carriers and airports for—

(1) the screening of catering supplies; and

(2) checking documents at security checkpoints.

* * * * * * *

SEC. 823. [49 U.S.C. 41718 note] GENERAL AVIATION FLIGHTS AT RONALD REAGAN WASHINGTON NATIONAL AIRPORT.

(a) SECURITY PLAN.—The Secretary of Homeland Security shall develop and implement a security plan to permit general aviation aircraft to land and take off at Ronald Reagan Washington National Airport.

(b) LANDINGS AND TAKEOFFS.—The Administrator of the Federal Aviation Administration shall allow general aviation aircraft that comply with the requirements of the security plan to land and take off at the Airport except during any period that the President suspends the plan developed under subsection (a) due to national security concerns.

(c) REPORT.—If the President suspends the security plan developed under subsection (a), the President shall submit to the Senate Committee on Commerce, Science, and Transportation and the House of Representatives Committee on Transportation and Infrastructure a report on the reasons for the suspension not later than 30 days following the first day of the suspension. The report may be submitted in classified form.

* * * * * * *

SEC. 825. NOISE CONTROL PLAN FOR CERTAIN AIRPORTS.

(a) IN GENERAL.—Notwithstanding chapter 475 of title 49, United States Code, or any other provision of law or regulation, a sponsor of a commercial service airport that does not own the airport land and is a party to a long-term lease agreement with a Federal agency (other than the Department of Defense or the Department of Transportation) may impose restrictions on, or prohibit, the operation of Stage 2 aircraft weighing less than 75,000 pounds, in order to help meet the noise control plan contained within the lease agreement. A use restriction imposed pursuant to this section must contain reasonable exemptions for public health and safety.

(b) PUBLIC NOTICE AND COMMENT.—Prior to imposing restrictions on, or prohibiting, the operation of Stage 2 aircraft weighing less than 75,000 pounds, the airport sponsor must provide reasonable notice and the opportunity to comment on the proposed airport use restriction limited to no more than 90 days.

(c) DEFINITIONS.—In this section, the terms "Stage 2 aircraft" and "Stage 3 aircraft" have the same meaning as those terms have in chapter 475 of title 49, United States Code.

* * * * * * *

SEC. 827. PRIVATE AIR CARRIAGE IN ALASKA.

(a) IN GENERAL.—Due to the demands of conducting business within and from the State of Alaska, the Secretary of Transportation shall permit, under the operating rules of part 91 of title 14 of the Code of Federal Regulations where common carriage is not involved, a company, located in the State of Alaska, to organize a subsidiary where the only enterprise of the subsidiary is to provide air carriage of officials, employees, guests, and property of the company, or its affiliate, when the carriage—

(1) originates or terminates in the State of Alaska;

(2) is by an aircraft with no more than 20 seats;

(3) is within the scope of, and incidental to, the business of the company or its affiliate; and

(4) no charge, assessment, or fee is made for the carriage in excess of the cost of owning, operating, and maintaining the airplane.

(b) LIMITATION ON STATUTORY CONSTRUCTION.—Nothing in this

subsection shall be construed as prohibiting a company from making intermediate stops in providing air carriage under this section.

* * * * * * *

SELECTED PROVISIONS OF THE AVIATION AND TRANSPORTATION SECURITY ACT

PUBLIC LAW 107-71

AVIATION AND TRANSPORTATION SECURITY ACT

[Public Law 107–71; 115 Stat. 597]

[As Amended Through P.L. 116–92, Enacted December 20, 2019]

AN ACT To improve aviation security, and for other purposes.

Be it enacted by the Senate and House of Representatives of the United States of America in Congress assembled,

SECTION 1. SHORT TITLE.

This Act may be cited as the "Aviation and Transportation Security Act".

TITLE I—AVIATION SECURITY

SEC. 101. TRANSPORTATION SECURITY ADMINISTRATION.

(a)

* * *

* * * * * * *

(g) TRANSITION PROVISIONS.—

(1)

* * *

* * * * * * *

(4) TRANSFER OF OWNERSHIP.—In recognition of the assumption of the financial costs of security screening of passengers and property at airports, and as soon as practical after the date of enactment of this Act, air carriers may enter into agreements with the Under Secretary to transfer the ownership, at no cost to the United States Government, of

SEC. 104. [49 U.S.C. 44903 note] IMPROVED
FLIGHT DECK INTEGRITY MEASURES.

AVIATION AND TRANSPORTAT
SECURITY

any personal property, equipment, supplies, or other material associated with such screening, regardless of the source of funds used to acquire the property, that the Secretary determines to be useful for the performance of security screening of passengers and property at airports.

SEC. 104. [49 U.S.C. 44903 note] IMPROVED FLIGHT DECK INTEGRITY MEASURES.

(a) IN GENERAL.—As soon as possible after the date of enactment of this Act, the Administrator of the Federal Aviation Administration shall—

(1) issue an order (without regard to the provisions of chapter 5 of title 5, United States Code)—

(A) prohibiting access to the flight deck of aircraft engaged in passenger air transportation or intrastate air transportation that are required to have a door between the passenger and pilot compartments under title 14, Code of Federal Regulations, except to authorized persons;

(B) requiring the strengthening of the flight deck door and locks on any such aircraft operating in air transportation or intrastate air transportation that has a rigid door in a bulkhead between the flight deck and the passenger area to ensure that the door cannot be forced open from the passenger compartment;

(C) requiring that such flight deck doors remain locked while any such aircraft is in flight except when necessary to permit access and egress by authorized persons; and

(D) prohibiting the possession of a key to any such flight deck door by any member of the flight crew who is not assigned to the flight deck; and

(2) take such other action, including modification of safety and security procedures and flight deck redesign, as may be necessary to ensure the safety and security of the aircraft.

(b) IMPLEMENTATION OF OTHER METHODS.—As soon as possible after such date of enactment, the Administrator of the Federal Aviation Administration may develop and implement methods—

(1) to use video monitors or other devices to alert pilots in the flight deck to activity in the cabin, except that the use of such monitors or devices shall be subject to nondisclosure

requirements applicable to cockpit video recordings under section 1114(c);

(2) to ensure continuous operation of an aircraft transponder in the event of an emergency; and

(3) to revise the procedures by which cabin crews of aircraft can notify flight deck crews of security breaches and other emergencies, including providing for the installation of switches or other devices or methods in an aircraft cabin to enable flight crews to discreetly notify the pilots in the case of a security breach occurring in the cabin.

(c) COMMUTER AIRCRAFT.—The Administrator shall investigate means of securing the flight deck of scheduled passenger aircraft operating in air transportation or intrastate air transportation that do not have a rigid fixed door with a lock between the passenger compartment and the flight deck and issue such an order as the Administrator deems appropriate to ensure the inaccessibility, to the greatest extent feasible, of the flight deck while the aircraft is so operating, taking into consideration such aircraft operating in regions where there is minimal threat to aviation security or national security.

* * * * * * *

SEC. 106. IMPROVED AIRPORT PERIMETER ACCESS SECURITY.

(a)

* * *

(b) [49 U.S.C. 44903 note] SMALL AND MEDIUM AIRPORTS.—

(1) TECHNICAL SUPPORT AND FINANCIAL ASSISTANCE.—The Under Secretary of Transportation for Security shall develop a plan to—

(A) provide technical support to airports, each of which had less than 1 percent of the total annual enplanements in the United States for the most recent calendar year for which data is available, to enhance security operations; and

(B) provide financial assistance to those airports to defray the costs of enhancing security.

(2) REMOVAL OF CERTAIN RESTRICTIONS.—

(A) CERTIFICATION BY OPERATOR.—If the operator of an airport described in paragraph (1), after consultation with the appropriate State and local law enforcement authorities, determines that safeguards are in place to sufficiently protect public safety, and so certifies in writing to the Under Secretary, then any security rule, order, or other directive restricting the parking of passenger vehicles shall not apply at that airport after the applicable time period specified in subparagraph (B), unless the Under Secretary, taking into account individual airport circumstances, notifies the airport operator that the safeguards in place do not adequately respond to specific security risks and that the restriction must be continued in order to ensure public safety.

(B) COUNTERMAND PERIOD.—The time period within which the Secretary may notify an airport operator, after receiving a certification under subparagraph (A), that a restriction must be continued in order to ensure public safety at the airport is—

(i) 15 days for a nonhub airport (as defined in section 41714(h) of title 49, United States Code);

(ii) 30 days for a small hub airport (as defined in such section);

(iii) 60 days for a medium hub airport (as defined in such section); and

(iv) 120 days for an airport that had at least 1 percent of the total annual enplanements in the United States for the most recent calendar year for which data is available.

* * * * * * *

(e) [49 U.S.C. 44903 note] AIRPORT SECURITY AWARENESS PROGRAMS.—The Under Secretary of Transportation for Security shall require scheduled passenger air carriers, and airports in the United States described in section 44903(c) to develop security awareness programs for airport employees, ground crews, gate, ticket, and curbside agents of the air carriers, and other individuals employed at such airports.

* * * * * * *

SEC. 109. [49 U.S.C. 114 note] ENHANCED SECURITY MEASURES.

(a) IN GENERAL.—The Under Secretary of Transportation for Security may take the following actions:

(1) Require effective 911 emergency call capability for telephones serving passenger aircraft and passenger trains.

(2) Establish a uniform system of identification for all State and local law enforcement personnel for use in obtaining permission to carry weapons in aircraft cabins and in obtaining access to a secured area of an airport, if otherwise authorized to carry such weapons.

(3) Establish requirements to implement trusted passenger programs and use available technologies to expedite the security screening of passengers who participate in such programs, thereby allowing security screening personnel to focus on those passengers who should be subject to more extensive screening.

(4) In consultation with the Commissioner of the Food and Drug Administration, develop alternative security procedures under which a medical product to be transported on a flight of an air carrier would not be subject to an inspection that would irreversibly damage the product.

(5) Provide for the use of technologies, including wireless and wire line data technologies, to enable the private and secure communication of threats to aid in the screening of passengers and other individuals on airport property who are identified on any State or Federal security-related data base for the purpose of having an integrated response coordination of various authorized airport security forces.

(6) In consultation with the Administrator of the Federal Aviation Administration, consider whether to require all pilot licenses to incorporate a photograph of the license holder and appropriate biometric imprints.

(7) Provide for the use of voice stress analysis, biometric, or other technologies to prevent a person who might pose a danger to air safety or security from boarding the aircraft of an air carrier or foreign air carrier in air transportation or intrastate air transportation.

(8) Provide for the use of technology that will permit enhanced instant communications and information between

airborne passenger aircraft and appropriate individuals or facilities on the ground.

(b) REPORT.—Not later than 6 months after the date of enactment of this Act, and annually thereafter until the Under Secretary has implemented or decided not to take each of the actions specified in subsection (a), the Under Secretary shall transmit to Congress a report on the progress of the Under Secretary in evaluating and taking such actions, including any legislative recommendations that the Under Secretary may have for enhancing transportation security.

SEC. 110. SCREENING.

(a)

* * *

* * * * * * *

(c) DEADLINE FOR DEPLOYMENT OF FEDERAL SCREENERS.—

(1) IN GENERAL.—Not later than 1 year after the date of enactment of this Act, the Under Secretary of Transportation for Security shall deploy at all airports in the United States where screening is required under section 44901 of title 49, United States Code, a sufficient number of Federal screeners, Federal Security Managers, Federal security personnel, and Federal law enforcement officers to conduct the screening of all passengers and property under section 44901 of such title at such airports.

(2) CERTIFICATION TO CONGRESS.—Not later than 1 year after the date of enactment of this Act, the Under Secretary shall transmit to Congress a certification that the requirement of paragraph (1) has been met.

* * * * * * *

SEC. 111. TRAINING AND EMPLOYMENT OF SECURITY SCREENING PERSONNEL.

[Subsections (a) and (b) omitted—amends other Acts]

(c) [49 U.S.C. 44935 note] TRANSITION.—The Under Secretary of Transportation for Security shall complete the full implementation of section 44935 (e), (f), (g), and (h) of title 49,

United States Code, as amended by subsection (a), as soon as is practicable. The Under Secretary may make or continue such arrangements for the training of security screeners under that section as the Under Secretary determines necessary pending full implementation of that section as so amended.

(d) [49 U.S.C. 44935 note] SCREENER PERSONNEL.—

(1) GENERAL AUTHORITY.—Except as provided in paragraph (2), and notwithstanding any other provision of law, the Under Secretary of Transportation for Security may employ, appoint, discipline, terminate, and fix the compensation, terms, and conditions of employment of Federal service for such a number of individuals as the Under Secretary determines to be necessary to carry out the screening functions of the Under Secretary under section 44901 of title 49, United States Code. The Under Secretary shall establish levels of compensation and other benefits for individuals so employed.

(2) EXCEPTIONS.—

(A) REEMPLOYMENT.—In carrying out the functions authorized under paragraph (1), the Under Secretary shall be subject to the provisions set forth in chapter 43 of title 38, United States Code.

(B) LEAVE.—The provisions of subchapter V of chapter 63 of title 5, United States Code, shall apply to any individual appointed under paragraph (1) as if such individual were an employee (within the meaning of subparagraph (A) of section 6381(1) of such title).

* * * * * * *

SEC. 113. FLIGHT SCHOOL SECURITY.

(a)

* * *

* * * * * * *

(c) [49 U.S.C. 44939 note] INTERNATIONAL COOPERATION.—The Secretary of Transportation, in consultation with the Secretary of State, shall work with the International Civil Aviation Organization and the civil aviation authorities of other countries to improve international aviation security through screening programs for

SEC. 117. [49 U.S.C. 44903 note] AIRLINE
COMPUTER RESERVATION SYSTEMS.

AVIATION AND TRANSPORTAT
SECURITY

flight instruction candidates.

* * * * * * *

SEC. 117. [49 U.S.C. 44903 note] AIRLINE COMPUTER RESERVATION SYSTEMS.

In order to ensure that all airline computer reservation systems maintained by United States air carriers are secure from unauthorized access by persons seeking information on reservations, passenger manifests, or other nonpublic information, the Secretary of Transportation shall require all such air carriers to utilize to the maximum extent practicable the best technology available to secure their computer reservation system against such unauthorized access.

* * * * * * *

SEC. 121. [49 U.S.C. 44903 note] AUTHORIZATION OF FUNDS FOR REIMBURSEMENT OF AIRPORTS FOR SECURITY MANDATES.

(a) AIRPORT SECURITY.—There is authorized to be appropriated to the Secretary of Transportation for fiscal years 2002 and 2003 a total of $1,500,000,000 to reimburse airport operators, on-airport parking lots, and vendors of on-airfield direct services to air carriers for direct costs incurred by such operators to comply with new, additional, or revised security requirements imposed on such operators by the Federal Aviation Administration or Transportation Security Administration on or after September 11, 2001. Such sums shall remain available until expended.

(b) DOCUMENTATION OF COSTS; AUDIT.—The Secretary may not reimburse an airport operator, on-airport parking lot, or vendor of on-airfield direct services to air carriers under this section for any cost for which the airport operator, on-airport parking lot, or vendor of on-airfield direct services does not demonstrate to the satisfaction of the Secretary, using sworn financial statements or other appropriate data, that—

(1) the cost is eligible for reimbursement under subsection (a); and

(2) the cost was incurred by the airport operator, on-airport parking lot, or vendor of on-airfield direct services to air carriers.

The Inspector General of the Department of Transportation and the Comptroller General of the United States may audit such statements and may request any other information necessary to conduct such an audit.

(c) CLAIM PROCEDURE.—Within 30 days after the date of enactment of this Act, the Secretary, after consultation with airport operators, on-airport parking lots, and vendors of on-airfield direct services to air carriers, shall publish in the Federal Register the procedures for filing claims for reimbursement under this section of eligible costs incurred by airport operators.

* * * * * * *

SEC. 127. [49 U.S.C. 40101 note] MAIL AND FREIGHT WAIVERS.

(a)[1] IN GENERAL.—During a national emergency affecting air transportation or intrastate air transportation, the Secretary of Transportation, after consultation with the Transportation Security Oversight Board, may grant a complete or
partial waiver of any restrictions on the carriage by aircraft of freight, mail, emergency medical supplies, personnel, or patients on aircraft, imposed by the Department of Transportation (or other Federal agency or department) that would permit such carriage of freight, mail, emergency medical supplies, personnel, or patients on flights, to, from, or within a State if the Secretary determines that—

---

[1]   Margin so in law.

---

(1) extraordinary air transportation needs or concerns exist; and

(2) the waiver is in the public interest, taking into consideration the isolation of and dependence on air transportation of the State.

(b) LIMITATIONS.—The Secretary may impose reasonable limitations on any such waiver.

* * * * * * *

SEC. 137. [49 U.S.C. 44912 note] RESEARCH AND DEVELOPMENT OF AVIATION SECURITY TECHNOLOGY.

(a) FUNDING.—To augment the programs authorized in section 44912(a)(1) of title 49, United States Code, there is authorized to be appropriated an additional $50,000,000 for each of fiscal years 2006 through 2011 and such sums as are necessary for each fiscal year thereafter to the Transportation Security Administration, for research, development, testing, and evaluation of the following technologies which may enhance transportation security in the future. Grants to industry, academia, and Government entities to carry out the provisions of this section shall be available for fiscal years 2006 through 2011 for—

(1) the acceleration of research, development, testing, and evaluation of explosives detection technology for checked baggage, specifically, technology that is—

(A) more cost-effective for deployment for explosives detection in checked baggage at small- to medium-sized airports, and is currently under development as part of the Argus research program at the Transportation Security Administration;

(B) faster, to facilitate screening of all checked baggage at larger airports; or

(C) more accurate, to reduce the number of false positives requiring additional security measures;

(2) acceleration of research, development, testing, and evaluation of new screening technology for carry-on items to provide more effective means of detecting and identifying weapons, explosives, and components of weapons of mass destruction, including advanced x-ray technology;

(3) acceleration of research, development, testing, and evaluation of threat screening technology for other categories of items being loaded onto aircraft, including cargo, catering, and duty-free items;

(4) acceleration of research, development, testing, and evaluation of threats carried on persons boarding aircraft or entering secure areas, including detection of weapons, explosives, and components of weapons of mass destruction;

(5) acceleration of research, development, testing and evaluation of integrated systems of airport security enhancement, including quantitative methods of assessing security factors at airports selected for testing such systems;

(6) expansion of the existing program of research, development, testing, and evaluation of improved methods of

education, training, and testing of key airport security personnel; and

(7) acceleration of research, development, testing, and evaluation of aircraft hardening materials, and techniques to reduce the vulnerability of aircraft to terrorist attack.

(b) GRANTS.—Grants awarded under this subtitle shall identify potential outcomes of the research, and propose a method for quantitatively assessing effective increases in security upon completion of the research program. At the conclusion of each grant, the grant recipient shall submit a final report to the Transportation Security Administration that shall include sufficient information to permit the Under Secretary of Transportation for Security to prepare a cost-benefit analysis of potential improvements to airport security based upon deployment of the proposed technology. The Under Secretary shall begin awarding grants under this subtitle within 90 days of the date of enactment of this Act.

(c) BUDGET SUBMISSION.—A budget submission and detailed strategy for deploying the identified security upgrades recommended upon completion of the grants awarded under subsection (b), shall be submitted to Congress as part of the Department of Transportation's annual budget submission.

(d) DEFENSE RESEARCH.—There is authorized to be appropriated $20,000,000 to the Transportation Security Administration to issue research grants in conjunction with the Defense Advanced Research Projects Agency. Grants may be awarded under this section for—

(1) research and development of longer-term improvements to airport security, including advanced weapons detection;

(2) secure networking and sharing of threat information between Federal agencies, law enforcement entities, and other appropriate parties;

(3) advances in biometrics for identification and threat assessment; or

(4) other technologies for preventing acts of terrorism in aviation.

* * * * * * *

SEC. 145. [49 U.S.C. 40101 note] AIR CARRIERS REQUIRED TO

HONOR TICKETS FOR SUSPENDED SERVICE.

(a) IN GENERAL.—Each air carrier that provides scheduled air transportation on a route shall provide, to the extent practicable, air transportation to passengers ticketed for air transportation on that route by any other air carrier that suspends, interrupts, or discontinues air passenger service on the route by reason of insolvency or bankruptcy of the other air carrier.

(b) PASSENGER OBLIGATION.—An air carrier is not required to provide air transportation under subsection (a) to a passenger unless that passenger makes alternative arrangements with the air carrier for such transportation within 60 days after the date on which that passenger's air transportation was suspended, interrupted, or discontinued (without regard to the originally scheduled travel date on the ticket).

(c) SUNSET.—This section does not apply to air transportation the suspension, interruption, or discontinuance of which occurs after November 30, 2006.

* * * * * * *

TITLES I AND II OF THE AIR TRANSPORTATION SAFETY AND SYSTEM STABILIZATION ACT

PUBLIC LAW 107-42

TITLE I AND TITLE IV OF THE AIR TRANSPORTATION SAFETY AND SYSTEM STABILIZATION ACT

[Public Law 107–42; 115 Stat. 230; 49 U.S.C. 40101 note]

[As Amended Through P.L. 116–34, Enacted July 29, 2019]

AN ACT To preserve the continued viability of the United States air transportation system.

Be it enacted by the Senate and House of Representatives of the United States of America in Congress assembled,

SECTION 1. [49 U.S.C. 40101 note] SHORT TITLE.

This Act may be cited as the "Air Transportation Safety and System Stabilization Act".

TITLE I—AIRLINE STABILIZATION

SEC. 101. [49 U.S.C. 40101 note] AVIATION DISASTER RELIEF.

(a) IN GENERAL.—Notwithstanding any other provision of law, the President shall take the following actions to compensate air carriers for losses incurred by the air carriers as a result of the terrorist attacks on the United States that occurred on September 11, 2001:

(1) [Repealed. Pub. L. 110-161, div. D, title I, Dec. 26, 2007, 121 Stat. 1974.]

(2) Compensate air carriers in an aggregate amount equal to $5,000,000,000 for—

(A) direct losses incurred beginning on September 11, 2001, by air carriers as a result of any Federal ground stop order issued by the Secretary of Transportation or any subsequent order which continues or renews such a stoppage; and

SEC. 102. [49 U.S.C. 40101 note] SPECIAL
RULES FOR COMPENSATION.

Title I and title IV of the Air Transports
Safety and System Stabilizatior

(B) the incremental losses incurred beginning September 11, 2001, and ending December 31, 2001, by air carriers as a direct result of such attacks.

(b) EMERGENCY DESIGNATION.—Congress designates the amount of new budget authority and outlays in all fiscal years resulting from this title as an emergency requirement pursuant to section 252(e) of the Balanced Budget and Emergency Deficit Control Act of 1985 (2 U.S.C. 901(e)). Such amount shall be available only to the extent that a request, that includes designation of such amount as an emergency requirement as defined in such Act, is transmitted by the President to Congress.

SEC. 102. [Repealed. Pub. L. 110-161, div. D, title I, Dec. 26, 2007, 121 Stat. 1974.]

SEC. 103. [49 U.S.C. 40101 note] SPECIAL RULES FOR COMPENSATION.

(a) DOCUMENTATION.—Subject to subsection (b), the amount of compensation payable to an air carrier under section 101(a)(2) may not exceed the amount of losses described in section 101(a)(2) that the air carrier demonstrates to the satisfaction of the President, using sworn financial statements or other appropriate data, that the air carrier incurred. The Secretary of Transportation and the Comptroller General of the United States may audit such statements and may request any information that the Secretary and the Comptroller General deems necessary to conduct such audit.

(b) MAXIMUM AMOUNT OF COMPENSATION PAYABLE PER AIR CARRIER.—The maximum total amount of compensation payable to an air carrier under section 101(a)(2) may not exceed the lesser of—

(1) the amount of such air carrier's direct and incremental losses described in section 101(a)(2); or

(2) in the case of—

(A) flights involving passenger-only or combined passenger and cargo transportation, the product of—

(i) $4,500,000,000; and

(ii) the ratio of—

(I) the available seat miles of the air carrier for the month of August 2001 as reported to the Secretary; to

SEC. 104. [49 U.S.C. 40101 note]
CONTINUATION OF CERTAIN AIR SERVICE.

Title I and title IV of the Air Transportation
Safety and System Stabilization Act

(II) the total available seat miles of all such air carriers for such month as reported to the Secretary; and

(B) flights involving cargo-only transportation, the product of—

(i) $500,000,000; and

(ii) the ratio of—

(I) the revenue ton miles or other auditable measure of the air carrier for cargo for the latest quarter for which data is available as reported to the Secretary; to

(II) the total revenue ton miles or other auditable measure of all such air carriers for cargo for such quarter as reported to the Secretary.

(c) PAYMENTS.—The President may provide compensation to air carriers under section 101(a)(2) in 1 or more payments up to the amount authorized by this title.

(d) COMPENSATION FOR CERTAIN AIR CARRIERS.—

(1) SET-ASIDE.—The President may set aside a portion of the amount of compensation payable to air carriers under section 101(a)(2) to provide compensation to classes of air carriers, such as air tour operators and air ambulances (including hospitals operating air ambulances) for whom the application of a distribution formula containing available seat miles as a factor would inadequately reflect their share of direct and incremental losses. The President shall reduce the $4,500,000,000 specified in subsection (b)(2)(A)(i) by the amount set aside under this subsection.

(2) DISTRIBUTION OF AMOUNTS.—The President shall distribute the amount set aside under this subsection proportionally among such air carriers based on an appropriate auditable measure, as determined by the President.

SEC. 104. [Repealed. Pub. L. 110-161, div. D, title I, Dec. 26, 2007, 121 Stat. 1974.]

SEC. 105. [49 U.S.C. 40101 note] CONTINUATION OF CERTAIN AIR SERVICE.

(a) ACTION OF SECRETARY.—The Secretary of Transportation

should take appropriate action to ensure that all communities that had scheduled air service before September 11, 2001, continue to receive adequate air transportation service and that essential air service to small communities continues without interruption.

(b) ESSENTIAL AIR SERVICE.—There is authorized to be appropriated to the Secretary to carry out the essential air service program under subchapter II of chapter 417 of title 49, United States Code, $120,000,000 for fiscal year 2002.

(c) SECRETARIAL OVERSIGHT.—

(1) IN GENERAL.—Notwithstanding any other provision of law, the Secretary is authorized to require an air carrier receiving direct financial assistance under this Act to maintain scheduled air service to any point served by that carrier before September 11, 2001.

(2) AGREEMENTS.—In applying paragraph (1), the Secretary may require air carriers receiving direct financial assistance under this Act to enter into agreements which will ensure, to the maximum extent practicable, that all communities that had scheduled air service before September 11, 2001, continue to receive adequate air transportation service.

SEC. 106. [49 U.S.C. 40101 note] REPORTS.

(a) REPORT.—Not later than February 1, 2002, the President shall transmit to the Committee on Transportation and Infrastructure, the Committee on Appropriations, and the Committee on the Budget of the House of Representatives and the Committee on Commerce, Science, and Transportation, the Committee on Appropriations, and the Committee on the Budget of the Senate a report on the financial status of the air carrier industry and the amounts of assistance provided under this title to each air carrier.

(b) UPDATE.—Not later than the last day of the 7-month period following the date of enactment of this Act, the President shall update and transmit the report to the Committees.

SEC. 107. [49 U.S.C. 40101 note] DEFINITIONS.

In this title, the following definitions apply:

(1) AIR CARRIER.—The term "air carrier" has the meaning

such term has under section 40102 of title 49, United States Code.

(2) [Repealed. Pub. L. 110-161, div. D, title I, Dec. 26, 2007, 121 Stat. 1974.]

(3) INCREMENTAL LOSS.—The term "incremental loss" does not include any loss that the President determines would have been incurred if the terrorist attacks on the United States that occurred on September 11, 2001, had not occurred.

* * * * * * *

TITLE IV—VICTIM COMPENSATION

* * * * * * *

SEC. 401. [49 U.S.C. 40101 note] SHORT TITLE.

This title may be cited as the "September 11th Victim Compensation Fund of 2001".

SEC. 402. [49 U.S.C. 40101 note] DEFINITIONS.

In this title, the following definitions apply:

(1) AIR CARRIER.—The term "air carrier" means a citizen of the United States undertaking by any means, directly or indirectly, to provide air transportation and includes employees and agents (including persons engaged in the business of providing air transportation security and their affiliates) of such citizen. For purposes of the preceding sentence, the term "agent", as applied to persons engaged in the business of providing air transportation security, shall only include persons that have contracted directly with the Federal Aviation Administration on or after and commenced services no later than February 17, 2002, to provide such security, and had not been or are not debarred for any period within 6 months from that date.

(2) AIR TRANSPORTATION.—The term "air transportation" means foreign air transportation, interstate air transportation, or the transportation of mail by aircraft.

(3) AIRCRAFT MANUFACTURER.—The term "aircraft manufacturer" means any entity that manufactured the aircraft or any parts or components of the aircraft involved in

the terrorist related aircraft crashes of September 11, 2001, including employees and agents of that entity.

(4) AIRPORT SPONSOR.—The term "airport sponsor" means the owner or operator of an airport (as defined in section 40102 of title 49, United States Code).

(5) CLAIMANT.—The term "claimant" means an individual filing a claim for compensation under section 405(a)(1).

(6) COLLATERAL SOURCE.—The term "collateral source" means all collateral sources, including life insurance, pension funds, death benefit programs, and payments by Federal, State, or local governments related to the terrorist-related aircraft crashes of September 11, 2001, or debris removal, including under the World Trade Center Health Program established under section 3001 of the Public Health Service Act, and payments made pursuant to the settlement of a civil action described in section 405(c)(3)(C)(iii).

(7) CONTRACTOR AND SUBCONTRACTOR.—The term "contractor and subcontractor" means any contractor or subcontractor (at any tier of a subcontracting relationship), including any general contractor, construction manager, prime contractor, consultant, or any parent, subsidiary, associated or allied company, affiliated company, corporation, firm, organization, or joint venture thereof that participated in debris removal at any 9/11 crash site. Such term shall not include any entity, including the Port Authority of New York and New Jersey, with a property interest in the World Trade Center, on September 11, 2001, whether fee simple, leasehold or easement, direct or indirect.

(8) DEBRIS REMOVAL.—The term "debris removal" means rescue and recovery efforts, removal of debris, cleanup, remediation, and response during the immediate aftermath of the terrorist-related aircraft crashes of September 11, 2001, with respect to a 9/11 crash site.

(9) ECONOMIC LOSS.—The term "economic loss" means any pecuniary loss resulting from harm (including the loss of earnings or other benefits related to employment, replacement services loss, loss due to death, burial costs, loss of business or employment opportunities, and past out-of-pocket medical expense loss but not future medical expense loss) to the extent recovery for such loss is allowed under applicable State law.

(10) ELIGIBLE INDIVIDUAL.—The term "eligible individual" means an individual determined to be eligible for compensation under section 405(c).

(11) IMMEDIATE AFTERMATH.—The term "immediate aftermath" means any period beginning with the terrorist-related aircraft crashes of September 11, 2001, and ending on May 30, 2002.

(12) NONECONOMIC LOSSES.—The term "noneconomic losses" means losses for physical and emotional pain, suffering, inconvenience, physical impairment, mental anguish, disfigurement, loss of enjoyment of life, loss of society and companionship, loss of consortium (other than loss of domestic service), hedonic damages, injury to reputation, and all other nonpecuniary losses of any kind or nature.

(13) SPECIAL MASTER.—The term "Special Master" means the Special Master appointed under section 404(a).

(14) WTC PROGRAM ADMINISTRATOR.—The term "WTC Program Administrator" has the meaning given such term in section 3306 of the Public Health Service Act (42 U.S.C. 300mm–5).

(15) WTC-RELATED PHYSICAL HEALTH CONDITION.—The term "WTC-related physical health condition"—

(A) means, subject to subparagraph (B), a WTC-related health condition as defined by section 3312(a) of the Public Health Service Act (42 U.S.C. 300mm–22(a)), including the conditions listed in section 3322(b) of such Act (42 U.S.C. 300mm–32(b)); and

(B) does not include—

(i) a mental health condition described in paragraph (1)(A)(ii) or (3)(B) of section 3312(a) of such Act (42 U.S.C. 300mm–22(a));

(ii) any mental health condition certified under section 3312(b)(2)(B)(iii) of such Act (42 U.S.C. 300mm–22(b)(2)(B)(iii)) (including such certification as applied under section 3322(a) of such Act (42 U.S.C. 300mm–32(a));

(iii) a mental health condition described in section 3322(b)(2) of such Act (42 U.S.C. 300mm–32(b)(2)); or

(iv) any other mental health condition.

(16) 9/11 CRASH SITE.—The term "9/11 crash site" means—

(A) the World Trade Center site, Pentagon site, and Shanksville, Pennsylvania site;

(B) the buildings or portions of buildings that were destroyed as a result of the terrorist-related aircraft crashes of September 11, 2001;

(C) the area in Manhattan that is south of the line that runs along Canal Street from the Hudson River to the intersection of Canal Street and East Broadway, north on East Broadway to Clinton Street, and east on Clinton Street to the East River;[1]

---

[1]   Probably should read "; and" at the end of subparagraph (C).

(D) any area related to, or along, routes of debris removal, such as barges and Fresh Kills.

SEC. 403. [49 U.S.C. 40101 note] PURPOSE.

It is the purpose of this title to provide full compensation to any individual (or relatives of a deceased individual) who was physically injured or killed as a result of the terrorist-related aircraft crashes of September 11, 2001, or the rescue and recovery efforts during the immediate aftermath of such crashes.

SEC. 404. [49 U.S.C. 40101 note] ADMINISTRATION.

(a) IN GENERAL.—The Attorney General, acting through a Special Master appointed by the Attorney General, shall—

(1) administer the compensation program established under this title;

(2) promulgate all procedural and substantive rules for the administration of this title; and

(3) employ and supervise hearing officers and other administrative personnel to perform the duties of the Special Master under this title.

(b) APPOINTMENT OF SPECIAL MASTER AND DEPUTY SPECIAL MASTERS.—The Attorney General may appoint a Special Master and no more than two Deputy Special Masters without regard to the provisions of title 5, United States Code, governing appointments in the competitive service. Any such employee shall serve at the pleasure of the Attorney General. The Attorney General shall fix the annual salary of the Special Master and the Deputy Special Masters.

(c) AUTHORIZATION OF APPROPRIATIONS.—There are authorized to be appropriated such sums as may be necessary to pay the administrative and support costs for the Special Master in carrying out this title.

SEC. 405. [49 U.S.C. 40101 note] DETERMINATION OF ELIGIBILITY FOR COMPENSATION.

(a) FILING OF CLAIM.—

(1) IN GENERAL.—A claimant may file a claim for compensation under this title with the Special Master. The claim shall be on the form developed under paragraph (2) and shall state the factual basis for eligibility for compensation and the amount of compensation sought.

(2) CLAIM FORM.—

(A) IN GENERAL.—The Special Master shall develop a claim form that claimants shall use when submitting claims under paragraph (1). The Special Master shall ensure that such form can be filed electronically, if determined to be practicable.

(B) CONTENTS.—The form developed under subparagraph (A) shall request—

(i) information from the claimant concerning the physical harm that the claimant suffered, or in the case of a claim filed on behalf of a decedent information confirming the decedent's death, as a result of the terrorist-related aircraft crashes of September 11, 2001, or debris removal during the immediate aftermath;

(ii) information from the claimant concerning any possible economic and noneconomic losses that the claimant suffered as a result of such crashes or debris removal during the immediate aftermath; and

(iii) information regarding collateral sources of compensation the claimant has received or is entitled to receive as a result of such crashes or debris removal during the immediate aftermath.

(3) LIMITATION.—

(A) IN GENERAL.—Except as provided by subparagraph (B), no claim may be filed under paragraph (1) after the date that is 2 years after the date on which regulations are promulgated under section 407(a).

(B) EXCEPTION.—A claim may be filed under paragraph (1), in accordance with subsection (c)(3)(A)(i), by an individual (or by a personal representative on behalf of a deceased individual) during the period beginning on the date on which the regulations are updated under section 407(b)(1) and ending on October 1, 2090.

(C) SPECIAL MASTER DETERMINATION.—

(i) IN GENERAL.—For claims filed under this title during the period described in subparagraph (B), the Special Master shall establish a system for determining whether, for purposes of this title, the claim is—

(I) a claim in Group A, as described in clause (ii); or

(II) a claim in Group B, as described in clause (iii).

(ii) GROUP A CLAIMS.—A claim under this title is a claim in Group A if—

(I) the claim is filed under this title during the period described in subparagraph (B); and

(II) on or before the day before the date of enactment of the James Zadroga 9/11 Victim Compensation Fund Reauthorization Act, the Special Master postmarks and transmits a final award determination to the claimant filing such claim.

(iii) GROUP B CLAIMS.—A claim under this title is a claim in Group B if the claim—

(I) is filed under this title during the period described in subparagraph (B); and

(II) is not a claim described in clause (ii).

(iv) DEFINITION OF FINAL AWARD

464

DETERMINATION.—For purposes of this subparagraph, the term "final award determination" means a letter from the Special Master indicating the total amount of compensation to which a claimant is entitled for a claim under this title without regard to the limitation under the second sentence of section 406(d)(1), as such section was in effect on the day before the date of enactment of the James Zadroga 9/11 Victim Compensation Fund Reauthorization Act.

(b) REVIEW AND DETERMINATION.—

(1) REVIEW.—The Special Master shall review a claim submitted under subsection (a) and determine—

(A) whether the claimant is an eligible individual under subsection (c);

(B) with respect to a claimant determined to be an eligible individual—

(i) the extent of the harm to the claimant, including any economic and noneconomic losses; and

(ii) subject to paragraph (7), the amount of compensation to which the claimant is entitled based on the harm to the claimant, the facts of the claim, and the individual circumstances of the claimant.

(2) NEGLIGENCE.—With respect to a claimant, the Special Master shall not consider negligence or any other theory of liability.

(3) DETERMINATION.—Not later than 120 days after that date on which a claim is filed under subsection (a), the Special Master shall complete a review, make a determination, and provide written notice to the claimant, with respect to the matters that were the subject of the claim under review. Such a determination shall be final and not subject to judicial review.

(4) RIGHTS OF CLAIMANT.—A claimant in a review under paragraph (1) shall have—

(A) the right to be represented by an attorney;

(B) the right to present evidence, including the presentation of witnesses and documents; and

(C) any other due process rights determined appropriate by the Special Master.

(5) NO PUNITIVE DAMAGES.—The Special Master may not include amounts for punitive damages in any compensation paid under a claim under this title.

(6) COLLATERAL COMPENSATION.—

(A) IN GENERAL.—The Special Master shall reduce the amount of compensation determined under paragraph (1)(B)(ii) by the amount of the collateral source compensation the claimant has received or is entitled to receive as a result of the terrorist-related aircraft crashes of September 11, 2001.

(B) GROUP B CLAIMS.—Notwithstanding any other provision of this title, in the case of a claim in Group B as described in subsection (a)(3)(C)(iii), a claimant filing such claim shall receive an amount of compensation under this title for such claim that is not greater than the amount determined under paragraph (1)(B)(ii) less the amount of any collateral source compensation that such claimant has received or is entitled to receive for such claim as a result of the terrorist-related aircraft crashes of September 11, 2001.

(7) LIMITATIONS FOR GROUP B CLAIMS.—

(A) NONECONOMIC LOSSES.—

(i) IN GENERAL.—Except as provided in clause (ii), with respect to a claim in Group B as described in subsection (a)(3)(C)(iii), the total amount of compensation to which a claimant filing such claim is entitled to receive for such claim under this title on account of any noneconomic loss—

(I) that results from any type of cancer shall not exceed $250,000; and

(II) that does not result from any type of cancer shall not exceed $90,000.

(ii) EXCEPTION.—The Special Master may exceed the applicable limitation in clause (i) for a claim in Group B as described in subsection (a)(3)(C)(iii) if the Special Master determines that the claim presents special circumstances.

(B) DETERMINATION OF ECONOMIC LOSS.—

(i) IN GENERAL.—Subject to the limitation described in clause (ii) and with respect to a claim in Group B as described in subsection (a)(3)(C)(iii), the Special Master shall, for purposes of calculating the amount of compensation to which a claimant is entitled under this title for such claim on account of any economic loss, determine the loss of earnings or other benefits related to employment by using the applicable methodology described in section 104.43 or 104.45 of title 28, Code of Federal Regulations, as such Code was in effect on the day before the date of enactment of the James Zadroga 9/11 Victim Compensation Fund Reauthorization Act.

(ii) ANNUAL GROSS INCOME LIMITATION.—In considering annual gross income under clause (i) for the purposes described in such clause, the Special Master shall, for each year of any loss of earnings or other benefits related to employment, limit the annual gross income of the claimant (or decedent in the case of a personal representative) for each such year to an amount that is not greater than the annual gross income limitation. The annual gross income limitation in effect on the date of enactment of the Never Forget the Heroes: James Zadroga, Ray Pfeifer, and Luis Alvarez Permanent Authorization of the September 11th Victim Compensation Fund Act is $200,000. The Special Master shall periodically adjust that annual gross income limitation to account for inflation.

(C) GROSS INCOME DEFINED.—For purposes of this paragraph, the term "gross income" has the meaning given such term in section 61 of the Internal Revenue Code of 1986.

(c) ELIGIBILITY.—

(1) IN GENERAL.—A claimant shall be determined to be an eligible individual for purposes of this subsection if the Special Master determines that such claimant—

(A) is an individual described in paragraph (2); and

(B) meets the requirements of paragraph (3).

(2) INDIVIDUALS.—A claimant is an individual described in

this paragraph if the claimant is—

(A) an individual who—

(i) was present at the World Trade Center, (New York, New York), the Pentagon (Arlington, Virginia), the site of the aircraft crash at Shanksville, Pennsylvania, or any other 9/11 crash site at the time, or in the immediate aftermath, of the terrorist-related aircraft crashes of September 11, 2001; and

(ii) suffered physical harm or death as a result of such an air crash or debris removal;

(B) an individual who was a member of the flight crew or a passenger on American Airlines flight 11 or 77 or United Airlines flight 93 or 175, except that an individual identified by the Attorney General to have been a participant or conspirator in the terrorist-related aircraft crashes of September 11, 2001, or a representative of such individual shall not be eligible to receive compensation under this title; or

(C) in the case of a decedent who is an individual described in subparagraph (A) or (B), the personal representative of the decedent who files a claim on behalf of the decedent.

(3) REQUIREMENTS.—

(A) REQUIREMENTS FOR FILING CLAIMS DURING EXTENDED FILING PERIOD.—

(i) TIMING REQUIREMENTS FOR FILING CLAIMS.—An individual (or a personal representative on behalf of a deceased individual) may file a claim during the period described in subsection (a)(3)(B) as follows:

(I) In the case that the Special Master determines the individual knew (or reasonably should have known) before the date specified in clause (iii) that the individual suffered a physical harm at a 9/11 crash site as a result of the terrorist-related aircraft crashes of September 11, 2001, or as a result of debris removal, and that the individual knew (or should have known) before such specified date that the individual was eligible to file a claim under this title, the individual may file a claim not later than the date that is 2 years after such specified date.

(II) In the case that the Special Master determines the individual first knew (or reasonably should have known) on or after the date specified in clause (iii) that the individual suffered such a physical harm or that the individual first knew (or should have known) on or after such specified date that the individual was eligible to file a claim under this title, the individual may file a claim not later than the last day of the 2-year period beginning on the date the Special Master determines the individual first knew (or should have known) that the individual both suffered from such harm and was eligible to file a claim under this title.

(ii) OTHER ELIGIBILITY REQUIREMENTS FOR FILING CLAIMS.—Except with respect to claims in Group B as described in subsection (a)(3)(C)(iii), an individual may file a claim during the period described in subsection (a)(3)(B) only if—

(I) the individual was treated by a medical professional for suffering from a physical harm described in clause (i)(I) within a reasonable time from the date of discovering such harm; and

(II) the individual's physical harm is verified by contemporaneous medical records created by or at the direction of the medical professional who provided the medical care.

(iii) DATE SPECIFIED.—The date specified in this clause is the date on which the regulations are updated under section 407(b)(1).

(iv) GROUP B CLAIMS.—

(I) IN GENERAL.—Subject to subclause (II), an individual filing a claim in Group B as described in subsection (a)(3)(C)(iii) may be eligible for compensation under this title only if the Special Master, with assistance from the WTC Program Administrator as necessary, determines based on the evidence presented that the individual has a WTC-related physical health condition, as defined by section 402 of this Act.

(II) PERSONAL REPRESENTATIVES.—An individual filing a claim in Group B, as described in subsection (a)(3)(C)(iii), who is a personal representative described in paragraph (2)(C) may be eligible for compensation under this title only if the Special Master, with assistance from the WTC Program Administrator as necessary, determines based on the evidence presented that the applicable decedent suffered from a condition that was, or would have been determined to be, a WTC-related physical health condition, as defined by section 402 of this Act.

(B) SINGLE CLAIM.—Not more than one claim may be submitted under this title by an individual or on behalf of a deceased individual.

(C) LIMITATION ON CIVIL ACTION.—

(i) IN GENERAL.—Upon the submission of a claim under this title, the claimant waives the right to file a civil action (or to be a party to an action) in any Federal or State court for damages sustained as a result of the terrorist-related aircraft crashes of September 11, 2001, or for damages arising from or related to debris removal. The preceding sentence does not apply to a civil action to recover collateral source obligations, or to a civil action against any person who is a knowing participant in any conspiracy to hijack any aircraft or commit any terrorist act.

(ii) PENDING ACTIONS.—In the case of an individual who is a party to a civil action described in clause (i), such individual may not submit a claim under this title—

(I) during the period described in subsection (a)(3)(A) unless such individual withdraws from such action by the date that is 90 days after the date on which regulations are promulgated under section 407(a); and

SEC. 406. [49 U.S.C. 40101 note] PAYMENTS TO ELIGIBLE INDIVIDUALS.

Title I and title IV of the Air Transportation Safety and System Stabilization Act

(II) during the period described in subsection (a)(3)(B) unless such individual withdraws from such action by the date that is 90 days after the date on which the regulations are updated under section 407(b)(1).

(iii) SETTLED ACTIONS.—In the case of an individual who settled a civil action described in clause (i), such individual may not submit a claim under this title unless such action was commenced after December 22, 2003, and a release of all claims in such action was tendered prior to the date on which the James Zadroga 9/11 Health and Compensation Act of 2010 was enacted.

SEC. 406. [49 U.S.C. 40101 note] PAYMENTS TO ELIGIBLE INDIVIDUALS.

(a) IN GENERAL.—Subject to the limitations under subsection (d), not later than 20 days after the date on which a determination is made by the Special Master regarding the amount of compensation due a claimant under this title, the Special Master shall authorize payment to such claimant of the amount determined with respect to the claimant.

(b) PAYMENT AUTHORITY.—For the purpose of providing compensation for claims in Group A as described in section 405(a)(3)(C)(ii), this title constitutes budget authority in advance of appropriations Acts in the amounts provided under subsection (d)(1) and represents the obligation of the Federal Government to provide for the payment of amounts for compensation under this title subject to the limitations under subsection (d).

(c) ADDITIONAL FUNDING.—

(1) IN GENERAL.—The Attorney General is authorized to accept such amounts as may be contributed by individuals, business concerns, or other entities to carry out this title, under such terms and conditions as the Attorney General may impose.

(2) USE OF SEPARATE ACCOUNT.—In making payments under this section, amounts contained in any account containing funds provided under paragraph (1) shall be used prior to using appropriated amounts.

(d) LIMITATIONS.—

SEC. 406. [49 U.S.C. 40101 note] PAYMENTS TO
ELIGIBLE INDIVIDUALS.

Title I and title IV of the Air Transport:
Safety and System Stabilizatior

(1) GROUP A CLAIMS.—

(A) IN GENERAL.—The total amount of Federal funds paid for compensation under this title, with respect to claims in Group A as described in section 405(a)(3)(C)(ii), shall not exceed $2,775,000,000.

(B) REMAINDER OF CLAIM AMOUNTS.—In the case of a claim in Group A as described in section 405(a)(3)(C)(ii) and for which the Special Master has ratably reduced the amount of compensation for such claim pursuant to paragraph (2) of this subsection, as this subsection was in effect on the day before the date of enactment of the James Zadroga 9/11 Victim Compensation Fund Reauthorization Act, the Special Master shall, as soon as practicable after the date of enactment of such Act, authorize payment of the amount of compensation that is equal to the difference between—

(i) the amount of compensation that the claimant would have been paid under this title for such claim without regard to the limitation under the second sentence of paragraph (1) of this subsection, as this subsection was in effect on the day before the date of enactment of the James Zadroga 9/11 Victim Compensation Fund Reauthorization Act; and

(ii) the amount of compensation the claimant was paid under this title for such claim prior to the date of enactment of such Act.

(2) GROUP B CLAIMS.—

(A) IN GENERAL.—The total amount of Federal funds paid for compensation under this title, with respect to claims in Group B as described in section 405(a)(3)(C)(iii), shall not exceed the amount of funds deposited into the Victims Compensation Fund under section 410.

(B) PAYMENT SYSTEM.—The Special Master shall establish a system for providing compensation for claims in Group B as described in section 405(a)(3)(C)(iii) in accordance with this subsection and section 405(b)(7).

(C) DEVELOPMENT OF AGENCY POLICIES AND PROCEDURES.—

(i) DEVELOPMENT.—

SEC. 406. [49 U.S.C. 40101 note] PAYMENTS TO ELIGIBLE INDIVIDUALS.

Title I and title IV of the Air Transportation Safety and System Stabilization Act

(I) IN GENERAL.—Not later than 30 days after the date of enactment of the James Zadroga 9/11 Victim Compensation Fund Reauthorization Act, the Special Master shall develop agency policies and procedures that meet the requirements under subclauses (II) and (III) for providing compensation for claims in Group B as described in section 405(a)(3)(C)(iii), including policies and procedures for presumptive award schedules, administrative expenses, and related internal memoranda.

(II) LIMITATION.—The policies and procedures developed under subclause (I) shall ensure that total expenditures, including administrative expenses, in providing compensation for claims in Group B, as described in section 405(a)(3)(C)(iii), do not exceed the amount of funds deposited into the Victims Compensation Fund under section 410.

(III) PRIORITIZATION.—The policies and procedures developed under subclause (I) shall prioritize claims for claimants who are determined by the Special Master as suffering from the most debilitating physical conditions to ensure, for purposes of equity, that such claimants are not unduly burdened by such policies or procedures.

(ii) REASSESSMENT.—Beginning 1 year after the date of enactment of the James Zadroga 9/11 Victim Compensation Fund Reauthorization Act, and each year thereafter until the Victims Compensation Fund is permanently closed under section 410(e), the Special Master shall conduct a reassessment of the agency policies and procedures developed under clause (i) to ensure that such policies and procedures continue to satisfy the requirements under subclauses (II) and (III) of such clause. If the Special Master determines, upon reassessment, that such agency policies or procedures do not achieve the requirements of such subclauses, the Special Master shall take additional actions or make such modifications as necessary to achieve such

SEC. 406. [49 U.S.C. 40101 note] PAYMENTS TO
ELIGIBLE INDIVIDUALS.

Title I and title IV of the Air Transport
Safety and System Stabilization

requirements.

(D) COMPENSATION REDUCED BY SPECIAL MASTER DUE
TO INSUFFICIENT FUNDING.—

(i) IN GENERAL.—In any claim in Group B as
described in section 405(a)(3)(C)(iii) in which, prior to
the enactment of the Never Forget the Heroes: James
Zadroga, Ray Pfeifer, and Luis Alvarez Permanent
Authorization of the September 11th Victim
Compensation Fund Act, the Special Master had
advised the claimant that the amount of compensation
has been reduced on the basis of insufficient funding,
the Special Master shall, in the first fiscal year
beginning after sufficient funding becomes available
under such Act, pay to the claimant an amount that
is, as determined by the Special Master, equal to the
difference between—

(I) the amount the claimant would have been
paid under this title if sufficient funding was
available to the Special Master at the time the
Special Master determined the amount due the
claimant under this title; and

(II) the amount the claimant was paid under
this title.

(ii) DEFINITIONS.—For purposes of this
subparagraph:

(I) INSUFFICIENT FUNDING.—The term
"insufficient funding" means funding—

(aa) that is available to the Special
Master under section 410(c) on the day before
the date of enactment of the Never Forget
the Heroes: James Zadroga, Ray Pfeifer, and
Luis Alvarez Permanent Authorization of the
September 11th Victim Compensation Fund
Act for purposes of compensating claims in
Group B as described in section
405(a)(3)(C)(iii); and

(bb) that the Special Master determines
is insufficient for purposes of compensating
all such claims and complying with

SEC. 406. [49 U.S.C. 40101 note] PAYMENTS TO ELIGIBLE INDIVIDUALS.

Title I and title IV of the Air Transportation Safety and System Stabilization Act

subparagraph (A).

(II) SUFFICIENT FUNDING.—The term "sufficient funding" means funding—

(aa) made available to the Special Master for purposes of compensating claims in Group B as described in section 405(a)(3)(C)(iii) through an Act of Congress that is enacted after the date on which the amount of the claim described in clause (i) has been reduced; and

(bb) that the Special Master determines is sufficient for purposes of compensating all claims in such Group B.

(e) ATTORNEY FEES.—

(1) IN GENERAL.—Notwithstanding any contract, the representative of an individual may not charge, for services rendered in connection with the claim of an individual under this title, more than 10 percent of an award made under this title on such claim.

(2) LIMITATION.—

(A) IN GENERAL.—Except as provided in subparagraph (B), in the case of an individual who was charged a legal fee in connection with the settlement of a civil action described in section 405(c)(3)(C)(iii), the representative of the individual may not charge any amount for compensation for services rendered in connection with a claim filed under this title.

(B) EXCEPTION.—If the legal fee charged in connection with the settlement of a civil action described in section 405(c)(3)(C)(iii) of an individual is less than 10 percent of the aggregate amount of compensation awarded to such individual through such settlement, the representative of such individual may charge an amount for compensation for services rendered to the extent that such amount charged is not more than—

(i) 10 percent of such aggregate amount through the settlement, minus

(ii) the total amount of all legal fees charged for services rendered in connection with such settlement.

(3) DISCRETION TO LOWER FEE.—In the event that the special master finds that the fee limit set by paragraph (1) or (2) provides excessive compensation for services rendered in connection with such claim, the Special Master may, in the discretion of the Special Master, award as reasonable compensation for services rendered an amount lesser than that permitted for in paragraph (1).

SEC. 407. [49 U.S.C. 40101 note] REGULATIONS.

(a) IN GENERAL.—Not later than 90 days after the date of enactment of this Act, the Attorney General, in consultation with the Special Master, shall promulgate regulations to carry out this title, including regulations with respect to—

(1) forms to be used in submitting claims under this title;

(2) the information to be included in such forms;

(3) procedures for hearing and the presentation of evidence;

(4) procedures to assist an individual in filing and pursuing claims under this title; and

(5) other matters determined appropriate by the Attorney General.

(b) UPDATED REGULATIONS.—

(1) JAMES ZADROGA 9/11 HEALTH AND COMPENSATION ACT OF 2010.—Not later than 180 days after the date of the enactment of the James Zadroga 9/11 Health and Compensation Act of 2010, the Special Master shall update the regulations promulgated under subsection (a) to the extent necessary to comply with the provisions of title II of such Act.

(2) JAMES ZADROGA 9/11 VICTIM COMPENSATION FUND REAUTHORIZATION ACT.—Not later than 180 days after the date of enactment of the James Zadroga 9/11 Victim Compensation Fund Reauthorization Act, the Special Master shall update the regulations promulgated under subsection (a), and updated under paragraph (1), to the extent necessary to comply with the amendments made by such Act.

SEC. 408. [49 U.S.C. 40101 note] LIMITATION ON LIABILITY.

(a) IN GENERAL.—

(1) LIABILITY LIMITED TO INSURANCE COVERAGE.—Notwithstanding any other provision of law,

476

liability for all claims, whether for compensatory or punitive damages or for contribution or indemnity, arising from the terrorist-related aircraft crashes of September 11, 2001, against an air carrier, aircraft manufacturer, airport sponsor, or person with a property interest in the World Trade Center, on September 11, 2001, whether fee simple, leasehold or easement, direct or indirect, or their directors, officers, employees, or agents, shall not be in an amount greater than the limits of liability insurance coverage maintained by that air carrier, aircraft manufacturer, airport sponsor, or person.

(2) WILLFUL DEFAULTS ON REBUILDING OBLIGATION.—Paragraph (1) does not apply to any such person with a property interest in the World Trade Center if the Attorney General determines, after notice and an opportunity for a hearing on the record, that the person has defaulted willfully on a contractual obligation to rebuild, or assist in the rebuilding of, the World Trade Center.

(3) LIMITATIONS ON LIABILITY FOR NEW YORK CITY.—Liability for all claims, whether for compensatory or punitive damages or for contribution or indemnity arising from the terrorist-related aircraft crashes of September 11, 2001, against the City of New York shall not exceed the greater of the city's insurance coverage or $350,000,000. If a claimant who is eligible to seek compensation under section 405 of this Act, submits a claim under section 405, the claimant waives the right to file a civil action (or to be a party to an action) in any Federal or State court for damages sustained as a result of the terrorist-related aircraft crashes of September 11, 2001, including any such action against the City of New York. The preceding sentence does not apply to a civil action to recover collateral source obligations.

(4) LIABILITY FOR CERTAIN CLAIMS.—Notwithstanding any other provision of law, liability for all claims and actions (including claims or actions that have been previously resolved, that are currently pending, and that may be filed) for compensatory damages, contribution or indemnity, or any other form or type of relief, arising from or related to debris removal, against the City of New York, any entity (including the Port Authority of New York and New Jersey) with a property interest in the World Trade Center on September 11, 2001

(whether fee simple, leasehold or easement, or direct or indirect) and any contractors and subcontractors, shall not be in an amount that exceeds the sum of the following, as may be applicable:

(A) The amount of funds of the WTC Captive Insurance Company, including the cumulative interest.

(B) The amount of all available insurance identified in schedule 2 of the WTC Captive Insurance Company insurance policy.

(C) As it relates to the limitation of liability of the City of New York, the amount that is the greater of the City of New York's insurance coverage or $350,000,000. In determining the amount of the City's insurance coverage for purposes of the previous sentence, any amount described in subparagraphs (A) and (B) shall not be included.

(D) As it relates to the limitation of liability of any entity, including the Port Authority of New York and New Jersey, with a property interest in the World Trade Center on September 11, 2001 (whether fee simple, leasehold or easement, or direct or indirect), the amount of all available liability insurance coverage maintained by any such entity.

(E) As it relates to the limitation of liability of any individual contractor or subcontractor, the amount of all available liability insurance coverage maintained by such contractor or subcontractor on September 11, 2001.

(5) PRIORITY OF CLAIMS PAYMENTS.—Payments to plaintiffs who obtain a settlement or judgment with respect to a claim or action to which paragraph (4) applies, shall be paid solely from the following funds in the following order, as may be applicable:

(A) The funds described in subparagraph (A) or (B) of paragraph (4).

(B) If there are no funds available as described in subparagraph (A) or (B) of paragraph (4), the funds described in subparagraph (C) of such paragraph.

(C) If there are no funds available as described in subparagraph (A), (B), or (C) of paragraph (4), the funds described in subparagraph (D) of such paragraph.

(D) If there are no funds available as described in

subparagraph (A), (B), (C), or (D) of paragraph (4), the funds described in subparagraph (E) of such paragraph.

(6) DECLARATORY JUDGMENT ACTIONS AND DIRECT ACTION.—Any claimant to a claim or action to which paragraph (4) applies may, with respect to such claim or action, either file an action for a declaratory judgment for insurance coverage or bring a direct action against the insurance company involved, except that no such action for declaratory judgment or direct action may be commenced until after the funds available in subparagraph (A), (B), (C), and (D) of paragraph (5) have been exhausted consistent with the order described in such paragraph for payment.

(b) FEDERAL CAUSE OF ACTION.—

(1) AVAILABILITY OF ACTION.—There shall exist a Federal cause of action for damages arising out of the hijacking and subsequent crashes of American Airlines flights 11 and 77, and United Airlines flights 93 and 175, on September 11, 2001. Notwithstanding section 40120(c) of title 49, United States Code, this cause of action shall be the exclusive remedy for damages arising out of the hijacking and subsequent crashes of such flights.

(2) SUBSTANTIVE LAW.—The substantive law for decision in any such suit shall be derived from the law, including choice of law principles, of the State in which the crash occurred unless such law is inconsistent with or preempted by Federal law.

(3) JURISDICTION.—The United States District Court for the Southern District of New York shall have original and exclusive jurisdiction over all actions brought for any claim (including any claim for loss of property, personal injury, or death) resulting from or relating to the terrorist-related aircraft crashes of September 11, 2001.

(c) EXCLUSION.—Nothing in this section shall in any way limit any liability of any person who is a knowing participant in any conspiracy to hijack any aircraft or commit any terrorist act. Subsections (a) and (b) do not apply to civil actions to recover collateral source obligations.

SEC. 409. [49 U.S.C. 40101 note] RIGHT OF SUBROGATION.

The United States shall have the right of subrogation with respect to any claim paid by the United States under this title, subject to the limitations described in section 408.

SEC. 410. [49 U.S.C. 40101 note] VICTIMS COMPENSATION FUND.

(a) IN GENERAL.—There is established in the Treasury of the United States a fund to be known as the "Victims Compensation Fund", consisting of amounts deposited into such fund under subsection (b).

(b) DEPOSITS INTO FUND.—There shall be deposited into the Victims Compensation Fund each of the following:

(1) Effective on the day after the date on which all claimants who file a claim in Group A, as described in section 405(a)(3)(C)(ii), have received the full compensation due such claimants under this title for such claim, any amounts remaining from the total amount made available under section 406 to compensate claims in Group A as described in section 405(a)(3)(C)(ii).

(2) The amount appropriated under subsection (c).

(c) APPROPRIATIONS.—There is appropriated, out of any money in the Treasury not otherwise appropriated, such sums as may be necessary for fiscal year 2019 and each fiscal year thereafter through fiscal year 2092, to remain available until expended, to provide compensation for claims in Group B as described in section 405(a)(3)(C)(iii).

(d) AVAILABILITY OF FUNDS.—Amounts deposited into the Victims Compensation Fund shall be available, without further appropriation, to the Special Master to provide compensation for claims in Group B as described in section 405(a)(3)(C)(iii).

(e) TERMINATION.—On October 1, 2092, or at such time thereafter as all funds are expended, the Victims Compensation Fund shall be permanently closed.

SEC. 411. [49 U.S.C. 40101 note] 9-11 RESPONSE AND BIOMETRIC ENTRY-EXIT FEE.

(a) TEMPORARY L-1 VISA FEE INCREASE.—Notwithstanding section 281 of the Immigration and Nationality Act (8 U.S.C. 1351) or any other provision of law, during the period beginning on the date of the enactment of this section and ending on September 30, 2027, the combined filing fee and fraud prevention and detection fee required to be submitted with an application for admission as a

SEC. 411. [49 U.S.C. 40101 note] 9-11 RESPONSE
AND BIOMETRIC ENTRY-EXIT FEE.

Title I and title IV of the Air Transportation
Safety and System Stabilization Act

nonimmigrant under section 101(a)(15)(L) of the Immigration and
Nationality Act (8 U.S.C. 1101(a)(15)(L)), including an application
for an extension of such status, shall be increased by $4,500 for
applicants that employ 50 or more employees in the United States
if more than 50 percent of the applicant's employees are
nonimmigrants admitted pursuant to subparagraph (H)(i)(b) or (L)
of section 101(a)(15) of such Act.

(b) TEMPORARY H-1B VISA FEE INCREASE.—Notwithstanding
section 281 of the Immigration and Nationality Act (8 U.S.C. 1351)
or any other provision of law, during the period beginning on the
date of the enactment of this section and ending on September 30,
2027, the combined filing fee and fraud prevention and detection
fee required to be submitted with an application for admission as a
nonimmigrant under section 101(a)(15)(H)(i)(b) of the Immigration
and Nationality Act (8 U.S.C. 1101(a)(15)(H)(i)(b)), including an
application for an extension of such status, shall be increased by
$4,000 for applicants that employ 50 or more employees in the
United States if more than 50 percent of the applicant's employees
are such nonimmigrants or nonimmigrants described in section
101(a)(15)(L) of such Act.

(c) 9-11 RESPONSE AND BIOMETRIC EXIT ACCOUNT.—

(1) ESTABLISHMENT.—There is established in the general
fund of the Treasury a separate account, which shall be known
as the "9–11 Response and Biometric Exit Account".

(2) DEPOSITS.—

(A) IN GENERAL.—Subject to subparagraph (B), of the
amounts collected pursuant to the fee increases authorized
under subsections (a) and (b)—

(i) 50 percent shall be deposited in the general
fund of the Treasury; and

(ii) 50 percent shall be deposited as offsetting
receipts into the 9–11 Response and Biometric Exit
Account, and shall remain available until expended.

(B) TERMINATION OF DEPOSITS IN ACCOUNT.—After a
total of $1,000,000,000 is deposited into the 9–11 Response
and Biometric Exit Account under subparagraph (A)(ii), all
amounts collected pursuant to the fee increases authorized
under subsections (a) and (b) shall be deposited in the
general fund of the Treasury.

(3) USE OF FUNDS.—For fiscal year 2017, and each fiscal year thereafter, amounts in the 9–11 Response and Biometric Exit Account shall be available to the Secretary of Homeland Security without further appropriation for implementing the biometric entry and exit data system described in section 7208 of the Intelligence Reform and Terrorism Prevention Act of 2004 (8 U.S.C. 1365b).

SELECTED PROVISIONS OF THE WENDELL H. FORD AVIATION INVESTMENT AND REFORM ACT FOR THE 21ST CENTURY

PUBLIC LAW 106-181

WENDELL H. FORD AVIATION INVESTMENT AND
REFORM ACT FOR THE 21ST CENTURY

[Public Law 106–181; 114 Stat. 61]

[As Amended Through P.L. 118–63, Enacted May 16, 2024]

AN ACT To amend title 49, United States Code, to reauthorize
programs of the Federal Aviation Administration, and for other
purposes.

*Be it enacted by the Senate and House of Representatives of the
United States of America in Congress assembled,*

SECTION 1. SHORT TITLE; TABLE OF CONTENTS.

(a) SHORT TITLE.—This Act may be cited as the "Wendell H.
Ford Aviation Investment and Reform Act for the 21st Century".

* * * * * * *

TITLE I—AIRPORT AND AIRWAY IMPROVEMENTS

Subtitle A—Funding

* * * * * * *

SEC. 103. FAA OPERATIONS.

(a)

* * *

(b) **[49 U.S.C. 106 note]** OFFICE OF AIRLINE
INFORMATION.—There is authorized to be appropriated from the
Airport and Airway Trust Fund to the Secretary $4,000,000 for

fiscal years beginning after September 30, 2000, to fund the activities of the Office of Airline Information in the Bureau of Transportation Statistics of the Department of Transportation.

* * * * * * *

[Sec. 106. Repealed. P.L. 108–176, sec. 104(c), 117 Stat. 2497.]

* * * * * * *

Subtitle B—Airport Development

* * * * * * *

SEC. 139. [49 U.S.C. 47104 note] DESIGN-BUILD CONTRACTING.

(a) PILOT PROGRAM.—The Administrator may establish a pilot program under which design-build contracts may be used to carry out up to 7 projects at airports in the United States with a grant awarded under section 47104 of title 49, United States Code. A sponsor of an airport may submit an application to the Administrator to carry out a project otherwise eligible for assistance under chapter 471 of such title under the pilot program.

(b) USE OF DESIGN-BUILD CONTRACTS.—Under the pilot program, the Administrator may approve an application of an airport sponsor under this section to authorize the airport sponsor to award a design-build contract using a selection process permitted under applicable State or local law if—

(1) the Administrator approves the application using criteria established by the Administrator;

(2) the design-build contract is in a form that is approved by the Administrator;

(3) the Administrator is satisfied that the contract will be executed pursuant to competitive procedures and contains a schematic design adequate for the Administrator to approve the grant;

(4) use of a design-build contract will be cost effective and expedite the project;

(5) the Administrator is satisfied that there will be no conflict of interest; and

(6) the Administrator is satisfied that the selection process will be as open, fair, and objective as the competitive bid system and that at least three or more bids will be submitted for each project under the selection process.

(c) REIMBURSEMENT OF COSTS.—The Administrator may reimburse an airport sponsor for design and construction costs incurred before a grant is made pursuant to this section if the project is approved by the Administrator in advance and is carried out in accordance with all administrative and statutory requirements that would have been applicable under chapter 471 of title 49, United States Code, if the project were carried out after a grant agreement had been executed.

(d) DESIGN-BUILD CONTRACT DEFINED.—In this section, the term "design-build contract" means an agreement that provides for both design and construction of a project by a contractor.

(e) EXPIRATION OF AUTHORITY.—The authority of the Administrator to carry out the pilot program under this section shall expire on September 30, 2003.

Subtitle C—Miscellaneous

* * * * * * *

SEC. 155. COMPETITION PLANS.

(a)

* * *

* * * * * * *

(d) [49 U.S.C. 47101 note] AVAILABILITY OF GATES AND OTHER ESSENTIAL SERVICES.—The Secretary shall ensure that gates and other facilities are made available at costs that are fair and reasonable to air carriers at covered airports (as defined in section 47106(f)(4) of title 49, United States Code) where a "majority-in-interest clause" of a contract or other agreement or arrangement inhibits the ability of the local airport authority to provide or build new gates or other facilities.

* * * * * * *

SEC. 158. [49 U.S.C. 47101 note] CONSTRUCTION OF RUNWAYS.

Notwithstanding any provision of law that specifically restricts the number of runways at a single international airport, the Secretary may obligate funds made available under chapters 471 and 481 of title 49, United States Code, for any project to construct a new runway at such airport, unless this section is expressly repealed.

SEC. 159. [49 U.S.C. 48103 note] NOTICE OF GRANTS.

(a) TIMELY ANNOUNCEMENT.—The Secretary shall announce a grant to be made with funds made available under section 48103 of title 49, United States Code, in a timely fashion after receiving necessary documentation concerning the grant from the Administrator.

(b) NOTICE TO COMMITTEES.—If the Secretary provides any committee of Congress advance notice of a grant to be made with funds made available under section 48103 of title 49, United States Code, the Secretary shall provide, on the same date, such notice to the Committee on Transportation and Infrastructure of the House of Representatives and the Committee on Commerce, Science, and Transportation of the Senate.

* * * * * * *

TITLE II—AIRLINE SERVICE IMPROVEMENTS

Subtitle A—Small Communities

SEC. 209. MAINTAINING THE INTEGRITY OF THE ESSENTIAL AIR SERVICE PROGRAM.

(a)

* * *

* * * * * * *

(c) [49 U.S.C. 41733 note] EFFECT ON CERTAIN ORDERS.—All orders issued by the Secretary after September 30, 1999, and before the date of the enactment of this Act establishing, modifying, or revoking essential air service levels shall be null and void beginning on the 90th day following such date of enactment. During the 90-day period, the Secretary shall reconsider such orders and shall issue new orders consistent with the amendments made by this section.

* * * * * * *

TITLE III—FAA MANAGEMENT REFORM

* * * * * * *

SEC. 304. [49 U.S.C. 44505 note] PILOT PROGRAM TO PERMIT COST-SHARING OF AIR TRAFFIC MODERNIZATION PROJECTS.

(a) PURPOSE.—It is the purpose of this section to improve aviation safety and enhance mobility of the Nation's air transportation system by encouraging non-Federal investment on a pilot program basis in critical air traffic control facilities and equipment.

(b) IN GENERAL.—Subject to the requirements of this section, the Secretary shall carry out a pilot program under which the Secretary may make grants to project sponsors for not more than 10 eligible projects.

(c) FEDERAL SHARE.—The Federal share of the cost of an eligible project carried out under the program shall not exceed 33 percent. The non-Federal share of the cost of an eligible project shall be provided from non-Federal sources, including revenues collected pursuant to section 40117 of title 49, United States Code.

(d) LIMITATION ON GRANT AMOUNTS.—No eligible project may receive more than $15,000,000 under the program.

(e) FUNDING.—The Secretary shall use amounts appropriated under section 48101(a) of title 49, United States Code, for fiscal years 2001 through 2003 to carry out the program.

(f) DEFINITIONS.—In this section, the following definitions apply:

(1) ELIGIBLE PROJECT.—The term "eligible project" means a project relating to the Nation's air traffic control system that is certified or approved by the Administrator and that promotes safety, efficiency, or mobility. Such projects may include—

(A) airport-specific air traffic facilities and equipment,

including local area augmentation systems, instrument landings systems, weather and wind shear detection equipment, lighting improvements, and control towers;

(B) automation tools to effect improvements in airport capacity, including passive final approach spacing tools and traffic management advisory equipment; and

(C) facilities and equipment that enhance airspace control procedures, including consolidation of terminal radar control facilities and equipment, or assist in en route surveillance, including oceanic and offshore flight tracking.

(2) PROJECT SPONSOR.—The term "project sponsor" means a public-use airport or a joint venture between a public-use airport and one or more air carriers.

(g) TRANSFERS OF EQUIPMENT.—Notwithstanding any other provision of law, project sponsors may transfer, without consideration, to the Federal Aviation Administration, facilities, equipment, and automation tools, the purchase of which was assisted by a grant made under this section. The Administration shall accept such facilities, equipment, and automation tools, which shall thereafter be operated and maintained by the Administration in accordance with criteria of the Administration.

(h) GUIDELINES.—Not later than 90 days after the date of the enactment of this Act, the Administrator shall issue advisory guidelines on the implementation of the program.

* * * * * * *

TITLE VI—TRANSFER OF AERONAUTICAL CHARTING ACTIVITY

* * * * * * *

SEC. 607. [49 U.S.C. 44721 note] PROCUREMENT OF PRIVATE ENTERPRISE MAPPING, CHARTING, AND GEOGRAPHIC INFORMATION SYSTEMS.

The Administrator shall consider procuring mapping, charting, and geographic information systems necessary to carry out the duties of the Administrator under title 49, United States Code, from private enterprises, if the Administrator determines that such procurement furthers the mission of the Federal Aviation

Administration and is cost effective.

* * * * * * *

TITLE VII—MISCELLANEOUS PROVISIONS

* * * * * * *

SEC. 707. DISCRIMINATION AGAINST HANDICAPPED
INDIVIDUALS.

(a)

* * *

* * * * * * *

(c) [49 U.S.C. 41705 note] ESTABLISHMENT OF HIGHER
INTERNATIONAL STANDARDS.—The Secretary shall work with
appropriate international organizations and the aviation
authorities of other nations to bring about the establishment of
higher standards for accommodating handicapped passengers in air
transportation, particularly with respect to foreign air carriers that
code-share with air carriers.

* * * * * * *

SEC. 726. [49 U.S.C. 47508 note] STANDARDS FOR AIRCRAFT AND
AIRCRAFT ENGINES TO REDUCE NOISE LEVELS.

(a) DEVELOPMENT OF NEW STANDARDS.—The Secretary shall
continue to work to develop through the International Civil Aviation
Organization new performance standards for aircraft and aircraft
engines that will lead to a further reduction in aircraft noise levels.

(b) GOALS TO BE CONSIDERED IN DEVELOPING NEW
STANDARDS.—In negotiating standards under subsection (a), the
Secretary shall give high priority to developing standards that—

(1) are performance based and can be achieved by use of a
full range of certifiable noise reduction technologies;

(2) protect the useful economic value of existing Stage 3
aircraft in the United States fleet;

(3) ensure that United States air carriers and aircraft

SEC. 732. [49 U.S.C. 44701 note] REGULATION
OF ALASKA GUIDE PILOTS.

WENDELL H. FORD AVIATION INVESTM
AND REFORM ACT FOR THE 21ST CENT

engine and hushkit manufacturers are not competitively disadvantaged;

(4) use dynamic economic modeling capable of determining impacts on all aircraft in service in the United States fleet; and

(5) continue the use of a balanced approach to address aircraft environmental issues, taking into account aircraft technology, land use planning, economic feasibility, and airspace operational improvements.

SEC. 732. [49 U.S.C. 44701 note] REGULATION OF ALASKA GUIDE PILOTS.

(a) IN GENERAL.—Beginning on the date of the enactment of this Act, flight operations conducted by Alaska guide pilots shall be regulated under the general operating and flight rules contained in part 91 of title 14, Code of Federal Regulations.

(b) DEFINITION OF ALASKA GUIDE PILOT.—In this section the term "Alaska guide pilot" means a pilot who—

(1) conducts aircraft operations over or within the State of Alaska;

(2) operates single engine, fixed-wing aircraft on floats, wheels, or skis, providing commercial hunting, fishing, or other guide services and related accommodations in the form of camps or lodges; and

(3) transports clients by such aircraft incidental to hunting, fishing, or other guide services.

SEC. 737. [49 U.S.C. 47106 note] COMPLIANCE WITH REQUIREMENTS.

Notwithstanding any other provision of law, in order to avoid unnecessary duplication of expense and effort, the Secretary may authorize the use, in whole or in part, of a completed environmental assessment or environmental impact study for new construction projects on the air operations area of an airport, if the completed assessment or study was for a project at the airport that is substantially similar in nature to the new project. Any such authorized use shall meet all requirements of Federal law for the completion of such an assessment or study.

* * * * * * *

SEC. 740. [10 U.S.C. 2576 note] AUTHORITY TO SELL AIRCRAFT AND AIRCRAFT PARTS FOR USE IN RESPONDING TO OIL SPILLS.

(a) AUTHORITY.—

(1) SALE OF AIRCRAFT AND AIRCRAFT PARTS.—Notwithstanding subchapter II of chapter 5 of title 40, United States Code, and subject to subsections (b) and (c), the Secretary of Defense may sell aircraft and aircraft parts referred to in paragraph (2) to a person or entity that provides oil spill response services (including the application of oil dispersants by air) pursuant to an oil spill response plan that has been approved by the Secretary of the Department in which the Coast Guard is operating.

(2) AIRCRAFT AND AIRCRAFT PARTS THAT MAY BE SOLD.—The aircraft and aircraft parts that may be sold under paragraph (1) are aircraft and aircraft parts of the Department of Defense that are determined by the Secretary of Defense to be—

(A) excess to the needs of the Department; and

(B) acceptable for commercial sale.

(b) CONDITIONS OF SALE.—Aircraft and aircraft parts sold under subsection (a)—

(1) shall have as their primary purpose usage for oil spill spotting, observation, and dispersant delivery and may not have any secondary purpose that would interfere with oil spill response efforts under an oil spill response plan; and

(2) may not be flown outside of or removed from the United States except for the purpose of fulfilling an international agreement to assist in oil spill dispersing efforts, for immediate response efforts for an oil spill outside United States waters that has the potential to threaten United States waters, or for other purposes that are jointly approved by the Secretary of Defense and the Secretary of Homeland Security.

(c) CERTIFICATION OF PERSONS AND ENTITIES.—The Secretary of Defense may sell aircraft and aircraft parts to a person or entity under subsection (a) only if the Secretary of Homeland Security certifies to the Secretary of Defense, in writing, before the sale, that the person or entity is capable of meeting the terms and conditions of a contract to deliver oil spill dispersants by air, and that the overall system to be employed by that person or entity for the delivery and application of oil spill dispersants has been sufficiently tested to ensure that the person or entity is capable of being included in an oil spill response plan that has been approved by the Secretary of the Department in which the Coast Guard is operating.

(d) REGULATIONS.—

(1) ISSUANCE.—As soon as practicable after the date of the enactment of this Act, the Secretary of Defense, in consultation with the Secretary of Homeland Security and the Administrator of General Services, shall prescribe regulations relating to the sale of aircraft and aircraft parts under this section.

(2) CONTENTS.—The regulations shall—

(A) ensure that the sale of the aircraft and aircraft parts is made at a fair market value, as determined by the Secretary of Defense, and, to the extent practicable, on a competitive basis;

(B) require a certification by the purchaser that the aircraft and aircraft parts will be used only in accordance with the conditions set forth in subsection (b);

(C) establish appropriate means of verifying and enforcing the use of the aircraft and aircraft parts by the purchaser and other operators in accordance with the conditions set forth in subsection (b) or pursuant to subsection (e); and

(D) ensure, to the maximum extent practicable, that the Secretary of Defense consults with the Administrator of General Services and with the heads of appropriate departments and agencies of the Federal Government regarding alternative requirements for such aircraft and aircraft parts before the sale of such aircraft and aircraft parts under this section.

(e) ADDITIONAL TERMS AND CONDITIONS.—The Secretary of Defense may require such other terms and conditions in connection with each sale of aircraft and aircraft parts under this section as the Secretary considers appropriate for such sale. Such terms and conditions shall meet the requirements of regulations prescribed under subsection (d).

(f) REPORT.—Not later than March 31, 2006, the Secretary of Defense shall transmit to the Committees on Armed Services and Commerce, Science, and Transportation of the Senate and the Committees on National Security and Transportation and

Infrastructure of the House of Representatives a report on the Secretary's exercise of authority under this section. The report shall set forth—

(1) the number and types of aircraft sold under the authority, and the terms and conditions under which the aircraft were sold;

(2) the persons or entities to which the aircraft were sold; and

(3) an accounting of the current use of the aircraft sold.

(g) STATUTORY CONSTRUCTION.—

(1) AUTHORITY OF ADMINISTRATOR.—Nothing in this section may be construed as affecting the authority of the Administrator under any other provision of law.

(2) CERTIFICATION REQUIREMENTS.—Nothing in this section may be construed to waive, with respect to an aircraft sold under the authority of this section, any requirement to obtain a certificate from the Administrator to operate the aircraft for any purpose (other than oil spill spotting, observation, and dispersant delivery) for which such a certificate is required.

(h) PROCEEDS FROM SALE.—The net proceeds of any amounts received by the Secretary of Defense from the sale of aircraft and aircraft parts under this section shall be covered into the general fund of the Treasury as miscellaneous receipts.

(i) EXPIRATION OF AUTHORITY.—The authority to sell aircraft and aircraft parts under this section expires on September 30, 2006.

* * * * * * *

TITLE VIII—NATIONAL PARKS AIR TOUR MANAGEMENT

SEC. 801. [49 U.S.C. 40128 note] SHORT TITLE.
This title may be cited as the "National Parks Air Tour Management Act of 2000"[49 U.S.C. 40128 note].

SEC. 802. [49 U.S.C. 40128 note] FINDINGS.
Congress finds that—

(1) the Federal Aviation Administration has sole authority to control airspace over the United States;

(2) the Federal Aviation Administration has the authority to preserve, protect, and enhance the environment by minimizing, mitigating, or preventing the adverse effects of aircraft overflights on public and tribal lands;

(3) the National Park Service has the responsibility of conserving the scenery and natural and historic objects and wildlife in national parks and of providing for the enjoyment of the national parks in ways that leave the national parks unimpaired for future generations;

(4) the protection of tribal lands from aircraft overflights is consistent with protecting the public health and welfare and is essential to the maintenance of the natural and cultural resources of Indian tribes;

(5) the National Parks Overflights Working Group, composed of general aviation, commercial air tour, environmental, and Native American representatives, recommended that the Congress enact legislation based on the Group's consensus work product; and

(6) this title reflects the recommendations made by that Group.

SEC. 803. [49 U.S.C. 40128 note] AIR TOUR MANAGEMENT PLANS FOR NATIONAL PARKS.

(a) IN GENERAL.—Chapter 401 (as amended by section 706(a) of this Act) is further amended by adding at the end the following:

"**SEC. 40128. Overflights of national parks**

"(a) IN GENERAL.

"(1) GENERAL REQUIREMENTS. A commercial air tour operator may not conduct commercial air tour operations over a national park or tribal lands except—

"(A) in accordance with this section;

"(B) in accordance with conditions and limitations prescribed for that operator by the Administrator; and

"(C) in accordance with any applicable air tour management plan for the park or tribal lands.

"(2) APPLICATION FOR OPERATING AUTHORITY.

"(A) APPLICATION REQUIRED. Before commencing commercial air tour operations over a national park or

496

tribal lands, a commercial air tour operator shall apply to the Administrator for authority to conduct the operations over the park or tribal lands.

"(B) COMPETITIVE BIDDING FOR LIMITED CAPACITY PARKS. Whenever an air tour management plan limits the number of commercial air tour operations over a national park during a specified time frame, the Administrator, in cooperation with the Director, shall issue operation specifications to commercial air tour operators that conduct such operations. The operation specifications shall include such terms and conditions as the Administrator and the Director find necessary for management of commercial air tour operations over the park. The Administrator, in cooperation with the Director, shall develop an open competitive process for evaluating proposals from persons interested in providing commercial air tour operations over the park. In making a selection from among various proposals submitted, the Administrator, in cooperation with the Director, shall consider relevant factors, including—

"(i) the safety record of the person submitting the proposal or pilots employed by the person;

"(ii) any quiet aircraft technology proposed to be used by the person submitting the proposal;

"(iii) the experience of the person submitting the proposal with commercial air tour operations over other national parks or scenic areas;

"(iv) the financial capability of the person submitting the proposal;

"(v) any training programs for pilots provided by the person submitting the proposal; and

"(vi) responsiveness of the person submitting the proposal to any relevant criteria developed by the National Park Service for the affected park.

"(C) NUMBER OF OPERATIONS AUTHORIZED. In determining the number of authorizations to issue to provide commercial air tour operations over a national park, the Administrator, in cooperation with the Director, shall take into consideration the provisions of the air tour

"SEC. 40128. [49 U.S.C. 40128 note] AIR TOUR MANAGEMENT PLANS FOR NATIONAL

WENDELL H. FORD AVIATION INVESTM! AND REFORM ACT FOR THE 21ST CENT!

management plan, the number of existing commercial air tour operators and current level of service and equipment provided by any such operators, and the financial viability of each commercial air tour operation.

"(D) COOPERATION WITH NPS. Before granting an application under this paragraph, the Administrator, in cooperation with the Director, shall develop an air tour management plan in accordance with subsection (b) and implement such plan.

"(E) TIME LIMIT ON RESPONSE TO ATMP APPLICATIONS. The Administrator shall make every effort to act on any application under this paragraph and issue a decision on the application not later than 24 months after it is received or amended.

"(F) PRIORITY. In acting on applications under this paragraph to provide commercial air tour operations over a national park, the Administrator shall give priority to an application under this paragraph in any case in which a new entrant commercial air tour operator is seeking operating authority with respect to that national park.

"(3) EXCEPTION. Notwithstanding paragraph (1), commercial air tour operators may conduct commercial air tour operations over a national park under part 91 of the title 14, Code of Federal Regulations if—

"(A) such activity is permitted under part 119 of such title;

"(B) the operator secures a letter of agreement from the Administrator and the national park superintendent for that national park describing the conditions under which the operations will be conducted; and

"(C) the total number of operations under this exception is limited to not more than five flights in any 30-day period over a particular park.

"(4) SPECIAL RULE FOR SAFETY REQUIREMENTS. Notwithstanding subsection (c), an existing commercial air tour operator shall apply, not later than 90 days after the date of the enactment of this section, for operating authority under part 119, 121, or 135 of title 14, Code of Federal Regulations. A new entrant commercial air tour operator shall apply for such authority before conducting commercial air tour operations over a national park or tribal lands. The Administrator shall make every effort to act on any such application for a new entrant and issue a decision on the application not later than 24 months after it is received or amended.

"(b) AIR TOUR MANAGEMENT PLANS.

"(1) ESTABLISHMENT.

"(A) IN GENERAL. The Administrator, in cooperation with the Director, shall establish an air tour management plan for any national park or tribal land for which such a plan is not in effect whenever a person applies for authority to conduct a commercial air tour operation over the park. The air tour management plan shall be developed by means of a public process in accordance with paragraph (4).

"(B) OBJECTIVE. The objective of any air tour management plan shall be to develop acceptable and effective measures to mitigate or prevent the significant adverse impacts, if any, of commercial air tour operations upon the natural and cultural resources, visitor experiences, and tribal lands.

"(2) ENVIRONMENTAL DETERMINATION. In establishing an air tour management plan under this subsection, the Administrator and the Director shall each sign the environmental decision document required by section 102 of the National Environmental Policy Act of 1969 (42 U.S.C. 4332) which may include a finding of no significant impact, an environmental assessment, or an environmental impact statement and the record of decision for the air tour management plan.

"(3) CONTENTS. An air tour management plan for a national park—

"(A) may prohibit commercial air tour operations in whole or in part;

"(B) may establish conditions for the conduct of commercial air tour operations, including commercial air tour routes, maximum or minimum altitudes, time-of-day restrictions, restrictions for particular events, maximum number of flights per unit of time, intrusions on privacy on tribal lands, and mitigation of noise, visual, or other impacts;

"(C) shall apply to all commercial air tour operations within ½ mile outside the boundary of a national park;

"(D) shall include incentives (such as preferred commercial air tour routes and altitudes, relief from caps and curfews) for the adoption of quiet aircraft technology by commercial air tour operators conducting commercial air tour operations at the park;

"(E) shall provide for the initial allocation of opportunities to conduct commercial air tour operations if the plan includes a limitation on the number of commercial air tour operations for any time period; and

"(F) shall justify and document the need for measures taken pursuant to subparagraphs (A) through (E) and include such justifications in the record of decision.

"(4) PROCEDURE. In establishing an air tour management plan for a national park or tribal lands, the Administrator and the Director shall—

"(A) hold at least one public meeting with interested parties to develop the air tour management plan;

"(B) publish the proposed plan in the Federal Register for notice and comment and make copies of the proposed plan available to the public;

"(C) comply with the regulations set forth in sections 1501.3 and 1501.5 through 1501.8 of title 40, Code of Federal Regulations (for purposes of complying with the regulations, the Federal Aviation Administration shall be the lead agency and the National Park Service is a cooperating agency); and

"(D) solicit the participation of any Indian tribe whose tribal lands are, or may be, overflown by aircraft involved in a commercial air tour operation over the park or tribal lands to which the plan applies, as a cooperating agency under the regulations referred to in subparagraph (C).

"(5) JUDICIAL REVIEW. An air tour management plan developed under this subsection shall be subject to judicial review.

"(6) AMENDMENTS. The Administrator, in cooperation with

the Director, may make amendments to an air tour management plan. Any such amendments shall be published in the Federal Register for notice and comment. A request for amendment of an air tour management plan shall be made in such form and manner as the Administrator may prescribe.

"(c) INTERIM OPERATING AUTHORITY.

"(1) IN GENERAL. Upon application for operating authority, the Administrator shall grant interim operating authority under this subsection to a commercial air tour operator for commercial air tour operations over a national park or tribal lands for which the operator is an existing commercial air tour operator.

"(2) REQUIREMENTS AND LIMITATIONS. Interim operating authority granted under this subsection—

"(A) shall provide annual authorization only for the greater of—

"(i) the number of flights used by the operator to provide the commercial air tour operations within the 12-month period prior to the date of the enactment of this section; or

"(ii) the average number of flights per 12-month period used by the operator to provide such operations within the 36-month period prior to such date of enactment, and, for seasonal operations, the number of flights so used during the season or seasons covered by that 12-month period;

"(B) may not provide for an increase in the number of commercial air tour operations conducted during any time period by the commercial air tour operator above the number that the air tour operator was originally granted unless such an increase is agreed to by the Administrator and the Director;

"(C) shall be published in the Federal Register to provide notice and opportunity for comment;

"(D) may be revoked by the Administrator for cause;

"(E) shall terminate 180 days after the date on which an air tour management plan is established for the park or tribal lands;

"(F) shall promote protection of national park resources, visitor experiences, and tribal lands;

"(G) shall promote safe commercial air tour operations;

"(H) shall promote the adoption of quiet technology, as appropriate; and

"(I) shall allow for modifications of the interim operating authority based on experience if the modification improves protection of national park resources and values and of tribal lands.

"(3) NEW ENTRANT AIR TOUR OPERATORS.

"(A) IN GENERAL. The Administrator, in cooperation with the Director, may grant interim operating authority under this paragraph to an air tour operator for a national park or tribal lands for which that operator is a new entrant air tour operator if the Administrator determines the authority is necessary to ensure competition in the provision of commercial air tour operations over the park or tribal lands.

"(B) SAFETY LIMITATION. The Administrator may not grant interim operating authority under subparagraph (A) if the Administrator determines that it would create a safety problem at the park or on the tribal lands, or the Director determines that it would create a noise problem at the park or on the tribal lands.

"(C) ATMP LIMITATION. The Administrator may grant interim operating authority under subparagraph (A) of this paragraph only if the air tour management plan for the park or tribal lands to which the application relates has not been developed within 24 months after the date of the enactment of this section.

"(d) EXEMPTIONS. This section shall not apply to—

"(1) the Grand Canyon National Park; or

"(2) tribal lands within or abutting the Grand Canyon National Park.

"(e) LAKE MEAD. This section shall not apply to any air tour operator while flying over or near the Lake Mead National Recreation Area, solely as a transportation route, to conduct an air tour over the Grand Canyon National Park.

"(f)) Definitions.—In this section, the following definitions apply:

"(1) COMMERCIAL AIR TOUR OPERATOR. The term "'commercial air tour operator'" means any person who conducts a commercial air tour operation.

"(2) EXISTING COMMERCIAL AIR TOUR OPERATOR. The term "'existing commercial air tour operator'" means a commercial air tour operator that was actively engaged in the business of providing commercial air tour operations over a national park at any time during the 12-month period ending on the date of the enactment of this section.

"(3) NEW ENTRANT COMMERCIAL AIR TOUR OPERATOR. The term "'new entrant commercial air tour operator'" means a commercial air tour operator that—

"(A) applies for operating authority as a commercial air tour operator for a national park or tribal lands; and

"(B) has not engaged in the business of providing commercial air tour operations over the national park or tribal lands in the 12-month period preceding the application.

"(4) COMMERCIAL AIR TOUR OPERATION.

"(A) IN GENERAL. The term "'commercial air tour operation'" means any flight, conducted for compensation or hire in a powered aircraft where a purpose of the flight is sightseeing over a national park, within ½ mile outside the boundary of any national park, or over tribal lands, during which the aircraft flies—

"(i) below a minimum altitude, determined by the Administrator in cooperation with the Director, above ground level (except solely for purposes of takeoff or landing, or necessary for safe operation of an aircraft as determined under the rules and regulations of the Federal Aviation Administration requiring the pilot-in-command to take action to ensure the safe operation of the aircraft); or

"(ii) less than 1 mile laterally from any geographic feature within the park (unless more than ½ mile outside the boundary).

"(B) FACTORS TO CONSIDER. In making a determination

of whether a flight is a commercial air tour operation for purposes of this section, the Administrator may consider—

"(i) whether there was a holding out to the public of willingness to conduct a sightseeing flight for compensation or hire;

"(ii) whether a narrative that referred to areas or points of interest on the surface below the route of the flight was provided by the person offering the flight;

"(iii) the area of operation;

"(iv) the frequency of flights conducted by the person offering the flight;

"(v) the route of flight;

"(vi) the inclusion of sightseeing flights as part of any travel arrangement package offered by the person offering the flight;

"(vii) whether the flight would have been canceled based on poor visibility of the surface below the route of the flight; and

"(viii) any other factors that the Administrator and the Director consider appropriate.

"(5) NATIONAL PARK. The term "'national park'" means any unit of the National Park System.

"(6) TRIBAL LANDS. The term "'tribal lands'" means Indian country (as that term is defined in section 1151 of title 18) that is within or abutting a national park.

"(7) ADMINISTRATOR. The term "'Administrator'" means the Administrator of the Federal Aviation Administration.

"(8) DIRECTOR. The term "'Director'" means the Director of the National Park Service."

(b) CONFORMING AMENDMENT.—The analysis for chapter 401 (as amended by section 706(b) of this Act) is further amended by adding at the end the following:

"40128. Overflights of national parks.".

(c) COMPLIANCE WITH OTHER REGULATIONS.—For purposes of section 40128 of title 49, United States Code—

(1) regulations issued by the Secretary of Transportation and the Administrator under section 3 of Public Law 100-91 (16

U.S.C. 1a-1 note); and

(2) commercial air tour operations carried out in compliance with the requirements of those regulations,

shall be deemed to meet the requirements of such section 40126.

SEC. 804. [49 U.S.C. 40128 note] QUIET AIRCRAFT TECHNOLOGY FOR GRAND CANYON.

(a) QUIET TECHNOLOGY REQUIREMENTS.—Within 12 months after the date of the enactment of this Act, the Administrator shall designate reasonably achievable requirements for fixed-wing and helicopter aircraft necessary for such aircraft to be considered as employing quiet aircraft technology for purposes of this section. If the Administrator determines that the Administrator will not be able to make such designation before the last day of such 12-month period, the Administrator shall transmit to Congress a report on the reasons for not meeting such time period and the expected date of such designation.

(b) ROUTES OR CORRIDORS.—In consultation with the Director and the advisory group established under section 805, the Administrator shall establish, by rule, routes or corridors for commercial air tour operations (as defined in section 40128(f) of title 49, United States Code) by fixed-wing and helicopter aircraft that employ quiet aircraft technology for—

(1) tours of the Grand Canyon originating in Clark County, Nevada; and

(2) "local loop" tours originating at the Grand Canyon National Park Airport, in Tusayan, Arizona,

provided that such routes or corridors can be located in areas that will not negatively impact the substantial restoration of natural quiet, tribal lands, or safety.

(c) OPERATIONAL CAPS.—Commercial air tour operations by any fixed-wing or helicopter aircraft that employs quiet aircraft technology and that replaces an existing aircraft shall not be subject to the operational flight allocations that apply to other commercial air tour operations of the Grand Canyon, provided that the cumulative impact of such operations does not increase noise at the Grand Canyon.

(d) MODIFICATION OF EXISTING AIRCRAFT TO MEET STANDARDS.—A commercial air tour operation by a fixed-wing or helicopter aircraft in a commercial air tour operator's fleet on the date of the enactment of this Act that meets the requirements designated under subsection (a), or is subsequently modified to meet the requirements designated under subsection (a), may be used for commercial air tour operations under the same terms and conditions as a replacement aircraft under subsection (c) without regard to whether it replaces an existing aircraft.

(e) MANDATE TO RESTORE NATURAL QUIET.—Nothing in this Act shall be construed to relieve or diminish—

(1) the statutory mandate imposed upon the Secretary of the Interior and the Administrator of the Federal Aviation Administration under Public Law 100-91 (16 U.S.C. 1a-1 note) to achieve the substantial restoration of the natural quiet and experience at the Grand Canyon National Park; and

(2) the obligations of the Secretary and the Administrator to promulgate forthwith regulations to achieve the substantial restoration of the natural quiet and experience at the Grand Canyon National Park.

SEC. 805. [49 U.S.C. 40128 note] ADVISORY GROUP.

(a) ESTABLISHMENT.—Not later than 1 year after the date of the enactment of this Act, the Administrator and the Director of the National Park Service shall jointly establish an advisory group to provide continuing advice and counsel with respect to commercial air tour operations over and near national parks.

(b) MEMBERSHIP.—

(1) IN GENERAL.—The advisory group shall be composed of—

(A) a balanced group of—

(i) representatives of general aviation;

(ii) representatives of commercial air tour operators;

(iii) representatives of environmental concerns; and

(iv) representatives of Indian tribes;

(B) a representative of the Federal Aviation Administration; and

(C) a representative of the National Park Service.

(2) EX OFFICIO MEMBERS.—The Administrator (or the designee of the Administrator) and the Director (or the designee of the Director) shall serve as ex officio members.

(3) CHAIRPERSON.—The representative of the Federal Aviation Administration and the representative of the National Park Service shall serve alternating 1-year terms as chairman of the advisory group, with the representative of the Federal Aviation Administration serving initially until the end of the calendar year following the year in which the advisory group is first appointed.

(c) DUTIES.—The advisory group shall provide advice, information, and recommendations to the Administrator and the Director—

(1) on the implementation of this title and the amendments made by this title;

(2) on commonly accepted quiet aircraft technology for use in commercial air tour operations over a national park or tribal lands, which will receive preferential treatment in a given air tour management plan;

(3) on other measures that might be taken to accommodate the interests of visitors to national parks; and

(4) at the request of the Administrator and the Director, safety, environmental, and other issues related to commercial air tour operations over a national park or tribal lands.

(d) COMPENSATION; SUPPORT; CHAPTER 10 OF TITLE 5, UNITED STATES CODE.—

(1) COMPENSATION AND TRAVEL.—Members of the advisory group who are not officers or employees of the United States, while attending conferences or meetings of the group or otherwise engaged in its business, or while serving away from their homes or regular places of business, may be allowed travel expenses, including per diem in lieu of subsistence, as authorized by section 5703 of title 5, United States Code, for persons in the Government service employed intermittently.

(2) ADMINISTRATIVE SUPPORT.—The Federal Aviation Administration and the National Park Service shall jointly furnish to the advisory group clerical and other assistance.

(3) NONAPPLICATION OF CHAPTER 10 OF TITLE 5, UNITED STATES CODE.—Section 1013 of title 5, United States Code, does

not apply to the advisory group.

SEC. 806. [49 U.S.C. 40128 note] PROHIBITION OF COMMERCIAL AIR TOUR OPERATIONS OVER THE ROCKY MOUNTAIN NATIONAL PARK.

Effective beginning on the date of the enactment of this Act, no commercial air tour operation may be conducted in the airspace over the Rocky Mountain National Park notwithstanding any other provision of this Act or section 40128 of title 49, United States Code.

SEC. 807. [49 U.S.C. 40128 note] REPORTS.

(a) OVERFLIGHT FEE REPORT.—Not later than 180 days after the date of the enactment of this Act, the Administrator shall transmit to Congress a report on the effects overflight fees are likely to have on the commercial air tour operation industry. The report shall include, but shall not be limited to—

(1) the viability of a tax credit for the commercial air tour operators equal to the amount of any overflight fees charged by the National Park Service; and

(2) the financial effects proposed offsets are likely to have on Federal Aviation Administration budgets and appropriations.

(b) QUIET AIRCRAFT TECHNOLOGY REPORT.—Not later than 2 years after the date of the enactment of this Act, the Administrator and the Director of the National Park Service shall jointly transmit a report to Congress on the effectiveness of this title in providing incentives for the development and use of quiet aircraft technology.

SEC. 808. [49 U.S.C. 40128 note] METHODOLOGIES USED TO ASSESS AIR TOUR NOISE.

Any methodology adopted by a Federal agency to assess air tour noise in any unit of the national park system (including the Grand Canyon and Alaska) shall be based on reasonable scientific methods.

SEC. 809. [49 U.S.C. 40128 note] ALASKA EXEMPTION.

The provisions of this title and section 40128 of title 49, United States Code, as added by section 803(a), do not apply to any land or waters located in Alaska.

* * * * * * *

SELECTED PROVISIONS OF THE FEDERAL AVIATION REAUTHORIZATION ACT OF 1996

PUBLIC LAW 104-264

FEDERAL AVIATION REAUTHORIZATION ACT OF 1996

[Public Law 104–264; 110 Stat. 3213]

[As Amended Through P.L. 118–63, Enacted May 16, 2024]

AN ACT To amend title 49, United States Code, to reauthorize programs of the Federal Aviation Administration, and for other purposes.

SECTION 1. SHORT TITLE; TABLE OF CONTENTS.

(a) SHORT TITLE.—This Act may be cited as the "Federal Aviation Reauthorization Act of 1996".

* * * * * * *

TITLE III—AVIATION SECURITY

* * * * * * *

[Sections 302, 307, 309, and 310 repealed by section 218(g) of Public Law 118–63.] [Sec. 308. Repealed. P.L. 108–176, sec. 143, 117 Stat. 2503.]

* * * * * * *

TITLE XII—MISCELLANEOUS PROVISIONS

* * * * * * *

[Section 1203 repealed by section 719(c)(1) of Public Law 118–63.]

SEC. 1205. REGULATIONS AFFECTING INTRASTATE AVIATION IN ALASKA.

In modifying regulations contained in title 14, Code of Federal Regulations, in a manner affecting intrastate aviation in Alaska, the Administrator of the Federal Aviation Administration shall consider the extent to which Alaska is not served by transportation modes other than aviation, and shall establish such regulatory distinctions as the Administrator considers appropriate.

* * * * * * *

SEC. 1214. CARRIAGE OF CANDIDATES IN STATE AND LOCAL ELECTIONS.

The Administrator of the Federal Aviation Administration shall revise section 91.321 of the Administration's regulations (14 C.F.R. 91.321), relating to the carriage of candidates in Federal elections, to make the same or similar rules applicable to the carriage of candidates for election to public office in State and local government elections.

* * * * * * *

SEC. 1221. HAWAII CARGO.

Notwithstanding any other provision of law, and for a period that shall not extend beyond September 30, 1998, an air carrier which commenced all-cargo turnaround service during November 1995 with Stage 2 aircraft with a maximum weight of more than 75,000 pounds may operate no more than one Stage 2 aircraft in all-cargo turnaround service and may also maintain a second such aircraft in reserve. The reserve aircraft may only be used as a replacement aircraft when the first aircraft is not airworthy or is unavailable due to closure of an airport at which the first aircraft is located in the State of Hawaii.

* * * * * * *

NOTAM Improvement Act of 2023

Public Law 118-4

NOTAM IMPROVEMENT ACT OF 2023

[(Public Law 118–4)]

[This law has not been amended]

AN ACT To establish a task force on improvements for notices to air missions, and for other purposes.

Be it enacted by the Senate and House of Representatives of the United States of America in Congress assembled,

SECTION 1. [49 U.S.C. 40101 note] SHORT TITLE.

This Act may be cited as the "NOTAM Improvement Act of 2023".

SEC. 2. FAA TASK FORCE ON NOTAM IMPROVEMENT.

(a) ESTABLISHMENT.—Not later than 180 days after the date of enactment of this Act, the Administrator of the Federal Aviation Administration shall establish a task force to be known as the FAA Task Force on NOTAM Improvement (in this section referred to as the "Task Force").

(b) COMPOSITION.—The Task Force shall consist of members appointed by the Administrator, including at least one member of each of the following:

(1) Air carrier representatives.

(2) Airport representatives.

(3) Labor union representatives of airline pilots.

(4) Labor union representatives of aircraft dispatchers.

(5) The labor union certified under section 7111 of title 5, United States Code, to represent FAA air traffic control specialists assigned to the United States NOTAMs Office.

(6) The labor union certified under section 7111 of title 5,

United States Code, to represent FAA aeronautical information specialists.

(7) General and business aviation representatives.

(8) Aviation safety experts with knowledge of NOTAMs.

(9) Human factors experts.

(10) Computer system architecture and cybersecurity experts.

(c) DUTIES.—The duties of the Task Force shall include—

(1) reviewing existing methods for publishing NOTAMs and flight operations information to pilots;

(2) reviewing regulations, policies, systems, and international standards relating to NOTAMs, including their content and presentation to pilots;

(3) evaluating and determining best practices to organize, prioritize, and present flight operations information in a manner that optimizes pilot review and retention of relevant information; and

(4) providing recommendations for—

(A) improving the publication and delivery of NOTAM information in a manner that prioritizes or highlights the most important information, and optimizes pilot review and retention of relevant information;

(B) ways to ensure that NOTAMs are complete, accurate, timely, relevant to safe flight operations, and contain pertinent information;

(C) any best practices that the FAA should consider to improve the accuracy and understandability of NOTAMs and the display of flight operations information;

(D) ways to work with air carriers, other airspace users, and aviation service providers to implement solutions that are aligned with the recommendations under this paragraph; and

(E) ways to ensure the stability, resiliency, and cybersecurity of the NOTAM computer system.

(d) REPORT.—Not later than 1 year after the date of the establishment of the Task Force, the Task Force shall submit to the Committee on Transportation and Infrastructure of the House of Representatives and the Committee on Commerce, Science, and Transportation of the Senate a report detailing—

(1) the results of the reviews and evaluations of the Task Force under paragraphs (1) through (3) of subsection (c);

(2) the best practices identified and recommendations provided by the Task Force under subsection (c)(4);

(3) any recommendations of the Task Force for additional regulatory or policy actions to improve the publication of NOTAMs; and

(4) the degree to which implementing the recommendations of the Task Force described under paragraph (2) will address National Transportation Safety Board Safety Recommendation A-18-024.

(e) APPLICABLE LAW.—Chapter 10 of title 5, United States Code, shall not apply to the Task Force.

(f) SUNSET.—The Task Force shall terminate on the later of—

(1) the date on which the Task Force submits the report required under subsection (d); or

(2) the date that is 18 months after the date on which the Task Force is established under subsection (a).

(g) AUTHORITY.—The Administrator shall have the authority to carry out the recommendations of the Task Force detailed in the report required under subsection (d).

(h) RULE OF CONSTRUCTION.—Nothing in this section may be construed to require the FAA to duplicate any prior, ongoing, or planned efforts related to the improvement of NOTAMs, including any efforts related to implementing any previously enacted requirements.

(i) DEFINITIONS.—In this section:

(1) FAA.—The term "FAA" means the Federal Aviation Administration.

(2) NOTAM.—The term "NOTAM" means a notice containing information (which is not known sufficiently in advance to publicize by other means) concerning the establishment, condition, or change in any component (including a facility, service, or procedure thereof) or hazard in the National Airspace System, the timely knowledge of which is essential to personnel concerned with flight operations.

SEC. 3. [49 U.S.C. 44701 note] ADDITIONAL REQUIREMENTS.

Not later than September 30, 2024, the Administrator of the Federal Aviation Administration shall make the following improvements:

(1) Complete implementation of a Federal NOTAM System (in this section referred to as a "FNS").

(2) Implement a back-up system to the FNS.

(3) Brief the Committee on Transportation and Infrastructure of the House of Representatives and the Committee on Commerce, Science, and Transportation of the Senate on a plan to enhance the capability to deliver information through the FNS that is machine-readable, filterable, and in the format used by the International Civil Aviation Organization (ICAO) to promote further global harmonization among neighboring Air Navigation Service Providers (ANSPs) and provide users of the National Airspace System with one consistent format for domestic and international operations.

Sections 352 and 367 of the Consolidated Appropriations Resolution, 2003

Public Law 108-7

CONSOLIDATED APPROPRIATIONS RESOLUTION, 2003-(FED. AVIATION RELATED)

[Division I of Public Law 108–7; 117 Stat. 384]

[This Act has not been amended]

AN ACT Making consolidated appropriations for the fiscal year ending September 30, 2003, and for other purposes.

* * * * * * *

Sec. 352. FAA NOTICE TO AIRMEN FDC 2/0199.

(a) IN GENERAL.—The Secretary of Transportation—

(1) shall maintain in full force and effect, for a period of 1 year after the date of enactment of this Act, the restrictions imposed under Federal Aviation Administration Notice to Airmen FDC 2/0199 and the restrictions that had been in effect on September 26, 2002 and that were imposed under local Notices to Airmen based on or derived from Notice to Airmen FDC 1/3353;

(2) shall rescind immediately any waivers or exemptions from those restrictions that are in effect on the date of enactment of this Act; and

(3) may not grant any waivers or exemptions from those restrictions, except—

(A) as authorized by air traffic control for operational or safety purposes;

(B) for operational purposes of an event, stadium, or other venue, including (in the case of a sporting event) equipment or parts, transport of team members, officials of the governing body and immediate family members and guests of such teams and officials to and from the event, stadium, or other venue;

(C) for broadcast coverage for any broadcast rights holder;

(D) for safety and security purposes of the event, stadium, or other venue; or

(E) to operate an aircraft in restricted airspace to the extent necessary to arrive at or depart from an airport using standard air traffic procedures.

(b) WAIVERS.—Beginning no earlier than 1 year after the date of enactment of this Act, the Secretary may modify or terminate such restrictions, or issue waivers or exemptions from such restrictions, if the Secretary promulgates, after public notice and an opportunity for comment, a rule setting forth the standards under which the Secretary may grant a waiver or exemption. Such standards shall provide a level of security at least equivalent to that provided by the waiver policy applied by the Secretary as of the date of enactment of this Act.

(c) FUNDING LIMITATION.—Unless and until the Secretary promulgates a rule in accordance with subsection (b) above, none of the funds made available in this Act or any other Act may be used to terminate or limit the restrictions described in paragraph (a)(1) above or to grant waivers of, or exemptions from, such restrictions except as provided in paragraph (a)(3) above.

(d) BROADCAST CONTRACTS NOT AFFECTED.—Nothing in this section shall be construed to affect contractual rights pertaining to any broadcasting agreement.

* * * * * * *

Sec. 367. LETTERS OF INTENT FOR AIRPORT SECURITY IMPROVEMENT PROJECTS.—

(a) The Under Secretary of Transportation for Security may issue a letter of intent to an airport committing to obligate from future budget authority an amount, not more than the Federal Government's share of the project's cost, for an airport security improvement project (including interest costs and costs of formulating the project) at the airport. The letter shall establish a schedule under which the Under Secretary will reimburse the airport for the Government's share of the project's costs, as amounts become available, if the airport, after the Under Secretary issues the letter, carries out the project without receiving amounts under

Chapter 471 of title 49.

(b) The airport shall notify the Under Secretary of the airport's intent to carry out the airport security improvement project before the project begins.

(c) A letter of intent may be issued under this section only if—

(1) The airport security improvement project to which the letter applies involves the replacement of baggage conveyer systems or the reconfiguration of terminal baggage areas in order to install explosive detection systems; and

(2) The Under Secretary determines that the project will improve security or will improve the efficiency of the airport without lessening security.

(d) A letter of intent issued under this section is not an obligation of the Government under section 1501 of title 31, and the letter is not deemed to be an administrative commitment for financing. An obligation or administrative commitment may be made only as amounts are provided in authorization and appropriations laws.

(e) The Government's share of the project's cost shall be 75 percent for a project at an airport having at least 0.25 percent of the total number of passenger boardings each year at all airports and 90 percent for a project at any other airport.

(f) Nothing in this section shall be construed to prohibit the obligation of amounts pursuant to a letter of intent under this section in the same fiscal year as the letter of intent is issued.

(g) The Under Secretary shall notify the House and Senate Committees on Appropriations, the House Transportation and Infrastructure Committee, and the Senate Commerce, Science, and Transportation Committee at least 3 days prior to the issuance of a letter of intent under this section.

(h) There is authorized to be appropriated to carry out this section $500,000,000 in each of fiscal years 2003, 2004, 2005, 2006, and 2007.

* * * * * * *

POPULAR TITLE NAMES

POPULAR TITLE NAMES

Act of June 29, 1940--(Washington Airports)
54 stat. 686

Act of October 31, 1945
Chapter 443 of 79th Congress
59 Stat. 553

Act of September 7, 1950--(Washington Airports)
Chapter 905 of 81st Congress 64
Stat. 770

Air Transportation Safety and System Stabilization Act
Pub. L. 107 42, Sept. 22, 2001,
115 Stat. 230 (49 U.S.C. 40101 note)

Aircraft Certification, Safety, and Accountability Act
Pub. L. 116 260, div. V, title I, Dec. 27, 2020,
134 Stat. 2309
Short title, see 49 U.S.C. 40101 note

Airline Safety and Federal Aviation Administration Extension Act of 2010
Pub. L. 111 216, Aug. 1, 2010,
124 Stat. 2348
Short title, see 49 U.S.C. 40101 note

Airport and Airway Improvement Act of 1982
Pub. L. 97 248, title V, Sept. 3, 1982,
96 Stat. 671

Airport Security Improvement Act of 2000
Pub. L. 106 528, Nov. 22, 2000, 1
14 Stat. 2517
Short title, see 49 U.S.C. 40101 note

Atomic Energy Defense Act
Pub. L. 107 314, div. D, as added Pub. L. 108 136, div. C, title XXXI, § 3141(b), Nov. 24, 2003,
117 Stat. 1753 (50 U.S.C. 2501 et seq.)
Short title, see 50 U.S.C. 2501 note

Aviation and Transportation Security Act
Pub. L. 107 71, Nov. 19, 2001, 1
15 Stat. 597
Short title, see 49 U.S.C. 40101 note

Aviation Medical Assistance Act of 1998

Pub. L. 105 170, Apr. 24, 1998,
112 Stat. 47 (49 U.S.C. 44701 note)

Bob Stump National Defense Authorization Act for Fiscal Year 2003
Pub. L. 107 314, Dec. 2, 2002,
116 Stat. 2458

Cape Town Treaty Implementation Act of 2004
Pub. L. 108 297, Aug. 9, 2004,
118 Stat. 1095
Short title, see 49 U.S.C. 40101 note

Clean Air Act
July 14, 1955, ch. 360,
69 Stat. 322 (42 U.S.C. 7401 et seq.)
Short title, see 42 U.S.C. 7401 note

Consolidated Appropriations Act, 2021
Pub. L. 116 260, Dec. 27, 2020,
134 Stat. 1182

Consolidated Appropriations Resolution, 2003
Pub. L. 108 7, Feb. 20, 2003,
117 Stat. 11

Death on the High Seas Act
Title 46, chapter 303 (§ 30301 et seq.) Mar. 30, 1920, ch. 111,
41 Stat. 537
Short title, see 46 U.S.C. 30301

Department of Housing and Urban Development Appropriations Act, 2006
Pub. L. 109 115, div. A, title III, Nov. 30, 2005,
119 Stat. 2440

Department of Transportation and Related Agencies Appropriations Act, 2000
Pub. L. 106 69, Oct. 9, 1999,
113 Stat. 986

European Union Emissions Trading Scheme Prohibition Act of 2011
Pub. L. 112 200, Nov. 27, 2012,
126 Stat. 1477 (49 U.S.C. 40101 note)

FAA Extension, Safety, and Security Act of 2016
Pub. L. 114 190, July 15, 2016, 1
30 Stat. 615
Short title, see 49 U.S.C. 40101 note

FAA Modernization and Reform Act of 2012
Pub. L. 112 95, Feb. 14, 2012,
126 Stat. 11
Short title, see 49 U.S.C. 40101 note

FAA Reauthorization Act of 2018
Pub. L. 115 254, Oct. 5, 2018,
132 Stat. 3186
Short title, see 49 U.S.C. 40101 note

Fairness for Pilots Act

Pub. L. 115-254, div. B, title III, subtitle C (Secs. 391-396), Oct. 5, 2018, 132 Stat. 3323

Short title, see 49 U.S.C. 40101 note

FAA Reauthorization Act of 2024

Pub. L. 118 63, May 16, 2024,
138 Stat. 1025

Short title, see 49 U.S.C. 40101 note

Federal Airport Act

May 13, 1946, ch. 251,
60 Stat. 170

Federal Aviation Act of 1958

Pub. L. 85 726, Aug. 23, 1958,
72 Stat. 731

Federal Aviation Reauthorization Act of 1996

Pub. L. 104 264, Oct. 9, 1996,
110 Stat. 3213

Short title, see 49 U.S.C. 40101 note

General Aviation Revitalization Act of 1994

Pub. L. 103 298, Aug. 17, 1994,
108 Stat. 1552 (49 U.S.C. 40101 note)

Homeland Security Act of 2002

Pub. L. 107 296, Nov. 25, 2002,
116 Stat. 2135 (6 U.S.C. 101 et seq.)

Short title, see 6 U.S.C. 101 note

Implementing Recommendations of the 9/11 Commission Act of 2007

Pub. L. 110 53, Aug. 3, 2007,
121 Stat. 266

Short title, see 6 U.S.C. 101 note

Intelligence Reform and Terrorism Prevention Act of 2004

Pub. L. 108 458, Dec. 17, 2004,
118 Stat. 3638

Short title, see 50 U.S.C. 3001 note

International Air Transportation Competition Act of 1979

Pub. L. 96 192, Feb. 15, 1980,
94 Stat. 35

International Security and Development Cooperation Act of 1985

Pub. L. 99 83, Aug. 8, 1985,
99 Stat. 190

Short title, see 22 U.S.C. 2151 note

John S. McCain National Defense Authorization Act for Fiscal Year 2019

Pub. L. 115 232, Aug. 13, 2018,
132 Stat. 1636

MAP 21 Also known as *Moving Ahead for Progress in the 21st Century Act*

Pub. L. 112 141, July 6, 2012,
126 Stat. 405

Short title, see 23 U.S.C. 101 note

Moving Ahead for Progress in the 21st Century Act also known as *MAP 21*
Pub. L. 112 141, July 6, 2012, 126 Stat. 405
Short title, see 23 U.S.C. 101 note

Narcotics Control Trade Act
Pub. L. 93 618, title VIII, as added Pub. L. 99 570, title IX, § 9001, Oct. 27, 1986,
100 Stat. 3207 164 (19 U.S.C. 2491 et seq.)
Short title, see 19 U.S.C. 2491

National Defense Authorization Act for Fiscal Year 2016
Pub. L. 114 92, Nov. 25, 2015,
129 Stat. 726

National Defense Authorization Act for Fiscal Year 2017
Pub. L. 114 328, Dec. 23, 2016,
130 Stat. 2000

National Emission Standards Act
July 14, 1955, ch. 360, title II, as added Pub. L. 89 272, Title I, § 101(8), Oct. 20,
1965,
79 Stat. 992
Short title, see 42 .S.C. 7401 note

National Parks Air Tour Management Act of 2000
Pub. L. 106 181, title VIII, Apr. 5, 2000,
114 Stat. 185
Short title, see 49 U.S.C. 40128 note

National Transportation Safety Board Amendments Act of 2000
Pub. L. 106 424, Nov. 1, 2000,
114 Stat. 1883
Short title, see 49 U.S.C. 1101 note

National Transportation Safety Board Reauthorization Act of 2003
Pub. L. 108 168, Dec. 6, 2003,
117 Stat. 2032
Short title, see 49 U.S.C. 1101 note134 Stat. 1182

National Transportation Safety Board Reauthorization Act of 2006
Pub. L. 109 443, Dec. 21, 2006,
120 Stat. 3297
Short title, see 49 U.S.C. 1101 note

NOTAM Improvement Act of 2023
Pub. L. 118 4, June 3,,2023, 137 Stat. 7
Short title, see 49,U.S.C. 40101 note

Railway Labor Act
May 20, 1926, ch. 347, 44 Stat. 577
(45 U.S.C. 151 et seq.)
Short title, see 45,U.S.C. 151

Safe, Accountable, Flexible, Efficient Transportation, Equity Act: A Legacy for Users
Also known as *SAFETEA LU*
Pub. L. 109 59, Aug. 10, 2005,

119 Stat. 1144
Short title, see 23 U.S.C. 101 note
SAFETEA LU Also known as *Safe, Accountable, Flexible, Efficient Transportation Equity Act: A Legacy for Users*
Pub. L. 109 59, Aug. 10, 2005,
119 Stat. 1144
Short title, see 23 U.S.C. 101 note
September 11th Victim Compensation Fund of 2001
Pub. L. 107 42, title IV, Sept. 22, 2001,
115 Stat. 237 (49 U.S.C. 40101 note)
TICKETS Act Also known as the *Transparency Improvements and Compensation to Keep Every Ticketholder Safe Act of 2018*
Pub. L. 115-254, div. B, title IV, Sec. 425, Oct. 5, 2018,
132 Stat. 3338 (49 U.S.C. note prec. 42301)
Trade Act of 1974
Pub. L. 93 618, Jan. 3, 1975,
88 Stat. 1978 (19 U.S.C. 2101 et seq.)
Short title, see 19 U.S.C. 2101
Transparency Improvements and Compensation to Keep Every Ticketholder Safe Act of 2018 Also known as the *TICKETS Act*
Pub. L. 115-254, div. B, title IV, Sec. 425, Oct. 5, 2018,
132 Stat. 3338 (49 U.S.C. note prec. 42301)
Trust Fund Code of 1981
Aug. 16, 1954, ch. 736, § 1(d) [Internal Revenue Title, subtitle I], as added Pub. L. 97 119, title I, § 103(a), Dec. 29, 1981,
95 Stat. 1636 (26 U.S.C. 9500 et seq.)
Vision 100 Century of Aviation Reauthorization Act
Pub. L. 108 176, Dec. 12, 2003,
117 Stat. 2490
Short title, see 49 U.S.C. 40101 note
Wendell H. Ford Aviation Investment and Reform Act for the 21st Century
Pub. L. 106 181, Apr. 5, 2000,
114 Stat. 61
Short title, see 49 U.S.C. 40101 note

INDEX

Index

A

535

G

H

I

R

W

Z

www.ingramcontent.com/pod-product-compliance
Lightning Source LLC
Chambersburg PA
CBHW060921120626
46557CB00003B/837